REGNUM STUDIES IN MISSION

Korean Diaspora and Christian Mission

REGNUM STUDIES IN MISSION

Series Preface

Regnum Studies in Mission are born from the lived experience of Christians and Christian communities in mission, especially, but not solely, in the fast growing churches among the poor of the world. These churches have more to tell than stories of growth. They are making significant impacts on their cultures in the cause of Christ. They are producing 'cultural products' which express the reality of Christian faith, hope and love in their societies.

Titles in the Regnum Studies in Mission series are the fruit of rigorous research to the highest international standards and always of authentic Christian engagement in the transformation of people and societies. These books have been created for the world. The formation of Christian theology, missiology and practice, in the twenty-first century, will depend to a great extent on the active participation of growing churches contributing biblical and culturally appropriate expressions of Christian practice to inform World Christianity.

Series Editors

A full listing of titles in this series appears at the end of this book

REGNUM STUDIES IN MISSION

Korean Diaspora and Christian Mission

Edited by

S. Hun Kim and Wonsuk Ma

First published 2011 by Regnum Books International
and
Korean Research Institute for Diaspora, Oxford

Regnum is an imprint of the Oxford Centre for Mission Studies
St. Philip & St. James Church
Woodstock Road, Oxford, OX2 6HR, UK

16 15 14 13 12 11 10   8 7 6 5 4 3 2 1

British Library Cataloguing in Publication Data
A catalogue record for this book is available from the British Library

ISBN 978-1-506477-96-1

Cover design by Words by Design
Typeset by RBI

Distributed by 1517 Media in the US and Canada

In honour of the many millions
who have been scattered as strangers
and yet live with a calling to the Kingdom

Contents

Forewords xi
Preface xv
Editorial Note xvii

Introduction 1
S. Hun Kim and Wonsuk Ma

Part 1 Foundations

A Millennial Shift of Global Christianity and Mission: An Initial Reflection 11
Wonsuk Ma

Identity Crisis for the Diaspora Community 25
Sungho Choi

Why People Move? A Prolegomenon to Diaspora Missiology 35
Tereso C. Casiño

Diaspora and Timely Hit: Towards a Diaspora Missiology 59
Min-young Jung

The Diasporic Politics of Asian-American Christianity 72
Jonathan Tran

The Korean Diaspora Models of a Missional Church 84
Steve Sang-cheol Moon

Korean Diaspora: From Hermit Kingdom to Kingdom Ministry 101
Enoch Wan

The Diaspora Experience of the Korean Church and its Implications for World Missions 117
Minho Song

Part 2 Setting the Stage

A Critical Appraisal of Korean Missionary Work 131
Julie C. Ma

Migrant Workers and 'Reverse Mission' in the West 146
S. Hun Kim

Korean Evangelicals' Responses to Muslim Neighbours 153
Matthew Keung-Chul Jeong

Mission Korea: The Contribution of Global Youth Mobilization 164
Chulho Han

New Missional Avenues for Asian Churches 171
Byung Yoon Kim

Part 3 Korean Diaspora in Mission

History of the Korean Diaspora Movement 181
Doug K. Oh

The Founding and Development of the Korean Diaspora Forum 197
Soon Keun Lee

A South Korean Case Study of Migrant Ministries 207
David Chul Han Jun

International Evangelical Student Mission Movement: UBF Case Study 223
Peter Chang

Kingdom-centred Identity: The Case of Bicultural Korean-Brazilians 242
Do Myung Chun

Mobilizing Senior Christians in Korea and among the Korean Diaspora for Mission 260
See-Young Lee

Business, Diaspora and the Future of Mission: Reflections on Shanghai Korean Business Forum **264**
Sam Cho

Point5: Serving the Returned Korean Diaspora **281**
Jae Ryun Chung

Postscript **287**
Wonsuk Ma and S. Hun Kim

Selected Bibliography **293**
Contributors **299**

Foreword

Not long ago, I was in Shanghai addressing a group of Korean businessmen and women working in China. They were committed to sharing God's word with whomever they came into contact, while making a profit through genuine business. In my travels, I have come across Korean people everywhere. What is gratifying to me is that many of these Koreans are firm believers in the Lord Jesus Christ and are passionate about proclaiming the gospel. Wherever they are, they begin prayer gatherings among themselves. They not only try to reach out to their own people living in diaspora, but also to the people of the host nations.

I have often stated that South Korea is, and will continue to be, a missionary-producing country of the highest order. Churches in Korea are mission-minded and the Korean disaspora congregations that are being formed around the world have a strong mission emphasis.

It is my prayer that both the Korean Christians in their homeland and the diaspora Korean believers will join forces and forge a strong partnership in order to advance the kingdom and together help fulfil the Great Commission.

This book will be a treat to those interested in diaspora studies. It contains historical, biblical, strategic, and case study approaches to the exploration of diaspora issues. It is replete with lessons for the future of missions.

Tetsunao Yamamori, Ph.D.
Senior Advisor, Lausanne Movement

Foreword

In the summer of 2008, onboard an Emirates flight from Kampala, Uganda to Dubai, United Arab Emirates, seated beside me was a well-mannered and well-dressed gentleman who I guessed was of Korean descent. Over lunch, we started talking and hoping to confirm my conjecture, I politely asked which part of the world he was living or working. He told me that he was from Tajikistan and then went on to say that his ancestors were from Korea. For over an hour, he gave me a lesson on how the Chinese and Russians banished thousands of Koreans from their homeland to Siberia and Central Asia. Just before we separated in Dubai, he said: 'Come visit me someday. I will tell you more about the Koreans in my homeland'. I discovered he was a professor of sociology specializing in migration. Apparently, there are thousands of ethnic Koreans in China, East Russia, and Central Asia who were pushed out during the Korean War and past regional conflicts.

The fact of the matter is that Koreans are all over the globe. Where there are products of Samsung and Hyundai there are Korean communities. To these communities they bring their 'kimchis' and 'bul go gis'! They also bring their spiritualities and religious practices. For Korean Christians in diaspora, they build churches and start up prayer movements. In the Philippines, for example, the Korean migrants and Christian workers set up 'prayer mountains' and retreat centres outside Metro Manila. In large urban centres such as Toronto and Los Angeles we find 'little Seoul' sprawled across city blocks. In Thailand, Korean Airlines unload thousands of tourists, many of whom come for the weekend just to play golf! Like the Japanese, Korean fishing boats are all over the South Pacific. The Korean diaspora is huge!

For many years, the Koreans abroad have formed their own ghettos and they have built only their own ethnic local churches. They have tended to reach out to their own people but this practice is changing rapidly thanks to the hundreds of teachers who are coming to South Korea especially to teach English as a second language. Once the Koreans learned the universal language, i.e. English, their voluntary migration seems to have accelerated. Today, Koreans on the move are fluent in English and many are businessmen and missionaries who are aggressively proclaiming the good news not only to their own people but also to many nations.

On the flip side, according to labour experts, close to 1 million migrant workers are now in South Korea. The Korean Peninsula has become a labour and economic hub for Vietnamese, Burmese, Nepalese, Indians, Filipinos, Chinese, Africans, Latinos, and even Westerners. In addition, there are thousands of American military personnel and consultants. The world has come to the 'door steps' of the Korean churches. For as long as the economy of Korea is strong, foreign workers will arrive. This has given the Korean churches a tremendous opportunity to usher thousands of people into the kingdom.

In May 2010, I was invited to speak at the Korean Diaspora Forum (KDF) and the International Forum for Migrant Mission in Seoul, South Korea. It was inspiring for me to see how many Koreans now appreciate their global dispersion and its implications for world evangelization. Some of the papers presented at the Spring 2010 conferences, along with other strategic documents, are now compiled in this volume. Rev. Hun Kim, a Korean scholar based in Oxford, UK, in collaboration with his colleagues, has done a wonderful job in producing this seminal work on Korean diaspora missiology. It is my prayer that the Korean believers will champion diaspora missions in all four corners of the globe where they are scattered and that they will open wide their church doors to the scattered people on the move who are now in living in the 'Land of the Morning Calm'.

As the Lausanne Movement Senior Associate for Diasporas, I count it a great privilege to endorse this book for anyone engaged in missions and evangelism. May the Global Church of Jesus Christ not only learn how the Koreans pray but also how they do diaspora missions.

Sadiri Joy Tira, D.Min., D.Miss.
Chairman, Global Diaspora Network, Lausanne Movement

Preface

An interesting journey began in summer of 2007 when Wonsuk Ma, the new Executive Director of Oxford Centre for Mission Studies invited Hun Kim of Wycliffe Bible Translators UK to join the leadership conference of the Lausanne Committee of World Evangelization held in Budapest. Hun was pioneering Wycliffe UK's new initiative to build a network among diaspora communities in Europe for missionary involvement. Both editors, being new to the Lausanne community, were instantly connected with the vast network of mission thinkers and practitioners. One benefit was for Hun to become part of the fledgling Diaspora Study Group. When Hun began his Ph.D. research on the diaspora movement in Europe, and then launched the Eurovision Forum for Korean-European Christian leaders, diaspora and mission became part of his life. Wonsuk Ma, on the other hand, continued to develop his mission leadership through the study centre, which culminated in the significant contribution both individually and institutionally to the Edinburgh 2010 process. This book project, in a way, is an expression of their newly developed mission understanding.

Providentially, 2004 was indeed a significant year on diaspora for three groups: the Korean Diaspora Forum in USA, the Filipino Diaspora Consultation in Seoul and the Lausanne Congress on World Evangelization (LCWE) in Thailand.

Arising from the latter two meetings, significant materials on diaspora emerged: 'Scattered' by the Filipino Diaspora and the Lausanne Occasional Paper No. 55, which have created an awareness of the importance of people on the move for Christian mission. In the same year, the Korean Diaspora Forum was inaugurated to enhance the strategic cooperation among Korean diaspora churches and missions world wide with an annual convention every 7 years. Already the Forum has submitted a pre-publication, *Korean Diaspora and Christiana Mission* to the third Lausanne Congress in South Africa, a volume that has become a tool to rekindle the hearts of other diaspora groups in global outreach at the Congress.

This present publication discusses Korean diaspora missions with evaluative appraisals and practical illustrations in the diasporic contexts in a more academic way than the one submitted to the Lausanne Congress. It is also commended for its diversity of research, in various aspects of ministries in the diaspora, comprising of three parts: foundations, broader contexts and case studies of Korean diaspora missions. However, due to our shortcomings and lack of resources, we are aware that it is not a comprehensive volume to accommodate every aspect of Korean diaspora missions. To attain this goal, we intend another volume to follow later.

The birth of a book of this nature is a shining testimony of cooperation. First of all, the contributors are to be acknowledged for their valuable studies, all borne out of their long-term experiences. Considering their various leadership responsibilities, they deserve much credit for the book. Our gratitude also goes to the Regnum team of Oxford Centre for Mission Studies, Oxford. Its editorial members supported the project from the inception. Our particular appreciation is expressed to Ms. Parrizad Pound, the managing editor of Regnum, for her efficient management of the project. Also, Mr. Tony Gray of Word by Design deserves our special thanks for his expert advice and helpful guidance throughout the editorial and production process. Mr. Ralph Bates, a Regnum team member, and Ms. Kaye Cole, a former missionary colleague of Wonsuk, spent countless hours proofreading the entire manuscript. They improved the original manuscripts significantly.

For this publication, we wish to acknowledge, with appreciation for financial support, the members of the Korean Diaspora Forum, the Korean Diaspora Missions Network, the United Bible Fellowship in Europe, and God's Will Church in Korea, and other Korean diaspora churches who supported us in their prayerful hearts.

This book is dedicated to the glory of our Lord who became a stranger to walk with us so that we can not only be reconciled with our God but also become partners of His mission to save the lost world.

Editors
Oxford
Spring, 2011

Editorial Note

The Romanisation standard of Korean names has gone through several revisions, and the latest one is still in dispute. The convention used in the book is a modification of the latest standard, as some Korean consonants were Romanized normally using stronger consonant values (e.g., ‘Kim’ for ‘Gim’ which is closer to the Korean pronunciation). Also, there is an uncertainty in the Romanization of some cases. As a result, although most personal and place names are according to the current system, some exceptions have become unavoidable. It is simply because names which were Romanized using different systems have already been used in various publications. To avoid confusion, as much as possible, the editors adopted the following rules for this book:

A personal name is presented in the order of the given name followed by the surname, which is the opposite of the normal Korean convention.

A given name, as well as many location names, (such as a place, a nation, etc.), often consists of two syllables, but is treated as one word. In some cases, to aid pronunciation, a dash (‘-’) is added. For this reason, the syllable after the dash is in a lower case. This convention is against some common practice which treats the two syllables as if they were two different words.

In the footnotes, as well as in the bibliography, only the English translations of the original Korean titles are provided, but not the transliterations of the Korean titles. The latter are deemed unnecessary, especially for non-Korean readers.

Introduction

S. Hun Kim and Wonsuk Ma

The Historic Journey of Diaspora Studies in Mission Circles

The world church celebrated the centenary of the epoch-making Edinburgh Missionary Conference of 1910. All the global gatherings, including those in Tokyo, Edinburgh and Cape Town, agreed that globalisation and the increasing mobility of people have made migration a critically important issue for mission. This does not imply that the role of Christian migrants or diaspora has not featured in mission circles. Nonetheless, it is unfortunately true that migration has been traditionally viewed as a political and social challenge. It is only in recent years that diaspora has been taken seriously as a unique missionary gift.

Lausanne Movement

The first concrete action was the founding of the Chinese Coordinating Committee for World Evangelization in 1976, in Hong Kong.[1] This was the fruit of the coming together of the Chinese participants in ICCOWE in Lausanne in 1974.[2] Following Lausanne II in Manila (1989), South Asian Concern was inaugurated, and, in succeeding years, the North American Consultation of South Asian Christians (NACSAC). The Lausanne Diaspora Movement was officially organised after the Manila Congress by Tom Houston, then the International Director, and the first international Diaspora Leadership Consultation was held in Edmonton, Alberta, Canada in 1998. At the LCWE Forum in September, 2004 in Pattaya, Thailand, there was a plan for diaspora leaders and a document was produced.[3] This was considered a watershed moment in evangelical mission thinking. Since then, the movement has accelerated to form the Lausanne Diasporas Leadership Team (LDLT) in 2009. In the meantime, the Filipino International Network (FIN) incidentally published a volume of Filipino diaspora after the Seoul Consultation in 2004.[4]

---

[1] The first part of the Lausanne Movement was excerpted from the outline of the Lausanne Diaspora Initiative provided by Rev. Tom Houston (Oxford, Feb 2011).

[2] For further information, see 'Kingdom Vision and Commission: A Reader of the CCCOWE Movement' (1989).

[3] Lausanne Occasional Paper No.55, 'The New People Next Door' (2004).

[4] Luis Pantoja, Sadiri Joy Tira, and Enoch Wan (eds), *Scattered: The Filipino GlobalPpresence* (Manila: Lifechange Publishing, 2004).

In 2007, Joy Tira, who was newly appointed as the Senior Associate for Diaspora for the Lausanne Committee, providentially encountered with us at the Leadership Conference in Budapest, Hungary and requested a comprehensive volume on Korean diaspora and Christian missions which would inspire other ethnic diaspora groups for world mission. For the past two years, the Korean Diaspora Forum (KDF) and the Korean Diaspora Missions Network (KODIMNET) have contributed on various research works through their close cooperation in order to produce a volume about the Korean diaspora mission in the world.

In two significant consultations in Manila and Seoul in 2009, the Lausanne Diaspora Leadership Team developed a relevant framework and in Manila laid a theological foundation for those who seek to formulate a strategy for Christian missions to the diaspora. In Seoul, in November 2009, the Lausanne Diaspora Educators Consultation formulated the 'Seoul Declaration on Diaspora Missiology'. A spin-off of the Seoul gathering was a diaspora conference held in Oxford, in April 2010, to explore specifically European cases.[5]

In a way, the Third Lausanne Congress in Cape Town, South Africa was a very encouraging occasion for Korean churches as *Korean Diaspora and Christian Mission*, covering various aspects of Korean diaspora and Christian missions, has been endorsed to be distributed among international delegates at the Congress. In fact, the issue of diaspora and its missiology was one of the predominant features of the whole programme and acclaimed as a paradigm for world evangelization. Consequently, in the middle of the Congress on 20th of October, 2010, the (Lausanne) Global Diaspora Network Advisory Board was formed in place of the Lausanne Diaspora Leadership Team.

World Council of Churches

One would intuitively think that various arms of the World Council of Churches (WCC) would have made concerted efforts regarding this subject, as migrantion often raises various justice issues. It is true that the Council has issued a good number of statements on the topic, especially when wars displace thousands of innocent people. A good number of programmes and projects have raised various issues related to migration. The description of the Migration and Social Justice Project, however, exemplifies the focus of the Council, which is in contrast to the evangelical interest, as highlighted by the Lausanne circles:

> Migration…raises new economic, political, cultural and ecclesial concerns in today's globalized world. New forms of migration, including trafficking and

[5] Some of the studies presented during the Oxford conference are found in *Transformation* 28:1 (January 2011).

> development-induced displacement, threaten the human dignity of millions of people. Xenophobia is increasing. Migration in a globalized world raises questions about inter-faith relations, identity, justice, racism, advocacy and diakonia.[6]

The Global Ecumenical Network on Migration, which has replaced the Global Ecumenical Network on Uprooted People, is another programme of the Council. This programme raises issues related to migration such as 'racism and xenophobia, and the effect of migration on changing ecclesial contexts'.[7] Unlike the evangelicals, the framework for discussions on migration among the WCC circles is found under the 'justice, diakonia and responsibility for creation' programme.

However, the most substantial and concerted effort in the Council is the publication of 'Mapping Migration, Mapping Churches' Responses'.[8] In spite of its limited scope to Europe, the book is a valuable resource. The first four chapters, relatively briefer than expected, provide an important perspective on migration in Europe. Two chapters are particularly useful: chapter three explores a theological approach to migration, and chapter four summarises the European churches' responses to migration. The bulk of the book, however, is dedicated to country profiles, including attitudes toward minority groups in each country. The profiles are extremely useful but they require regular updating. Equally desirable are similar studies for other continents, although the Council's financial difficulties may leave the current volume as the first and the last.

Growing Regional Studies

The appearance of new research on diaspora is extremely encouraging. For regional and national levels, such initiatives will continue in the future. Two recent publications may serve as good examples.

The first is Jehu Hanciles' *Beyond Christendom*,[9] the fruit of a five-year research project on African Christian immigrants in North America. Hanciles contends that immigrant communities play a decisive role in the impact Christianity on the host nation, North America in this case, and ultimately the shaping of global Christianity. The Samuel-Eli model is particularly attractive

---

6 www.oikoumene.org/programmes/justice-diakonia-and-responsibility-for-creation/migration-and-social-justice.html, accessed on 25 January, 2011.

7 www.oikoumene.org/programmes/justice-diakonia-and-responsibility-for-creation/migration-and-social-justice/gem-network.html, accessed on 25 January, 2011.

8 Darrel Jackson and Alessia Passarelli, *Mapping Migration, Mapping Churches' Responses: A Europe Study* (Geneva: Churches' Commission for Migrations in Europe, World Council of Churches, 2008).

9 Jehu J. Hanciles, *Beyond Christendom: Globalization, African Migration, and the Transformation of the West* (Maryknoll, NY: Orbis, 2006).

in illustrating the significant potential of immigrant Christian communities to make an impact on the host churches.[10] The model is used to describe immigrant Christians in mainline established churches in the United States. The dynamic and younger form of spirituality brought by the immigrants can potentially replace or rejuvenate the waning and ageing Christian life of the host churches, just as Samuel replaced Eli. The model is also useful to illustrate the same potential on the national level. It will require a clear missionary vision by leaders of immigrant Christians, in order for this formidable mandate to be realized. Hanciles argues that this is not just a dream, but it can also be a reality. I recently learned that an African minister now leads a historic British Pentecostal denomination, founded in 1916, as a result of the Welsh revival.[11] In fact, three out of seven executive national leaders of the denomination are African immigrants. In this case, the black Samuels may strengthen and rejuvenate the church by replacing, or working with, the white Elis.

The second is Währisch-Oblau's work on Christian immigrant communities in Germany which has had a very different journey from the first example, as this research was part of her doctoral work.[12] Her research initiatve was augmented by her involvement in the 'Program for Cooperation between German and Foreign Language Churches' (since 1998) of the United Evangelical Misison (UEM) and the Evangelical Church in the Rhineland, Germany. The combined nine-year journey of the mission agency and the researcher has been one of learning. The result of extensive field research, involving more than 100 churches and their leaders, is an astonishing self-portrait of the diaspora community: defining themselves not as 'victimized and in need of assistance, but as expatriate agents with a clear calling and a vision to change the continent they now live in'.[13] This study, we are convinced, must have surprised both the host church as well as the diaspora group in Germany, and this may be applicable to many other diaspora settings.

Korean Christianity

The last quarter of the twentieth century witnessed a significant change in the global Christian landscape. Many studies testify to this fact. Indeed, a convincing argument has been put forward by mission statisticians that this shift is following a global pattern approximately in approximately every

---

[10] Hanciles, *Beyond Christendom*, 327.

[11] Apostolic Church, 'Leadership' (www.apostolic-church.org/leadership.phtml), accessed on 20 Feb 2011.

[12] Claudia Währisch-Oblau, *The Missionary Self-Perception of Pentecostal/Charismatic Church Leaders from the Global South in Europe: Bringing Back the Gospel* (Leiden: Brill, 2009).

[13] The back cover of Währisch-Oblau, *The Missionary Self-Perception of Pentecostal/Charismatic Church Leaders.*

millennium throughout church history.[14] The trajectory of the centre of gravity of global Christianity, despite questions of its precision, is quite illuminating on the rise and waning of churches in the Global South and the North.[15]

The experience of Protestant Christianity in Korea fits well into this particular argument. In the 1970s and 1980s, the Korean church achieved a record growth, and this was the time when the mission movement was born. This is the time when global Christianity, according to the trajectory, intensified its southward direction but more significantly, in 1970 to be precise, made a drastic eastward turn.[16] This period of growth is also true with other East and Southeast Asian countries, such as China, the Philippines, Indonesia, Malysia, Singapore, Myanmar, and others. However, the growth of Christianity does not always produce a missionary movement. For this reason, it is significant to note that the growth of the national church in Korea was accompanied by the strengthening of its missionary movement. The development of the Korean mission movement was a witness to local congregations actively engaging in mission as well as in the growing number of mission organizations.

This was also the period when the nation began its impressive economic development, and its success began to attract labour migrants. In the beginning, the favoured labour group was Korean-Chinese, coming predominantly from northeastern China. Through China's policy on minorities, the Korean-Chinese have maintained the Korean language and cultural heritage, albeit with obvious gap in the culture of South Korea. Another interesting group of Korean migrants, who attracted much media attention, were adopted Koreans, particularly to European countries. The Korean War, coupled with extreme poverty, made Korea the number one 'exporter' of babies for adoption. World Vision and Compassion International were intiated to rescue these post-war babies from grinding poverty and social instability. Now in their early thirties, the adopted Koreans began to trace their roots back to Korea, while Korea also began to become increasingly aware of its place in the global context. This was also the period when a small number of immigrants in North America decided to return home, as Korea offered more opportunities than when they left the country. Such stories caught the nation's imagination.

The growing missionary movement in Korea and the widespread overseas Koreans began to find ways of complementing each other. In spite of its large missionary contingent, numbering over 20,000 in 2009, its language and cultural barriers have limited its important contribution to global mission

---

[14] Todd M. Johnson and Sun Young Chung, 'Christianity's Centre of Gravity, AD 33-2100', in *Atlas of Global Christianity*, 50-51.

[15] Todd M. Johnson and Sun Young Chung, 'Christianity's Centre of Gravity, AD 33-2100: Chrisian Expansion by UN Region, AD 100-2100', in *Atlas of Global Christianity*, 53.

[16] Johnson and Chung, 'Christianity's Centre of Gravity, AD 33-2100', 53.

discussions. One glowing picture was found in the Lausanne Leaders' Gathering in Budapest in 2007. Out of 300 or so delegates, encompassing three generations of the Lausanne leadership, (that is, the old and pioneering Lausanne generation, the current Manila generation and the future Cape Town generation), were intentionally brought together. Considering the global shift of Christianity and its missionary feat, there was a general expectation for the Korean church to exercise a significant leadership role. By the time the Cape Town Congress was concluded, this expectation was happily met, not by mission leaders of the Korean church, but predominantly by Korean-American missionaries, all in their thirties and twenties.

This, among others, highlights the unique set of gifts which immigrant Christian communities can exercise not only in their 'home' (in this case, Korean) churches and missionary initiatives, but more importantly in global mission leadership. Of course, the rise of a diaspora leadership has also been paralleled by the growing awareness of diaspora among the Korean mission leadership. To explore the missional implications of diapora, since 2004, the Korean Diaspora Forum and the Korean Diaspora Missions Network have held annual consultations and forums respectively, and many of the contributors for this volume were part of a critical mass to conduct research on the various issues of Korean diaspora missions worldwide.

The Book

With a scarcity of serious research on diaspora from theological and missiological perspectives, the gathering of studies, reflections and experiences of mission players in diaspora is a valuable contribution. In the midst of a growing cry for mission studies by the Global South, the Korean church is in a position to take up such a challenge for the sake of other emerging missionary churches. In addition, the book is a challenge to other churches, especially those in the South, many of which have large contingents of migrants, to take a new perspective on their own Christian migrant communities as a missional gift. If the book can further encourage diaspora communities in their self-identity as missionary people, and in their awareness of their unique opportunities and gift, the book will accomplish something far beyond the editors' modest prayers.

In this volume, the contents are divided into three parts: foundations, broad context, and case studies. The first part is intended to provide a theological framework for the Korean diaspora in this contemporary century and its missiological implications for world missions. Furthermore, the chapters in this part provide observations on relevant models of a missional church on the legitimate basis of cross-cultural contexts.

The second part takes the reader closer to the Korean scene by setting a broader context for Korean diaspora studies. The chapters attempt to explore broader subjects that may affect current ministries in their respective realms:

Korean missionary work; migrant workers; Korean Evangelicals and Muslim neighbours; global youth mobilization; and ministry for Asian churches. From this research, we become aware of how significant a multi-ethnic ministry is in a diasporic context.

The third part presents various case studies of the Korean diaspora mission. A study explores a diachronic perspective on Korean diaspora history, particularly Korean migrant churches in recent centuries and five different cases are illustrated. All the cases are 'live' testimonies, born out of ministry experiences, and they are still continuing. We expect to benefit greatly from their successes as well as their shortcomings. Each case has its own originality and uniqueness so that we are able to reflect on our own ministries through their diverse aspects and their trials and errors. The categories of ministries comprise of a mission forum for Korean migrant churches; a ministry for foreign workers; international student mission overseas; mobilization of senior Christians in and out of Korea and a business as mission in the creative access area.

Beyond the Book

The editors and partners are well aware of the complexity of the subject matter, and it will be naïve to think that theological explanations will be sufficient to turn the immigrant Christian communities into an effective missionary force. It is important to recognize that immigrant life is seldom rosy as envisioned by many. In fact, there are rapidly increasing forced migrants such as refugees due to wars and natural disasters. For this reason, mission leaders will need to learn a great deal from the mass of sociological, economic and political studies on migration. By nature, however, this book is intended to be more theologically and missiologically orientated.

Also, it is important to recognize that migration is not always a one-way traffic: it is increasingly a two-way phenomenon. For example, Korea was traditionally a 'migrant-out' country, that is, people left the country, but now, it receives, more than it sends. Often the 'out' group is much simpler in their motivation than the 'in' group. Again, for Korea, it ranges from highly educated professionals seeking work opportunities in large companies, universities and government agencies, to low paid factory workers and North Korean refugees. This 'messy' situation has created new missionary challenges and opportunities. Churches need to learn from other disciplines, as theology alone will not solve complex social challenges.

As already alluded to above, the Korean church needs to take an older brother's role in facilitating, resourcing and empowering other developing missional churches especially from the Global South by its examples, sharing its experiences, and helping them to undertake serious research. This critical call, however, is not unachievable if it learns to effectively utilize the broad network of its missionaries all over the world.

Part 1

Foundations

A Millennial Shift of Global Christianity and Mission: An Initial Reflection

Wonsuk Ma

The year 2010 was an extremely illustrious year for global mission circles with the commemoration of the historic 1910 Edinburgh Missionary Conference, the watershed of the modern missionary movement. As various mission gatherings found their way of reflecting on the century of global Christianity and its mission, the most agreed and obvious difference between the two points of mission history is the mega-shift of global Christianity. Causes for this have been studied both by Westerners as well as 'Southerners,' and the impact of the growth of Christianity in the Global South, although still in its initial stage of its global influence, has been strongly felt on various fronts.

The present study purports to open up the changing landscape of global Christianity in the context of the millennial shift theory recently argued, and to discuss the implications of this global shift for mission theory and practice, particularly for churches in the Global South. Within this global mission framework, as a concluding reflection, I suggest the unique place of diaspora as a significant factor in God's mission in the coming days.

By nature, therefore, this study attempts to draw a larger framework of global Christianity and its mission, so that the significance of migrant Christians is examined as an intentional mission agenda and resource. As the global church has been grappling with this sweeping change in our own lifetime, observations and predictions abound. My own reflection has emerged as an Asian mission thinker and practitioner, witnessing with awe the rapid change of the Christian landscape regionally and globally over several decades. This reflection, therefore, represents an extremely formative phase of initial thoughts and convictions.

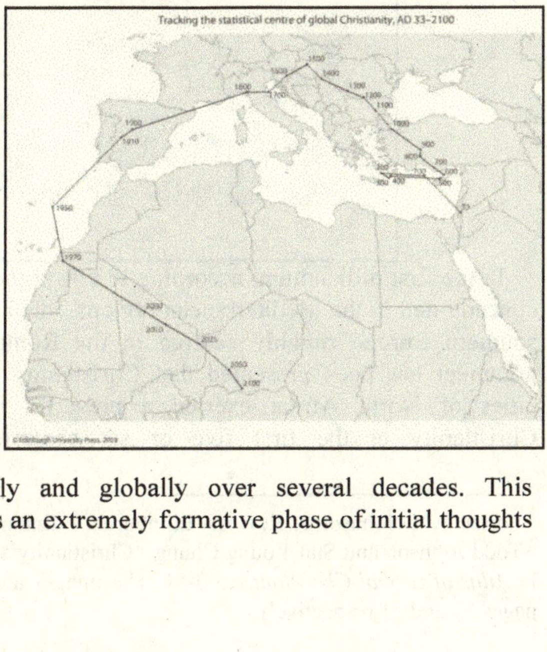

As the nature of this discussion is global in scope, over-generalization cannot be avoided and some tentative conclusions may not be applicable to every local context. Nonetheless, I hope that the study will encourage diaspora Christian communities, especially in the West, to develop their self-understanding as mission orientated. Here, the word 'diaspora' is used to refer to dispersed or migrated Christians and their communities.

Millennial Shifts of Global Christianity

One of the Edinburgh 2010 publications, *Atlas of Global Christianity*[1] was launched during the centenary gathering in June 2010. This atlas is the first of its kind including full graphic features in the accompanying media material on the provincial level. One of the most significant contributions of the *Atlas*, in my view, is the presentation of the North-South shifts of global Christianity in each millennium of church history.[2] Although the precise method, by which the centre of Christian gravity is calculated, is not clear and the accuracy of specific figures can be questioned, the presentations are extremely useful in tracing the trajectory of the development of global Christianity. The starting point of the Christian movement is, of course, Jerusalem, and the pivot between East and West, as well as North and South is calculated to identify the centre of gravity of global Christianity in each major historical period. There are several visual presentations to illustrate the oscillation of global Christianity between South and North.

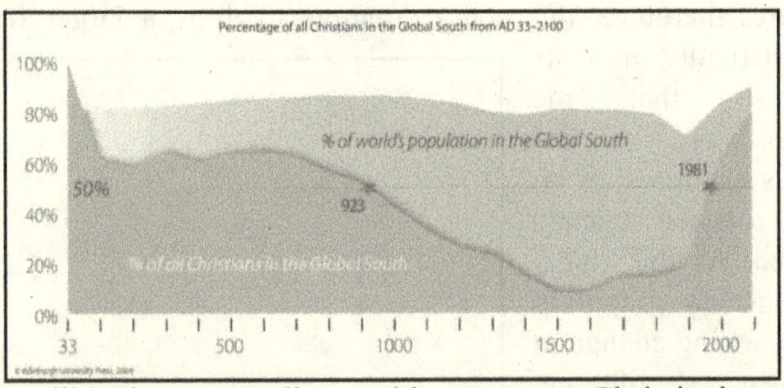

In the first millennium, according to this argument, Christianity was heavily concentrated in the Mediterranean regions, including Asia, northern Africa and southern Europe roughly centred in the Roman Empire. In fact, a strong argument has been presented that Christianity centred around two principal cities of North Africa exerted a powerful influence in the shaping of Christianity in the first five or six centuries: Alexandria in Orthodox

[1] Edited by T. Johnson & K. Ross (Edinburgh: Edinburgh University Press, 2010).

[2] Todd Johnson and Sun Young Chung, 'Christianity's Centre of Gravity, AD 33-2100', in *Atlas of Global Christianity*, 50-51. The images are from the same writing found in pages 53 and 51 respectively.

Christianity and Carthage in Western Christianity.[3] In spite of the rise of Islam, in the seventh century, global Christianity was a religion of the South. The existence of vibrant Christian centres in India, Ethiopia and Egypt to this day is a stark reminder of this fact.

In the second millennium or precisely from 923, according to Stott and Chung, Christians in the global North steadily grew and eventually outnumbered its southern counterpart.[4] Global Christianity began to expand in the North of the Mediterranean, as the Roman Church grew in strength with the rise of the Middle Ages in Europe. Reformation further brought renewed missionary impetus to European Christianity. This north- and westward move was accelerated on the one hand by European colonial expansion and the discovery of new lands, including the Americas, and on the other hand, by the shrinking influence of the Eastern Church in Asia and Africa as Islam practically took most of their Christian strongholds in the two regions. The flourishing of Orthodox Christianity in new territories such as Eastern Europe and Russia accelerated the speed of the north-westward shift. Western civilization flexed its muscles in various ways, but often in the Constantinian sense. For example, the Crusades are a prime example of the cross and sword going hand in hand, and the missionary movement was often associated with the paths of the sword.

The third millennium has just dawned on us, and global Christianity made another millennial turn in 1981, according to Stott & Chung.[5] A steep southward momentum was recorded in the 1950s. It was in the following decades, when the majority of African nations gained independence, and also several important revivals were recorded. The birth of the African Independent Church movement also rose during this period. Then, in the 1970s, according to the Stott & Chung trajectory, global Christianity's southward move also gained a distinct eastward turn. This is the time churches in Asia grew significantly: in China, Korea, the Philippines, Singapore, Malaysia, Indonesia, Myanmar and India. They grew not only in numbers but also in missionary awareness. Eventually, many of these churches have become substantial new missionary churches. It is estimated that, some time in the 1990s, the total number of non-Western missionaries topped their Western counterparts. Many revivals during this period and ensuing church growth exhibited unmistakable Pentecostal-Charismatic features, particularly in worship and their openness to the work of the Holy Spirit.

---

[3] Thomas C. Oden, *How Africa Shaped the Christian Mind: Rediscovering the African Seedbed of Western Christianity* (Downer's Grove, IL: IVP Books, 2007), 42-61 specifically lists the seven most significant contributions of African Christianity in the first five centuries of Christian history.

[4] Stott & Chung, 'Christianity's Centre of Gravity', 50.

[5] Stott & Chung, 'Christianity's Centre of Gravity', 50.

While churches in Asia, Africa, Latin America and post-Communist Eastern Europe have gained a new impetus in vitality and missionary zeal, the churches in the West have steadily lost their strength at the onslaught of secularism, pluralism, and materialism. Once powerful missionary churches in the West may now transfer their leadership to the new mission players. Following Walls' painful historical pattern of the serial move of Christianity, the West will eagerly wait for the new energy to come from the churches in the Global South.[6] Today, the largest churches in Europe and the United Kingdom, where many historic churches are now devoid of people, are African-led.

These latest global shifts took place in the present generation, and the gap in the South-North divide will continue to grow. As the theory of the millennial shift appears to be validated, the churches in the South as well as the North face tremendous challenges and opportunities, requiring enormous adjustments of our assumptions and practices, both in being a church and in doing mission. Christian immigrants from the South to the West, therefore, have the potential to serve as the first line of engagement between the growing South and the waning North.

Business as Usual? Challenges to Established Mission Thinking

As mentioned earlier, one quite useful means, by which to observe the drastic changes in global Christianity over a century, are the reference points between the Edinburgh Missionary Conference of 1910 and its centenary celebrated in June, 2010.[7] The contrast highlights the changes that took place between the two gatherings.

The turn of the twentieth century was arguably at the height of the Western colonial era, and also the culminating point of the great century of Christianity and mission. Thus, the first historic 'ecumenical' missionary conference was a strategic gathering among 'Christian' (thus, mostly Western) nations with the firm conviction that the world could be evangelised in their own generation. Every means, be it political, economic, military, and, of course, Christian were at their disposal. However, in their own generation, it was not world evangelization but the most destructive wars, two of them, and among Christian nations, that devastated the West's missionary hopes. These were followed by a series of events not anticipated in the 1910 gathering: the end of the colonial era, the independence of many former colonies, the Cold War period, the waning of the Western churches, and the rise of the churches in the Global South. The meagre size of the centenary gathering, only one-fifth of the 1910

[6] Andrew F. Walls, 'Christianity across Twenty Centuries', in *Atlas of Global Christianity*, 48.

[7] The aim of the Atlas was precisely to formulate the trajectory of global Christianity in the last hundred years between the two Edinburgh gatherings: Todd M. Johnson and Kenneth R. Ross, 'Preface', *Atlas of Global Christianity*, x.

meeting reflects the fragile state of the Western church, in comparison to the Lausanne Congress in Cape Town of the same year, which drew more than 4,000 delegates, more than half of whom were from the Global South.

A quick comparative glance sees the new ways of missionary engagement and a new set of theological assumptions to support them. One hundred years ago, about 80% of global Christians lived in the global North, particularly in the North Atlantic region, although South America was also considered Christian. But today, close to 70% of world Christians live in the Global South, that is, Africa, Asia, Latin America and Eastern Europe. It was graphically visible in the conference delegates. Hundred years ago, less than 20 of the 1200 conference delegates came from the non-Western world, or from Asia to be precise. But in the Edinburgh 2010 conference, over 50% of delegates came from the Global South, while the 2010 Lausanne Congress reports even a higher proportion drawn from the South.

Understandably almost all the missionaries, at the turn of the twentieth century, were from the Western nations. As discussed above, today more than half of the world's missionary force is from the emerging churches in the South. If we revise the definition of 'missionaries' to include cross-cultural workers within a 'country', I am sure those from the new churches have far exceeded the Western missionaries. For example, most of the so-called BRICs countries, namely Brazil, Russia, India and China with their large populations, growing economies, and the growth of Christianity, are potentially 'super' missionary-sending countries.

The following discussion is to challenge several key mission assumptions developed in the West, particularly in the last two centuries. Often, mission in a 'business usual' mode has unknowingly shaped a strong set of assumptions and they in turn impacted on missionary 'rules of engagement'. That is, the assumptions and rules have been shaped by the Western social and religious context. Often, these paradigms are not questioned for their theological validity, and, unfortunately, this uncritical acceptance is influencing new missionary churches in the Global South. For this reason, several established 'missionary myths' need to be challenged in the light of the shift in global Christianity, and also how the early church practiced its mission.

Only Christian Nations Do Mission

The series of questions deal with qualifications or the 'right' for mission. The 1910 Edinburgh Conference was planned, organized and run by Western churches, with a small group of delegates and invitees from some mission 'fields', or beneficiaries of missionary activities. Although the term 'Christendom' may have not been used during the conference, in the back of everyone's mind, it must have assumed that only after a country has been fully evangelized, or Christianized, does the nation earn a right to be a missionary nation. That is, only when 'home' has been reached, a 'foreign mission' can begin, or mission moves from a Christian 'centre' to fringes. One hundred years ago, such were Western Europe, North America and Oceania and it seems reasonable and logical. However, it is a sheer myth.

Today, this assumption is challenged by two realities. First, it is no longer 100% Christianized nations that send out their missionaries. Many new missionary mega-powers like Korea, China, and India are not 'Christian' countries, although countries like Brazil, the Philippines, Nigeria and others have more of a Christian population than others. In fact, India and China claim less than 10% of their populations as Christian. However, they could be well among the top five missionary-sending nations, if we view it per capita. According to the seventh edition *Operation World*,[8] several fascinating facts can be extracted. Regardless of the accuracy of the figures, I picked several top missionary-sending countries and calculated how many believers it takes to send a cross-cultural missionary. USA takes 263 (or 93,500 missionaries out of 246,553,000 belivers) to send one cross-cultural and international missionary,[9] South Korea takes 698 (or 21,500 missionaries out of 15,011,000 belivers),[10] China takes 870 believers (or 120,000 missionaries—both working within and without China—out of 105,382,000 belivers),[11] and the United Kingdom takes 5787 (or 6,405 missionaries out of 37,067,000 believers).[12]

The second, this time, a reverse argument also proves the challenge. Not all 'Christian' nations are missionary entities. Although this notion has much to do with the definition of mission, some African nations, for example, which have more than an impressive 80% Christianization success, are not necessarily strong missionary countries. This of course challenges us with a deep question: what makes a church missional?

Now we can turn our attention to the early church. The missionary impetus of the early church was not based on the two-step plan of evangelization: home and abroad. The church by nature, thus, from its birth, is missionary. The Jerusalem church was given a missionary plan before it was born (Act 1:8), and the Antioch church was a missionary church, while 'home' remained a missionary challenge. It is plausible that the missionary 'failure' of Jerusalem church may have come from the programmatic or progressive understanding of mission: only when Jerusalem is reached, can they move to Judea, Samaria and, at the last, to the ends of the earth. The intention could have been a simultaneous missionary move, that is, while the church struggles in Jerusalem, the church is to be an active missionary agent. The Antioch church lived in a mission field, while far-reaching in mission. In fact, the Antioch church

[8] Jason Mandryk, *Operation World: The Definitive Prayer Guide to Every Nation*, 7th ed. (Gerrards Cross, UK: WEC International, 2011).

[9] Mandryk, *Operation World*, 862.

[10] Mandryk, *Operation World*, 509-510.

[11] Mandryk, *Operation World*, 215-16.

[12] Mandryk, *Operation World*, 851-52.

provides a useful parallel to today's emerging missionary churches, as mission has to take place at home as well as 'abroad'.

This comes with an enormous new opportunity as well as challenges. To begin with, the understanding of what is mission has to be seriously revisited from the perspective of the new mission players. It will inevitably be holistic in scope, encompassing proclamation and justice with everything in between. The place of a Christian community, as a sign of God's kingdom, will be a significant 'missionary' presence in many Christian-minority places. Even if marginalized and sometimes persecuted, the presence of a local congregation itself is a powerful declaration that God is the Lord and He has an answer to every issue with which the society struggles. Consequently, missionary engagement will be profoundly affected as the missioners are now in the 'field'. For instance, issues of other faiths will have a radically different light, when those, who are surrounded by other religions as a minority, set the rules of missionary engagement. The 'Antioch' model of the church opens new horizons for mission, and the millennial shift of global Christianity has presented us with this rare opportunity.

Only Resource-Rich Countries Can Do Mission

I am sure not even the slightest suggestion has been made that only rich countries can do mission. However, the mission players of the last two hundred years of the previous century were all from economically resourceful countries. One may argue that the cause and effect should be reversed, that is, mission commitment resulted in God's blessing. To the eyes of the rest of the world, however, finance has become an assumed priority requirement for mission, and this has often been the first excuse of Christian-rich countries not engaging in mission. This image is often created by the image of a Western, often white male, missionary, fully 'armed' with expensive gadgets, acting as a benefactor to local churches and communities. This has inevitably influenced the understanding of mission and missionaries. This emphasis on resources, even if shaped unintentionally, has serious consequences as we see today. Dependency, for example, is an ongoing challenge to many emerging nations and their churches. Equally serious is that the pattern of mission engagement among the new missionary churches of the South often uncritically follows the established notion of resources as a missionary prerequisite.

Today, in spite of criticism that new missionary churches tend to follow the old 'established' Western missionary paradigm, signs abound to suggest that the new emerging churches do not wait to have a certain economic level before they begin missionary engagement. One such example is diaspora. The life of immigrants as a social and cultural minority is never easy. In spite of the urgency of survival in a new environment, stories abound that such communities become the lifeline for the fragile churches back home, often under oppressive political and social systems. For years, for example, Nepali immigrants on the Indian-Nepali borders exerted their concerted efforts in evangelism, training, and Bible translation for their homeland, while the churches were persecuted by a socialist regime and a Hindu social system. A similar effort has been present in the Bhutan communities on the Indian side of the border. I am sure that many Eastern European immigrant communities in Western Europe were the major source of strength in maintaining persecuted churches 'back home' during the Cold War era. The diaspora communities have also shown their unique missionary potential, this time, to the host countries, in spite of their own fight for survival. The story of Sunday Adelaja of the Embassy of God Church in Ukraine is a well-known example. Adelaja, a Nigerian student in Kiev found the Christian faith during his study, and eventually established the largest single congregation in Europe. The church's significant influence on Ukrainian society has been studied by many observers.[13] If one compares the two countries, the mission should have taken the other direction, from the Western and traditionally Christian and Ukraine to the under-developed African Nigeria. But it does not have to be so. Understandably, however, the new mission players are found in South-to-South settings, such as Ethiopian missionaries working in Pakistan, and Filipino missionaries in Cambodia.

The story of the early church's expansion in the first century would be more according to this paradigm, with Galilean fishermen reaching out to Roman citizens. The apostles' instance on work-and-preach may be an indication of their subsistence, as much as of their principle of self-support (2 Cor. 11:8). The 'nameless' missionaries recorded in Acts 11 may shed light on our discussion, when fleeing the persecution in Jerusalem, some 'travelled as far as Phoenicia, Cyprus and Antioch' (11:19). The impression is such that from Jerusalem they were reaching the ends of the earth (Acts 1:8). As the three places mentioned are all north of Jerusalem, one can easily assume that these 'refugees' were either Jewish diaspora or pilgrims from these regions.[14] As they reached out to the Greek-speaking population, these Jews no longer enjoyed an ethnic acceptance among fellow Jews. Their disadvantage could also have been felt in gaps in the social status between these missionaries and the societies such as Antioch where they preached the gospel. That Paul often debated with local intellectuals, such as in Athens (Acts 17:16-34), serves as an illustration. It is quite clear that in their missionary context, the missionaries did not come with ready resources to offer assistance to the people in the 'field', nor strengthened their position with material wealth. Rather they often came with subsistence or out of need.

---

[13] For example, J.K. Asamoah-Gyadu, 'African Initiated Christianity in Eastern Europe: Church of the "Embassy of God" in Ukraine', *International Bulletin of Missionary Research* 30:2 (2006), 73-75.

[14] However, among them were 'men from…Cyrene', North Africa (11:20) indicating a more intentional missionary motivation.

This paradigm shift has a serious practical implication: the primary resource of mission is a transformed life through the gospel, but not material riches or technology. If a missionary symbol is a satellite linked to a wireless communication gadget in a deep mountain village which does not have electricity, it is quite wrong. If new mission players also continue this trend, this is hopelessly fatal. But missionaries regardless of their national origin identify themselves with the people they minister to in every aspect of their lives, and that is called 'incarnational mission' after our Lord.

Mission is by the Developed to the Developing or Underdeveloped

Related to the preceding points is the notion that the developed, civilised or 'first-world' nations do mission to the 'heathen', uncivilised or underdeveloped 'third world'. At least the last two hindered years of Christian mission was undertaken by so called 'first' world nations, developed in politics, economics, culture and education. This practice and notion of mission is deeply rooted in the racial supremacy of the West and colonial imperialism. Politically, the West took the rest of the world as its 'subject', while the extremely unbiblical and counter-humanistic claim of a 'white man's burden' was viewed quite natural during the 'great [missionary] century. One of the mission aims was in 'civilizing' the heathens, by introducing medicine, education and 'proper' (that is, 'Western') ways of living. There is perfectly legitimate in introducing new ways to improve life, but this approach often creates a value system which privileges the Western paradigms while bringing a harsh judgement upon indigenous culture. This cultural imperialism sometimes produces rather humorous images. One of them is what I encountered in the Northern Philippines among the Igorot mountain tribes. An Igorot young man has 'proper' attire with a necktie and a suit, but with bare feet and a loin cloth, called a g-string, for the lower half of his body. However, there were many serious cases. When Catholicism was first introduced to Korea, thousands of early believers were executed by the state for refusing ancestor rites and (for men) cutting their long hair. Christianity was misunderstood as requiring a Western lifestyle, with a deep confusion between Christianity and the missionary's culture.

Today, about two-thirds of global Christians live in the Global South, or developing or under-developed world. As there are more missionaries from these churches than those from the traditional Western churches, mission workers from 'under-developed' countries are now found working in other 'underdeveloped' or developing countries as well as developed ones. Without much reflection, the flow of mission from relatively 'developed' to less developed is also observed. For instance, the majority of Korean missionaries are concentrated in Asia and Africa, where Korea, in general, can play a 'superior' role. Often motivated by pragmatic reasons, this pattern has unfortunately continued the unhealthy and unbiblical notion of mission flowing from civilised to 'heathen'. Missionary movements from South to South often ignore cultural and economic differences, as now Chinese missionaries are found in a number of central Asian nations. However, an increasing number of missionaries from the 'South' are found in the West, as well as diaspora communities serving as a vanguard of emerging and dynamic Christianity of the Global South in the midst of secular Western societies where Christianity has been weakening. In fact a large number of Filipino migrants in the Middle East and the West, for example, have demonstrated the possibility of 'reverse' mission, that is, from the developing to the developed. If the flow of mission has to be from gospel rich to the gospel poor, the 'received' notion of mission from the developed to the developing world is a sheer coincidence for the last two centuries.

As alluded to above, the move of the early church's missionary centre from Jerusalem to Antioch was a revolutionary development. When Christian mission moved beyond the Jewish racial framework, Jewish Christians no longer enjoyed their cultural acceptability and privilege in the face of the 'Gentiles'. In fact, some groups may have viewed Jews as racially and culturally inferior to theirs, as often illustrated in Paul's encounters with social elites in various cities. Ultimately, who reached the Roman elite families with the Christian faith? Early missionary forces may have been slaves, merchants, manual workers, and the like whose life and work manifested the new found religion. Early Christians did not have, in general, the cultural or social advantages over their 'mission field'.

Summary: The Issue of Power

The core of the paradigm shift in Christian mission is the issue of power: is mission achieved by power or powerlessness? In one sense, the gospel is the power of salvation, and this power can be manifested in various ways as witnessed in the life of Jesus: from the precarious suffering and death to the demonstration of power in healing and exorcism. In fact, many aspects of mission demonstrate this power through the work of the Holy Spirit. However, it is important to note that God's power is manifest through the total obedience of the vessels, often in their weakness. Without the ultimate sacrifice of Christ, through his death, the power of redemption cannot be accomplished. The demonstration of his power and authority over principalities and powers has its place, but not as a substitute for his obedience through total surrender. Paul's understanding of God's power, through his own weakness (2 Cor 12:10), attests to the same principle.

The 'established' mission paradigm in the nineteenth and twentieth centuries is that of mission with power, be it political, cultural, economic or military. It also includes 'Christian' power. Mission with superiority, or with an upper hand, however, is far from the testimony of the life of Jesus. Although the Jerusalem church may have perceived mission in connection with superiority or power, this was quickly replaced by the Antiochian model, mission undertaken with a new paradigm, mission with weakness. It was possible because Antioch was not a 'centre' of Christianity, but still remained as a 'mission field', surrounded by culture and forces challenging and even threatening the Christian presence.

The argument that, although hard to independently verify, the total Muslim converts in the Middle East through Filipino domestic helpers far outnumber the converts through duly deployed missionaries in the region is revealing.[15] If the two groups of mission players are compared to each other, in the places of origin (still predominantly from the West), training, resources, support, and the like, the former cannot outperform the latter. The most striking difference is that the domestic helpers are there to serve but not to instruct and teach. The place of weakness plays such a powerful role in mission, and our observation of the scriptures proves that this is how mission is to be approached. The new mission players from 'mission fields', struggling with resources, and culturally and politically 'weak' places have the potential not only to revitalize Christian mission but also to restore the right 'rules of missionary engagement' as informed by the New Testament. This potential will be realized, only if the mission players and their churches know that the 'established' or 'received' mission paradigm is to be critically evaluated before adoption or rejection, as it was the product of the West's own golden missionary age and socio-political context. One thing they need to avoid is the 'business as usual' mindset. It requires a serious reflection on the scriptural and historical practices and principles that informed the practices. This is where an entirely new breed of missiologists is needed, and the higher education systems which will raise them.

Implications

Then what are some of the implications of the millennial shift of global Christianity for mission? The change in the mission paradigm discussed above has the potential to transform mission thinking and practice altogether. The following list will be only representative and the will inevitably increase as more participate in this journey of exploratory thinking.

First, what constitutes mission will require serious probing. The old dichotomy between proclamation and social engagement will be broken once and for all, as missiology is constructed by the new mission players. This

---

[15] Melba Padilla Maggay made this comment during her verbal presentation of her study, although her published chapter does not include this: 'Early Protestant Missionary Efforts in the Philippines: Some Intercultural Issues', in Wonsuk Ma and Julie C. Ma (eds), *Asian Church and God's Mission: Studies Presented in the International Symposium on Asian Mission in Manila, January 2002* (Quezon City, Philippines: OMF Lit., 2003), particularly 39.

dichotomy, found between the ecumenical and evangelical circles, and also later among evangelicals since the Lausanne Congress of 1974, is simply irrelevant. The subsequent discussions of the Lausanne circles, especially led by mission leaders of the emerging churches, resulted in the formation of a network called the International Fellowship of Mission Theologians in the Two-Thirds World (INFEMIT), and this circle has championed the concept of holistic mission for evangelical mission.[16] The 'Antiochian' reality of the Global South, that is, mission taking place in a mission field, will embrace a vast range of social and cultural issues in mission.

Second, as our discussion has struggled with the issue of power, the new missionary paradigm will wrestle with a new set of powers. This will include spiritual powers found in their indigenous as well as dominant religions. More often than not, it will be political powers which Christian mission needs to deal with, especially the oppressive and corrupt ones, as well as justice issues.

Third, peace and reconciliation will become a critical part of Christian mission, as new mission players find themselves surrounded by often 'hostile' forces, unlike the Western churches in the midst of Christendom. Engaging with other faiths will be no longer viewed as an exotic discussion on the 'other side of the river', as now many Christians are living in the midst of other faiths.[17] A peaceful life becomes a priority for everyone, and Christian mission will take this extremely seriously. Ecumenism, on the other hand, will also be viewed as a part of Christian reality, if the issue is left to the new churches. To begin with, their predominantly relational and holistic orientation of life will take the issue in a different direction.

Fourth, the rise of the new missionary churches has created a new missionary 'order', that is, from everywhere to everywhere.[18] This multi-directional flow of mission is a stark contrast to the previous one: from the West to the rest. Former mission powers are rapidly becoming a desperate mission field, while the old mission field is now for missionary-sending players. However, because of many new missionary churches that find themselves in the midst of a 'mission field', potentially every nation can be missionary-sending as well as a receiving body.

Fifth, perhaps most importantly for the expansion of global Christianity, evangelism and church growth will be seen in an entirely new light. The Edinburgh 2010 celebration was marked by the 'sophistication' of mission discussions, particularly in comparison with its original gathering. The earlier one made it clear that the evangelisation of the world was the foremost mission

---

[16] For its historical development, see Al Tizon, *Transformation after Lausanne: Radical Evangelical Mission in Global-Local Perspective* (Oxford: Regnum Books, 2008).

[17] A Korean expression, 'Watching a fire on the other side of the river' refers to an indifferent attitude toward a deeply troubled reality, but which is not one's own.

[18] For example, Samuel Escobar, *The New Global Mission: From Everywhere to Everyone* (Downer's Grove, IL: InterVarsity Press, 2003).

agenda. One hundred years later, evangelism was hardly discussed, and the presentation of the largest congregation in the world was with met hushed voices of 'so what' predominantly from the Western delegates. In fact, it is sadly amusing to hear comments such as 'I am glad that we still have one-third of the world as Christian'. It is important for all of us to ask the foundational question: do we want to see world Christianity continue to decline as seen in the West, or do we want to see it finally cross the one-third barrier of the world's population? Unless the world allows the new mission players to bring their stories of various encounters with God and take the lead in mission, one hundred years later, we may be astonished to have Christianity still around, not to mention its proportion or its impact. Without celebrating the growth of individual congregations and the unashamed presentation of the gospel even in hostile environment, the future of global Christianity will continue in its survival mode. The West must help the rest not to repeat its fatal error in taking Christianity on the path of decline. In fact, it is the turn of the churches in the Global South to revive the Western church, and the role of the diaspora, therefore, in the midst of the secular West, is critically important.

This list must go on, and many need to join this exploration. Do I present Christianity in the emerging South as the ideal form close to the scriptural model? By no means, as in the first generation of the global tilt of Christianity, forms of mediocrity and abuses have sprung up in virtually every part of the Southern continents. The prosperity in its worst forms is found there, and so does a fierce entrepreneurial model of churches. Korea has now more than one hundred Presbyterian denominations and most of them are 'home-made'. The worst scenario will be a Christian dinosaur, with a massive body but practically a brain as big as an egg. What I presented above is the best case scenario, with the full potential of the emerging movement finally realised.

The future of 'Southern Christianity' and, consequently, global Christianity will hinge on several key components. Just two are worth our immediate attention. The first is the role of the Western churches in this changing balance of global Christianity. It is important to begin a serious inventory of its gifts to further strengthen the emerging churches, as well as the mistakes, so that the rest will not repeat the same fate. The second is theological education. How to nurture its leaders in various levels of influence on the churches in the Global South will determine its future. If my observation is right, theological education is where the West has made the most profound impact, good as well as no so good. If an African theological seminary operates with a curriculum suitable for a future pastor who will work in the heart of Western Europe, everyone fails. On the other hand, if key and global leaders trained in the West are equipped to be authentically relevant in their context in the South, while gaining full competence to exercise their leadership for global Christianity, we can live with the expectation of the best future for the global church and its mission. The West has unique resources to assist, encourage and even facilitate the

development of theological minds, while the South can bring its dynamism and commitment to the world.

Identity Crisis for the Diaspora Community

Sungho Choi

Introduction

This paper attempts at examining briefly the concept of diaspora in the formation of biblical thinking and how it contributes to the overall understanding of Israel's identity in the Bible. After discussing this within the biblical context I shall examine how the concept has a profound relevance in contemporary society and how one is to define his/her identity in a so-called diaspora environment. Although the paper is ultimately concerned with the modern contemporary understanding of diaspora and the relevance it has for Christian communities worldwide, it is nevertheless important to have some awareness of the biblical background of the emerging phenomenon. The reason for the inclusion of a biblical discussion of the concept is that any missiological model or strategy should be anchored firmly in the Bible. The outline of the paper can thus be divided as follows; first, I shall lay the foundation of this discussion by surveying the role of the diaspora in the redemptive history of Israel. Secondly, I shall examine how Israel dealt with an identity crisis throughout her turbulent relationship with Yahweh and how she continued to define her identity within the context of a foreign environment. Thirdly, on the basis of biblical evidence, I shall direct my attention to our modern contemporary setting and discuss how one is to define his/her identity in a diaspora community and the role of the Church in nurturing one's identity in Christ.

Biblical Survey: Centrality of Diaspora in the Redemptive History of Israel

The term diaspora is commonly understood as being scattered or dispersed from the homeland which is indeed what characterizes Israel's history as she was constantly invaded by foreign oppressors. The nation of Israel was forced into a series of exiles by the Assyrians (722 BCE) and Babylon (597 BCE), and later dispersed throughout the Roman Empire to Egypt, Asia Minor, Greece and Italy.[1] Although there is no technical Hebrew equivalent for the Greek word *diaspora* the history of Israel in the Old Testament is made up of stories of

[1] Cf. Narry F. Santos, 'Survey of the Diaspora Occurrences in the Bible and of their Contexts in Christian Missions in the Bible', in Luis Pantoja, Jr., Sadiri Joy Tira, Enoch Wan (eds), *Scattered: The Filipino Global Presence* (Lifechange Publishing, 2004), 53.

Yahweh's chosen nation in constant expulsions from the homeland.[2] In the ancient historical context of Israel, the term diaspora is related to the pain and sorrow of being forcefully led away or deported from the homeland. In other words, in the history of Israel, diaspora is perceived as a substitute for exile or banishment from the homeland which is a prevalent theme within the prophetic tradition of the Old Testament. It is also within Israel's diaspora setting from which Israel matured in faith and the Jewish belief of the Messiah precipitated during the times of exile. Therefore, the diaspora environment, while it was perceived as suffering in a sense that Israel had to be expelled and dispersed across the nations was nonetheless a crucial setting in the formation of Israel's religious and national identity.

The coming of the Messiah, who will restore the covenantal relationship between Yahweh and Israel, is the central message that the prophets preached in response to the threat of exile. The national theology of Israel and the messianic expectation are products of Israel's political crisis which resulted in her diaspora. During the Assyrian invasion, prior to the Babylonian captivity, the national theology of Israel which was anchored in the affirmation of Yahweh's choice of Zion and his promise to the Davidic dynasty of an everlasting reign were thrown into the crisis. The prophetic response to the national crisis seems somewhat varied. Bright notes that Jeremiah utterly rejected the national confidence in the Davidic promises. He did not deny its theoretical validity nor did he reject the institution of the monarchy as such. But he was convinced that, since the existing state had failed in its obligations, neither it nor its kings would know anything of promises.[3] Ezekiel on the other hand spoke of the greater New Exodus (20:33-38) as he eagerly anticipated the restored nation under the Davidic kingship (34:23-24; 37:15-28).

The time of the exilic plight for Israel was a testing time not just for the political tenacity of the state but also for her faith in Yahweh's redemptive plan. On the one hand, the period could be seen as a judgment upon an unfaithful Israel which was guilty of breaching the covenantal relationship with Yahweh and, therefore, it was a well-deserved punishment for her stubborn and unrepentant heart. On the other hand, it could be argued that the period had a didactic purpose for Israel as the crisis of the exile forced her to reassess her faith in Yahweh. It provided an opportunity to purge Israel of sin and look to a new future of national restoration.[4] The era of diaspora, due to the exile, was

---

[2] Santos, 'Survey of the Diaspora Occurrences', 57 notes that in Deuteronomy 30:4, the Hebrew root is *ndt*, which in the niphal means, 'expelled, driven out'. The nearest Hebrew term, which may correspond to diaspora is *golah*, or *galot*, or the emphatic *galota* (from the Aramaic root *galo*).

[3] J. Bright, *A History of Israel*, rev. ed. (London: SCM, 1972), 334.

[4] Bright, *A History of Israel*, 350, argues that the cultic laws which comprise the bulk of the so-called priestly code, and which reflect the practice of the Jerusalem Temple were likewise collected and codified in a definitive form at about this time. Also, the priestly

undoubtedly the most challenging time for Israel, but it was also the time when she grew in spiritual maturity. In Deutero-Isaiah, the entire prophecy is dominated by the consolation and conviction that Yahweh, as Israel's true King, will come and redeem his people scattered throughout the nations. Those who returned from the Babylonian exile under the leadership of Zerubbabel, were obviously eager to reinstitute the cult of Israel and reconstruct the Temple but the early years of the restoration community (538-522 BCE) again proved bitterly disappointing (cf. Hag. 1:2-11; 2:15-17). In this dire predicament, the prophets Haggai and Zechariah gave a message of comfort and encouragement that Yahweh would not abandon Zion and affirmed the fulfilment of Yahweh's promise in the national theology of Israel and the Davidic dynasty. The prophet Haggai charged people with the conviction that Yahweh would defeat the enemy nations and would shortly restore Israel (cf. Hag. 2:20-23). With this encouragement the Temple was completed and dedicated in 515 BCE (Ezra 1-6), marking the beginning of Second Temple Judaism.[5]

Despite the difficulties and challenges of the exilic environment, the prophets did not give up their hopes. They continued to assert that Yahweh would establish the greater New Exodus event through which He would gather and redeem the true remnants of Israel from the nations. What is significant here is that despite countless disappointments and failures, Jewish religion never detached itself from the messianic hope of Israel and still managed to maintain its identity by upholding the Davidic dynasty and, in the end, that Yahweh would fulfil his promises by sending the Messiah to establish salvation for the elect.[6]

From this brief survey of Israel's diaspora in the Old Testament period which was the direct result of the series of exilic plights, we may come up with two observations: First, the exile, which is primarily perceived as the demise of the Israelite nation, was in fact a crucial period in which the messianic hope was more pervasive than is usually the case.[7] In other words, from a missiological perspective, diaspora, although it is often characterized in terms of challenges and difficulties of living as aliens in foreign environments, can be a strategic missionary asset in the expansion of God's kingdom. The exilic and post-exilic periods were a time when Israel fervently looked for the strong

---

narrative of the Pentateuch (P) was composed, probably during the sixth century BCE and probably in the period of exile.

[5] E. Ferguson, *Backgrounds of Early Christianity*, 2nd ed. (Grand Rapids, MI: Eerdmans, 1993), 377 notes that the great work of Ezra was the restoration of the law (cf. Neh. 8-10). The post-exilic community was dedicated to the study of the law.

[6] Bright, *A History of Israel*, 456, notes that Obadiah looked (vs. 15-21) for a restoration of the Davidic boundaries on the Day of Yahweh, and even the Chronicler desired a rehabilitation of the national-cultic institutions after the order of David (Ezra 3:10; Neh. 12:45).

[7] Ronald de Vaux, *Ancient Israel-Its Life and Institutions*, trans. John McHugh (London: Darton, Longman & Todd, 1973), 110.

intervention of Yahweh in the midst of the oppression and the deportation from the homeland. The context of diaspora, therefore, provided an exposure for the people of Israel through which their faith in Yahweh intensified. This is also the case in the New Testament era when the diaspora takes on a more missionary outlook. Narry F. Santos notes that in the Book of Acts, diaspora relates to the scattering of the Christians of the Hellenistic Jewish origin, Greek-speaking Jewish Christians in areas where there was a non-Jewish majority (Acts 11:19). Here, Santos also points out that those who were scattered played essential roles in the expansion of early Christianity or to missions (Acts 8:4-8, 40; 11:19-21).[8] I shall discuss in more detail later on how the diaspora community in the contemporary world can be utilized as a strategic missionary asset.

Secondly, from our survey, it is clear that the prophetic tradition placed a heavy emphasis upon Israel's national as well as religious identity. There are constant doubts and criticisms at the failures of Israel's monarchy but Israel never detaches herself from its Jewish identity. This is the major point which I need to discuss in greater detail. It is evident that the Bible constantly emphasizes the Jewish identity in the context of foreign domination and the emphasis continues to the New Testament era, as Jesus' origin is thoroughly embedded within Israel's royal genealogy. This also is an interesting point for discussion within the context of modern contemporary diaspora communities and the implications it generates for churches.

Identity Crisis? Emphasis on the Jewishness in the Bible

Taking into account that the Gospels were also composed in a Hellenistic diaspora setting, it naturally directs our attention to the social setting of the first century. This is an important period since the first followers of Christ, who had Jewish identity, had to cope with the pressures of foreign oppression as well as the Jewish authorities.

In the Gospels, it is evident that Jesus and his followers were constantly in conflict with the Jewish authorities which may suggest that they had separated from mainstream Judaism to form a sectarian group called Christians. However, it is becoming increasingly acknowledged that Jesus' attitude and the early Christian interpretation of his teachings remained within the broad spectrum of Judaism. Jesus still upheld the Jewish identity which, according to E.W. Stegemann and W. Stegemann, remained constitutively related to the central social institutions of the Israel of their time.[9] It seems that there was a fine balance between defining oneself within the Jewish legacy and at the same time repudiating its fundamental principle, which is what characterizes the

---

[8] Santos, 'Survey of the Diaspora Occurrences', 56.

[9] E.W. Stegemann and W. Stegemann, *The Jesus Movement: A Social History of its First Century*, trans. O.C. Dean, Jr. (Edinburgh: T & T Clark, 1999), 102.

social setting of the early Christian diaspora community. The relationship between the early Christians and Judaism is somewhat paradoxical in that while their identity is derived from the parent body of Judaism their movement implies a certain level of deviance. Schwartz explains the unique context of first century Christianity by applying the theories of social memory.[10] He argues that society changes constantly but social memory endures because new beliefs are superimposed upon- rather than replaced- old ones. This is, in fact, how the early Jewish-Christians defined themselves, as they did not seek to discard their Jewish heritage thereby creating a new religion of their own but they continued to define their faith in Christ on the basis of their Jewish sacred text. According to the theory of social memory, one may surmise that the past memory of God's redemptive promises becomes a decisive driving force in the present reality of the early Christian setting. Even though the circumstances of the first century were evidently different from the original context in which the Old Testament texts were written, the Jewish ethos more or less maintained its relevance. Therefore, the Jewish identity, which is defined in terms of the faith in Yahweh's redemptive act, functioned as a decisive element in the formation of early Christian identity. The past was reinterpreted to serve new power distributions, institutional structures, values, interests and needs.[11] This demonstrates that the early Christians in the diaspora setting did not discard their Jewish identity but rather maintained it and re-interpreted it in newly-emerging movement. The Gospel writers take for granted that Jesus and his followers should attend the synagogue on the Sabbath (Mat. 4:23; 12:9-14; cf. also Mk. 1:21, 39; 3:1; 6:2; Lk. 4:15-16) which is also taken for granted by John who records Jesus celebrating major Jewish festivals such as the Passover, the Festival of Booths, and the Festival of Dedication (Jn. 2:23; 5:1; 7:2-11; 10:22). All this evidence suggests that the early Christians identified themselves as Jewish and not with the dominant Hellenistic culture. Nowhere does Jesus deny the fundamental ethos of the Jewish religion and challenge Israel's status as God's elect.[12] Jesus' stance toward the law and the prophet makes it clear that he affirmatively accepts the authority of the Torah (Mat. 5:17-20; cf. Mk. 12:28-34).

This shows that the early Jewish Christians in their diaspora setting firmly rooted their identity within Israel and the fundamental character of this national

---

[10] B. Schwartz, 'Christian Origins: Historical Truth and Social Memory', in A. Kirk and T. Thatcher (eds), *Memory, Tradition and Text: Uses of the Past in Early Christianity*, SBL/Semeia Studies 52 (Atlanta, GA: Society of Biblical Literature, 2005), 44, 46, 53.

[11] Schwartz, 'Christian Origins', 44.

[12] Stegemann & Stegemann, *The Jesus Movement*, 208 notes that it is true that there are provocative arguments with the witness of Gentiles in the judgment, the participation of Gentiles in the kingdom of God, and the exclusion of the 'sons of the kingdom', as well as the exemplary faith of a non-Jew. This presupposes, nonetheless, the election of Israel. There is no programmatic turning of Jesus' attention toward non-Jews.

/ religious identity was never compromised by external influences. Of course, as the early Christians began to evangelize the Gentiles who presumably had very limited knowledge of Judaism it became inevitable and indeed necessary that their image as an independent religious movement had to be clearly delineated. Although early Jewish Christian diaspora communities would undoubtedly have been influenced in some ways by the surrounding Hellenistic culture, they nevertheless regarded themselves as Jewish. Hence, it is generally impossible to deny the Jewish mindset of the New Testament writers. The early Jewish Christians, in the midst of oppression and conflict, looked to the promises of God that were originally made to Israel. This gave a particular understanding of promises which they believed have been fulfilled in Christ Jesus.[13] The re-visitation of that past by (Jewish) Gospel writers is thus an act of re-validation of the history of Israel and God's redemptive activity manifested in the Old Testament.

The tenacity of Jewish identity in the context of diaspora can also be seen in the writings of Paul. In Acts 16:1-3 Luke records that Paul circumcised a disciple. Again the issue of identity is crucial here as the early Christians must have faced constant problems in maintaining Jewish identity as well as embracing foreign cultures. This is precisely what is at stake in these verses of Acts as Paul's act of circumcision seemed to be in striking contradiction to what he preached in Galatians 2:3-4. In the latter, Levinskaya notes that Paul talks about his visit to Jerusalem to discuss with the Jerusalem leaders his mission to the Gentiles and Titus, an uncircumcised Greek, was there with him. This apparently occasioned a fierce debate amongst the leaders in Jerusalem, but in the end Paul won his case and Titus did not have to submit to circumcision.[14] Levinskaya points that the easiest way to resolve this contradiction seems to be through the difference in the ethnicity of Titus and Timothy – the former was a Greek and thus was exempted from circumcision, while the latter was a Jew and thus was not.[15]

This has an interesting implication for the diaspora community of early Christians, as Paul emphasized the importance of maintaining the ethnic identity of Israel but in a way that did not interfere with the gospel mission. Here, in the story of Timothy, an identity crisis is clearly a pressing issue as he was at the same time Jewish because of his mother (an ethnic definition of Jewishness) and non-Jewish because he was not circumcised (a religious

---

[13] Alan Kirk and Tom Thatcher (eds), *Memory, Tradition and Text: Uses of the Past in Early Christianity* SBL / Semeia Studies No. 52 (2005); Jens Schroter, 'The Historical Jesus and the Sayings Tradition: Comments on Current Research', *Neotestamentica* 30 (1996), 151-68, cited in Alan Kirk and Tom Thatcher, *Jesus Tradition as Social Memory*, 39.

[14] Irina Levinskaya, *The Book of Acts in its First Century Setting*, vol. 5, *Diaspora Setting* (Grand Rapids, MI: Eerdmans, 1996), 12.

[15] Levinskaya, *The Book of Acts*, 13.

definition). These two principles of Jewish self-identification were in conflict in the person of Timothy.[16] It is further noted that circumcision is an act symbolic of becoming a part of the chosen people, a sign of Jewishness. Timothy was called formally uncircumcised, but if he was Jewish in Luke's eyes, then the circumcision only confirms the status which he had before as a son of a Jewish mother. This act was not impossible for the Paul of Acts, with his respect for the law. What was absolutely impossible was to circumcise a Gentile.[17]

Paul must have realized the importance of identity crisis as a Jew in the diaspora setting. In the same line, these biblical passages have a profound relevance for modern contemporary Christians, who also face problems of an identity crisis in a global society. The issues of inter-marriage and diaspora communities in foreign environments naturally lead to the questions of identity especially for the next generation which the early Christians must also have faced in a Gentile milieu.[18]

Having considered the biblical evidence concerning the identity issues I shall now move onto the contemporary setting and how we are to accommodate the increasing demands of the diaspora community.

Contemporary Setting: Defining Identity in a Diaspora Community

The issues of identity crisis continue to be hugely relevant in our modern contemporary world both at political and religious levels. The issue of an identity crisis, of course, is not exclusively confined within Christian communities but is widely extended to other religious communities. Recently, Choi's dissertation tackles the issue of Islamic radicalism in the UK.[19] He argues that all the global trends of Islam and its revivals boil down to one thing: identity.[20] An important observation is made as Choi remarks that some of the radicalized Muslims are actually found within the British environment that are born in the UK and have received a British education from a very early age until adulthood. In other words, their identity within their diaspora setting has been strengthened by the common ideal which gave rise to serious clash of civilizations. An identity crisis is an extremely important matter, to which the churches need to pay more attention. Especially, in our modern context of the rapid processes of economic, demographic, social, political, cultural and

---

[16] Levinskaya, *The Book of Acts*, 16.
[17] Levinskaya, *The Book of Acts*, 16.
[18] Levinskaya, *The Book of Acts*, 17.
[19] Jaeho Choi, 'Islamic Radicalism in the UK: An Inevitable or an Avoidable Phenomenon?' (M.Sc. thesis, Cranfield University, 2008).
[20] Choi, 'Islamic Radicalism', 36.

environmental change rising from decolonization, modernization and uneven development, the issue of identity crisis becomes a critical issue.[21]

There are various forms and factors of diasporas, for as Wan notes, they occur among people in many countries and continents including Chinese, Jewish, South Asian, Hispanic, Caribbean, due to many factors, such as economic betterment, social instability, political conflict, conquest or oppression, natural catastrophes.[22]

As in biblical times, a diaspora environment is characterized in terms of uncertainty, challenges of settling in an unfamiliar place, difficulties of getting along with the foreign people and often discrimination due to racial / cultural differences. The exilic plight of ancient Israel was a deeply challenging time as her faith was put to the test. However, we have seen that this was also the time when Israel's faith in Yahweh intensified and matured. This was the period when the messianic belief was firmly established in Israel. In the same light, diaspora in the modern world, despite its challenges and difficulties, also provides opportunities for mission and the expansion of God's kingdom. The early Christians, who were scattered in the diaspora, experienced severe persecution but they still preached the gospel wherever they went. Santos notes that these Christians used their own diaspora outside Jerusalem to be the setting for their missionary efforts. In other words, it was their context of persecution that enabled them to fulfil Jesus' commissions that they bear witness in all Judea and Samaria (Acts 1:8).[23]

The diaspora, therefore, has a far-reaching strategic significance for global missions.[24] To be more specific, the diaspora gives rise to a new generation, that is often bi-lingual and bi-cultural, that can access the core of the local culture as well as its own ethnic culture. Moreover, Wan also observes that the phenomenon of diaspora provides a new intermediate state between 'local' and 'global'.[25] In other words, the diaspora has provided a new paradigm of a generation that is without borders. This generation of diaspora is indeed trans-national and one that can freely access different cultures with ease. According to Hanciles, this new paradigm suggests that even though migrants invest socially, economically, and politically in their new society, they may continue to participate in the daily life of the society from which they emigrated but which they did not abandon. Transmigrants are often bilingual, can lead

[21] S. Castles and M.J. Miller, *The Age of Migration: International Population Movements in the Modern World* (New York: Guilford Press, 1998), 139.

[22] Enoch Wan, 'The Phenomenon of Diaspora: Missiological Implications for Christian Missions', in *Scattered: The Filipino Global Presence*, 105.

[23] Santos, 'Survey of Diaspora Occurrences', 60.

[24] Cf. also Santos, 'Survey of Diaspora Occurrences', 62.

[25] Wan, 'The Phenomenon of Diaspora', 108.

dual lives, move easily between cultures, frequently maintaining homes in two countries, and are incorporated as social actors in both.[26]

This new generation, produced by diaspora,is often blurred and ambiguous in ethnic identity as it tends to be culturally mixed, which can at times lead to a serious confusion regarding identity.[27] I have begun this section of the paper with a brief mention of radical Islamic terrorists who are in fact born and bred in the diaspora setting. Often these Muslims do not speak their own language and are officially registered as British citizens. But they turn more radical and extreme than their counterparts in their homeland. Why? This is precisely because of the identity crisis within a diaspora setting, which is at times simply neglected or improperly nurtured. It is absolutely vital that the churches of ethnic minorities living in the diaspora address these serious issues of identity for this second generation. As we have seen in our brief survey of biblical evidence, the Israelites, in the diaspora context, have never abandoned their original identity. This is true of the exilic Jews of the Old Testament as well as the early Christians in the New Testament period. Even Jesus was portrayed primarily within the Jewish context. This has an important implication for the modern Christian diaspora communities. It is absolutely vital that the churches need to educate the second generation of a diaspora community with a correct understanding of its ethnic and religious identity. Without the healthy understanding of self-identity these new generations of diaspora are likely to have a negative impact upon society. The example of Islamic radicals, who are born and bred in the UK, is an appropriate illustration of the gravity of this issue. The biblical model encourages or indeed promotes such self-awareness as Israel firmly maintained her Jewish identity. Without this fundamental self-identity, it is extremely doubtful whether Israel could have survived the diaspora or indeed sustained its religious belief system. Of course, it would be unwise for the diaspora churches to stress adhering to the values of their culture without appreciating the complexities of a multi-cultural environment. The balance between maintaining one's own identity, as well as being able to appreciate and embrace its surrounding culture, is essential. Georgiou has also commented that the value of a diaspora does not erase the importance of concepts such as ethnicity and migration. Rather, diaspora has become an

---

[26] J. Hanciles, 'Migration and Mission: Some Implications for the 21st Century Church', *International Bulletin of Missionary Research* 27:4 (2003), 146-153.

[27] Wan, 'The Phenomenon of Diaspora', 109 also notes that the phenomenon of diaspora, which accelerates the process of mixing, resulted in the necessity of a new paradigm of an ambiguous ethnic identity or cultural 'hybridity', as an alternative to the traditional concept of 'homogeneity'.

additional concept. It is a useful concept that helps us understand the complexities of multi-cultural Europe.[28]

With a firm sense of identity, the new second generation of diaspora can indeed produce positive results for mission in a global world. For instance, the so-called Third World communities living as a diaspora in the West, where the churches are currently experiencing a painful decline, are a fresh injection, as their passion for the gospel is an instigator of spiritual revival in Europe, North America and so on. The common perception of Christian mission is fast-changing as the West is turning into a hard mission field because its culture is becoming simply indifferent toward the gospel. Within this world, Christians from old and new churches are called to new partnerships.[29] Wan aptly states that the global mission movement requires the cooperation and partnership of traditional missionary forces from the West with local ethnic Christians.[30] The synergy created from these gospel partnerships between the host countries and the diaspora communities will indeed make a significant contribution to the expansion of Christianity.

Conclusion

I have briefly conducted a survey of the concept of diaspora and the role it played in the formation of Israelite religion. From this we have learned that Israel placed an emphasis on maintaining her identity in God as well as preserving her national identity. Because of Israel's strong sense of identity, she was able to survive the tough conditions of diaspora and was able to launch her faith on the nations. I have attempted to apply these fundamental principles of diaspora in the Bible to the modern contemporary world. Diaspora can be a very strategic missionary asset in the global world. I have specifically identified the second generation of diaspora to be an important area of concern for the churches. This is due to the challenges of an identity crisis that this generation will unavoidably face in a diaspora environment. If a healthy understanding of self-identity based on the biblical model is taught, then it could be an important bridge in creating gospel partnerships between the diaspora community and the host country

[28] Myria Georgiou, 'Thinking Diaspora: Why Diaspora Is a Key Concept for Understanding Multicultural Europe', *More Color in the Media: The Multicultural Skyscraper Newsletter* 1:4 (2001).

[29] Samuel Escobar, 'The Global Scenario at the Turn of the Century', in William D. Taylor (ed.), *Global Missiology for the 21st century* (Grand Rapids, MI: Baker, 2000), 25-46 ('Gatherings in Diaspora: Religious Communities and the New Immigration').

[30] Wan, 'The Phenomenon of Diaspora', 114. Cf. also Hanciles, 'Migration and Mission, 146-153 notes that 'Christianity is a migratory religion, and migration movements have been a functional element in its expansion'.

Why People Move?
A Prolegomenon to Diaspora Missiology[1]

Tereso C. Casiño

The history of civilization is replete with the geographical mobility of peoples or individuals. In the first quarter of 2010 alone, an estimated 200 million people moved around the world.[2] Just a decade ago, 155 million were reportedly considered international migrants. It is estimated that by mid-2010, 104 million of these would be women, with only 109 million men. These figures reflect only the number of people who move internationally, but reports on how many people move domestically or internally within the homeland still have to be established. In the final piece of his twelve volumes *A Study of History*, British historian Arnold Toynbee projected global diasporas, rather than local national states, to be the way of the future.[3] Interestingly, Toynbee's last volume is focused on worldwide diasporas as a phenomenon to reckon with in the future.

This essay explores the mobility of people in both geographic and demographic forms in five sections. The first surveys major determinants of people's mobility; the second relates diaspora to trans-national migration; the third identifies salient points of geographical and demographical mobility; the fourth states basic theological considerations regarding diaspora; and the fifth discusses the implications of people's mobility to diaspora missiology. This study seeks to establish the relationship between the diasporic flow of people and individuals in general and the redemptive acts of God in the world.

Determinants of People's Mobility

The study of global diaspora relates to the study of migration, although diaspora technically serves as an umbrella term that covers all types of movements. Since a major aspect of this study focuses on the mobility of people in geographical and demographic terms, migration and the theories or

---

[1] An earlier version of the study was published under the same title in *Torch Trinity Journal* 13:1 (May 2010), and used with permission.

[2] United Nations, Department of Economic and Social Affairs, Population Division, 'The International Migrants Stock: The 2008 Revision' (http://esa.un.org/migration/p2k0data. asp), accessed April 7, 2010.

[3] See A.J. Toynbee, *A Study of History*, 12 vols. (New York: Oxford University Press, 1964). An abridged 1987 paperback edition by D.C. Somervell is available from the original publisher.

models that have developed to understand diaspora will be discussed.[4] Migration theories, from the past, lacked coherence and 'connection with a more general social theory'.[5] Oxford University's International Migration Institute, as an academic discipline, currently classifies migration theory under economics, anthropology, sociology, geography, and law.[6] Accordingly, migration theory is seen as:

> [D]ivided between approaches that examine the initiation of migration and those that look at how migration processes develop their own momentum once started. Migration research has its roots in social scientific approaches developed in the epoch of nationalism; in an era of globalisation the dynamics of social relations transcend borders and so must the theories and methods used to study them.[7]

Thus, migration and diasporic flows of people or individuals have been viewed differently by experts in the field.[8] The pioneering theory of geographical mobility in an academic discipline was developed by Ernest George Ravenstein, an English geographer. Based primarily on an economic framework, Ravenstein's theory metamorphosed later into what became known as the 'push-pull' factors in migration flows. Using a decadal census in England and Wales, between 1871 and 1881, Ravenstein observed that migration was governed by two conditions. They were: 1) unfavourable conditions in one place e.g., oppressive laws, heavy taxation, and a lack of jobs or accessible healthcare, which then 'pushed' people out; and 2) favourable conditions outside and beyond the original location. In a nutshell, Ravenstein claimed that 'the primary cause for migration was better external economic opportunities; the volume of migration decreases as distance increases; migration occurs in

---

[4] For an excellent study on factors behind migration and their corresponding relevant methodologies, see Michael J. Greenwood, 'Human Migration: Theory, Models, and Empirical Studies', *Journal of Regional Science* 25:4 (1985), 521-44.

[5] International Migration Institute, Oxford University, 'Migration Theory' (http://www.imi.ox. ac.uk/themes/migration-theory), accessed April 7, 2010.

[6] A sketch is available online. See, 'Migration - Theories of Migration', *JRank: Marriage and Family Encyclopedia* (http://family.jrank.org/pages/1170/ Migration-Theories-Migration. html# ixzz0j vdi9BjM), accessed: April 2, 2010); Susan Thieme, *Social Networks and Migration: Far West Nepalese Labour Migrants in Delhi*, Culture, Society and Environment 7 (Münster: LIT Publishing, 2006), 49-56.

[7] International Migration Institute, Oxford University, 'Migration Theory' (http://www.imi.ox.ac.uk/themes/migration-theory), accessed April 7, 2010.

[8] In Douglas S. Massey et al., 'Theories of International Migration: A Review and Appraisal', *Population and Development Review* 19:3 (September 1993), 432: 'Current patterns and trends in migration, however, suggest that a full understanding of contemporary migratory process will not be achieved by relying on the tools of one discipline alone, or by focusing on one single level of analysis. Rather, their complex, multifaceted nature requires a sophisticated theory that incorporates perspectives, levels, and assumptions'.

stages instead of one long move; population movements are bilateral; and migration differentials e.g., gender, social class, age, influence a person's mobility'.[9]

The concepts of absorption and dispersion were central to Ravenstein's earlier model of geographical mobility.[10] By absorption, Ravenstein meant a nation that took more people in (i.e., non-natives) as compared to a nation from which people (i.e., natives) moved out or away. By dispersion, Ravenstein had in mind the native inhabitants who moved out from their original place of settlement rather than those who continued to stay (i.e., countrymen). Using census data on the birthplace of each person, Ravenstein succeeded in sorting out 'basic population flows' between dispersion nations and absorption nations. His decadal study established that absorption areas 'are the chief seats of commerce and industry', while the places of dispersion were almost all agricultural.[11]

Ravenstein's empricial studies and observation developed into 'seven laws of migration'. These 'laws' became foundational to later generations of migration theorists:

> 1) Most migrants only proceed a short distance, and toward centres of absorption. 2) As migrants move toward absorption centres, they leave `gaps' that are filled up by migrants from more remote districts, creating migration flows that reach to `the most remote corner of the kingdom'; 3) The process of dispersion is inverse to that of absorption; 4) Each main current of migration produces a compensating counter-current; 5) Migrants proceeding long distances generally go by preference to one of the great centres of commerce or industry; 6) The natives of towns are less migratory than those of the rural parts of the country; and 7) Females are more migratory than males.[12]

Ravenstein formulated these 'migration laws' during a time of intense internal and migration flows, using data taken from the national census.

After Ravenstein, theories of geographical mobility evolved, many of which are variants of the ground-breaking economic model. In 1966, Everett Lee

---

[9] Massey et al., 'Theories of International Development', 432.

[10] John Corbett, 'Ernest George Ravenstein: The Laws of Migration, 1885' (,http://www.csiss.org/classics/content/90), accessed: March 31, 2010.

[11] Corbett, 'Ernest George Ravenstein'.

[12] Corbett, 'Ernest George Ravenstein' refers to the following works: Ernest George Ravenstein, 'The Laws of Migration', *Journal of the Statistical Society of London* 48:2 (June 1885), 167–235; 'The Laws of Migration', *Journal of the Royal Statistical Society* 52:2 (June 1889), 241–305; 'The Birthplace of the People and the Laws of Migration', *The Geographical Magazine* 3 (1876), 173–177, 201–206, 229–233. Corbett also cites W. Tobler, 'Migration: Ravenstein, Thorntwaite, and Beyond', *Urban Geography* 16:4 (1995), 327–343; R. Lawton, 'Population Changes in England and Wales in the Later Nineteenth Century: An Analysis of Trends by Registration District', *Transactions of the Institute of British Geographers* 44 (1968), 55–74.

reformulated Ravenstein's traditional theory and emphasized the 'push factors' or 'internal factors'.[13] According to Lee:

> Migration is defined broadly as a permanent or semipermanent change of residence. No restriction is placed upon the distance of the move or upon the voluntary or involuntary nature of the act, and no distinction is made between external and internal migration.[14]

However, Lee conceded that such a definition did not include all kinds of spatial mobility. He opted to exclude several types of people such as nomads (who continually moved around), migratory workers (who have short term residences), and vacationers. Lee also outlined the impact that intervening obstacles have on the migration process. He argued that variables (such as distance, physical and political barriers, and having dependents) can either impede or prevent migration where the process of migration can become selective ascribable to differentials (such as age, gender, and social class). These differentials affected how persons responded to push-pull factors and shaped their ability to overcome intervening obstacles.[15] Furthermore, personal factor, for example a person's education, knowledge of a potential receiver population, and family ties, facilitated or retarded the migration process. Lee, therefore, concluded, 'No matter how short or how long, how easy or how difficult, every act of migration involves an origin, a destination, and an intervening set of obstacles'.[16]

Neo-classical economic theory of migrations added a new twist. Migration flows have been classified into macro and micro theories.[17] On the one hand, macro-theory 'was developed originally to explain labor migration in the process of economic development'.[18] Mobility here, both local and international, was 'caused by geographic differences in supply of and demand for labor'.[19] On the other hand, micro-theory, as proposed by Larry A. Sjaastad and Michael Todaro, echoed macro-theory in that international migration related to 'the global supply and demand for labor'.[20] They asserted that

---

[13] Everett Lee, 'A Theory of Migration', *Demography* 3:1 (1966), 47-57.

[14] Lee, 'A Theory of Migration', 49.

[15] 'Migration—Theories of Migration', *JRank: Marriage and Family Encyclopedia.*

[16] 'Migration—Theories of Migration', *JRank: Marriage and Family Encyclopedia*

[17] See Massey et al., 'Theories of International Migration', 433-434.

[18] Massey et al., 'Theories of International Migration', 433.

[19] Massey et al., 'Theories of International Migration', 433.

[20] Larry A. Sjasstad, 'The Costs and Returns of Human Migration', *Journal of Political Economy* 70:5 (1962), 80-93; Michael P. Todaro, 'A Model of Labor Migration and Urban Unemployment in Less developed Countries', *The American Economic Review* 59 (1969), 138-48; 'Internal Migration in Developing Countries: A Survey', in Richard A. Easterlin (ed), *Population and Economic Change in Developing Countries* (Chicago, IL: University of Chicago Press, 1980), 361-401.

'nations with scarce labor supply and high demand will have high wages that pull immigrants in from nations with a surplus of labor'.[21] Micro-theory, however, diverged from macro-theory because of its emphasis on 'individual choice'. Massey and others explained:

> In this scheme, individual rational actors decide to migrate because a cost-benefit calculation leads them to expect a positive net return, usually monetary, from movement. International migration is conceptualized as a form of investment in human capital. People choose to move to where they can be most productive, given their skills; but before they can capture the higher wages associated with greater labor productivity they must undertake certain investments, which include the material costs of traveling, the costs of maintenance while moving and looking for work, the effort involved in learning a new language and culture, the difficulty experienced in adapting to a new labor market and the psychological costs of cutting old ties and forging new ones.[22]

Moreover, the micro-economics model argued that people moved in response to economic incentives. As a 'rational choice', moving takes place as a result of a 'careful cost benefit calculation'.[23] Thus, people moved because they wanted to maximize their individual return.[24]

Michael J. Piore applied labour-market approach to migration flows.[25] As a labor economist, Piore theorized that the economies of the economically advanced nations have been structured to require a 'certain level of immigration'. Thus, economies in developed nations were dualistic with a 'primary market of secure, well-remunerated work and a secondary market of low-wage work'. The main argument of the segmented labor-market model is that immigrants were needed to work in the 'secondary labor market' because a nation's citizens considered the jobs too demeaning and unpleasant to fill.[26]

---

[21] 'Migration - Theories of Migration'.

[22] Massey et al., 'Theories of International Migration', 434.

[23] Jialong Tang, 'What Drives Migration and Who Migrates: Migration Selectivity in the Late 1990s in China' (Master's thesis, Hong Kong University of Science and Technology, 2005), 9.

[24] Tang, 'What Drives Migration and Who Migrates', citing S. Bowles, 'Migration as Investment: Empirical Tests to the Human Investment Approach to Geographical Mobility', *The Review of Economics and Statistics* 52:4 (1976), 356-62; L.A. Sjaastad, 'The Costs and Returns of Human Migrations', *Journal of Political Economy* 70:5 (1962), 80-93.

[25] See Michael J. Piore, 'The Dual Labor Market: Theory and Implications', in S.H. Beer and R.E. Barringer (eds), *The State and the Poor* (Cambridge, MA: Winthrop Publishers, 1970), 55-59.

[26] 'Migration- Theories of Migration'. For a fuller treatment, see Michael J. Piore, 'Notes for a Theory of Labor Market Stratification', in R.C. Edwards, M. Reich, and D. Gordon (eds), *Labor Market Segmentation* (Lexington, MA: D.C. Heath and Co., 1975), 125-150.

Piore also found a relationship in the transition from mass production to flexible specialization. Central to Piore's work was 'the social, institutional, and cognitive dimensions of economic activity'.[27]

A Dutch scholar, Saskia Sassen, introduced the world-systems theory. She asserted that 'migration is a natural growth of disruptions and dislocations that inevitably occur in the process of capitalist development'.[28] Sassen was well-known for her emphasis on globalization and trans-national migration.[29] She viewed the 'spatial, or scalar, realities of globalization as a process that restructures space and place' and argued that international migration is a by-product of global capitalism.[30] According to her, 'Contemporary patterns of international migration tend to be from the periphery (poor nations) to the core (rich nations) because factors associated with industrial development in the First World generated structural economic problems, and thus push factors, in the Third World'.[31] Regarding Sassen's theory, William Robinson observed:

> The emergence of a global economy therefore contributed both to the creation abroad of pools of potential emigrants and to the formation of linkages between industrialized and developing countries that subsequently were to serve as bridges for international migration, facilitated further by the liberalization of immigration policy in most developed countries. Paradoxically, the very measures thought to deter immigration – foreign investment and the promotion of export-oriented growth in developing countries – have had precisely the opposite effect.[32]

---

[27] See Michael J. Piore and C. Sabel, *The Second Industrial Divide* (New York: Basic Books, 1984); Michael J. Piore and S. Berger, *Dualism and Discontinuity in Industrial Societies* (Cambridge, England: Cambridge University Press, 1980); Michael J. Piore, *Birds of Passage: Migrant Labor and Industrial Societies* (Cambridge, England: Cambridge University Press, 1979).

[28] Massey et al., 'Theories of International Migration', 445. For Saskia Sassen's works, see *The Mobility of Capital and Labor: A Study in International Investment and Labor Flow* (Cambridge: Cambridge University Press), 1988; *A Sociology of Globalization* (New York: W.W. Norton, 2007); *The Global City*, rev. ed. (Princeton: Princeton University Press, 2001); *Cities in a World Economy*, 2nd ed. (Thousand Oaks: Pine Forge, 2000); *Guests and Aliens* (New York: The New Press, 1999).

[29] For a critique, see William I. Robinson, 'Saskia Sassen and the Sociology of Globalization: A Critical Appraisal', *Sociological Analysis* 3:1 (Spring, 2009), 5-29.

[30] Robinson, 'Saskia Sassen', 5. Although influenced by world-systems theory, William I. Robinson calls for a rethinking of the 'relationship between space and development and a new conception of development based not on territory but on social groups'. See William I. Robinson, 'Remapping Development in Light of Globalization: From a Territorial to a Social Cartography', *Third World Quarterly* 23:6 (2002), 1048; William I. Robinson, 'Social Theory and Globalization: The Rise of a Transnational State', *Theory and Society*, 30:2 (April 2001), 157-200.

[31] 'Migration- Theories of Migration'.

[32] Robinson, 'Saskia Sassen and the Sociology of Globalization', 9.

Other migration theories also emerged based on non-economic theories. In 1958, William Petersen introduced typology as a theory of geographic mobility. Petersen argued that 'migration is not unitary; it differs from fertility and mortality in that it cannot be analyzed, even primarily in terms of supra-cultural, physiological factors but must be differentiated even at the most abstract level with the social conditions obtaining'.[33] Petersen's theory, of course, was a reaction against Ravenstein's theory of 'laws of migration'. He pointed out that 'the most general statement that one can make concerning migration must be in the form of a typology, rather than a law'.[34] Petersen typology was divided into five classes: primitive, impelled, forced, free, and mass. Each category has two types, namely, 'conservative migration, in which the mover changes residence to maintain his present standard of living, and innovative migration where the move is made in order to improve the living standards'.[35]

Petersen's typology was based on the original work of Henry P. Fairchild that appeared in 1925.[36] Petersen lamented that 'most studies of international migration are focused on the movement from or to one particular country, and virtually all of the other, somewhat broader works are concerned with a single historical era'.[37] Also, the 'emphasis is more on description rather than analysis, so that the theoretical framework into which these limited data are fitted is ordinarily rather primitive'.[38] This study was an attempt to bring into one typology some of the 'more significant analyses of internal and international migration' that would result in a formulation of a more general theory of migration. Typology then was developed based on ecological push, migration policy, people's aspirations, and social momentum. The emphasis, thus, is on the types of movements, causes and resultants of various forms of mobility.[39]

---

[33] John S. Mahoney cites William Petersen, *Population* (Mew York: Macmillan, 1969), 229 (*sic*, 299). John S. Mahoney, 'General Theories of Geographic Mobility' (Virginia Commonwealth University, http://www.people.vcu.edu/~jmahoney/migration.htm), accessed: April 20, 2010.

[34] Mahoney, 'General Theories'.

[35] Mahoney cites Kenneth C.W. Kammeyer, in his study on the United States migration flow, observes that most moves are 'free' and 'innovative'. See Kenneth C.W. Kammeyer, *An Introduction to Population* (San Francisco, CA: Chandler Publishing, 1971). Mahoney, 'General Theories'.

[36] Henry P. Fairchild, *A world movement and its American significance,* rev. ed. (New York: Macmillan, 1925).

[37] William Petersen, 'A General Typology of Migration', *American Sociological Review* 23:3 (June 1958), 256.

[38] Petersen, 'A General Typology of Migration', 256.

[39] See P. Krishnan and D. Odynak, 'A Generalization of Petersen's Typology of Migration', *International Migration* 25:4 (1987), 385–97.

In 1940, Samuel A. Stouffer introduced 'gravitational models' that emphasized the 'theory of intervening opportunities'.[40] Stouffer pointed out the relationship between mobility and distance that Ravenstein was famous for in his pioneering study on migration. Stouffer affirmed this relationship:

> Distance is such an important factor that it needs more explicit study than it has received. Whether one is seeking to explain 'why' persons go to a particular place to get jobs, 'why' they go to trade at a particular store, 'why' they go to a particular neighborhood to commit crime, or 'why' they marry the particular spouses they choose, the factor of spatial distance is of obvious significance.[41]

But Stouffer formulated a framework that rejected the connection between mobility and distance. He first introduced the concept of 'intervening opportunities', and proposed that 'the number of persons going a given distance is directly proportional to the number of opportunities at that distance and inversely proportional to the number of intervening opportunities'.[42] This sociological model has been tested in the United States.[43] Stouffer asserted that 'the relation between mobility and distance may be said to depend on an auxiliary relationship, which expresses the cumulated (intervening) opportunities as a function of distance'.[44] Margaret L. Bright and Dorothy S. Thomas noted Stouffer's theory as useful in 'its applicability to the determination of spatial patterning and its value particularly in throwing light on the nature and direction of specific departures from the observed general patterning'.[45]

Family decision processes also influence geographic mobility, as Peter Rossi's work in 1955 pointed out, with a special reference to elderly migration.[46] Rossi stated that a motivational approach to a decision-making process consisted of a multiplicative interaction of four variables, namely,

---

[40] Samuel A. Stouffer, 'Intervening Opportunities: A Theory Relating Mobility and Distance', *American Sociological Review* 5 (1940), 845-67.

[41] Stouffer, 'Intervening Opportunities', 845.

[42] Stouffer, 'Intervening Opportunities', 846.

[43] For a full treatment of Stouffer's theory of intervening opportunities that does not represent all migration flows with testing in the Unite States, see Robert H. Freymeyer and P. Neal Ritchey, 'Spatial Distribution of Opportunities and Magnitude of Migration: An Investigation of Stouffer's Theory', *Sociological Perspectives* 28:4 (October 1985), 419-40. See also David K. Foot and William J. Milne, 'Net Migration Estimation in an Extended, Multiregional Gravity Model', *Journal of Regional Science* 24 (1984), 119-133.

[44] Stouffer, 'Intervening Opportunities', 847.

[45] Margaret L. Bright and Dorothy S. Thomas, 'Interstate Migration and Intervening Opportunities', *American Sociological Review* 6:6 (December 1941), 773.

[46] Peter Rossi, *Why Families move: A Study in the Social Psychology of Urban Mobility* (New York: Macmillan, 1955).

availability, motive, expectancy, and incentive.[47] A variant of Rossi's original framework argued that these elements embodied the life-course theory with respect to people's mobility; the life course 'posits that causes and consequences of migration behavior ensue from transitions in family and socio-economic status that occur over the life course'.[48] Gordon F. De Jong and Deborah R. Graefe observed that in reference to younger adults, life course theory of mobility is primarily due to the age-related 'character family demographic transitions and social mobility transitions'.[49] In addition, they noted that 'logic of migration as triggered by family demographic processes focuses on the impact of such vital events as marriage, childbearing, divorce, separation, and death'.[50] Finally, they reasoned, 'Because of time-series data limitations, Rossi and many subsequent researchers have not been able to use direct life-course measures, and instead have characterized households by age of the head and number of children or household size'.[51]

Diaspora and Transnational Migration

Interest in the connection between diaspora and transnational migration has grown significantly in recent years, and more studies on globalization, global economics, international relations, global politics, international conflict resolutions, and foreign diplomacy have been produced. Whereas the design of transnational migration is not new, its influence and form dramatically expanded over the years. As Peggy Levitt notes:

> The assumption that people will live their lives in one place, according to one set of national and cultural norms, in countries with impermeable national borders, no longer holds. Rather, in the twenty-first century, more and more people will belong to two or more societies at the same time.[52]

---

[47] Ralph R. Sell and Gordon F. De Jong, 'Toward a Motivational Theory of Migration Decision Making', *Population & Environment* 1:4 (December 1978), 313-35.

[48] Gordon F. De Jong and Deborah Roempke Graefe, 'Family Life Course Transition and the Economic Consequence of Internal Migration' (A paper presented at the annual meeting of the Population Association of America, New York, March 2007), 4, available on http://paa2007.princeton.edu/ download.aspx?submissionId=72019 (accessed: April 26, 2010).

[49] De Jong and Graefe, 'Family Life Course Transition', 4.

[50] De Jong and Graefe, 'Family Life Course Transition', 4.

[51] De Jong and Graefe, 'Family Life Course Transition', 4.

[52] Peggy Levitt, 'Transnational Migrants: When "Home" Means More Than One Country' (http://www.migrationinformation.org/Feature/display. cfm?id=261), accessed: April 29, 2010. See also, Peggy Levitt, *The Transnational Villagers* (Berkeley, CA: University of California Press, 2001); Ewa Morawska, 'Immigrant Transnationalism and Assimilation: A Variety of Combinations and the Analytic Strategy It Suggests', in C.

This is possible because of advanced technologies in modern transportation and communications. According to Stephen Castles, 'some people develop a transnational consciousness, and maintain economic, cultural and social relationships in several places'.[53]

Oliver Blackwell echoes Levitt's assertion by viewing diaspora through the lens of migrants and transnationals. Accordingly, diaspora becomes a 'social form' that focuses 'upon an identified group characterised by their relationship-despite-dispersal'.[54] He states that the 'set trans-nationals do not necessarily consist exclusively of migrants and many migrants may not maintain trans-national activities'.[55] Blackwell perceives diaspora 'as a subset of trans-nationals, and both the sets of transnationals and diasporas intersect with the set of migrants'. Defining diasporas by their 'transnational character', Blackwell asserts that the term diaspora be 'reserved for particular people living in distinctive relationships with each other and a homeland'.[56] For Blackwell:

> Not all migrants become diasporas and not all diasporas can be considered as migrants (although their ancestors may have been so). Likewise, not all those who engage in trans-national practices are necessarily diasporic; they may simply be operating as networks of people with limited relationships to any place (real or imaginary).[57]

Echoing Blackwell's point, Levitt observes:

> Moreover, not all migrants are transnational migrants, and not all who take part in trans-national practices do so all the time.... Most migrants are occasional trans-national activists. At some stages in their lives they are more focused on

---

Joppke and Ewa Morawska (eds), *Toward Assimilation and Citizenship: Immigrants in Liberal Nation-States* (Basingstoke: Palgrave Macmillan, 2003), 133-176.

[53] Stephen Castles, 'Will Labour Migration Lead to a Multicultural Society in Korea?' (A Paper Presented at Global Human Resources Forum, October 23-25, 2007, Seoul, Korea), 3.

[54] A pre-published copy is found on: Oliver Blackwell, 'In Search of the Diasporas within Africa' (International Migration Institute, University of Oxford, http://www/imi.ox.uk/about-us/people/oliver-bakewell/), accessed: May 11, 2010.

[55] Blackwell, 'In Search of the Diasporas', 4.

[56] Blackwell, 'In Search of the Diasporas', 3.

[57] Blackwell, 'In Search of the Diasporas', 3. The relationship to place is what distinguishes transnationalism from diaspora, argues Blackwell, as he cites N. Nyberg-Sorensen, 'Introduction', in N. Nyberg-Sorensen (ed), *Living across Worlds: Diaspora, Development and Transnational Engagement* (Geneva: International Organization for Migration, 2007), 7 to support his case: 'Migrants' transnational practices have been understood to dissolves fixed assumptions about identity, place and community, whereas diasporic identity-making has been understood to evolve around attempts to "fix" and closely knit identity and community'.

> their countries of origin while at others they are more involved in their countries of reception. Similarly, they climb two different social ladders, moving up, remaining steady, or experiencing downward mobility, in various combinations, with respect to both sites.[58]

Broadly speaking, diaspora refers to the global phenomenon of the dispersion or scattering of people in various parts of the world, occurring either by a voluntary act or coerced condition in both domestic and global contexts. Migration facilitates geographical or demographic mobility that eventually results in diasporic conditions. Migration basically involves geographic and demographic flows of people or individuals, taking both internal and international directions. It is important to view the inherent connection between diaspora and migration because of their symbiotic relationship.[59] However, while both are complementary, they are not identical or interchangeable.

Therefore, diaspora refers to the overarching structure under which all forms of mobility take place, while migration serves as a tool to account for a diasporic process or condition. In *Global Diasporas: An Introduction*, Robin Cohen identifies the following features of diasporas: they are often traumatically dispersed from an original homeland; they leave their homeland in search of work, pursuit of trade, or to further colonial ambitions; they share a collective memory and myth about the homeland; and they possess an idealization of the supposed ancestral home. There is also a return movement or at least a continuing connection observed among them. They tend to have a strong ethnic group consciousness sustained over a long time and a troubled relationship with host societies. They share a sense of co-responsibility with co-ethnic members in other countries and possess the possibility of a distinctive creative, enriching life in tolerant host societies.[60]

---

[58] Levitt, 'Transnational Migrants: When 'Home' Means More Than One Country'.

[59] Patrick Iroegbu, 'Migration and Diaspora: Craze, Significance and Challenges' (http://www.hollerafrica.com/showArticle.php?artId=121&catId= 1&page=1), accessed: April 30, 2010, argues that 'migration or diasporism is substantially a human capital issue involving an individual or group. It is also structural in terms of forces that push people around for safety and income as the dual market theory suggests. That is, people move with the hope to be better off than they were before. Staying at home is to be the same, where chances of progress are known far ahead. But moving brings about a change, a change hoped to be better- therefore security, empowerment and opportunities will be filled with choices'.

[60] Robin Cohen, *Global Diasporas: An Introduction* (London: UCL Press, 2008), 17. Cohen identifies the following five major types of diaspora with their respective examples: 1) Victim-Jews, Africans, Armenians; 2) Labour-indentured Indians; 3) Imperial-British; 4) Trade-Lebanese, Chinese; and 5) Deterritorialized-Carribean peoples, Sindhis, Parsis (17-18).

Salient Features of People's Mobility

Factors behind the mobility and scattering of people vary from one group to another, depending on the circumstances, timing, and location of those involved. People move because (causal) of various reasons; they also move for (motive) similar reasons such as natural, social, political, economic, personal, educational, religious, or missional. Economic theories of migration developed within the framework of 'push-pull factors' to account for geographic and demographic mobility. In recent times, Nicholas Van Hear proposed to understand mobility as either proactive or reactive within the context of five types of orientation: outward, inward, return, onward, and stay-put.[61]

Mobility can be voluntary or involuntary, temporary or permanent. People move voluntarily when they do so without coercion or external factors that cause their displacement or relocation. Involuntary factors involve any life-threatening circumstances, including but not limited to religious, political, economic, social circumstances and natural calamities. People's mobility can be temporary or permanent. This depends on what drives people to abandon their original society and what attracts them to adopt the target homeland. One stresses motivation as that which drives individuals to leave their homeland; the other highlights incentive as that which attracts people to a new land.

People's move could be occasioned by natural factors, especially those that relate to environment or ecology. This may include natural calamities: floods, earthquakes, tsunamis, typhoons, cyclones, and hurricanes. In sub-Saharan Africa, for example, climate change causes drought, flooding, and desertification, which in turn drives migration.[62] Inversely, people's mobility can also contribute to:

> …agricultural transformation in a positive way as international migrant households often show a relatively high willingness to invest in agriculture. Nevertheless, the development potential of migration has not yet been fully realized due to a number of social, economic, legal, institutional, and infrastructural obstacles.[63]

In some quarters, religious persecutions trigger both small and large-scale mobility flow. People with strong particular religious convictions, for example, may find themselves ostracized by a society that is not sympathetic or sensitive to their particular belief systems and aspirations. Likewise, some people

[61] For a fuller discussion, see Nicholas Van Hear, *New Diasporas: The Mass Exodus, Dispersal and Regrouping of Migrant Communities* (London: University College London, 1988).

[62] Nancy Palus, 'Experts Say Climate Change Drives Migration in Sub-Saharan Africa' (http://www1.voanews.com/english/news/a-13-2008-03-20-voa33-66 809 527.html), accessed: March 30, 2010.

[63] See Hein de Haas, *Migration and Agricultural Transformations in the Oases of Morocco and Tunisia* (Utrecht: KNAG, 2001), 3.

abandon their homeland to avoid compromising their cultural traditions and value systems. Whenever the prospect of being assimilated into and absorbed by the mainstream society is high, people fear the possibility of losing their original ethnic identity.[64] On a grander scale, conflict could lead into religious wars, which would eventually produce refugees forced into dislocation and displacement.[65]

Parallel to religious persecution is political oppression. Dissension establishes a lasting animosity among people whose political orientations are different or diametrically inconsistent with those in power. Authorities may employ threats, physical violence, verbal abuse, and even death-threats to curb dissenters. In this case, the minority are marginalized from the political scene or banished to obscurity, or completely eradicated. Other issues regarding minorities concern interracial integration and national identity. Integration becomes difficult when some people see incoming migrants as a threat to national security and identity. This may inevitably lead to the clash of civilizations and cultures in their neighborhood.[66]

Alongside people's mobility are hopes to live in a 'greener pasture'. When a nation's economy bubbles and pops, people may react by looking for a 'promised land'. Those from the Global South may be attracted to move to the Global North to fulfil their 'dreams' in countries such as Canada, the United States, and Europe. The economic boom across the Asian region also lures people and individuals to move into more urbanized areas in search of a stable economy or even to increase political power. Among Asians, there is a growing passion to live out their 'dreams' in Japan, Korea, Singapore, Taiwan, or Hong Kong. One force that drives them to relocate into these strategic places is

---

[64] S. Castles, 'Will Labour Migration Lead to a Multicultural Society in Korea?', argues that 'more open and diverse societies do not have to mean loss of social cohesion, cultural identity and core values'. The idea of multiculturalism appeals to Castles as one creative way to avoid vague integration. In 1971, Canada became one of the first countries to officially adopt multiculturalism as a national policy.

[65] See Meic Pearse, *The Gods of War: Is Religion the Primary Cause of Violent Conflict?* (Downers Grove, IL: Inter-Varsity, 2007); Mary Jane Engh, *In the Name of Heaven: 3,000 Years of Religious Persecution* (New York: Prometheus Books, 2007).

[66] Samuel Huntington, *The Clash of Civilizations and the Remaking of World Order* (New York: Simon & Schuster, 1996) posits two major manifestations of the clash of civilizations- fault line conflicts and core state conflicts. A concise but insightful critique on Huntington's ideas applicable to the immigration experience in the United States is given in Luis Rivera-Pagan, 'Xenophobia or Xenophilia: Towards a Theology of Migration' (http://www.artofthesermon. org/index.php? option=comcontent& task=view&id =143&Itemid=1), accessed: April 18, 2010. See also, Andrej Tusicisny, 'Civilizational Conflicts: More Frequent, Longer, and Bloodier?' *Journal of Peace Research* 41:4 (2004), 485-98; Seizaburo Sato, 'Clash of Civilizations or Self-Renovation through Mutual Learning' (http://www.sbpark.com/inn60.html), accessed: April 29, 2010.

economic; many want to have a 'better life', economically speaking. Professional or highly specialized trade and labor skills have become tools to achieve one's dream. The effects and consequences of the exodus of professionals and skilled workers could cause a 'brain drain' for the homeland and a 'brain gain' for the host society.[67] There is also the lure of interracial marriages. Women are most likely to marry men from affluent societies and stable economies as a way of 'improving' their lives. Of course, not all intermarriages are caused by purely economic reasons. However, many who marry through third-party agents under a mail-order bride scheme or pre-arranged marriage programmes have economics as their prime motive.

People also move for personal reasons. Constants here include personal ambitions or just naïve adventurism. Ambitions in life involve a higher education, life-long career, and success in selected professions. For example, people who leave their homeland to study overseas belong to this category. This move could be temporary, depending on the length of one's studies, but it could also be irreversible as graduates decide to become permanent residents and consequently citizens of their host country. Those who eventually return to their homeland after accomplishing their goals in their adopted society do so for more nationalist reasons, not to mention socio-economic, political, or religious motivations.[68]

From an evangelical perspective, the study of people on the move goes beyond numbers, ethnicity, or demographics. While mobility involves natural, social, political, economic, personal, educational, and religious factors, some people may interpret dispersion providentially, or, more specifically, missiologically. Within this context, all movements of individuals and peoples are considered providential. In other words, these movements do not simply happen naturally. Rather, they occur under God's lordship and direction. Biblically speaking, providential movements are missional acts. As Tom

---

[67] For a fuller treatment, see Ronald Skeldon, 'Of Skilled Migration, Brain Drains and Policy Responses', *International Migration* 47:4 (November 2008), 3-29.

[68] Patrick Iroegbu, 'Migration and Diaspora: Craze, Significance and Challenges' (http://www.hollerafrica.com/showArticle.php?artId=121&catId=1&page=5), accessed: April 30, 2010, insightfully writes, 'Diasporism makes sense because it may forge stronger ties between the homeland and outside individuals. Diaspora communities show that diaspora issues are an important category to initiate and seek out ideas and accommodation of ways and forms in which intercultural and international relations between homeland and settled ethnic nationalities can strengthen one another. As a fact, it can help in sustaining new democratic nation states with the flow of ideas and social obligations in agreement with the home-inward and the home-outward. The meaning of diaspora therefore resonates with, but not limited to, the connection and feeling of asking those in diaspora how and when they would go back home and be relevant?'

Houston and others write, 'God controls these movements. The Bible is full of examples, from Genesis to Revelation of God using them for his purposes'.[69]

People's mobility advances the gospel. Whenever people move, the gospel moves. God opens up opportunities for the advancement of the good news. In the history of world evangelization, the dispersion of people or individuals plays a strategic role in fulfilling the Great Commission. There are two underlying basic principles relevant to this claim.

First, God's grace precedes any geographical mobility or demographic flow. With respect to diaspora, God's grace prepares people's hearts and creates an environment for divine-human encounters. God's grace precedes all undertakings involving evangelism.[70] Divine grace always operates ahead of any human mobility. This evangelistic aspect is crucial to see God's initiations that draw souls within the framework of a theology of diaspora. In other words:

> A theology of global diaspora unfolds the universal dispersal of God's grace and the availability of God's love in all corners of the world. Divine grace permeates the mobility of peoples around the world. God's grace goes wherever people go and operates wherever people are situated so that the divine missionary intent and redemptive purpose will be fulfilled. By his grace, God allows the scattering of peoples around the world; God also gathers peoples through his grace and for his grace.[71]

Secondly, migration flows provide providential opportunities for people to gain access to the gospel. This goes both ways: believers in diasporic contexts may influence the nationals of the host countries with their testimonies of God's love and forgiveness, and non-believers may move to areas where the gospel is readily accessible. Some people can encounter Christ in the process of moving or migrating even without the direct or sustained contact with believers; others can hear the good news for the first time as they become acquainted with believers in times of need. Migration flows, in fact, could serve as natural conduits for fulfilling God's missionary intention among people on the move.

---

[69] Tom Houston et al., 'The New People Next Door: A Call to Seize the Opportunities', Occasional Paper 55 (New Delhi: South Asian Concern/ Lausanne Committee for World Evangelization, 2005), 10.

[70] John Wesley, *The Works of John Wesley*, 3rd ed. (Grand Rapids, MI: Baker, 1978), VI, 512, calls the operation of grace before and during the 'gospel call' as prevenient grace. Alister E. McGrath, *Evangelicalism and the Future of Christianity* (Downers Grove, IL: InterVarsity Press, 1995), 179, laments how contemporary theology of mission often overlooks the doctrine of prevenient grace in world evangelization.

[71] Tereso C. Casiño, 'Global Diaspora: Basic Frameworks for Theological Construction' (A Paper Presented at the Global Diaspora Consultation, Taylor University College, Edmonton, Alberta, Canada, October 15-16, 2006), 16.

Furthermore, ministry-sensitive Christians will find migration as a strategic channel for doing their own share of the missionary task. Geographical mobility, whether forced or unforced, voluntary or involuntary, may be interpreted as a God-given opportunity to spread the good news. However, it does not follow that God orchestrates cruel and oppressive initiations or facilitations of diasporic movements. The fact remains that the missionary God is in total control over everything, and that adverse events and circumstances currently taking place would not be able to thwart his missionary intention in the world.[72]

Basic Theological Considerations for Global Diaspora

Any attempt to describe diaspora as a missiological concern needs to consider locating the theme first within a broader theological framework. The diaspora phenomenon can be grounded theologically, but not without scriptural validity and historical demonstrability. It is phenomenal when people scatter across continents and within homeland boundaries. The act of scattering points to a theological truth that dispersions accentuate God's redemptive plan that has been progressively unfolding with his reconciling acts in the world. It is, therefore, crucial to construct a 'theology of global diaspora', no matter how preliminary, upon which diaspora missiology could stand. I define 'theology of global diaspora' as:

> the dynamic process of articulating and systematizing the fundamental tenets of the missionary intentions and works of God as interpreted and implemented by God's covenant people among diaspora communities and situations around the world through the lens of the Scripture and the historical formulations of doctrines, using both traditional and contemporary speech-forms, symbols and metaphors'.[73]

Five major theological considerations can be stated in this regard. First, a global diaspora phenomenon situates Adam and Eve in the Garden of Eden and their eventual departure from their 'original homeland'. Disobedience caused this permanent departure and catapulted Adam and Eve to an irreversible exilic migration. In this sense, the diaspora may be perceived as a form of divine

[72] Houston et al., 'The New People Next Door', 16, write, 'God's control is not limited to "His" people: It extends to the rise and fall of the world's political and military powers. The vision of the empires in Daniel 2 and 7 demonstrates a philosophy of history: God is in supreme control-morally and spiritually, politically and militarily. Isaiah and Jeremiah emphasized that Egypt and Assyria, Babylon and Persia were instruments that God used for His purposes, and were themselves subject to His judgment (Is 10:5; 45:1; Jer 25:9-12). He directed the movement not only for Israel but of other nations as well (Am 9:7)'.

[73] Casiño, 'Global Diaspora', 1.

retribution.[74] Enoch Wan and Sadiri Joy Tira somberly note, 'Adam and Eve's expulsion from the Garden because of sin is the first recorded involuntary migration'.[75] When divine punishment was meted out, Adam and Eve had to leave their original domicile, and the loss of their original homeland also meant the alteration of their identity as citizens of the Garden of Eden. The exit from the Garden of Eden was thus the first recorded geographic mobility in biblical history, but caution is necessary in making it the prototype for succeeding diasporic experiences.[76]

Second, the breadth of global diaspora links historically with extreme Jewish nationalism. With Israel's perennial exclusivist tendency as the backdrop, the Jewish diaspora may be construed as a form of hermeneutical corrective to check nationalistic particularism. In their zeal to establish Yahweh as the God of Abraham, Isaac, and Jacob, some Jews tried to domesticate Yahweh within their borders. They thought Yahweh was 'located' with them, but not with other nations outside their borders. Yahweh's redemptive plan for all nations was supplanted by the Jews who stubbornly localized his presence within the boundaries of Israel and Judah.[77] Many Jews persisted with this exclusivist stance even during the New Testament times and beyond.[78]

---

[74] Enoch Wan and Sadiri Joy Tira, 'Diaspora Missiology', in Sadiri Joy Tira and Enoch Wan (eds), *Missions in Action in the 21st Century* (Ontario, Canada: Prinbridge, 2008), 44.

[75] Wan & Tira, 'Diaspora Missiology', 44.

[76] Using the twin metaphors of 'scattering' and 'gathering', Wan & Tira, 'Diaspora Missiology', 38-39, argue that such diasporic conditions are traceable to a war between the forces of God and Lucifer or Satan. The defeat of Satan led to his eviction from heaven. Satan continues to wage war against God and seeks to inflict pain and suffering upon the believers. However, in the battle of Armageddon, Satan and his evil forces will eventually meet their fate end up in hell for eternal punishment. Wan and Tira conclude, 'The supernatural suffering and gathering for the evil forces are both divine punishment, i.e., being forced out of heaven and being gathered in hell'. For a fuller treatment, see Gregory A. Boyd, *God at War: The Bible and Spiritual Conflict* (Downers Grove, IL: InterVarsity Press, 1997), specifically chapters 1-5.

[77] The prophet Jonah depicts the tension between Yahweh's universalism and the Jews' nationalist particularism. Called to proclaim Yahweh's message to the people in Nineveh, Jonah lamented over the universal scope of Yahweh's love and justice, even after the demonstration of God's power that swept across the nation in the aftermath of his preaching. For an extensive treatment, see Uriel Simon, *Jonah*, JPS Bible Commentary, trans. L.J. Schramm (Philadelphia, PA: Jewish Publication Society, 1999).

[78] God, of course, used the Jewish Diaspora even at the early stage of gospel advancement. Tuvya Zaretsky, 'A Missiological Study of Jewish Diaspora' (A paper presented at Global Diaspora Consultation, Taylor University College, Edmonton, Alberta, Canada, November 15-18, 2006), 4, emphatically writes, 'The mission of the church started in the Jewish homeland, under the power of the Holy Spirit. During the Jewish festival of Shavuot (Pentecost), Diaspora Jews and proselytes made pilgrimages to Jerusalem from Mesopotamia, Asia Minor, Northern Africa, the Mediterranean

Third, a global diaspora phenomenon accentuates the reality of divine justice. In this strict sense, the dispersal of the Jews in particular and the scattering of people in general, may be interpreted as a form of divine judgment. People were scattered in many places, going in many directions after the confusion of languages at the Tower of Babel. The Jews went into exile after a series of lapses in their spiritual devotion to Yahweh, not to mention the grave mistakes and miscalculations made by many leaders of Israel and Judah. Nevertheless, the exilic presence of the Jews in an environment of dispersion paved the way for a cross-cultural engagement, multiculturalism in the host country, and, eventually, cultural transformation.[79]

Fourth, a global diaspora phenomenon signifies the grand redemptive plan of God for all nations. Here, diaspora functions as a form of divine strategy to fulfil the universal missionary mandate. Again, God's sovereignty encompasses the scattering of people from various quarters of the world for an expressed missionary intention. Doors of opportunities for evangelism open up as people move. Given the emerging realities of transnational migration, people in dispersion can have direct access to the gospel without fear of losing their ethnic identity.[80]

Finally, global diaspora is a central theological frame for interpreting God's redemptive acts in the world based on the triune God's revelatory nature. The

---

regions, Southern Europe and the Arabian Peninsula. They heard the gospel message and believed it. After the festival, they carried the gospel back to their home Diaspora communities'.

[79] For an insightful analysis, see Leo G. Perdue, 'The Crisis of Judah and the Cultural Turn: Inculturation, Religious Transformation, and Intercultural Engagement in Second Temple Judaism' (A Paper Presented at the International Conference Celebrating the 10th Anniversary of Soongsil Graduate School of Christian Studies, Seoul, Korea, November 17, 2008), 44-65.

[80] Recent advancements in missionary strategies have introduced 'insider movements', which means that new believers can be obedient to Christ and yet 'remain integrated with or inside their natural community'. See Rebecca Lewis, 'Insider Movements: Retaining Identity and Preserving Community', in Ralph D. Winter and Steven C. Hawthorne (eds), *Perspectives on the World Christian Movement: A Reader*, 4th ed. (Pasadena, CA: William Carey Library Publishers, 2009), 673-75. Frank Decker, 'When "Christian" Does Not Translate', *Mission Frontiers*, September-October 2005, 8, argues, 'These "insider movements" are not intended to hide a believer's spiritual identity, but rather to enable those within the movement to go deeper into the cultural community – be it Islamic, Hindu, or Buddhist– and be witnesses for Jesus within the context of that culture'. For other opinions, see Biblical Missiology, 'What Is Wrong with the Insider Movement?' (http://biblical missiology.org/2010/01/07/what-is-wrong-with-the-insider-movement), accessed: April 30, 2010; Greg H. Parsons, 'Insider Movement: A New Phrase for an Old Idea' (http://www.lausanne worldpulse.com/research.php/418/07-2006), accessed: April 30, 2010; John Travis and Anna Travis, *Appropriate Christianity* (Pasadena, CA: William Carey Library, 2005), specifically chapter 23.

diaspora 'has shaped Jewish identity and history'.[81] In a similar vein, if Christian identity and history could be viewed as diasporic, then the rest of human identity and history could follow. In other words, diasporas cannot be monopolized by the Jews or Christians because the rest of humanity belongs to global diaspora communities. Central to this inclusive view of diaspora missiology is the incarnation of Jesus Christ, the concomitant of his uniqueness as the universal Redeemer and Lord. Wan and Tira assert that Christ's incarnation serves as a theological model of 'purposeful migration'.[82] Equally important themes include the universal workings of the Spirit of God, the spiritual state of humanity, the universal reality of sin, God's salvific works around the world, the diasporic orientation of the missionary mandate, the identity and calling of the church, and the realities involving millennialism in particular and eschatology in general.[83] All of these are based on scriptural foundations which then can offer global diasporas a coherent framework.

To state precisely, global diaspora is best construed as a 'theological form' that accentuates God's missionary intention for people on the move and the redemptive acts that go along with it, both domestically and globally.[84] The overall diasporic experience and paradigm involve a homeland, an adopted society, and the initiating and resultant circumstances, along with their corresponding factors, events, and processes. Theologically, between a given people's original homeland and their adopted country, there exists somewhere God's universal presence that operates in the lives of people as they face challenges in life and maximize the creative possibilities in their diasporic environment.[85]

---

[81] Zaretsky, 'A Missiological Study', 4. For a differing view that argues for exile (*galut*) instead of diaspora that shapes Jewish identity, see Howard Wettstein, ed., *Diasporas and Exiles: Varieties of Jewish Identity* (Berkeley, CA: University of California Press, 2002).

[82] Wan & Tira, 'Diaspora Missiology', 45. In an effort to locate contemporary diaspora missions in the incarnation of Christ, Wan and Tira write, 'Throughout his earthly life he exercised humility (Phil. 2:5-11) and is a model for future kingdom workers (e.g., tentmakers and missionaries) who willingly leave their homes for kingdom work. However, displaced diaspora people can also relate to his life experience as an "exile"' (45).

[83] Casiño, 'Global Diaspora', 2.

[84] Howard Wettstein, 'Coming to Terms with Exile', in Howard Wettstein (ed), *Diasporas and exiles: Varieties of Jewish identity* (Berkeley, CA: University of California Press, 2002), 47-59, argues that diaspora is a political idea that suggests geopolitical dispersion.

[85] Three significant dates are engraved in the memory of Israel related to diaspora are as follows: 22 BC (fall of Samaria); 586 BC (fall of Jerusalem); and 70 AD (destruction of Jerusalem). These major dates altered the history and identity of the Jewish people forever. Cohen, *Global Diasporas*, 22, argues that what befell on Judah in 586 BC 'created the central folk memory of the pessimistic, victim diaspora tradition—in

Implications for Diaspora Missiology

A theology of global diaspora generates a 'missiology of diaspora', and consequently, 'diaspora missiology'. In recent times, attempts have been made to define 'diaspora missiology' in some quarters. Wan defines diaspora missiology as 'a missiological study of the phenomena of diaspora groups being scattered geographically and the strategy of gathering for the kingdom'.[86] Tuvya Zaretsky refers to diaspora missiology as 'the science of mission that studies the phenomenon of diaspora or people scattered or in transition'.[87] Consultations on diaspora missiology were conducted in the last decade, but they did not produce a coherent definition of diaspora missiology. However, in November 2009, the Lausanne Movement Diasporas Leadership Team invited and convened selected missiologists and theological educators from major theological institutions in Europe, Oceania, America, and Asia at Torch Trinity Graduate School of Theology in Seoul, Korea. After three full days of scholarly discussions and debates on subjects related to diaspora mission and global diaspora studies, participants finally drafted, approved, and released a document entitled, 'Seoul Declaration of Diaspora Missiology'. Noting how 'diaspora missiology' emerges as a biblical and strategic field of missiology, the document defines diaspora missiology as 'a missiological framework for understanding and participating in God's redemptive mission among people living outside their place of origin'.[88] Evidently, all these efforts to define diaspora missiology point to the fact that the global diaspora phenomenon both embraces and transcends sociology, demographics, law, economics, anthropology, migration, and labor. Global diaspora missiology integrates 'many related disciplines on how God's mission is accomplished through the diaspora peoples'.[89] In this regard:

particular the experience of enslavement, exile, and displacement'. Narry Santos, 'Survey of the Diaspora Occurrences in the Bible and of their Contexts in Christian Missions', in Luis Pantoja Jr., Sadiri Joy Tira, and Enoch Wan (eds), *Scattered: The Filipino Global Presence* (Manila: LifeChange Publishing, 2004), 54-55, observes that in the New Testament, the term diaspora (*διασπορα*) appears only in three instances, which refers to the Jewish minority living amongst other religions (John 7:35), Jewish Christians scattered among the nations (James 1:1), and the scattered Christian communities outside Palestine (1 Peter 1:1).

[86] Enoch Wan, 'Diaspora Missiology', *Occasional Bulletin of EMS* 20:2 (2007), 3.

[87] Zaretsky, 'A Missiological Study', 3.

[88] For the full declaration, see Lausanne Diasporas Leadership Team, 'Seoul Declaration on Diaspora Missiology' (http://www.gatheredscattered.com/ component/ content/article/7), accessed: April 30, 2007. Previous consultations on diaspora missiology under the sponsorship of the Lausanne Movement Diasporas Track prior to the 'Seoul Declaration' were held in Canada, USA, Thailand, and the Philippines.

[89] Wan & Tira, 'Diaspora Missiology', 30.

> The mobility of God's people in particular, and the movements of communities, tribes, or nations, in general, help to cement the complimentary characteristics of both theology and diaspora missiology. Missiology is inherently theological as theology is indispensably missions-oriented. To construe global diaspora missiology through the lens of theology is therefore a logical necessity.[90]

Theology and missiology are inseparable; their relationship leads to five major implications for contemporary missiology.

First, the geographical and demographical mobility of people and individuals bears a strong missiological currency. Underlying the journeys and sojourns of people from their homelands to new places is divine providence, or to be exact, the reality of redemptive history. Diasporic movements unfold God's missionary intention for all nations. Regardless of the factors that initiate and facilitate a people's pilgrimage from their homeland, whether voluntary or involuntary, permanent or temporal, the fact remains that all movements can function as witnessing opportunities.

Second, given the missiological orientation of people's geographical mobility—both internally and internationally—diasporas appear to be a divine appointment.[91] Church history and its wider canvass, history of civilizations, show that the gospel moves whenever and wherever people move. In many parts of the world, the mobility of people at various circumstances e.g., war, labor flow, displacement because of persecution or ecological reasons, or economic migration, unfolds the introduction and expansion of biblical missions.[92]

Third, global diasporas open doors for more innovative missionaries to serve in different parts of the world, particularly the tentmakers. Many Christian professionals have seen their employment overseas as a fulfilment of their missionary vocation and calling. The Philippines, for example, is paving the way by producing tentmakers who would serve in different areas of the world, including places that seem hostile to the gospel. Tentmakers can live and work creatively where 'regular missionaries' have difficulty with entry. In 2010 alone, Filipino evangelicals are preparing to send out 200,000 tentmakers

---

[90] Casiño, 'Global Diaspora', 1.

[91] Some forced diasporic conditions like exiles and people's eventual return to their homeland could be considered as a missiological strategy for gospel witnessing, either directly or unintentionally. For a fuller treatment, see Alain Epp Weaver, *States of Exile: Visions of Diaspora, Witness, and Return*, foreword by Daniel Boyarin (Scottdale, PA: Herald Press, 2008).

[92] In his study of Christian diaspora, John Howard Yoder, cited in Roger E. Hedlund, *Building the Church* (Madras, India: Evangelical Literature Society, 1982), 79, observes that the good news has been brought to new parts of the world for centuries 'primarily by migration of financially independent Christians'.

around the world.[93] With an average of a million Filipinos leaving the country annually, the idea of diaspora missions is not far from reality. In fact, it has already happened in many parts of the world with Koreans, Chinese, Indians, Africans, and Hispanics. The departures of millions of Filipinos split families, drain personal resources, strain inter-personal relations and kinship ties, and affect family values back home; nevertheless, many Filipinos consider working overseas to be a 'divine gift'. Even though it is difficult to go abroad, Filipinos find creative ways to fulfil their missionary mandate.[94]

Fourth, global diaspora liberates the universal church from the trappings of traditional missiology. It transcends the former clear distinctions between 'home missions' and 'foreign missions', or 'local missions' and 'overseas missions'. A theology of global diaspora renders the popular notion of mission as 'primarily cross-cultural' to be biblically inconsistent and missiologically deficient.[95] Over the years, migrations, displacements, and dislocations of peoples from all quarters have already blurred the traditional way of distinguishing the missionary mandate from their homeland to a foreign land, or, as Johannes Blauw sees it, from centripetal (OT) to centrifugal (NT) directions of mission.[96] Missionary work within the realities of global diaspora has essentially become multi-directional and multi-faceted; it is no longer just the Global North sending out missionaries to the Global South or believers from one culture reaching out to people from different cultures.[97] Diaspora

---

[93] See David S. Lim, 'Vignettes of Filipino Tertmakers' (http://www.Tentmakernet.com/articles/vignettes.htm), accessed: April 30, 2010; Robert Ferdinand K. Lopez, 'The Philippine Missions Association (PMA) Tentmaking Agenda: Raising an Army of Outstanding Filipino Witnesses', in *Scattered: The Filipino Global Presence*, 197-208.

[94] Roman Catholic Bishop, Precioso D. Cantillas, in recognizing the strategic role that Overseas Filipino Workers (OFW) play in world evangelization writes, 'More than considering the migrant workers as modern heroes, the Church considers the migrants, and wants them to consider themselves too, as evangelizers and missionaries of their faith among the peoples they live and work. As the Church continues to empower the lay members to be protagonists of their faith and in the life of the Church, she sees in the migrants the prospect of active and effective lay evangelizers of the faith if and when they are properly trained and formed. The Church therefore looks at migration not only as a new and great pastoral challenge but also a new and a great tool for evangelization'. See 'Overseas Filipinos beyond Remittances' (http://www.cfo.gov.ph/index.php?option=com_content&view=article&id=362&Itemid=137), accessed April 30, 2010.

[95] See, for example, Robert Claro, *A Higher Purpose for your Overseas Job* (Makati, Philippines: CrossOver Books, 2003, 23, who asserts that 'missions is reaching people who are culturally different from me.

[96] Johannes Blauw, *The Missionary Nature of the Church: A Survey of the Biblical Theology of Mission* (Cambridge: Lutherworth Press, 2003), sees the discontinuity in the way mission was done in the Old Testament and New Testament.

[97] Reflecting on the emerging theologies of non-Western hemisphere, Justo L. Gonzales, *The Story of Christianity: The Reformation to the Present Day* (New York: HarperOne, 1985), II, 397, remarks that the 'lands that a century before were considered the `ends of

missiology calls for equal evangelistic concern for all peoples regardless of their ethnic background, place of origin, and social, economic, political, and religious circumstances. Diasporas continue to serve as catalysts for global socio-political economic dynamics, inundated with both theological and missiological implications. The mobility of people and individuals is a historic inevitability; it has, in fact, become an integral part of human history.

Lastly, global diaspora is an eschatological reality, that is, the march of the nations towards final judgment.[98] It is the moving of people from different ethno-linguistic groups and nations towards meeting God. A people's mobility serves as a matrix of divine-human encounters in both happy and adverse circumstances, either in displacements or dislocations, or in voluntary dispersions or involuntary migrations. Diaspora sets the broader canvas, on which the redemptive acts of God in history make their imprint, as people from various nations and tribes interact together.

Therefore, missionary efforts among people on the move are biblically valid, theologically consistent, and historically grounded. Under the redemptive plan of God, people move because the migratory or diasporic flows and transitions provide them with opportunities to encounter more of God's redemptive acts. People move because God calls them to move to bless the receiving communities of other nations.[99] The gospel moves with people. The dispersions of people, both internally and internationally, and purposely or unintentionally, happen under the lordship of Christ. The global diaspora phenomenon takes place under the sovereignty of 'one God and Father of all, who is over all and through all and in all' (Eph 4:6).

Conclusion

The geographical and demographical mobility of people- internal/external or domestic/international- has always been concomitant with the rise and fall of civilizations. It is logical to assume that in every era of world history, there were people groups or individuals who moved from one place to another.

---

the earth' will have an opportunity to witness to the descendants of those who had earlier witnessed to them'.

[98] Grant R. Osborne, *Revelation*, Baker Exegetical Commentary on the New Testament (Grand Rapids, MI: Baker Academic, 2002), 319, sees the connection between passages in the Book of Revelation and the Book of Isaiah regarding the long and generational march of nations of the world to God .

[99] The view that God is the 'director', but not necessarily the 'direct cause' of *all* forms of geographic and demographic mobility, finds support in the preeminence of the triune God regarding missionary work. 'Mission *is missio Dei*', argues David J. Bosch', *Transforming Mission: Paradigm Shifts in Theology of Mission* (Maryknoll, NY: Orbis Books, 1991), 529, which seeks to subsume into itself the *missiones ecclesiae*, the missionary programme of the church. It is not the church which 'undertakes' mission; it is the *missio Dei* which constitutes the church'.

Clearly, moving transcends cultural, ethnic, and geographical lines because human beings have the natural propensity to migrate domestically, regionally, or internationally. Integrative academic disciplines have established that people move because of institutional systems, economics, labor markets, political ideologies, and religious convictions, to name a few. At the very least, mobility involves an original homeland and an adopted home. It includes forces, events, and circumstances that cause and facilitate such transitions.

Theories of migration representing various disciplines are important to the missiological study of diasporas. They are integral to understanding people's demographic and geographic mobility. Their insights and contributions are crucial to formulating a diaspora missiology that is scripturally sound, theologically coherent, historically consistent, and contextually relevant. Diaspora thus functions as a 'theological framework' through which God's missionary plan, purpose, and redemptive acts can be deciphered and interpreted. Employing multi-disciplinary methodologies and approaches to migration theories can produce an instrument to elucidate global diasporas. Diaspora missiology refers to the process of interpreting the phenomena of global dispersions of people from every background. It presupposes the possibility of divine-human encounters in the course of demographic shifts caused by internal and international migrations, dynamic cultural engagements, clash of dissonant worldviews, and the rise and fall of civilizations.

Diaspora and Timely Hit: Towards a Diaspora Missiology

Min-young Jung

But when the fullness of the time was come, God sent forth his Son (Gal. 4:4, KJV)

This study is intentionally unconventional. Instead of pre-conditioning or prejudicing it with existing (mostly Western) scholarly works on diaspora and mission, I tried to put together miscellaneous thought-pieces that have come to my mind in the course of promoting, dialoguing, and collaborating missions movements among various Asian (mostly Korean) diaspora Christian communities. Having said that, I cannot but acknowledge that there is no such thing as truly original writing as I have been inevitably influenced by existing theological frameworks. Yet, by now, they bear quite different, perhaps richer and fuller, meanings viewed through the lens of diaspora movements. This paper is specifically Korean due to my Korean identity as well as the juxtaposition of diaspora concepts vis-à-vis Korean diaspora history.[1]

National Disgrace and Edinburgh 1910: Coincidence or Divine Conspiracy?

1910 is a landmark year in the modern mission history when the first Edinburgh conference was held. The blossom of 'Edinburgh Conferences' including the 3rd Lausanne Committee on World Evangelization (Cape Town, Oct. 16-25, 2010) celebrating the centennial anniversary proves its historic significance. Incidentally, it was the year Korea was humiliated by the Japanese takeover of her sovereignty. Would it be too much to try and find a possible correlation between these seemingly random incidents? If it is true that God is in charge of both church and secular histories – 'For from him and through him and to him are all things' (Rom. 11:36) – and that even a sparrow will not fall to the ground apart from his will (Mat. 10:29), I believe it is worth trying to connect the dots from the *missio Dei* perspective.

[1] I first wrote a short essay, 'A Call for a Worldwide Korean Diaspora Missions Network', which was featured in the compendium for Symposium on Korean-American Mission Mobilization (2003). It eventually led to the formation of KODIMNET (Korean Diaspora Missions Network) in 2004.

The national disgrace in 1910 is especially perplexing when we consider the fact that Korea not only received the gospel for the first time in her history[2] but also the new-born Korean church was in the middle of exponential growth. In 1907, Korea experienced the historic Pyungyang Revival which resulted in not only a tangible social transformation – a qualitative sign of any authentic revival – but also a quantitative church growth. The estimated number of Korean Christians was less than 200,000 in 1907, but the Million Souls Campaign launched in 1909 reveals a lot about the leaps-and-bounds growth caused by this significant revival.

But the socio-political situation of Korea at that time was quite bleak. The strategic location of the Korean peninsula, bridging the Asian continent (especially China and Russia) and the Pacific (Japan), has long been a geo-political target by ambitious world powers both nearby (China, Japan, Russia) and far off (France, Britain, the US, etc.). Korea did not open her gates voluntarily to outsiders, while the surrounding countries opened up to expedite their modernization process by welcoming Western civilization. The seclusion policy effectively blocked external influences including Christianity for decades until Korea was forced to open up. There were numerous cases of commercial pressure[3] and military invasion[4] to pry open this 'Hermit Nation'[5] in an attempt to preempt an advantageous stance to secure this strategic beachhead for further expansion. Japan finally took the upper hand by winning both the Sino-Japanese War (1894-1895) and the Russo-Japanese War (1905-1905).[6]

The fate of Korea at that time was not determined by her own people or government, but by the competitive 'chess game' of greedy world powers.[7] With the Chinese military weakened after the Sino-Japanese War, the European powers took advantage of the situation by occupying strategic areas of Manchuria. The Russians also occupied a good part of Manchuria along with the entire Liaodong peninsula, deploying over 100,000 soldiers after the Boxer

[2] The first Protestant missionaries, Horace G. Underwood and Henry G. Appenzeller, came to Korea in 1885. Depending on the definition of a missionary, some think Horace N. Allen, a medical doctor and American diplomat who came to Korea in 1884, to be the first.

[3] Such as the General Sherman Incident, or the Battle of Keupsa Gate (1866), in which an armed merchant steamer, the General Sherman, pushed its way upstream the Daedong River near Pyungyang, and was destroyed by the Korean (Chosun) army. A Welsh missionary, Robert J. Thomas, along with others onboard, was killed in this incident.

[4] The invaders included France (1866), the US (1871), Britain (1885), China (the Qing Dynasty), and Japan.

[5] William E. Griffis, *Corea, the Hermit Nation* (New York: Scriber's Sons, 1894).

[6] 'The Hermit Kingdom: A bone of contention, coveted by Russia and Japan', *The Illustrated London News*, November 7, 1903.

[7] *The Illustrated London News*, January 16, 1904.

Rebellion. A series of treaties were signed between Japan and European countries to check the growing Russian power in the Far East by recognizing the control of the Korean peninsula by Japan.[8] It eventually led to the Russo-Japanese War, and the victory by Japan gave them the undisputed control of not only the Korean peninsula but all of Manchuria as well. The Russo-Japanese War was officially ended with the signing of the Treaty of Portsmouth in the United States between the Russian and Japanese representatives. This agreement effectively recognized that the US would not interfere with Japanese ambitions in Korea and Manchuria and that Japan would not interfere with American ambitions in the Philippines. With this development, Japan manipulated a unilateral treaty in 1905[9] to annex Korea, which was realized in 1910.[10]

Why would such a terrible thing happen to Korea in the middle of the great spiritual revival? Why did not God protect Korea, which was the top prayer topic and expectation of the Korean Christians at that time, from the invasion of world powers and specifically from the 'un-Christian' Japan? What did God accomplish, if intended, through this permissive providence?

Dispersion of Nations and *Missio Dei*

It takes a diaspora missiology to comprehend such a seemingly contradictory history. The Bible is full of such clashes – i.e. the conflict of interests between human expectations regarding God and divine providence. When I think about the bleak situation of Korea a century ago, it reminds me of the similar situation Jews had when Christ came to Palestine two thousand years ago. The Jews, especially Jesus' disciples, would have expected this Jewish Messiah to deliver their nation from the occupation of the ungodly Roman Empire. So we see this constant conflict of interests between the Jews' expectation of a political Messiah to recover 'the kingdom of Israel' and the divine intention to establish 'the kingdom of God' (Acts 1:6-8). As a fellow human being, let alone a fellow Christian, I can fully sympathize with the painful disappointment disciples must have felt at the hapless death of Christ without doing anything about the liberation of Israel. Yet, Paul says that God sent Christ 'when the fullness of the time was come' (Gal. 4:4). What did he mean by that? What exactly made the timing of Christ's birth most opportune, and for what?

The continuing dispersion of Jews in the wake of the Greco-Roman Empire was among a few prominent things God did during the inter-testamental period. The German church historian, Adolf von Harnack, presents a list wherein the Christian mission was indebted to the Jewish mission which preceded it, all of which are related to diaspora, i.e. a field tilled all over the empire; religious

---

[8] E.g., the Anglo-Japanese Alliance against the Franco-Russian Alliance.

[9] Eulsa Forced Treaty (乙巳勒約, 1905)

[10] Gyeongsul National Disgrace (庚戌國恥, 1910)

communities already formed everywhere in the towns; the preliminary knowledge of the Old Testament; the habit of regular worship and control of private life; an impressive apologetic on behalf of monotheism, historical teleology, and ethics; and the feeling that self-diffusion was a duty.[11] According to Arthur Glasser, the growing missionary concern for the peoples of the Gentile world in the Jewish diaspora was a divine providence setting the stage for the 'fullness of time' when salvation history turned from the particular to the universal.[12] Through diaspora, God brought Israel onto the centre stage of his redemptive drama, observed by the nations, bathed in the light of grace that shone on it through election and covenant.[13]

It is appropriate to regard the Synagogue, the Septuagint (LXX), monotheism, and high ethical standards as prominent factors of the diaspora's contribution to Christian mission.[14] The Synagogue, which was well established by the time the Temple was destroyed, not only catered to the needs of the believing diaspora community but also adapted consciously to the needs of the foreigner.[15] Korean diaspora churches in many parts of the world have had similar experiences, such as religious decentralization or independence (from major denominations in Korea), circumstantial freedom or reorientation in terms of lay movements, and awareness or acceptance of foreigners in their congregations. The Greek Bible translation (LXX) became the great apostle, the missionary of the Hebrew Bible.[16] The Korean Bible, first translated by a group of early Korean diaspora converts under the leadership of John Ross, a Scottish missionary to Manchuria, has been crucially instrumental for the spiritual vitality of the Korean diaspora communities.[17]

---

[11] Adolf von Harnack, *The Mission and Expansion of Christianity in the First Three Centuries* (New York: Harper and Brothers, 1961), 15.

[12] Arthur F. Glasser, *Kingdom and Mission* (Pasadena: Fuller Theological Seminary, School of World Mission, 1989), 137. This missionary motif is found also in the Apocrypha: 'Praise him, you Israelites, before the Gentiles, for though he has scattered you among them, he has shown you his greatness even there. Exalt him before every living being, because he is the Lord our God, our Father and God forever' (Tobit 13:3-4). Cf. 'I will sow her for myself in the land. I will also have compassion on her who had not obtained compassion. And I will say to those who were not my people, "You are My people!" And they will say, "You are my God!"' (Hos. 2:23, NASB).

[13] Richard R. de Ridder, *Discipling the Nations* (Grand Rapids: Baker Book House, 1975), 58.

[14] Hojin Jeon, *Introduction to Mission* [in Korean] (Seoul: Reformed Faith and Life, 1985), 55. God-fearers and Gentile proselytes mentioned in Acts 2:10, 6:5, 10:2, 13:43 are especially noteworthy.

[15] De Ridder, *Discipling the Nations*, 78.

[16] De Ridder, *Discipling the Nations*, 84.

[17] It was translated and published then smuggled into Korea in the early 1880s, even before the first Protestant missionaries ever set foot on Korean soil, resulting in the first communities of Korean believers. See the Appendix.

The presence of believing communities throughout the world brought together in loyalty to the Truth, the availability of the Scriptures in translation and interpretation in the synagogues, the relative simplicity of the synagogue service, the synagogue itself…ties with Jerusalem which directed Jew and proselyte eyes and hearts to the City of God… – these are but a few, though major, benefits from which Christianity would profit when the time was fulfilled that God 'sent forth his Son, born of woman, born under law, to redeem…' (Gal. 4:4).[18]

Formulation of a Diaspora Missiology

By allowing the national disgrace upon receiving the gospel, God opened up Korea, the land of the Morning Calm, to disperse her people all over the world with a missional purpose.[19] The covenant as prototype of the gospel (Gal. 3:8) clearly shows this formula, i.e. the missionary God sending (dispersing) Abraham and his descendants, the covenant community, with a missional purpose. In fact, such was the very content and perspective of Abraham's faith, the very core of Christian religion:

> By faith Abraham, when called to go to a place he would later receive as his inheritance, obeyed and went, even though he did not know where he was going. By faith he made his home in the promised land like a stranger in a foreign country; he lived in tents, as did Isaac and Jacob, who were heirs with him of the same promise. For he was looking forward to the city with foundations, whose architect and builder is God. By faith Abraham, even though he was past age—and Sarah herself was barren—was enabled to become a father because he considered him faithful who had made the promise. And so from this one man, and he as good as dead, came descendants as numerous as the stars in the sky and as countless as the sand on the seashore. All these people were still living by faith when they died. They did not receive the things promised; they only saw them and welcomed them from a distance. And they admitted that they were aliens and strangers on earth. People who say such things show that they are looking for a country of their own. If they had been thinking of the country they had left, they would have had opportunity to return. Instead, they were longing for a better country—a heavenly one. Therefore God is not ashamed to be called their God, for he has prepared a city for them (Heb. 11:8-16).

The diaspora nature of the Christian religion is in stark contrast with secularism and/or worldly religions as the table below:

Secularism / World Religions	Christianity

[18] De Ridder, *Discipling the Nations*, 127.

[19] 'When people move, they carry their ideas, beliefs, and religious practices with them'. Jehu J. Hanciles, *Beyond Christendom: Globalization, African Migration, and the Transformation of the West* (New York: Orbis Books, 2008), 8.

Human-centred	God-centred
Human Desire: Fortress on earth	God's Plan: Pilgrimage (diaspora)
Tower of Babel	Dispersion (diaspora)
Security in self/world: e.g. 'American Dream'	Security in God/heaven: 'Kingdom Dream'
'Restless wanderer' (Gen. 4:12, 14)	Purpose-driven pilgrim/diaspora
Settlement in Mesopotamia, one of the four major human civilizations	Covenant call (Heb. 11:8) to live in tents in a foreign country (Heb. 11:9)
Settlement in Goshen	Exodus
Settlement in Canaan	Exile (diaspora)

The fundamental distinctiveness of Christianity that makes it stand out among world religions, I believe, is its God-centred orientation as against the human-centredness of others. Whereas any given humanistic religion aims at satisfying human desires by appropriating or manipulating supernatural powers, Christianity is of, about, and for God. Conversion is transformation from sinful, human-centred perspective to a God-centred worldview. Without an authentic conversion, therefore, there is no point talking about worshipping God with the nations, or about the purpose of the sovereign God in dispersing his people.

Human desire, as epitomized in the story of the Tower of Babel, is to build a fortress on earth, whereas God's plan for his people is to send them out with a purpose. These two different agenda are in constant conflict against each other, not only in the biblical narratives but also in our routine lives. People seek worldly security by accumulating wealth (building a fortress) in this world, like the American Dream, the European Dream, or even the Korean Dream, whereas the Bible says God himself is the true security, the fortress (2 Sam. 22:2, Ps. 48:3, 59:9), and the great reward (Gen. 15:1).

Every man without God is 'a restless wanderer on the earth' (Gen. 4:12, 14). The world without God will continue to wander purposelessly till it finds its creator. Without purpose there is no meaning, and without meaning there is no value. Any teleological argument cannot stand without presupposing God. 'Without God, life has no purpose, and without purpose, life has no meaning. Without meaning, life has no significance or hope'.[20]

The problem of the Tower of Babel lies in its underlying atheistic worldview and motivation, not the civilization per se. The divine intervention to disperse the tower builders throughout the face of the earth was not only God's judgment but also his grace, in that it kept their sin from reaching its full measure, thereby preventing divine wrath. Grace has always been ingrained in the divine providence of scattering his people with a purpose. The people's

[20] Rick Warren, *The Purpose Driven Life: What on Earth Am I Here for?* (Grand Rapids: Zondervan, 2002), 21.

choice was the Shinar Plain, where they wanted to build their fortress, Babel, but God's gracious choice was elsewhere.

Likewise, we have the case of Abraham, the covenantal forefather of faith. God's calling him out of, and leading him away from Mesopotamia is noteworthy. Why would God want to remove him from his comfort zone, the favourite place for anyone at that time? The region is famous as one of the four riverine civilizations where writing was first invented, along with the Nile Valley in Egypt, the Indus Valley in the Indian subcontinent, and the Yellow River Valley in China. Instead of making him prosper at the place of his choice, God called him out to live in tents, as a sojourner rather than a permanent resident, in foreign soils (Heb. 11:8-9).

We see the repetition of the same paradigm in the ensuing biblical narratives: from settlement in Goshen, the fertile Nile Delta, to Exodus towards wilderness and Palestine; from settlement in Canaan, the promised land of 'milk and honey', to exile into the lands of Gentile empires. The covenant call was not about building a fortress on earth, after all, but to become and form a purpose-driven pilgrim community for God's kingdom.

Diaspora, the Seed for God's Kingdom

> When the Lord brought back the captives to Zion, we were like men who dreamed. Our mouths were filled with laughter, our tongues with songs of joy. Then it was said among the nations, 'The Lord has done great things for them'. The Lord has done great things for us, and we are filled with joy. Restore our captivity, O Lord, like streams in the Negev. Those who sow in tears will reap with songs of joy. He who goes out weeping, carrying seed to sow, will return with songs of joy, carrying sheaves with him (Psalm 126:1-6).

This is one of the favorite Psalms frequently recited in Korean churches during the month of August when the whole country celebrates its liberation from the Japanese occupation. I cannot help noticing the sudden shift of flow from celebration of liberation to prophecy of a future harvest. How are these seemingly random themes related? What logical connections can we make between the two? Here the psalmist is adumbrating the dispersion of Jews in captivity to the sowing in tears in view of an upcoming harvest. Just as God dispersed his people (Israel) for the kingdom harvest, he pried open the Korean Peninsula for Korean Christians to be scattered in tears.[21]

The fact that the Greek noun *diaspora* is composed of the preposition *dia* ('through') and the verb *speirein* ('to sow', Mat. 13:3) is especially revealing. The concept of diaspora as God's intentional act of sowing for his kingdom is embedded in the kingdom parables, especially the parable of sower (Mat.

---

[21] Asian Diaspora Initiative, Wycliffe International, recently produced a promotional DVD, *Korean Diaspora: The Seed of God's Kingdom.* (See Appendix for the script.)

13:3-8). It does not take a sage to put sowing (or planting) together with harvest, as there is an apparent logical connection. In this parable, as well as other teachings, Jesus explains the nature of God's kingdom through the imagery of farming, sowing, God as the farmer, various harvest fields, etc.

This leads to the divine providence of gathering and dispersing. Billy Graham is said to have classified various biblical commands into two major categories, i.e. 'come and go'.

Come / Gathering	Go / Dispersion
Fellowship of the Triune God	Sending of Christ & the Holy Spirit (*missio Dei*)
Early church community: Gathering & fellowship	Diasparentes ('dispersed', Acts 8:4, 11:19)
Antioch church: multi-racial community	Sending Paul & Barnabas

Christians come to (a local) church in order to be empowered to go out into the world rather than to stay there, just as the Triune God in intimate fellowship sent the Son and the Holy Spirit on mission. The concept of a missional church comes into this scene, which makes going and spreading out in the world a norm, a default, rather than an exception. The early church as a close-knit community gathered frequently for mutual fellowship. But it was only after God scattered them (diasparentes) through persecution that they became witnesses to Samaria and beyond. It eventually led to the birth of the first multiracial church in Antioch, to whom the Holy Spirit further instructed to send out their top leaders, Paul and Barnabas, as their missionaries. The future of church depends on outsiders in terms of whether they would be reached or not, rather than insiders and/or their younger generation.

Let us dig a little deeper into the imagery of sowing related to diaspora. According to John (chapter 15), God the farmer sows seed, which is an intentional act in view of an upcoming harvest at the right places (not random) in the right season (not random) – 'the fullness of time' (Gal. 4:4)[22] – and in right ways, i.e. in his sovereign and mysterious ways. Thus God sowed seed by allowing Gentile empires (permissive providence) to invade, thereby scattering, Israelites. His purpose? Spiritual harvest for his kingdom (Mat. 9:37-38), of course! Diaspora, therefore, whether scattered voluntarily or involuntarily, can define their spiritual identity as 'the kingdom seed'.[23]

---

[22] 'If something happens in the fullness of time, it will happen when the time is right and appropriate'. (http://www.usingenglish.com/reference/idioms/fullness+of+time.html)

[23] Christians often recognize their missional identity upon migration: 'The extraordinary African migrations in the last three decades have, more than any single factor, helped to foment a new epoch of African missionary expansion, transcending Africa from a mission field to missionary force'. Hanciles, *Beyond Christendom*, 218.

Conclusion: Diaspora, the Final Sprinter

Paul often employs sports imagery – a race – to explain the nature of Christian ministry. Missions are more like a relay than a sprint in that the baton of more than two thousand years of church history has been passed down from one group of sprinters to another. Diaspora is where they are not by chance, not by human plan in pursuit of worldly dreams, not by unfortunate random twist of history. They are there for a reason, for a great purpose, for the ultimate cause. The final sprint is set, waiting for them. The final sprinter should be the best. Who else is more qualified than a multi-lingual and multi-cultural diaspora for God's mission? The question is, will they take or drop the baton?

As a modern Christian, the phrase 'fullness of time' reminds me of a 'timely hit' in baseball game, one of the most schematic ballgames, i.e. it is more strategic than physical. In this game, timely hit, as against sporadic hits, is probably the most important feat especially at full base. In God's eternal providence, diaspora was sent ahead without their knowing to occupy all three bases, and God sent Jesus Christ, the top hitter, to make the most crucial timely hit in human history (Gal. 4:4). In the same way, God has deployed his people, including the Korean diaspora, who have been scattered 'weeping' (Ps. 126:5-6), and made another full base at this eschaton of human history. The lyric of a devotional song on the providential history of Korea sounds prophetic in this regard:[24]

Dark at night deep in thought, at history's dark hours
The morning star shines East, heralding nation's dawn
People of the Morning Calm, renewed in the light
Life in this light, builds tower of life for the land

Rooted deep in fertile soil, stems and branches shoot up
Countless branches and leaves, all people live by its fruit
People of the Morning Calm, God calls for workers
Be the kingdom seed, continue the life of history

Clean fountains gush up, streams soak dry lands
Fertile green plains, eye-opening spectacles
People of the Morning Calm, new heaven and new earth
Never stop shining, burn the torch for human race

There was a miracle during the 2008 Olympiad – to everyone's surprise, the Korean baseball team won the gold medal. When the final innings was over, the stadium literally exploded with overwhelming bliss. As a fellow kingdom builder, I would like to encourage my Korean diaspora brothers and sisters:

---

[24] This is my rough translation, originally written in Korean by Jaejoon Kim (1966), and composed by Donghoon Lee.

When you guys, the final sprinter of world mission relay, touch the end line by reaching the last of 6,000 UPGs, make the final hit by reaching the last of 2,000+ UPGs without God's word in their heart language, there sure will be a joyful and glorious celebration from above, the very climax of the whole human history, and long awaited eternity in heaven will finally be realized. Go, diaspora, go! Make God's day! Maranatha!

Appendix

Korean Diaspora, the Seed of God's Kingdom (DVD Script)

One hundred and twenty years ago, the power of God's word came to Chosun [Korea], a small country in East Asia. Chosun was then known only as the remote edge of China. A handful of missionaries had a heart for the land and prayed, but the door remained closed. The power of God's word was at work to awaken Chosun, not from inside but from outside first.

John Ross and John MacIntyre

The seclusion policy prevented the two missionaries from entering Chosun, so they began preaching the gospel to Koreans living in Shenyang and Manchuria. This is when they met a merchant named Sang-ryoon Suh. After receiving Jesus as his Savior, Suh worked with Eung-chan Lee, Hong-joon Baek and Sung-ha Lee to help Ross translate the books of the New Testament. In 1882, 'The Gospel of Jesus Christ according to Luke' was published. This was three years before any missionary ever set foot in Chosun. In 1887 the first Korean New Testament 'The Holy Bible of Jesus' was translated.

In Japan, Soo-jung Lee, with the help of Western missionaries there, translated 'The Gospel of Mark of the New Testament' in 1885. Horace T. Underwood and Henry G. Appenzeller, the first Protestant missionaries to Korea, brought this Gospel of Mark when they first came to Chosun. Even before the foreign missionaries began their ministry, many Koreans were already reading the Korean Bible distributed by a few dedicated Christians. This laid the foundation for the early missionary movement in Korea. Despite persecution, Korean Bibles were printed in Manchuria and smuggled across the border into Korea. Sang-ryoon Suh risked his own life to carry over 15,000 copies of the Korean Bible in his backpack within three years. God's work marched on by the sacrifice of these courageous early believers.

As a result, Underwood found a community of believers in Seoul when he first arrived, and baptized tens of people after just two years of ministry. Underwood wrote to his mission board at home: 'Instead of sowing seed, we are already harvesting what has been already sown'. The Korean Bible enabled the Korean church to grow as a healthy and rapidly multiplying indigenous church.

Revival and Trial

In 1907, God brought forth a great revival in Korea. It began in Pyongyang and swept the whole nation in just two years with the 'Million People Salvation Movement'. The revival movement seemed unstoppable. People expected and hoped that God would protect the nation from the threats of world powers. But the Japanese imperial regime subjugated Korea in 1910. Missionaries were driven out, and the Korean church was forced to worship Japanese Emperor abdicating their Christian faith. Why such a terrible ordeal despite the enthusiastic reception of the gospel and the amazing spiritual revival?

God began an amazing work through this tribulation. He began scattering the people of this 'hermit kingdom' throughout the world. The number of people who left Korea in the wake of the Japanese occupation was unprecedented in the Korean history. And that was just a beginning.

In 1903, over 7,000 Korean laborers to sugar cane plantations in Hawaii.

In 1905, over 1,000 Korean contract laborers to henequen farms in Mexico.

In 1937, more than 180,000 Koreans in the Maritime Provinces of Siberia relocated forcibly to Central Asia.

In 1945, over 8 million man-days were forced to be deployed throughout the Asia-Pacific during World War II.

Even after liberation, the pace of migration only accelerated due to the political and social turmoil in Korea including the Korean War. Afterwards, military dictatorship and the Vietnam War further scattered Koreans overseas. The last 100 years have indeed been a period of great Korean dispersion – nurses and coal miners to Europe, agricultural workers to Latin America, deep-sea fishery, overseas investment, the construction boom in the Middle East, the flood of Korean international students, and the recent Korean retirees to Southeast Asia.

'Those Who Sow in Tears Will Reap with Songs of Joy' (Psalm 126:5)

Why did God disperse Koreans throughout the world? We can find the answer from the case of the Jewish diaspora. God prepared the coming harvest of his kingdom by dispersing Israelites among Gentile nations through the invasion of Babylonia and other powerful empires. The Jewish diaspora became the seed for the kingdom harvest.

Extended trials and suffering led the Jewish diaspora to drop its Jewish exclusiveness to be reborn as a cosmopolitan community. This enabled them to prepare for the coming of Christ and his mission found in the book of Acts. The major players in the days of the Apostles, such as Paul, Barnabas, Silas, Luke, Timothy and Apollos, were all from the diaspora community. God worked in a similar fashion with Koreans who were as ethnocentric as the Jews. Just as God prepared Jews for the days of the Apostles by scattering them, he did the same thing to Koreans for his kingdom by scattering them throughout the world. The Jewish diaspora network was vital for the ministry of Paul and Barnabas. In the same way, the worldwide Korean diaspora network has been a strategic beachhead for the Korean missions movement since the 1970s.

Interview: Rev. Hyeon-soo Lim (Senior Pastor of a Korean Diaspora Church)

> It is quite obvious that God scattered Koreans for world mission. Although our immigration history is 100 years shorter than that of China and Japan, I believe we've been scattered by God's special providence for world mission. Accordingly, my church ministry focuses on world mission.

Two thousand years ago, the Jewish diaspora played the leading role in the early days of mission. Now it is time for the Korean diaspora to carry the torch. The Korean diaspora is not simply a victim of tragic history. They are not pursuers of the American Dream either. They are the seed that God has intentionally sown for the purpose of his kingdom harvest.

Interview: Rev. Minho Song (Senior Pastor of a Korean Diaspora Church)

> In Exodus 19:5-6, God calls his people 'my special possession'. In Hebrew, the word 'possession' means movable goods, in contrast to real estate that cannot be moved. It emphasizes mobility. Therefore, we are to be moved whenever and wherever God desires. As a diaspora, we are to be dispersed at God's will, and we believe this is our identity.

The Remaining Task and the Korean Diaspora

Asian, African and Latin American churches have been the beneficiaries of mission for a long time. But now, they are expanding their roles to be senders and partners in world mission. Who should play the leading role in the 21st century, perhaps the final century of world mission? God has brought amazing spiritual revivals in Korea and other non-Western churches in the last century. And now He desires to use them for the harvest.

Interview: Kirk Franklin, Executive Director, Wycliffe International

> It is a unique opportunity at this point of time for the Korean diaspora church and Christians, who are already located all around the world to engage in the Bible

> translation ministry, with a particular focus on Vision 2025. Together we can look at the remaining needs, the remaining people groups that still don't have Scriptures in their own language, and make this the priority for the Korean church.

The diaspora is a special envoy, strategically appointed by God, to spread the gospel in different cultures and languages. Their minds have been opened through living overseas, away from their homelands. They have adjusted to multi-cultural and multi-lingual societies. They are the most effective and strategic resource for world mission.

Currently, there are more than 2,000 language groups that still don't have even one verse of the Bible in their own language. How much longer should they wait? Wycliffe has a goal called Vision 2025 to start a translation project in every language group needing one by the year 2025. And there are already many among diaspora communities responding obediently to this call.

God has sown kingdom seed among Koreans through tribulation and suffering. This seed, scattered from the country of the Morning Calm, will return with a global harvest. Who shall respond to God's earnest call in these final days of world mission? Should it not be the Korean diaspora, the seed of the gospel that God has strategically sown for such a time as this? Korean diaspora! Rise and respond to God's call, and carry the torch of redemptive history!

The Diasporic Politics of Asian-American Christianity

Jonathan Tran

The following offers an account of the diasporic politics of Asian-American Christianity. My account here follows a single trajectory while highlighting two specific moments. First, it will show how the church has historically been a gathering point for Asian-American immigrant identity. Second, it will demonstrate how these immigrant churches can mobilize Asian-American political activity. By giving this account, I hope to make a wider argument about the church as politics and its cultivation of Asian-American as well as Christian identity, that is, Asian-American Christian identity. What will be critical to notice, within my account, is the ways the gathering of Asian-American Christianity provides the critical moral formation for the church's political organization, firstly the formation of a collective cultural identity and then the mobilization of that identity toward political action. Rather than seeing this as two distinct moments, one ecclesial and the other political, I trace a single *political* vector through the entire process: the church's politics intensifies, first as a gathering and then outwardly toward *further* political expression. Another way to speak of this single trajectory is to frame the church's ecclesial life in terms of sacramental presence which gathers the church into the world and mobilizes it. Conceptualizing the church in sacramental terms helps us understand these two moments- gathering and mobilizing- as one: the church as God's presence in the world, the church as God's activity in the world. Also critical is noticing how this politics is made possible by a uniquely immigrant comportment toward diaspora as a communal identity on the move.

My account follows the story of one particular Christian immigrant community, believing this example broad enough to illumine the experiences of various other Asian-American immigrant communities. No doubt every community has its own story to tell and the experience of this particular group of Asian-American Christian immigrants differs considerably from that of Korean-American Christians, who came to this country a decade before for entirely different reasons, or Chinese or Japanese immigrants whose presence in America dates from the nineteenth century. Still, I hope that by focusing on this one group of Christians, we will discover features common to all as well as encourage greater fealty to each particular community's story.

A Village Called Versailles

During and after Hurricane Katrina in 2005, the media was quick to report the storm's effects on two familiar parts of New Orleans: the tourist-driven, largely white-owned and operated French Quarter District and the historically poor black communities. In doing so, the American media continued business as usual, polemicizing American social life along the caricatured axis of rich and poor, white and black. No doubt such construals do reflect certain realities of American life, and New Orleans has always displayed quite well, especially with its locale in the historic South, the United States as largely bifurcated. The iconic rapper Kanye West was simply highlighting this reality, though perhaps crudely, when he charged, 'George Bush doesn't care about black people'. The media's now familiar images of armed soldiers corralling hoards of homeless and destitute African Americans into the crowded bladder of the New Orleans Superdome, where they would be kept for days, seemed to confirm the West's crude pronouncement. Such is life in America. The storm simply washed away all pretension that America is, or has ever been, anything other.

If America does not care about black people, black and white people, equally, in the days and even years following Katrina, did not care about yellow people. The media's white/black polemics blinded it to the plight of the tens of thousands of Vietnamese Americans who had for over three decades made their home in New Orleans East, in the shadow of Bourbon Street's monied economy and alongside those African Americans later shuttled into the belly of the Superdome. Again, this continued business as usual for the American media, and consequently, sadly, the American public who have historically rendered invisible the lives of Asian Americans. If one looks at an official map of New Orleans, one will not likely find Versailles, which just happens to be the densest concentration of Vietnamese anywhere outside of Vietnam. During the reconstruction that followed Katrina, city planners mapped out their vision of the new New Orleans, which prioritized bringing back the best of the old New Orleans. Nowhere on that map were their any plans to rebuild Versailles or resettle the thousands of Vietnamese who had called New Orleans home for over 30 years. As one resident claimed, 'We were never on the map'.

The critically acclaimed documentary A Village Called Versailles tells the story of how these blighted Vietnamese Americans claimed their place in New Orleans.[1] In an interview about his interest in Versailles, the film's maker, S. Leo Chiang, reflected:

---

[1] *A Village Called Versailles*, Walking Iris Films, 2009, directed by S. Leo Chiang. Many thanks to Billy Vo who first introduced me to this documentary and K. Christine Pae and James McCarty III whose 'Unavoidable Burden of Race: (Under)represented Asian/Asian Americans in the Public Ethical Discourse', presented at the 2011 Society of Christian Ethics meetings, spurred my own reflections here.

> I think that this particular story for me struck a chord because in the post-Katrina time, most of the images that you see on the mainstream television are really this, you know, sort of black versus white conflict that was emphasized over and over again. And I think that there upwards of 30-40,000 Asian-Americans [sic] along the Gulf Coast, whose stories really was not told. So when I found out about this particular story, I felt like it was an important missing piece to the history about the impact of Hurricane Katrina and the floods.[2]

A Village Called Versailles documents the Versailles community's efforts back into New Orleans East. At the centre of Versailles, and Chiang's documentary, stands Mary Queen of Vietnam, a Roman Catholic diocese. Unlike most Vietnamese Americans, the people of Versailles were Christian, and equally surprisingly, their Christianity is generations old, having been inherited in North Vietnamese villages, carried through the war, and planted in New Orleans East, when Vietnamese war refugees founded Versailles in New Orleans East in the late 1970s.

One of the documentary's most poignant moments occurs shortly after Katrina, at a point when New Orleans East was under a 'look and leave' order: residents were told to return to survey the damage of their wrecked communities and homes only to leave because of the extent of damage. They could not stay. If they wanted to begin the process of restoring their communities they could do so but they could not stay. This led to what the documentary called a 'Catch-22' where recovery could not begin because there was no infrastructure and no infrastructure could be built unless recovery began. This bind met another, which the film characterized as the cart and horse conundrum: no businesses would return to the wrecked neighbourhoods because no people were there and no people would return because no businesses were there. This double bind left the devastated city not only wrecked but also abandoned without a hope of reconstruction. Queen Mary, the original impetus for the community's settlement many years ago, now became the impetus for the community's return. As Father Vien Nguyen, the pastor of Mary Queen, states, 'The understanding was that we would lead the way back'. And so they did. Father Nguyen found a place for his parishioners to stay during the first stages of rebuilding and, equally critically, did what he and Mary Queen always did, they celebrated the Mass. Following Father Nguyen's lead, one of the parishioners summoned the community: 'Put out a call to all the people in Houston, and West Bank and Baton Rouge, and let them know we are going to hold the first Mass this Sunday'. In the first week 300 congregants gathered for the Mass, followed the next week by 800, and when Mary Queen invited the rest of New Orleans East, 2200 white, Latino, and African Americans gathered with Vietnamese Americans at Mary Queen of Vietnam to celebrate the Eucharist, under the banner, 'Welcome to the Resurrection of

[2] National Public Radio (NPR) interview dated May 25, 2010. http://www.npr.org/templates/story/story.php?storyId=127113878

New Orleans East Mass'. The documentary portrays the amazing scene when the worshipping community prays together in the very midst of Katrina's aftermath: 'Thy kingdom come, thy will be done…'. In the years that followed, as people tried to rebuild their lives, they celebrated the Mass. 'Didn't matter what kind of day it would be: 10:00 am, there will be Mass on Sunday'.

Before turning to how this community gathered around the Eucharist ushered forth a politics strong enough to resist and even overcome a failed municipal government and the tides of environmental racism, we should first examine how the story of Mary Queen, as amazing as it is, reflects but one instance of the church's political gathering of Asian-American immigrants. Akin to Mary Queen, the Christian church in America has led the way for Asian Americans in the long pilgrimages of immigration. Hurricane Katrina proved an especially powerful and difficult moment in this development, yet Mary Queen's critical role follows upon its enduring presence in Versailles; because of that endurance, its parishioners expected the church to lead the way, trusted it to provide a home, believed that amidst destruction its Mass was something to be celebrated, and understood themselves as constituted by this community. The ground for the recovery of Versailles had been nurtured Mary Queen. Moreover, as A Village called Versailles tells the story of Mary Queen, so Mary Queen tells the story of the Asian American Church, the sacramental gathering of Asian Americans amidst immigrant movements of despair and hope, struggle and achievement, a story captured by the passions of that which enables and embodies that story: the Asian American Church.

Strangers from a Different Shore

The history of Asian immigration to America can largely be told around U.S. immigration legislation. The Vietnamese spoken of in *A Village Called Versailles* came by way of a Congressional allowance following the emergency evacuation as the American war in Vietnam abruptly ended in 1975. The Orderly Departure Program initiated immigration allowances for the Vietnamese in subsequent waves from 1975 through the early 1990s. Much of America's history with Asian immigrants follows this course, that is, recurring moments of generosity, when borders would be opened, and protectionism, when borders would be closed. Indeed, Ronald Takaki's iconic history *Strangers from a Different Shore* organizes itself around the twin themes of extravagance and necessity.[3] Takaki's history chronicles the struggles met by first Chinese and Japanese immigrants to America and later Filipinos, Koreans, Vietnamese, Indian and other Asians and Pacific Islanders. Takaki's overarching thesis describes how these immigrants, unlike European immigrants, met intractable prejudice not because they were immigrants

[3] Ronald Takaki, *Strangers from a Different Shore: A History of Asian Americans* (Boston: Little, Brown and Company, 1989).

(America's history is primarily a history of immigration) who came from other shores (since every American, save the Native Americans, had come from other shores) but because they came from different shores. Because they were not Europeans, they were seen as consummate outsiders, forever foreigners, even after generations in America. Takaki's suggestion might be a bit overstated to the extent that many Europeans, such as the Irish, the Italians, or Eastern Europeans, also faced tremendous prejudice in America as Nathan Frye Jacobson's *Whiteness of a Different Color* ably demonstrates.[4] Still, Takaki helps us understand the character of the prejudice faced by Asian immigrants in America, and reading Takaki and Jacobson together reveals the unique travails of non-Caucasian immigrants. In Jacobson's account, those who were not hitherto countenanced as 'white' could achieve its privileged fraternity and power by socially enacting whiteness (by way of violence against non-white Americans, social performances of whiteness, and physically altering endeavors that helped one pass into whiteness). To the extent that Asian immigrants could not become white in these ways (try as they may) they found themselves continuously on the outside looking in.[5] No doubt racialized descriptions like 'white' and even ostensibly biological and eugenic notions such as 'Caucasian' were at best social constructions, but even so, such social constructions expressed themselves and were stabilized by cultural practices, social forms, and legislation that inculcated these social constructions into the everyday infrastructure of American civic life. We recall the social theorist Michel Foucault's comment that while such constructions are not real, they are as real as their effects.[6] Hence, the legacy of Asian immigration to America can be traced through subsequent legislation such that the Foreign Miners' Tax, the 1870 Naturalization Act, The Chinese Exclusion Act, *Fong Yue Ting versus The United States and Ozawa versus U.S.*, the Asiatic Exclusion League, the Alien Land Law, the Cable Act of 1922, the Hare-Hawes-Cutting Act, and the Angel Island Detention Center are hallmarks of America's attempts to limit Asian immigration and segregate and discriminate against Asian Americans largely based on racist-driven modes of protectionism. President Franklin Roosevelt's infamous Executive Order 9066, which mandated the forcible internment of

---

[4] Matthew Frye Jacobson, *Whiteness of a Different Color: European Immigrants and the Alchemy of Race* (Cambridge: Harvard University Press, 1998).

[5] For further theological work on these issues, see Jonathan Tran, 'Living Out the Gospel: Asian American Perspectives and Contributions', *Annual of the Society of Asian North American Christian Studies* 2 (2010), 13-56 and 69-73.

[6] Specifically, Foucault states, 'We can certainly say that madness "does not exist", but this does not mean it is nothing. All in all, it was a matter of doing the opposite of what phenomenology has taught us to say and think, the phenomenology that said, roughly: Madness exists, which does not mean that it is a thing'. Michel Foucault, *Security, Territory, Population: Lectures at the Collège de France 1977-1978*, ed. Arnold I. Davidson, trans. Graham Burchell (New York: Picador, 2007), 118.

nearly 120,000 Japanese Americans, epitomized, perhaps at its nadir, the tremendous difficulties faced by Asian immigrants in America.

Takaki identifies World War II as the Asian-American 'watershed moment' (357-405). During the Japanese American internment, non-Japanese Asian Americans found provisions for greater access into American life, namely by defining themselves over against Japanese Americans and by participating in the racial violence toward Japan and Japanese Americans. 'I'm not a Jap' purchased for Chinese and Filipino Americans a passage into the wider culture. Later when interned Japanese Americans went on to serve America with great distinction during the war, the Internment came to be understood by the rest of the nation as a mistake, helping America begin to see its errors in dealing with these 'strangers from a different shore'. After Civil Rights, America increasingly came to define itself beyond whiteness, which in turn proffered greater generosity toward immigrants from non-European nations. The next decades would see the arrival of hundreds of thousands of Filipinos, Chinese, Koreans, Vietnamese, and Indians.

Much has been made of the 'Model Minority' notion of Asian Americans and increasingly much has been made of the mythic power and social inaccuracy of its suggestion. When the children of Asian immigrants in America came of age and achieved astonishing academic success, America took notice, especially as the media in the decades following Civil Rights focused on this sterling example of what it meant to be a minority in America: academically successful, economically self-sufficient, and politically quiet. No doubt the myth found traction insofar as it pitted the 'model minorities' against those minorities who did not so easily fit the mould: academically under-serviced, economically dependent, and politically confrontational. The model minority became a rallying cry on behalf of whites for non-Asian minorities to get in line, and for Asian minorities to stay in line. Of course the main problem with the model minority myth was simply that it was not true. For every Asian academic prodigy, there remained many Asian immigrants who struggled to learn English or receive the benefits of education; the focus on Asian Americans who had 'made it' as physicians and lawyers covered over the reality that thousands of Asian Americans, at a rate often higher than historically disenfranchised African Americans, relied on welfare and other state-sponsored services. Even those astonishing academic superstars who went off to schools like Harvard and Stanford faced new versions of anti-Asian legislation, a prohibitive glass-ceiling that sequestered Asian Americans to middle management despite their Harvard and Stanford diplomas. The myth had the double effect of creating a backlash when non-Asian Americans presupposed that Asian Americans received breaks the rest of America did not, thereby cutting off struggling Asian Americans from benefits now earmarked for those minorities who 'really' needed help. The myth not only suggested what was not the case, but its power lay in its ability to simultaneously call Asian Americans to its false promises while silencing Asian Americans from protesting against impediments to those promises. The myth disappeared from the purview of the American public of the actual reality of Asian America. These realities are only now coming to the fore as the myth is dispelled and Asian Americans tell their stories beyond the stereotypes.

Immigration as Diaspora

In their celebrated sociological study *Growing up American*, Min Zhou and Carl Bankston report how religion fosters inculcation not only into Asian American communities but also helps create the basis for thriving within American life.[7] In their study of Vietnamese Christians in New Orleans East, Zhou and Bankston describe religion 'as a social institution that serves as a focal point for organizing relations and establishing identities among the Vietnamese'.[8] Zhou and Bankston's analysis focuses on the aforementioned Mary Queen of Vietnam, describing how the church serves as the centre of the whole community's civic life:

> Virtually all community organizations and activities have a church connection. For example, the local Vietnamese Voters Association, which helps to prepare eligible community members for the test for U.S. citizenship, holds all its meetings on the grounds of the church, and a priest serves as its advisor. The church also provides the site for community meetings at irregular intervals to discuss problems and goals. Every Saturday morning, the church grounds become an open-air market, where all Vietnamese in the Versailles neighborhood can sell their goods. The entire church parish divides itself into zones each of which has a 'zone leader', an influential person, who represents zone residents at meeting held at the church to decide both secular and religious activities and policies. All these continuing church-centred activities provide ample opportunities for ethnic interaction and thus help strengthen ties among members while also reinforcing the leadership roles of religious institutions and community-based organizations.[9]

Considering its historical constitution through immigration, America has an ironic and even tragic posture toward immigrants. Because of the logic of late capitalist cultures, Americans view immigrants as threats to limited resources. The very opportunities immigrants come for (vocational, educational and social) are seen as scare commodities of a zero-sum social imaginary. While Americans have largely moved beyond their racist reasons for fearing strangers from different shores, they tend to hold onto economic reasons for fear, which in turn resurrect racist sentiments. Thus in much of America, it is still not okay to be an immigrant. And yet, in the Mary Queen of Vietnam, it is okay to be an

---

[7] Min Zhou and Carl L. Bankston III, *Growing up American: How Vietnamese Children adapt to Life in the United States* (New York: Russell Sage Foundation, 1998).

[8] Zhou and Bankston, *Growing up American*, 19.

[9] Zhou and Bankston, *Growing up American*, 103.

immigrant. Indeed, not only is it okay, such places recast for its constituents and others what it means to be *American*, stating anew what America *is*. This happens not primarily through extraordinary events like those portrayed in *A Village Called Versailles,* but rather the regular ordinary day-to-day life described by Zhou and Bankston. Such ordinary life is where America is passed on from one generation to the next, renewed and restated in each respective American ethnic community: white, black, Chinese, Vietnamese, so on and so forth. What makes possible the extraordinary stories reported in *A Village Called Versailles* are the regular formative processes of *Growing up American.*

One of the more interesting discoveries made by Zhou and Bankston is that while ethnic immigrant communities serve as staging areas for success in broader American life, leaving behind one's immigrant culture is not a perquisite for that success, as some might suppose. One might guess that 'becoming American' means something like leaving behind one's immigrant status, even literally shedding ethnic identity markers. In some ways, such practices allow one to be more successful in a country that so highly values cultural homogeneity. Yet Zhou and Bankston found that those who retained their immigrant identities and continued concretely ethnic practices tended to achieve greater success in American life. In their study of Vietnamese-American youth, they found that students who held deep allegiances to Vietnamese cultural values while critical of what they understood to be 'Americanized' values tended to have greater educational success. This bucks the notion that American values such as independent thinking are prerequisites for success within America, therefore requiring immigrants to be 'Americanized' in order to succeed.[10] Moreover, Zhou and Bankston report that those who spoke both Vietnamese and English attained higher levels of mental and social adjustment, better academic success, and greater promise for the future. While one might think that success in an English-dominated culture would require forgetting native languages, again Zhou and Bankston found the opposite.[11] As the church served as the centre of this life (teaching congregants both English and Vietnamese, encouraging American and traditionally Vietnamese values, creating Vietnamese American modes of social life, etc.), it helped create the content and form of an entirely novel mode of life, affirmed and cultivated from one generation to the next. In contrast, Zhou and Bankston's evidence found overwhelmingly that Vietnamese Americans who were isolated from such communal interactions tended to fare worse in American life.

Later, when Katrina physically devastated Versailles, the cultural community created around Versailles would endure and come to re-gather the hurricane- dispersed Vietnamese Americans. Father Nguyen's invocation of the regularity of the Mass—'Didn't matter what kind of day it would be: 10:00 am,

---

[10] Zhou and Bankston, *Growing up American*, 71-92.

[11] Zhou and Bankston, *Growing up American*, 108-129.

there will be Mass on Sunday'—provided the basis for the community's return and renewal. Without such regularity, not only would reconstruction be less likely, no community would have been created in the first place. Their life at Mary Queen *as their life in America* gave the Vietnamese a reason to return to New Orleans East, even while many stayed away. And it was their immigrant identity that gave them the cultural currency to understand their plight. As one Versailles resident said, 'I fled three times. This is the third time. When I fled here from Vietnam I had no hope of returning. This hurricane is different. I also had to flee, but it's different. I had hopes of returning… I still had hope as I fled, the hope to return'.[12]

Mary Queen's story helps belie the now tired dichotomy between ecclesial and political concerns. The notion of democracy as centralized, bureaucratized, and representative is re-theorized as local, relational, and direct. Recent trends in academic Christian ethics follow on the work of radical democratic theorists and have come to the fore in recent public conversations between theological ethicists and religious philosophers.[13] However, all of that theoretical work is at best a second-order reflection on the historic reality of the church as politics, where the church has always served as a critical juncture of its resident community's civic life. That the Mary Queen of Vietnam served this purpose for Vietnamese refugees in the twentieth century simply follows suit of what the church has always done for its people throughout the centuries. But such reception is not the whole of the church's politics. Indeed, unlike other communities, the Christian church understands its politics as both hospitality and mission, its gathering of God's people for the sake of the world. It is in the second part of the story told in *A Village Called Versailles* that we see this first moment of gathering extended toward a politics of political resistance.

A Place at the Table

After Katrina, Mary Queen gathered its people back to New Orleans East. By providing homes and familiar life practices, it began rebuilding New Orleans.

[12] *A Village Called Versailles.*

[13] See William T. Cavanaugh, *Theopolitical Imagination: Discovering the Liturgy as a Political Act in an Age of Global Consumerism* (London: T & T Clark, 2002); Romand Coles, *Beyond Gated Politics: Reflections for the Possibility of Democracy* (Minneapolis: University of Minnesota Press, 2005); Jeffery Stout, *Democracy and Tradition* (Princeton: Princeton University Press, 2004); Sheldon S. Wolin, *Politics and Vision: Continuity and Innovation in Western Political Thought* (Princeton: Princeton University Press, 2004); Romand Coles and Stanley Hauerwas, *Christianity, Democracy, and the Radical Ordinary: Conversations between a Radical Democrat and a Christian* (Eugene: Cascade, 2008); and Richard Rorty, Cornel West, Stanley Hauerwas, and Jeffrey Stout, 'Pragmatism and Democracy: Assessing Jeffrey Stout's Democracy and Tradition', *Journal of the American Academy of Religion* 78:2 (June 2010), 413-48.

As stated, such gathering continued what had always been the case, the immigrant church as the centre of the immigrant community's life; as Mary Queen returned to New Orleans to rebuild, so its people returned to New Orleans to rebuild. During the rebuilding process, Mary Queen confronted a reality that had always been implicit within the greater civic life of America generally and New Orleans specifically: Asian Americans were rendered politically irrelevant, and hence politically impotent, in relation to the broader local politics. When 'the new New Orleans' was unveiled it was not a new development to find Versailles nowhere on the map, for as Father Nguyen said, 'We were never on the map'. Still, the community was shocked since even though they had always been passed over by the city, at least in their minds, Versailles was the centre of New Orleans life. To be completly left off any rebuilding plans seemed to suggest that their lives and residency simply did not matter. Insult was added to injury when the city organized their rebuilding efforts around a landfill imposed less than two miles from Versailles. While the city would not help Versailles rebuild, in its efforts to rebuild the parts of the city that mattered, the city was quite willing to stack their trash by the Vietnamese, whose political impotence made them good people to dump on, quite literally. We see here how the historic injustices against Asian immigrants returned, though in more subtle even if still legal forms. Just as Franklin Roosevelt had used Executive Order 9066 to intern the Japanese, so the mayor of New Orleans used an emergency executive order to circumvent due process in instituting the landfill. We also see here how the model minority myth proliferated an image of Asian Americans as politically irrelevant and hence easy political pickings. And here is where the Eucharistic gathering of the church and its mission to the nations would overcome these executive powers and stereotyping myths.

Regularly, the Bring New Orleans Back Commission can expect an audience of 10 or 20 concerned New Orleans citizens as it goes about its business reconstructing the city. Not so after the Commission's unwillingness to take into consideration Versailles. Behind 400 protesting Vietnamese, Father Nguyen told the Commission, 'We were never invited to the table. We have the right to be part of this community driven process'. A community that had for years 'remained silent, never protested, never raised its voice', now mobilized for the sake of its and the entire New Orleans East community. In the years that followed, the Versailles community would challenge the environmental racism behind the landfill, taking the mayor's executive order to any court that would hear its cause. As K. Christine Pae and James McCarty observe, 'Vietnamese Americans' resistance to environmental racism in New Orleans East in the aftermath of Hurricane Katrina illustrates how their Catholic parish has sustained Vietnamese identity and mobilized the organized protest against the city's decision to build the toxin landfill in their neighborhood'.[14] Behind the rallying cry, 'we are united and we are powerful' the gathered community used what Pae and McCarty call a 'counter-public' to force a conversation the city initially refused. At one point, when the dumping continued unabated, the Vietnamese youth gathered with elders to physically impede the progress of dump trucks, laying down their lives for the sake of justice. The same church that in recent years had struggled to bridge gaps between generations of immigrants and their children for the 'first time ever' saw the youth leading the elderly, and helped the children see Versailles and their immigrant Asian community as a place to stay, even build and protect. As the documentary's director Chiang says;

> You know, I think that Katrina made a lot of the first generation folks who arrived as refugees in the community realize that, hey, you know, we're no longer guests in this country. This is our home. Vietnam is not home anymore. This is our home. And I think that Katrina triggered that switch in terms of folks beginning to, you know, embrace and claim their unique American identity. And here comes this landfill that challenges that. And I think that it almost came at the right time for the folks to really kind of band together across generations and rise up and speak up and to decide to participate in a democratic process, which is to make their voices heard, to tell the city, to the tell the government that, hey, this is not okay what you're doing. And that transformation, you know, was so incredible to witness and in many ways happened so fast, probably because a lot of that was brewing underneath and events that happened after Katrina sort of provided the perfect platform for them to express that.

Versailles' political activity culminated the Vietnamese Christians' long diaspora from exile to the promised land, from guests to hosts, from immigrants to missionaries. As Father Nguyen says, 'This is my land; I am connected to this land. We are Americans; New Orleans East is home'.

The many difficulties of these 'strangers from a different shore' developed the resilience necessary to surviving those difficulties. As importantly, the lives that those immigrants built through those difficulties helped them know that this was their home and a home worth defending. Like the interned Japanese Americans who would go on to serve America during the war despite the cruel injustices they suffered in America, so the Vietnamese of Versailles understood New Orleans as theirs to rebuild even if they were not initially given a place at the table. The church played a central role by gathering immigrants around a table when no other tables were offered. At the table where the Versailles community celebrated the one body of Christ, it became the one body of Christ

[14] K. Christine Pae and James McCarty III, 'The Unavoidable Burden of Race: In Search of Justice-Oriented Asian American Christian Public Discourse' (Presented at The Society of Christian Ethics Meetings, 2011 in the 'Asian and Asian-American Working Group'), 12.

in the world, gathered for worship, mobilized as politics. Just as the Eucharist speaks in the material language of its worshippers, embodied as this bread and this wine in this place and time, so the congregants of Mary Queen could not help but see the Risen Christ as one risen in places like Hurricane Katrina-ravaged New Orleans East. And because they understood the ravaged world as risen in Christ's mission to the nations, they could not easily abide the world's injustice. Eventually they found a place at the table of New Orleans politics because they were first given a place at the Lord's Table amidst their diasporic pilgrimage home.

The Korean Diaspora Models of a Missional Church

Steve Sang-cheol Moon

Research Problem

Argumentations surrounding the concept of a missional church need to be expressed in concrete terms based on empirical research, so as to drive a movement to recover the essence of the church. This study attempts at identifying and introducing models of a missional church among Korean diaspora churches. Adopting a qualitative research approach limits the study to only four cases.

The research process begins with the step of identifying the criteria of missional churches, then to identify presently available models of a missional church among Korean diaspora churches. A preliminary observation of the churches is that diaspora churches in the mission field realize the theoretical characteristics of a missional church. They are at least proactively approaching neighbours and local people in a friendly way. Four churches, namely, the Yohan Tokyo Christian Church, the Korean Presbyterian Church of Thailand, the Shanghai Korean Community Church, and the Beijing Twenty-first Century Korean Church (Beijing 21KC) were finally selected and visited from January 2009 through March 2010 for interviewing and observation.

The research method is composed of an appreciative inquiry and the grounded theory approaches so that individual cases are first described and analyzed to be followed by the procedure of identifying commonalities and patterns.[1] At the same time, an attempt was made to understand schemas in the consciousness of informants behind the phenomena.[2]

---

[1] Scott Johnson and James D. Ludema (eds), *Partnering to Build and Measure Organizational Capacity: Lessons from NGOs around the World* (Grand Rapids, MI: Christian Reformed World Relief Committee, 1997), 74-76; Barney G. Glaser and Anselm L. Strauss, 1967. *The Discovery of Grounded Theory: Strategies for Qualitative Research* (New York: Aldine De Gruyter, 1967).

[2] Bradd Shore, *Culture in Mind: Cognition, Culture, and the Problem of Meaning* (Oxford: Oxford University Press, 1996), 47, 344, 362-65, 366-71; Eviatar Zerubavel, *Social Mindscapes: An Invitation to Cognitive Sociology* (Cambridge, MA: Harvard University Press, 1997), 3, 24, 31-32, 48, 88-89, 113, 116, 119, 124, 126; Claudia Strauss and Naomi Quinn, *A Cognitive Theory of Cultural Meaning* (Cambridge: Cambridge University Press, 2008), 50-51. Refer to Figure 1.

Interview protocol included items of consideration for church analysis, criteria of missional churches, and readiness factors of missional leadership. The total number of informants was 34 persons, the sample of which considers the ratio of men and women, pastors and lay people.

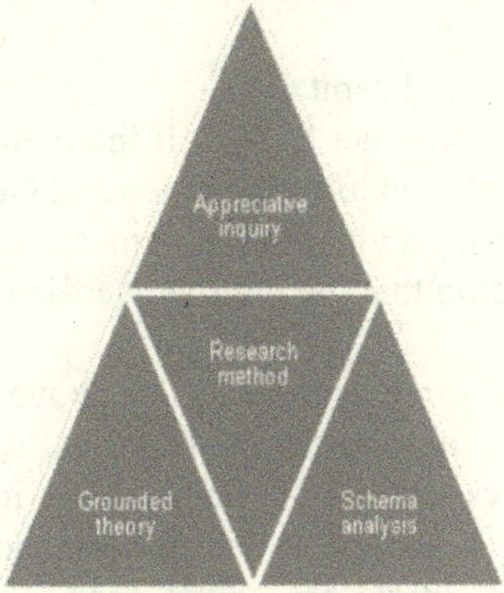

(Figure 1)

The Criteria of Missional Churches

The process of a literature review focused on identifying the criteria of missional churches. Craig van Gelder suggests seven internal factors and four external factors of church analysis. Seven internal factors include membership size, ministry style, programme model, organizational structure, volunteer involvement, the physical plant, and financial resources. Four external factors include the location, traffic patterns, population characteristics, and community needs.[3]

Twelve hallmarks of missional churches suggested by the Gospel and Our Culture Network are comprehensive as follows:[4]

1) The missional church proclaims the gospel.
2) The missional church is a community where all members are involved in learning to become disciples of Jesus.
3) The Bible is normative in this church's life.
4) The church understands itself as different from the world because of its participation in the life, death, and resurrection of its Lord.

[3] Craig van Gelder, *The Essence of the Church: A Community Created by the Spirit* (Grand Rapids, MI: Baker Books, 2000), 19.

[4] Michael Frost and Alan Hirsch, *The Shaping of Things to Come: Innovation and Mission for the 21st Century Church* (Peabody, MA: Hendrickson Publishers, 2003), 11-12.

5) The church seeks to discern God's specific missional vocation for the entire community and for all of its members.
6) A missional community is indicated by how Christians behave toward one another.
7) It is a community that practices reconciliation.
8) People within the community hold themselves accountable to one another in love.
9) The church practices hospitality.
10) Worship is the central act by which the community celebrates with joy and thanksgiving both God's presence and God's promised future.
11) This community has a vital public witness.
12) There is recognition that the church itself is an incomplete expression of the reign of God.

Frost and Hirsch add three criteria to the above items. First, the missional church is incarnational, not attractional, in its ecclesiology. Secondly, the missional church is Messianic, not dualistic, in its spirituality. Thirdly, the missional church adopts an apostolic, rather than a hierarchical, mode of leadership.[5] These three criteria are added ones, but they also summarize the above 12 items. This research was driven with a total 15 items in describing and analyzing the selected churches.

This study attempts at a deep analysis about missional leadership as part of a missional church. The leadership typology of poet, prophet, apostle, pastor, and abbot/abbess by Roxburgh is helpful, and used in this research.[6] Readiness factors of missional leadership can be listed in 16 items in four domains. The four domains are the factors of self-readiness, people-readiness, congregation-readiness, and community-readiness. Self-readiness factors include personal maturity, conflict resolution skills, personal courage, and developing trust. People-readiness factors contain creating missional thinking, cultivating growth, enabling change, and creating coalitions. Congregation-readiness factors include fostering church integration, cultivating missional culture, cultivating missional practices, and practicing missional theology. Community-readiness factors include understanding of the society, fostering church membership engagement, developing a missional future, and fostering a biblical foundation for change.[7] In light of these readiness factors, we need to apply an appropriate approach focusing on such questions as: what kind of strengths/weaknesses and characteristics does each leadership model display? How do those characteristics bear fruits in actual ministries?

[5] Frost & Hirsch, *The Shaping of Things to Come*, 12.

[6] Alan J. Roxburgh, *The Sky is Falling!?! Leaders Lost in Ttransition* (Eagle, Idaho: ACI Publishing, 2005), 163-83.

[7] Alan J. Roxburgh and Fred Romanuk, *The Missional Leader: Equipping Your Church to Reach a Changing World* (San Francisco, CA: Jossey-Bass, 2006), 185.

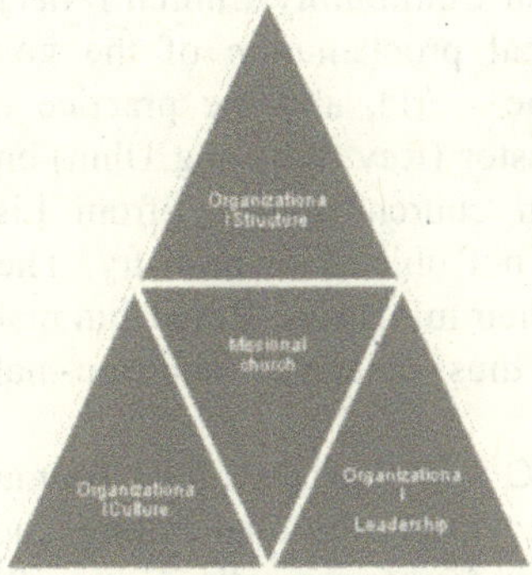

(Figure 2)

The Characteristics of Korean Diaspora Missional Churches

The procedures of literature review and data analysis posits the need for analyzing the domains of organizational structure, organizational culture, and beliefs of leadership. A balanced understanding of these three domains in their interactions is needed. Figure 2 summarizes this well.

The Structural Characteristics

Frost and Hirsch argue that missional churches should be apostolic rather than hierarchical in their structures. Being apostolic means a dynamic vitality driven by creative leaders.

The Yohan Tokyo Christian Church pursues the gospel proclamation, discipleship training, normativeness of the Bible, missionary calling in its mission and values a dynamic organizational structure. Church structure is designed to support substructures creatively and actively through which pastors and lay people communicate intimately and smoothly. Such a dynamic nature of church structure expresses the purpose-driven nature of the church and not merely a structure for itself. This structural vitality enables dynamic operations of church ministries and programmes so that many people are faithfully engaged in church activities in one way or another.

The Korean Presbyterian Church of Thailand focuses on the gospel proclamation, discipleship training, missionary call, and public witness in its mission, but pursues a church structure that pursues autonomy and personal intimacy as its strength over dynamic group power. The delegation characterizes the structure of this church in a significant way, but sometimes organizational interactions seem to be too horizontal, which reduces orderliness in an organization. The Korean Presbyterian Church of Thailand seems to be loosely structured, but the strength is its organizational flexibility, which then raises the level of a voluntary spirit among the church members.

The Shanghai Korean Community Church reflects the purposes of ministry such as a Christological proclamation of the gospel, discipleship training, distinctiveness from the world, and the practice of missional calling in its programmes. Senior Pastor (Rev. Kiyoung Uhm) emphasizes the participation of church members in church ministry from his firm belief that church members are subjects, not objects of ministry. The Church staff expresses a sense of ownership in their ministries. Rev. Uhm makes efforts not to centralize decision making and thus delegates decision-making to the lower levels systematically.

The Beijing 21KC emphasizes the normativeness of the Bible, distinctiveness from the world, missional calling, and actions toward each other in ministry structurally and systematically. Especially, the normativeness of the Bible is empathasized, based on the senior pastor's observation that traditions not words support authoritarian structures. This aspect becomes evident in the organizational culture, which encourages lay people's creative efforts for the church in ministry. The horizontal teamwork of the church staff prevents structural rigidity, which results in the purpose-driven structure and operations. This kind of structural flexibility results in better performance not just remaining as an idealistic experimentation, it would be a new alternative.

A common characteristic of the four churches is that their structures are not rigid, but flexible. The four churches seem to have Presbyterian-type church structures, but they are not typical Presbyterian churches in that their decision-making is not centralized in the elders' committee. One of the strengths of this kind of structure is that decisions are made in a fast and dynamic way. Systematic effectiveness is pursued over systematic stability in the four model churches.[8]

The four churches pursue structural renewal to overcome structural fundamentalism. These efforts, as they mature, suggest alternative structures in this postmodern era. The point is to suggest a structure dynamically led by the purpose and mission of the organization, not a top-down hierarchical structure as shown in Figure 3.

---

[8] James W. Sipe and Don M. Frick, *Seven Pillars of Servant Leadership: Practicing the Wisdom of Leading by Serving* (New York: Paulist Press, 2009), 130-154.

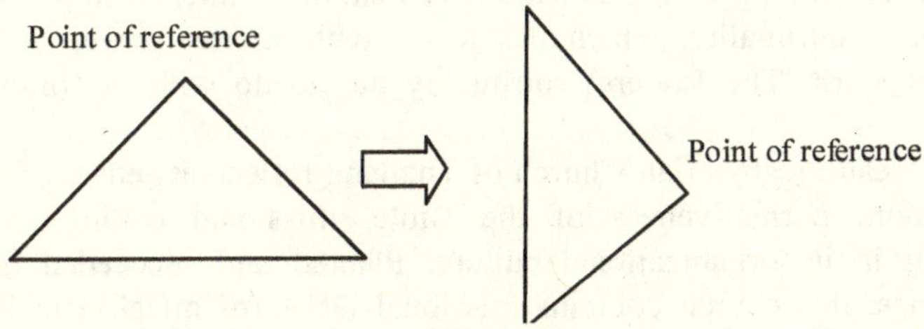

(Figure 3)

The missional church structures need to move beyond the process of structural unfreezing toward refreezing in order to suggest a new structural alternative.[9] If a new kind of organization is not suggested in the process of unfreezing and refreezing, it would only remain as a deconstruction. Missional church leaders may need to delve into organizational theories and lead discussions and argumentations on the structural issues. We need missional imagination for this kind of work, too.

The Cultural Characteristics

Geert Hofstede researched cultural differences of IBM company workers depending on their countries of origin. Hofstede analyzes cultural difference in terms of power distance, individualism vs. collectivism, masculinity vs. femininity, uncertainty avoidance vs. acceptance, long-term vs. short-term orientation.[10] I am going to use these categories in describing and analyzing the corporate cultures. Frost and Hirsch's notion of Messianic spirituality means integral spirituality. An attempt will be made to analyze the above four churches in terms of integral spirituality.

The Yohan Tokyo Christian Church manifests the importance of the gospel proclamation, discipleship training, normativeness of the Bible, distinctiveness from the world, and missional calling in its organizational culture. Diligent and passionate church members, who firmly believe in personal salvation and witnessing life, characterize the organizational climate of the church. Senior pastor and church staff set an example of a wartime lifestyle. Power distance in the Yohan Tokyo Christian Church seems to be shorter than in the average Korean church, but is longer than the other three models of a missional church in our study. This aspect is affected by Rev. Kim's personal journey of faith and background of the Campus Crusade for Christ. The organizational culture of the church is also characterized by collectivism, masculinity, uncertainty

---

[9] Edgar H. Schein, *Organizational Culture and Leadership* (San Francisco: Jossey-Bass, 1992), 298-303.

[10] Geert Hofstede, *Cultures and Organizations: Software of the Mind*, trans. Jaeho Cha and Eunyoung Nah (Seoul: Hakjisa, 1995), 47-206, 233-56.

avoidance, and a long-term orientation. The church is integral in its expressions of corporate spirituality, which has to do with shorter power distance and communal spirit. The leaders' spirituality has to do with the organizational culture.

The Korean Presbyterian Church of Thailand reflects its ethos of the gospel proclamation, normativeness of the Bible, missional calling, and public witnessing in its organizational culture. Planted and succeeded by Korean missionaries, this church contains missional DNA (or mDNA) in its culture, which is also an expression of the spirituality of the leaders. Especially, partnership ministries with the Seventh Presbytery are challenging and moving. The church is only behind the scenes in this partnership, but makes an invaluable contribution to the churches in Thailand. Rev. Kim's commitment to fellowship and partnership with other parts of the body of Christ is consistent. The power distance is very short in this church. Individual autonomy is valued over collective cohesiveness. It is balanced between masculinity and femininity, uncertainty avoidance and acceptance, long-term and short-term orientations. In spirituality, dualism is overcome to express an integral spirituality. Autonomy and intimate relationships within the church have to do with the senior pastor's spirituality.

The Shanghai Korean Community Church maintains an organizational culture that emphasizes proclaiming the gospel, discipleship training, the normativeness of the Bible, distinctiveness from the world, missionary calling, and the centrality of worship. The organizational culture resonates with the ministry philosophy based on the theology of the kingdom of God. Power distance is shorter than in the average Korean church. The church culture is balanced between individualism and collectivism, masculinity and femininity, and uncertainty avoidance and acceptance. It is pursuing long-term orientation. This balanced standpoint is reflecting both the Korean and Chinese cultures, and both the missionary culture and pastoral philosophy of the senior pastor. The evangelical ecumenism is rooted in the church's original ethos and the present senior pastor's inclusive leadership. Dualism is effectively overcome in the ministry philosophy and teaching, which results in fruits such as the Business As Mission (hereafter BAM). The church leader's spirituality and worldview are expressed well in the ministry programmes in this church.

The Beijing Korean Church expresses its communal vision in four items: the proclamation of the gospel, discipleship training, the normativeness of discipleship, and missional calling. The four visions are expressed not only in the church's structures, but also in its organizational culture. SR 300 (the missionary vision for reaching the cities and peoples along the Silk Road) is rooted in the culture of the young adults and adults. It is internalized in informal and dynamic forms within the church community. The power distance in the church is very short, maybe the shortest among the four churches in this study. It is not true that power distance is better for being shorter even in this postmodern age, but when it comes to this church, there are many strengths observed. Sometimes, the church culture seems to show both individualistic and collectivistic orientations. It is overall balanced between masculinity and femininity, and uncertainty avoidance and acceptance. It is somewhat long-term orientated rather than short-term oriented. Emphasis on the lordship of Christ in life helps overcome dualism to lead to integral spirituality. The senior pastor often teaches about the organic nature of the relationships between Christians. Cultural sensitivity and adeptness are symbolically expressed in the senior pastor's interest in iPad. The Beijing Korean Church's organizational culture is conservative, on the one hand, as can be seen in SR 300, but is progressive in its approaches to fulfil its mission which is conservatively defined.

The four churches emphasize balance and harmony in their organizational culture as a pattern. There is no extreme tendency in their cultural orientation. The concept of power distance, when applied in the analysis, helps us observe that the relationships between leaders and members are very intimate and personal, which can be interpreted as a strength rather than a shortcoming. When it is too short, we are concerned about protecting leaders from exhaustion. The balance between masculinity and femininity makes the church bold and subtle at the same time in this postmodern cultural climate where femininity is needed much more than before. This is a matter of both and, not of either or. A balance is required between uncertainty avoidance and acceptance, however uncertainty avoidance is often needed to help the churches to plan and prepare ministry well from a good sense of contingency and urgency. The four churches need reinforcement in this aspect. A similar emphasis is needed toward the short-term orientation to make the organizational culture more sensitive to environmental changes with roadmaps for a long-term perspective.

The four churches embody communality in their organizational culture under the leadership of the senior pastors. This aspect signifies the striving toward communality, overcoming the individualistic culture of the world. When a church loses this kind of balance and leans over toward collectivism too much, then there are the dangers of a weak autonomy and creativity. A continuous effort is needed to keep the balance between the two poles.

Behind an integral organizational culture are an integral spirituality and a wholesome worldview of a leader. In a voluntary organization, an integral spirituality based on a wholesome worldview is taught and transmitted and accepted through the medium of its organizational culture. Leaders create organizational cultures, which define leadership later on in a reciprocal way. That is the reason why we have to observe and diagnose how the organizational cultures ebb and flow, what kind of changes they go through with interest and a keen mind. We also need to watch if the organizational cultures receive too much input from the outer world overwriting the influence from the leaders.

The Characteristics of Leadership Beliefs

Missional leadership interacts with a leadership structure and an organizational culture. Especially leaders' beliefs form the deepest levels of organizational structure and culture. According to Sipe and Frick, beliefs are at the deeper level of an organization than events, strategies, and culture.[11] We will focus our analysis on the leadership beliefs for a better description and analysis.

Frost and Hirsh emphasize that missional churches should be incarnational rather than attractional in the sense that local churches need to approach their neighbours in their community proactively. Permeating the local communities with the gospel is a hallmark of missional churches. This point has to do with leadership characteristics.

Rev. Kyudong Kim, of the Yohan Tokyo Christian Church, exercises leadership with an emphasis on the centrality of God's words in Christian life. His leadership is also characterized by personal maturity, conflict resolution skills, and courage. He firmly believes in the centrality of God's words which results in building trust, creating missional thinking, encouraging growth, enabling changes, causing unity, integrating churches, but sometimes he exercises flexibility. The fundamentals are not changing, but methods and approaches are changing as influenced by environmental changes. His leadership is principle-centred, but is also realistic enough. His leadership enables creating a missional culture, developing missional practice and theology, and pioneering missional future. Planning the Gospel Concert for evangelistic purposes, separating the Yohan Washeda Christian Church for the Japanese congregation, and starting the Japanese Theological Seminary are all cases of a creative imagination. Understanding local society, facilitating church member's engagement, and laying down of the biblical foundations for change are the loci of his competency, which are reinforced by his insightful leadership. These competencies result in voluntary commitment. He knows what it means to create a balance between biblical faithfulness and contextual sensitivity. His lifestyle is rooted in the concept of simple lifestyle. His strategies are reflections of his worldview.

Rev. Kyudong Kim's leadership style is integral leadership with apostolic leadership characteristics prominent. As an integral leader, he is excellent in understanding people's potential and locating them properly. As an apostolic leader, he shows a dynamic capability to cross-culture and leads a multi-cultural church. His leadership team functions as a team. Often it is said that Rev. Kim does not try contextualization, but my analysis is that he attempts a needs-based contextualization at a deeper level. It is true that his contextualization is not just a matter of either the Korean or Japanese style, but a matter of critical contextualization with an emphasis on the need for transforming worldviews.

---

[11] Sipe & Frick, *Seven Pillars of Servant Leadership*, 133.

Rev. Young Sup Kim, of the Korean Presbyterian Church of Thailand, emphasizes balance and diligence as well as a long-term perspective in his leadership. This kind of leadership style finds an expression in a charisma based on personal maturity. He seeks to resolve conflicts with faith not with interpersonal skills. He builds trust with church staff and members, and motivates and influences them to grow. He enables change, coalition, the church integration with flexible leadership. He accepts suggestions and proposals for creating missional thinking, culture, and practice. He delegates properly, and influences people around him. Mission education programmes, such as Mission Exposure, are the result of this kind of leadership. He seeks consultation from other church leaders and members when he makes decisions for practicing missional theology and developing a missional future based on the concept of a multi-cultural church. His strategy of urban mission is derived from his appropriate understanding of local society. Rev. Kim tries to base his rationale for changes on the Bible and theological doctrines. One of the important aspects of his leadership is his approach to incarnational leadership. The case of cooperation with the Presbyterian Church of Thailand shows a good example of cross-cultural partnership based on an ecumenical spirit. His lifestyle maintains consistency and faithfulness rooted in a missionary spirit and philosophy. His attitude toward people reflects a sense of servant leadership, which seems to be based on his Christian worldview.

Rev. Kim's leadership type is an integral one which values listening to people and making group decisions. At the same time, he characterizes a type of leadership as a poet, which is often described as a caring and loving leadership. His leadership philosophy is far from authoritarianism, and is rooted in the concept of Christo-centric servant-hood. The location of the church building and use of space all explain what kind of spirit, ministry philosophy and missiological principles are driving the church. The church is far from the pursuit of organizational prosperity. He knows what it means to contextualize ministry approaches with balance and realism. His contextualization approach is not pursuing a transformation-oriented contextualization, but a culturally appropriate and sensitive contextualization. He is a respectful and courteous pastor and missionary. His expression of the Christian worldview is a caring and encouraging one. This kind of worldview expression is not a weak one, but a strong and wise one. How the leadership team can be more solid and cohesive with more balance and diversity is a good question to examine for further growth.

Rev. Uhm of the Shanghai Korean Community Church exercises leadership as a reflective practitioner. His ministry philosophy is clear and intentionally expressed in actual ministries. Enduring, bearing, embracing, and waiting attitude describes his personality well, which often results in peace-making, courageous, trust-building leadership qualities. In facilitating personal growth, enabling changes, causing unity, and integrating the church, he approaches the problem intellectually. There are both firmness in the core beliefs and flexibility in expressions. Rev. Uhm is proactive in networking, which is a good foundation for organizational learning. There is a logical consistency in creating missional thinking, culture, practice, and theology. The logical consistency lays the foundation for BAM Forum, recruiting missionaries in the church, and teaching church members to lead an integral life in their workplaces. The church's annual catchphrases are not instantaneously designed, but planned on a long-term basis expressing a sense of balance between being and doing of Christian faith and life. He is a good example of a 'reflective practitioner'.[12]

Rev. Uhm's leadership style is basically an integral one, which enables positioning people appropriately according to their potentials. At the same time, his leadership is that of a poet, the type of which drives ministry creatively and is future-oriented. His poetical leadership is more of an intellectual poet than of an affective one. Combined with philosophical reflection, his leadership produces logical strategies. It is wise for him to approach ministry issues faithfully to the biblical principles and sensitively to the local cultural contexts. His leadership basis is the grand unifying theory of the kingdom of God. His contextualization strategies are basically critical approaches with sensitivity to the biblical norms and contextual realities. His worldview overcomes parochialism, and thus is more than Korean or Chinese idiosyncrasies. Church members share an awareness of the church based on a sound biblical worldview. In contrast with this aspect, he is easy to talk to, comfortable, and kind. His beliefs in contextualization result in an incarnational lifestyle and the changed life of church members.

Rev. Park of the Beijing Korean Church exercises leadership based on personal maturity. A pure and humble personality leads to a leadership of self-discipline and conscious effort, which influences people in and outside the church. Self-discipline and accepting leadership qualities make him a courageous leader with balance. He bases his decisions for the church's future direction and new projects on personal trust. Patience and endurance for facilitating people's growth, enabling changes, and building unity are expressed in his ministry strategies. Individual imagination is combined with co-leadership and teamwork in the church. The phenomena of church integration by vision, driving ministry programmes through missional culture rather than structure, and a vital missional imagination resulting in subtle and proactive practices characterize his leadership and ministry. Creativity is expressed well in involving church members in ministry with his missional theology which emphasizes the work of the Holy Spirit, servant-hood, and unity. His leadership is a visionary leadership. In preparing the biblical

[12] William D. Taylor, ''From Iguassu to the Reflective Practitioners of the Global Family of Christ', in William D. Taylor (ed), *Global Missiology for the 21st Century: The Iguassu Dialogue* (Grand Rapids, MI: Baker Academic, 2001), 5-6.

foundation for changes, he strengthens and expresses his original thinking with his beliefs in co-workership.

Rev. Park's leadership type is that of an integral one with the type of poet primarily explicit. An integral leadership finds an expression in the teamwork of his leadership team. The sense of ownership shared among associate pastors is evidence of his deep understanding of personal characteristics and the nature of team ministry. His poetical imagination results in a visionary creativity, which is a good foundation of missional leadership among the younger generations in this postmodern age. Behind this phenomenon is his worldview, which enables incarnational ministry through the medium of a missional imagination for new generations and is embodied in a warm spirituality and a friendly personality. This is a good basis for worldview evangelism.

What is common among the four models of missional leadership is an incarnationally permeating proactiveness. There are clues and evidence for such leadership qualities in organizational cultures, strategies, and incidents. Their leadership beliefs are expressions of their worldview. The fruits of ministry and the performance of their programmes are surface phenomena of their deep beliefs on the worldview level. The leadership beliefs interact with structural and cultural characteristics within the church organization or community. These three domains dynamically interact with one another through the medium of a worldview. In summary, these four missional churches are characterized by the qualities of the permeation in their structural dynamics, cultural integration, and leadership beliefs (Figure 4).

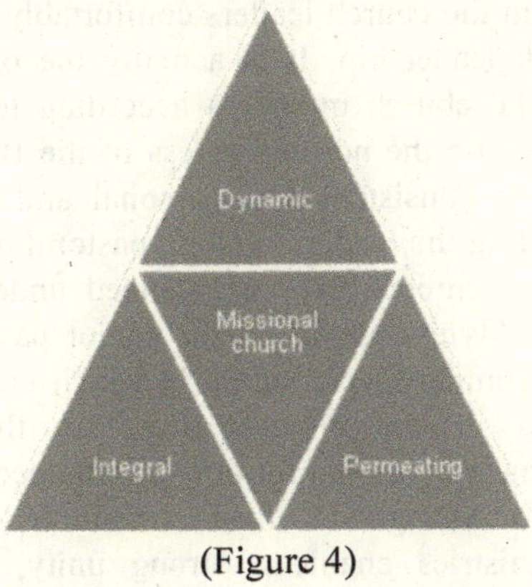

(Figure 4)

The Characteristics of Congregations

The characteristics of congregations display the churches' nature and ethos systematically. The maturity of a congregation is related to the maturity of leadership. Dennis D. Moses summarizes the condition of mature congregations in four points: firstly, a unified group of people; secondly, a group of listening people; thirdly, a group of supporting people; fourthly, a group of praying people.[13] In summary, a congregation should be 'a community of spiritually unified, supporting, and learning people'.

The congregation of the Yohan Tokyo Christian Church is a group of unified people. They are unified for the evangelization of Japan and Asia influenced by the vision of leaders. In other words, they are unified according to the missionary calling. This aspect is expressed in actions toward each other, the practice of reconciliation, and an accountability of love. The listening and learning attitude is practiced in discipleship training programmes. Especially, JMTC is being run by the vision of raising Christian workers, who are eager to learn. The supporting attitude toward church leaders is widely shared among the church members, which is extended to other Yohan churches in other cities. This aspect of church culture can be attributed to the ministry focus of the normativeness of the Bible. Rev. Kim's example of Christian life motivates church members to follow it. The congregation of the Yohan Tokyo Christian Church emphasizes prayer. Worship services and prayer meetings are filled with a passionate and touching spirituality and atmosphere. The centrality of God's presence and promised future is affirmed and assured again and again in this church. In summary, the Yohan Tokyo Christian Church is a congregation characterized by training, commitment, and a unified vision.

The congregation of the Korean Presbyterian Church of Thailand is united voluntarily. Mostly probably influenced by the local culture, church members are united in a subtle and soft atmosphere. Church members can express different opinions from the church leaders comfortably in this church, which is never a sign of weak leadership. It is actually the opposite. Teachability is rather weak among the church members according to the church leadership team, but the emphasis on the normativeness of the Bible is very strong. The spiritual atmosphere is consistent and personal and voluntary, which finds expressions in supporting the leaders' vision, pastoral philosophy, and ministry programmes. Church members have a balanced understanding about prayer according to their worldview taught by the senior pastor. The congregational size of the church is comparatively small, in which interpersonal relationships are well established in the congregation. As the church grows, the congregation's learning and passion for prayer will need to be strengthened.

The congregation of Shanghai Korean Community Church is intellectually united. Teaching ministries enable a strong unity, in which the pastoral philosophy is connected to the congregation's beliefs. This church's catchphrases carry pastoral directions well, and unite the congregation with the same sense of purpose. Preaching, discipleship training, and the normativeness of the Bible play important roles in uniting the congregation. Teaching with an

---

[13] Dennis D. Moses, *Leadership and Church Structure in the Pulpit and Out* (Columbus, GA: Brentwood Christian Press, 2000), 147-53.

emphasis on the kingdom of God unites the congregation dynamically. This church is a passionate learning community, which finds expressions in the seminar on the kingdom of God. The learning in this church is not just an intellectual process, but leads on to a mature practice. The church's purpose of 'becoming a mature congregation of the citizens of the kingdom of God' presupposes this kind of learning and practice. The characteristics of a holistically learning and practicing congregation are expressed in BAM ministries. The support for the leadership team is reinforced through the proclamation of the gospel, the normativeness of the Bible, and the distinctiveness from the world. The praying attitude is consistent with the theological teaching and transmission of the biblical worldview. The cohesiveness of the Shanghai Korean Community Church is impressive, since it is composed of various kinds of people with different denominational backgrounds. The centripetal power of the biblical worldview makes this possible.

The Beijing (21C) Korean Church is a well-united congregation notable for its freedom and friendliness. It is united not by an authoritarian and charismatic leadership but by a personal attractiveness mixed with spiritual charisma. The leadership team is a strong one composed of atypical Korean pastors. The learning attitude looks rather weak, but creativity characterizes its leadership and organizational culture, which then seems to express the affective dimension better than the cognitive dimension. This church stresses the importance of teaching the Bible, but takes various approaches to ministry strategy. All Nations School, SR300, and DVD are the products of such a creative approach, to which the congregation agree and give support. The support for the leaders is impressive, propelled by Rev. Park's personality and spirituality. When it is systematized by sharing the vision and pastoral philosophy, it will be more balanced and powerful. The corporate prayer is focused on realizing the vision and ministry purpose. A pious life in the daily routine is well emphasized in the congregational teaching. This church is united somewhat relationally, driven by the love and support for the leadership team, which produces a fresh congregational culture and performance.

The four churches are characterized by unity, support for leadership, and fervent prayer. There is no significant weakness in these areas in the four churches. The communal aspect of the churches is certainly a strength. There seems to be a possible weakness in corporate learning. A leaning atmosphere across disciplines is desirable in these churches. There seems to be a need for a systematic effort for organizational learning in order for the churches to be flagships in this postmodern age. Learning and working need to be balanced in the church. If learning is not enough for the ministry, people are liable to discouragement and a sense of fatigue.

Worldview transmission from the leaders to the church members has to do with the ministry period of the senior pastor in the church. However, when a pastor makes a conscious effort for a worldview understanding and transmission, the followers are better aware of the biblical worldview. The issue is how to understand the biblical worldview at a deep level and apply it in real life to transform cultural worldviews. The four churches need to grow more according to the biblical standards.

Research Findings and Implications

This descriptive study's major findings, as intended by the appreciative inquiry, are related to highlighting the positive characteristics of the four model churches. However, we will also attempt at fleshing out some of the developmental issues of the churches where reinforcements are needed. Both aspects of the evaluation are important for other churches that want to learn from case studies.

Common Strengths of the Model Churches

An idiographic description was attempted previously to introduce the strengths of the four churches. We now need to analyze common characteristics of the churches at the deep level of worldview.

First of all, the four model churches express the integrity of the worldview shared by the church leaders and members. Secondly, these four model churches exhibit a sense of balance in understanding the biblical worldview shared by the leaders and members (Figure 5).

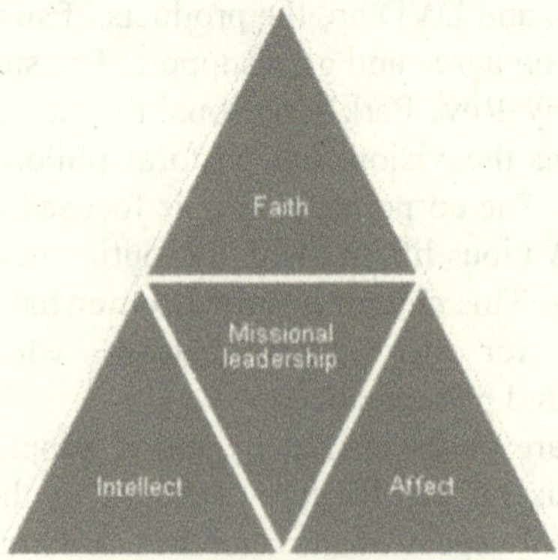

(Figure 5)

Thirdly, these four model churches experience the impact of a worldview transformation from the church leaders to the members, which also affects the local communities both directly and indirectly.

An emerging pattern in the analytical process is that the church members' worldview is related to the leaders' worldview to a significant degree. The leaders' worldview begins its formation from the conversion experience later to be fully developed and explained. The four leaders had opportunities for worldview transformation and experiential clarification, which motivates their missional leadership to bear the fruit of the reproduced biblical worldview among the church members. More detailed empirical research is needed in this line of thinking.[14]

In summary, there is a pattern of missional churches in possessing three characteristics of worldview, such as integrity, balance, and transformation at the worldview level. When these three components are combined in their interactions for dynamic synergy, there are really fruitful missional congregations. An integral worldview keeps balance. When an integral and balanced worldview is expressed wholly in cognitive, affective, and volitional dimensions, then there is transformation and reproduction of the biblical worldview. A person and a society can be changed at the deepest level in this way. We need to understand these interactions and transformation processes more deeply through more rigorous analysis. My theoretical standpoint at this point is summarized in Figure 6 as follows.

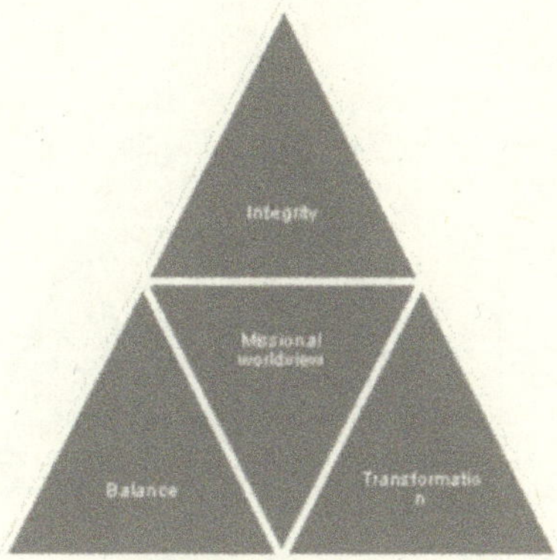

(Figure 6)

Recommendations for the Model Churches

When we recognize the status of churches as a community of pilgrims which is incomplete, we will pursue the continuous maturation of churches. Firstly, the four churches need to stress the importance of organizational learning based on their strengths of integrity, balance, and transformation at the worldview level. Secondly, the four churches need to stress the importance of protecting and caring leadership teams based on their strengths of integrity, balance, and transformation at the worldview level. Thirdly, the four churches need to stress the importance of passing on the spiritual heritage to the next generation based on their strengths of integrity, balance, and transformation.

---

[14] Paul G. Hiebert, *Transforming Worldviews: An Anthropological Understanding of How People Change* (Grand Rapids: Baker, 2009).

These four churches need to continue to be models of a missional church in the next generations, for which the churches need to make conscious efforts to transmit the biblical worldview.[15] This conclusive concept can be expressed visually in Figure 7.

In conclusion, the Yohan Tokyo Christian Church, the Korean Presbyterian Church of Thailand, the Shanghai Korean Community Church, and the Beijing 21KC are good models of missional church. They are not perfect in their worldview and practices, but they have a lot of strengths and positive characteristics. The patterns of positive characteristics of the churches show in which direction to go for other churches, and the patterns of weakness indicate in what areas the churches need to grow and be reinforced. There are other models of missional churches among Korean and Korean diaspora churches. We need more research directed on the description and analysis of other missional churches in the years ahead.

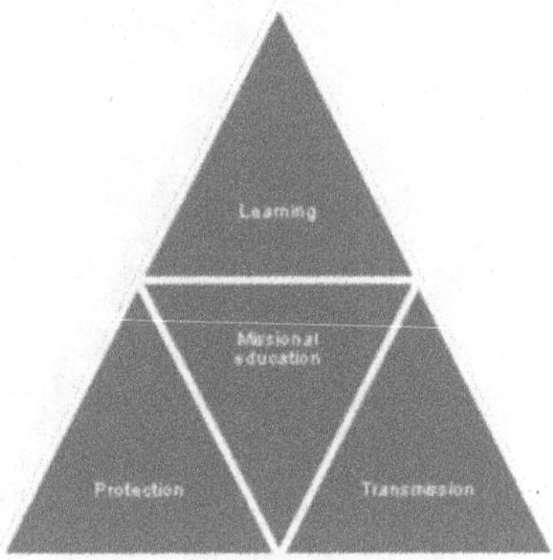

(Figure 7)

[15] Kiyoung Uhm, *The Kingdom of God: Christian Freedom* (Shanghai: Shanghai Korean Community Church, n.d.), 9.

Korean Diaspora:
From Hermit Kingdom to Kingdom Ministry

Enoch Wan

Introduction

The dual purposes of this study are to present an ethnographic description of Korean diaspora and propose two new paradigms for their engagement in kingdom ministry.

Koreans diaspora (i.e. Korean residing outside of their homeland in Korea) are culturally akin and psychologically attached to their country of origin , 'the Hermit Kingdom': yet they are to be challenged to actively be engaged in kingdom ministry.

In this study, 'diaspora' is a reference to 'people living outside their place of origin' and 'diaspora missiology' is 'a missiological framework for understanding and participating in God's redemptive mission[1] among diaspora groups'.[2] 'Diaspora missions' is 'the Christian's participation in God's redemptive mission to evangelize their kinsmen on the move and through them to natives in their homeland and beyond'.[3]

The 'inter-disciplinary methodology'[4] in this study combines historical, ethnographic and missiological approaches. It begins with a historical overview of the Korean cultural heritage (i.e. 'Hermit Kingdom'), continues with an ethnographic description of Korean diaspora, and ends with challenging the Korean diaspora to be actively engaged in kingdom ministry by proposing two new paradigms for consideration by Korean Christians.

---

[1] 'Mission' is defined as the *missio Dei* of the Triune God'.

[2] See 'The Seoul Declaration on Diaspora Missiology' http://www.lausanne.org/documents/seoul-declaration-on-diaspora-missiology.html (retrieve March25, 2010)

[3] Enoch Wan, 'Global People and Diaspora Missiology' (Plenary presentation at Tokyo 2010 Global Mission Consultation, Tokyo, May 13, 2010), 1.

[4] For 'Inter-disciplinary methodology' see Enoch Wan, 'Rethinking Missiological Research Methodology: Exploring a New Direction' (Global Missiology at www.globalmissiology.net, Oct. 2003).

Ethnographic Description of Korean Diaspora

Historical Review

There are about seven million Koreans in the diaspora, who are recent expatriates and descendants of early emigrants from the Korean peninsula, about four-fifths of whom find residence in the countries of China, Japan, and the United States. Figure 1 shows their distribution in the top three countries.

Figure 1: Korean diaspora in top three countries [5]

Country	2009 Statistics	Proportion of Korean Diaspora	Adopted Koreans		Local Census Statistics	Year of Census
			Number	Year range		
USA	2,102,283	30.81%	107,145	1953-2007	1,555,293	2007
China	2,336,771	34.25%	Not available			
Japan	912,770	13.38%	226	1962-1982	Not available	

Due to the limitation of this study, the ethnographic description of Korean diaspora will be delimited to those residing in the US as a case study[6] of the Korean diaspora in many lands.

The term 'Hermit Kingdom'[7] is used in this study as a descriptive term referring to pre-modern Korea, particularly to the Chosun Dynasty of approximately five centuries (1392–1897) with its rich classical Korean culture, trade, science, literature, technology and Confucian ideals. The reason for using the Chosun Dynasty as a backdrop for the ethnographic description of this study is due to the fact that the cultural legacy of the Chosun Dynasty left a strong imprint on modern Korean language, etiquette, cultural norms and social attitudes.

The Korean hierarchical relationship (by age and gender) and the values of 'politeness/courtesy' can be linguistically discerned, yet historically can be traced back to the Confucian influence of the Chosun Dynasty. Confucian elements are still dynamic forces shaping contemporary Korean society in several aspects: the moral system, national laws, and general way of life in Korea, as well as the underlying consciousness of many contemporary Koreans. The high values placed on education, family, loyalty, honor, filial piety, authoritarian social structure, reciprocity (obligation towards others) are the cultural heritage of the Chosun Dynasty.

---

[5] (South Korean) Ministry of Foreign Affairs and Trade, 'Current Status of Overseas Compatriots'http://www.mofat.go.kr/consul/overseascitizen/compatriotcondition/index6.jsp?TabMenu=TabMenu6, 2009, Retrieved: 21 May, 2009.

[6] For discussion on the case study method, see Robert K. Yin, *Case Study Research: Design and Methodology*, 4th ed. (London: Sage, 2009).

[7] See the 1882 classic of William Elliot Griffis, *Corea: The Hermit Nation*.

Ethnographic Description of the Korean Diaspora

PERSONAL RELATIONSHIPS AND SOCIAL NETWORK

The ethnographic profiling of the Korean diaspora has to begin with Koreans in the historical past in their native land. The Korean sense of 'community/cooperation (*jeong* or 情) can be attributed to a centuries-long agricultural history and to communal living. There is also the time-honored high value placed on developing relational skills and cultivating /nurturing relational networks. The solidarity of group and collective identity (e.g. family, clan and nation) are the natural outcome of the linguistic, racial and cultural homogeneity of Korean society over many centuries. The positive side of this group solidarity is patriotism and the sense of ethnic solidarity and pride. It can also account for the economic accomplishment of South Korea over the last 60 years.[8] However, on the negative side are parochialism and racism and, among the Korean diaspora, the tendency to be socially isolated from other ethnic groups and difficulties in cultural adaptation.

The Korean's sense of *Kibun* can be described in terms of pride, face, mood, or state of mind and it permeates every facet of Korean life. The imperative to show the proper respect and avoid causing loss of face will ensure social harmony. *Inhwa* is the Korean version of the Confucian concept of harmony that requires consensus in decision-making and collective efforts. 'Smooth personal relationships' (SPR) based on mutual trust and benefits are to be nurtured and reinforced at all cost. SPR and social networks are essential to success in both business and ministry.

Korean companies and congregations share the same vertical social structure, based on age, gender and social status. The organizational arrangement is highly centralized, with authority and decision-making concentrated in senior levels. Personal ties (e.g. kinship, schools, birthplaces, etc.) often take precedence over job seniority, rank or other factors (e.g. performance and productivity), thus having significant influence on the structure and management of Korean companies and congregations. The rule of reciprocity (e.g. gift-giving, favor, etc.) is to be followed closely to maintain harmonious relationships and social networks. In summary, SPR and social networks are of primary importance, both in Korean traditional culture and contemporary society at home and abroad (i.e. among native Koreans and the Korean diaspora).

Korean society is constituted of a myriad of extended/overlapping relational networks and that is also true of the Christian sub-culture. Whenever there is a relational problem within the networks, the discord and disharmony will have a severe negative impact on the wider system of the organization or congregation. This can help explain the frequent occurrence of conflicts and

---

[8] The rapid economic development of South Korea in today's modern world economy is indeed impressive, becoming the largest in Asia after Japan and China.

fthe ragmentation of Korean organizations. A case in point is the schism within the Korean Presbyterian church between Hap-dong (合同) and Tong-hap (統合), with the irony that all four characters in the two names have the implicit meaning of unity/harmony).

ETHNIC-LINGUISTIC-CULTURAL HOMOGENEITY

In Korea, an average Korean grows up within a homogeneous environment without the complexity and challenges of a multi-cultural reality as other Asians such as Singaporeans, Indians, etc. Most Koreans can survive and flourish within Korean society without acquiring a second language, unlike post-colonial and multi-lingual societies such as Malaysia, India, etc. Koreans are not like Europeans and other Asians, who by necessity have to acquire more than one language and operate within a context of multi-culturalism and poly-ethnicity to survive, especially when striving for personal accomplishment and social advancement.

KOREAN DIASPORA CONGREGATION

In comparison to other ethnic groups, the first generation (not 1.5) Korean immigrants in the US are relatively less likely to be assimilated due to socio-objective factors (e.g. language barrier, racial discrimination, visible minority, social isolation, etc.) and psycho-subjective factors (e.g. linguistic and cultural homogeneity, internal ethnic-solidarity, psychological aversion to losing-face or risk-taking, etc.). Subsequently, ethnic Korean congregations in the US (hereafter referred to as KDC – Korean diaspora congregation) have multiple functions: as the centre of social activities, language (Korean) school for children, 'home away from homeland', etc.

Korean Diaspora for Kingdom Ministry: Proposing Two New Paradigms

In order to challenge the Korean diaspora to become actively engaged in kingdom ministry and before proposing two new paradigms, a theological understanding of the phenomenon of the Korean diaspora is in order.

Theological Understanding of the Korean Diaspora

The many factors leading to the phenomenon of the Korean diaspora over many decades may be summarized into two categories: the push and pull factors.[9] The push factors for the Korean diaspora are: the threat of the communist regime in the North, the political instability and economic hardship in South Korea in the last century, etc.; whereas the pull factors are: the political stability

[9] For a detailed discussion on the 'push-and-pull' factors of international migration or diaspora, please see Enoch Wan, 'Diaspora Missiology', *Occasional Bulletin*, Spring 2007

and economic opportunities overseas, the strong desire for their children to enjoy educational and economic opportunities abroad, etc.

On the surface and from merely a human perspective, it is tragic for Koreans to leave their homeland of familiarity and security in exchange for a sojourner's hardship abroad. Yet nothing that happens (both the fortunate and unfortunate kinds) in life escapes the sovereignty of God, as Joseph reflected on his diaspora experience in Egypt (Gen. 45:1-6) and the apostle Paul's confession in Rom. 8:28. Theologically, we can see the hand of God scattering the Korean diaspora abroad for the purpose of the kingdom.[10]

For a systematic discussion on the themes listed below, please consult earlier publications: scattering (dispersion) in the OT;[11] gathering (calling) in the OT;[12] scattering (dispersion) in the NT; [13] and gathering (calling, covenant, ecclesiology) in the NT.[14]

To summarize the biblical framework, we conclude that 'scattering' in the OT is not always a consequence of sin. In fact, it was God's design that human kind was 'to scatter' as indicated within the blessings of Adam and Eve by God before the Fall (i.e. 'Let them have dominion…and over all the earth…and replenish the earth', Gen. 1:26-28) and was reaffirmed to Noah after the flood ('be fruitful and multiple, and replenish the earth…bring forth abundantly in the earth', Gen. 9:1, 7) and by refusing to do so, in God's judgment, was being rebellious at the Tower of Babel (Gen. 11:1-9).

---

[10] See two other works: Enoch Wan, 'Rethinking Missiology in the Context of the 21st Century: Global Demographic Trends and Diaspora Missiology', *Great Commission Research Journal*, Sept. 2010, 11. The 'Seoul Declaration', see www.lausanne.org/documents/seoul-declaration-on-diaspora-missiology.html). For more discussion on diaspora and mission, see Enoch Wan, 'Mission among the Chinese Diaspora: A Case Study of Migration and Mission', *Missiology: An International Review* 31:1 (January 2003); Tuvya Zaretsky (ed), *Jewish Evangelism: A Call to the Church* (LCWE 2004); also 'A Fresh Approach for Ministry to American Jewish-Gentile Couples', in Enoch Wan and Joy Tira (eds) *Missions Practice in the 21st Century.* (Pasadena: William Carey International University Press, 2009). Enoch Wan and Tuvya Zaretsky, *Jewish-Gentile Couples: Trends, Challenges and Hopes* (Pasadena: William Carey Library, 2004); Sadiri Joy Tira and Enoch Wan, 'Filipino Experience in Diaspora Missions: A Case Study of Christian Communities in Contemporary Contexts' (Commission VII, Christian Communities in Contemporary Contexts, Edinburgh, June 12-13, 2009).

[11] See a detailed chart on 'Scattering (dispersion) in the OT' in *Missions Practice in the 21st Century*, 36.

[12] See a detailed chart on 'Gathering (calling) in the OT' in *Missions Practice in the 21st Century*, 36.

[13] See a detailed chart on 'Scattering (dispersion) in the NT' in *Missions Practice in the 21st Century*, 37.

[14] See a detailed chart on 'Scattering (dispersion) in the NT' in *Missions Practice in the 21st Century*, 37.

Otherwise, scattering of people in the OT often occurred as the consequence of sin, e.g. the fall of man at the Garden of Eden (Gen. 3:22-24); the murderous act of Cain (Gen. 4:13-15); the plot of rebellion at the Tower of Babel (Gen. 11); the idolatry of the Israelites (Ps 78:54-64; Is 1-5).

The Great Commission is God's design for Christians in the NT to scatter, bearing the good news to all nations (Mat. 28:18-20; Mark 16:15-17; Luke 24:46-49; John 17:18; Acts 1:8). Failing to do so incurs the punishment of being 'scattered' (Acts 9, 11). However, the scattering of Christians could be God's provision of outreach and church planting (Acts 18; 1 Peter and 2 Peter).

Calling in the OT is God's way of gathering his choice people, e.g. Noah (Gen. 7-8; Heb. 11:7), Abraham (Gen. 12, 14, 17; Heb. 11:8-12), Isaac (Gen. 21), Jacob (Gen. 28), the Israelites (Book of Joshua, Heb. 11), the remnant (Is. 40-45), and the church (Eph. 1-2; 1 Pet, 2:1-11). The calling of people unto himself is a matter of grace.

Due to the limitation of this study, no detailed explanation and discussion on God's sovereignty and the human tragedy of diaspora in Christian missions can be presented here.[15] However, missiologically speaking, though the life of the Korean diaspora is a harsh reality, characterized by suffering and hardship in strange lands, and the sad separation from the extended family in the homeland and long-time sojourning abroad, it is clearly God's way of scattering them from the 'Hermit Kingdom of Korea' for the divine purpose of kingdom ministry. They are the modern version of cases of diaspora in the Bible: Abraham the wanderer towards Ur, Egypt, and Canaan; Joseph moving from slave to prime minister in Egypt; Daniel from captive to court officer in Babylon; Priscilla and Aquila from political refugee from Rome to Corinth, to church planting in Ephesus and Rome.[16]

Theoretical Framework for Kingdom Ministry: Relational Paradigm

There are many philosophical and theological paradigms that are optional for evangelical Christians (e.g. existentialism, rationalism, etc.), but of all of them, the 'relational paradigm' is the best fit for Korean Christians due to its strong emphasis on relationship in Korean culture. A detailed explanation of the 'what', 'how' and 'why' of the 'relational paradigm' cannot be elaborated in this brief study, as it is elsewhere.[17] It is suffice to use the following diagram to

---

[15] See the unpublished paper '"Diasporas" and God's Mission: A Position Paper', by Lausanne Diasporas Leadership Team, drafted by Enoch Wan and Elias Medeiros, 2009.

[16] See a detailed chart on 'Gathering (calling, covenant, ecclesiology) I, the Scattering (dispersion) in the NT', in Enoch Wan and Joy Tira (eds), *Missions Practice in the 21st Century*, 37.

[17] Detailed explanation on the content and distinctiveness of 'relational paradigm' was presented in a lecture at OCMS (Oxford Centre of Missions Studies) on April 16, 2010. For further study on 'relational paradigm', see the following articles: Enoch Wan,

introduce Yahweh (the great 'I AM' of Ex 3:14; cf. John 8:24, 28, 58) and Christian (lower case - 'i am').[18]

Parallel to the emphasis on 'reason' in rationalism, 'relationship' is the focus of the 'relational paradigm' both vertically with the Triune God and horizontally within the created order of angels and human society as shown in the several charts and long discussion found in earlier publications of mine. For the integration of the five elements in 'diaspora missiology' with the 'relational paradigm' see Figures 3 and 5 of an earlier work.[19]

Missiogical Strategy for Kingdom Ministry: Diaspora Missiology/Missions

The new paradigm of 'diaspora missiology' is proposed in this study to supplement that of the 'traditional missiology' in formulating a strategy for the Korean diaspora. 'Traditional missiology' is represented by organizations such as the American Society of Missiology with the journal Missiology, and the Evangelical Missiological Society with the publication Occasional Bulletin and monograph published annually.[20]

At the 'Commission VII: Christian Communities in Contemporary Contexts', Sadiri Joy Tira and Enoch Wan clearly stated:

> The integration of migration research and missiological study has resulted in practical 'diaspora missiology' - a new strategy for missions. Diaspora mission is a providential and strategic way to minister to the nations 'by the diaspora and through the diaspora'.[21]

In the last few decades, Korean missions have been surging upward to compensate for the lapse of mission forces from the sending countries of the

---

'Relational Theology and Relational Missiology', *Occasional Bulletin of Evangelical Missiological Society* 21:1 (Winter 2007), 1-7; Enoch Wan, 'The Paradigm of "Relational Realism"', *Occasional Bulletin* 19:2 (Spring 2006), 1-4' Enoch Wan, 'A Missio-Relational Reading of Romans', *Occasional Bulletin* 23:1 (Winter 2010), 1-8. Also published in www.GlobalMissiology.org 'Relational Study' April 1, 2010.

[18] For more references on 'relational paradigm', see Enoch Wan and Mark Hedinger, 'Understanding "Relationality" from a Trinitarian Perspective', *Global Missiology, Trinitarian Studies,* January 2006 (www.GlobalMissiology.com); Enoch Wan, 'The Paradigm of "Relational Realism"', *Occasional Bulletin* 19:2 (Spring 2006), 1-4; Enoch Wan, 'Relational Theology and Relational Missiology', *Occasional Bulletin* 21:1 (Winter 2007), 1-7; Enoch Wan, 'A Missio-Relational Reading of Romans', *Occasional Bulletin* 23 (Winter, 2010), 1-8. For a detailed discussion on 'relational paradigm' and the several helpful charts, please consult an earlier publication, Wan and Tira (eds), *Missions Practice in the 21st Century*, 14-19.

[19] Enoch Wan, 'Global People and Diaspora Missiology' (Plenary presentation at Tokyo 2010 Global Mission Consultation, May, 2010), 7, 10.

[20] See websites: ASM - http://www.asmweb.org and EMS - www.EMSweb.org

[21] Tira & Wan, 'Filipino Experience in Diaspora Missions'.

West. However, their major thrust has been following the traditional missiology paradigm of the Western churches. In lthe ight of the phenomenal increase of the Korean diaspora and the new demographic reality of the twenty-first century, diaspora missiology is to be explored and the paradigm of diaspora missions should be employed to supplement the traditional approach.

How can Korean churches send out thousands of missionaries abroad to engage in foreign missions, yet ignore the many disapora groups God has sent to their doorstep in Korea? These transient people on Korean soil are geographically on the move from their homeland and are moved by the Holy Spirit spiritually to become receptive to the gospel and reachable domestically in Korea. The Great Commission cannot be fulfilled only by Korean missionaries serving overseas.

Korean Christians are to practice diaspora missions at home. They are to show holistic Christianity, integrating evangelism with Christian charity to the sojourners and practice 'mission on our doorstep'.[22] There are diaspora people from the 10/40 windows on Korean soil, so they are no longer 'unreached people', as designated by traditional mission. Korean Christians are to view and follow God's way of providentially moving people spatially to Korea and spiritually within reach in the Korean peninsula. Remember, it is God who determines where people will live at certain times, so that wherever they are in the universe, they can call upon God and find him (Acts 17:26-28).

In the NT, Jesus Christ systematically taught his disciples and the multitude the vertical and horizontal dimensions of responsibility and accountability (Mt 5-7; Mark 9:33-55; Luke 6, 11; John 13-15). Deriving from the fact that the apostle Paul served in Ephesus for other elders to follow (Act 20:17-35), we learn that he was accountable to God vertically and for shepherding the flock horizontally. The Corinthian Christians are to be followers of the apostle Paul horizontally, as he is a follower of Christ vertically (2.Cor. 11:1).

We learn from the Pauline Epistles that Christian leaders are accountable to God vertically in calling, and are faithful and exemplary horizontally in the contexts of fellow-Christians or among members of his household or non-Christians (1 Tim. 3-4; Tit. 2; 1 Pet. 5:1-6). The apostle Peter also addressed the issue of leadership and accountability vertically and horizontally (i.e. shepherding and modeling horizontally while accountable to the chief shepherd vertically, 1 Pet. 5:1-6). Christians are vertically accountable to God in integrity and not to be a stumbling to God's people horizontally (Rom. 14; 1 Cor. 10:23-33). Korean churches are to be reminded of their relational accountability to God due to his endowment upon them of the rich resources of personnel, finance and ministerial opportunities in Christian mission.

In the 'code of household', both the apostles Paul (Eph. 5:21-6:9; Col. 3:18-4:6; 1 Tim. 6:1-2; Tit 2) and Peter (1 Pet. 3:1-7) addressed the vertical dimension to God and the horizontal dimension in membership and

[22] Wan, 'Global People and Diaspora Missiology', 11.

accountability. Relational accountability is the understanding and practice of accountability within the relational paradigm of both vertical and horizontal dimensions. 'Relational paradigm' is a good alternative for Korean churches, for their cultural context is part of the missions in the majority world.[23] The popularity of the cell group approach[24] in Korean churches is in line with the post-modernist, high-tech and high-touch orientation of the twenty-first century, more so than the traditional 'modernist' and 'rationalist orientations'.

There are precedents in the OT illustrative of relational accountability. For example, Joseph was faithful in the household of Potiphar in Egypt to God (Gen. 32) and later in the entire country of Egypt (Gen. 42-45). He was vertically accountable to God (Gen. 45:1-15) and horizontally both to Pharaoh (Gen. 41:37-57) and for the well-being of his family (Gen. 50:15-25). In similar manner, Moses was found faithful in the household of God (Heb. 3:2) and was held accountable to God for his ministry vertically (2 Cor. 3:1-18), including his failure to honor God as leader of the Israelites horizontally by disobediently striking the rock for water (Deut. 20:10-13; 34:1-8). Koreans are very keen on relationships and often strive to cultivate and maintain relational networks to be honorable, not shameful. Korean Christians, therefore, are to be reminded of the biblical truth of stewardship and accountability when engaging in diaspora missions.

Missiological Implications and Call for Action

In this section, several missiological implications are derived from the ethnographic descriptions of the Korean diaspora and the two proposed paradigms. These implications are presented in the format of a call for action, so that the Korean Christians can come out of the cocoon of the 'Hermit Kingdom' to be involved in global missions and be engaged in kingdom ministry. Passages from the Pastoral Epistles (as a biblical foundation) will be used for this section.

Pursue the Study of Diaspora Missiology and Promote It

By definition, diaspora missiology is a missiological framework for understanding and participating in God's redemptive mission among diaspora groups. There is a relational dimension in the Great Commission which is *missio Dei* (God's mission) and we are his co-rulers/laborers (2 Tim. 2:12, cf. 2 Cor. 5:17-6:1). God is moving the diaspora spatially and spiritually on a global

---

[23] See Enoch Wan and Michael Pocock (eds), *Missions in the Majority World* (Pasadena: William Carey Library, 2009).

[24] People are starving for relationship as evidenced by the cell-group movement within the Church and the thriving of the virtual community in the twenty-first century. A relational approach is, therefore, most relevant.

scale and we are to move along with God by seizing the opportunity to reach a receptive diaspora who are both transient and sojourning. This kind of theological understanding of God, moving people geographically and spiritually, (both historically in the OT, NT and contemporary society), is 'a sound doctrine' (2 Tim. 4:3) that is to be pursued in study (2 Tim. 2:14-15) and entrusted 'to those who can teach others' (2 Tim. 2:2). Korean Christians at home and the diaspora Korean abroad are to: 1) Discern the theological soundness of diaspora missiology; 2) Disseminate the demographic information of the Korean diaspora on a global scale; 3) Deliver the education of diaspora missiology through theological institutions and lay-training programmes inside Korea and overseas so as to motivate and mobilize Korean churches for Christian missions both in the traditional way and the new paradigm on diaspora missiology; 4) Develop a contextualized version of diaspora missiology that is culturally sensitive to the Korean heritage and adaptable to diaspora Koreans anywhere; and 5) Dare to raise up a new generation of Korean missiologists and mission leaders who are i) attuned to the socio-cultural shift (e.g. globalization, post-modernist, demographic trends, etc.), ii) ready to contextualize the relational paradigm for the Korean context in Korea and abroad, iii) be engaged in diaspora missions.

Parting with 'Unscriptural' Aspects of Korean Cultural Tradition

Evangelical Christians are to distinguish 'biblical' and 'scriptural' elements in any cultural system and filter out 'unscriptual' elements. In the relevant literature, the word 'biblical' and 'scriptural' are usually used interchangeably, but not in the present study. The two words are being distinguished carefully and being used technically as shown in the figure below.

Figure 2: Comparison between 'biblical' and 'scriptural'[25]

BIBLICAL	SCRIPTURAL
Descriptive: Recorded/reported in the Bible	Prescriptive: Prescribed by the Incarnate & enscriptured Word
Precedent in the Bible	Principle of 'the whole counsel of God'
particular: time and place specific	Universal: transcending time & space
culturally & contextually specific	Neither culturally nor contextually specific

[25] For a detailed discussion on 'biblical' and 'scriptural' see Enoch Wan, 'Core Values of Mission Organization in the Cultural Context of the 21st Century' (www. GlobalMissiology.org, January 2009).

The Bible is full of 'description' (row 1 in Figure 2) of the behavior and practice of major figures in biblical times, but is not 'prescription' for us nowadays. For example, the Bible recorded/reported the patriarch Abraham and King David as polygamists; but it is prescriptive for us to be monogamists by the teaching of Jesus (Mt 19; Mk 10; Lk 16) and consistent teaching (Gen. 1:14; Deut 24:13; Mal. 2:15). Row 2 in Figure 2 ('casting lots', Acts 1) is merely 'biblical' not 'scriptural' (row 3). King David's confession and the hymn based on Ps 51, though 'biblical' is not 'scriptural' because it contradicts the promise of Jesus that the Holy Spirit will 'be with you forever' (Jn 14:16). According to row 4, the ceremonial law and sacrificial system of the OT is 'biblical' as revealed by God in the OT period but it is not 'scriptural' and thus not applicable to NT Christians as the 'scriptural teaching' of Hebrews of NT applicable to all people at all times.

The 'Hermit Kingdom' orientation of 'isolationism' is merely 'culturally Korean' but not 'scriptural'. Therefore, it should be replaced by 'kingdom orientation' that is all-embracing and inclusive in its gospel outreach. Therefore, it should not become a hindrance to Korean Christians participating in global mission. It is in this sense that the Great Commission Korean churches should part ways with the traditional Korean 'Hermit Kingdom' orientation of 'isolationism' and replace it with the kingdom orientation of inclusiveness, i.e. 'making disciples of all nations'.

Korean society has been historically and culturally homogeneous, so it is 'cultural' for Koreans to avoid the challenge of cultural adjustment, language acquisition and the costly involvement in cross-cultural evangelism and engagement in a kingdom agenda. This 'cultural' orientation is not 'scriptural' and should be avoided at all cost.

Truly, Korean Christians are passionate about evangelizing fellow Koreans in Korea and diaspora Koreans overseas. It is so tempting to evangelize Koreans only (and not non-Koreans), just like the scattered Jewish Christians of Acts 11:19 evangelized 'Jews only' but not non-Jews. It is culturally Korean to be 'pragmatic', obsessive with quantifiable accomplishments, quick successes measured by budgets and numerical growth – both in Korean secular business and global mission. Their outcome-based orientation can be culturally explained, for it is expedience in evangelizing Koreans only, for that would not require crossing cultural and linguistic barriers but it is not 'scriptural'.

Koreans should avoid the mistake of some Chinese Christian leaders, who misuse Paul's sentiment for his (Jewish) 'kinsmen' in Rom. 9, misquote Paul's statement about evangelizing the Jews first (Rom. 1:16) and his practice of going to the synagogue to reach fellow Jews with the gospel (e.g. Acts 14:1; 17:1-2; 18:4, etc.). Chinese Christians have the tendency to exclusively reach diaspora Chinese evangelistically and ignore non-Chinese in the host country and elsewhere. This phenomenon is 'cultural' and their insistence of following Paul's precedence is only 'biblical' but not 'scriptural'.

In a similar manner, the Korean diaspora overseas tends to socially interact with fellow Koreans and strongly resists cultural adaptation and clusters to form a 'Korean town'. Korean Christians abroad will first start a Korean diaspora congregation' (KDC), followed by a Korean language school for the 1.5 and second generation. The involvement of cross-cultural mission among the Korean diaspora is relatively low, in comparison to that within Korea. Again, this is only a 'cultural' tendency and 'cultural' practice among Koreans but it is not 'scriptural'.

Proceed onto a 'Kingdom Agenda' with a 'Kingdom Orientation'

A 'kingdom orientation' (i.e. not parochial but embracing the perspective, sentiment and motivation of the kingdom) should be embraced when conducting diaspora missions, in which division is minimized between the host and the diaspora, the sending West and thriving Global South. Kingdom orientation is to replace denominations and parochialism. Genuine partnership is best practiced along with kingdom orientation that permeates all facets of Christian mission with the Korean churches, both inside Korea and overseas, for though it is not traditionally 'cultural' it is 'scriptural'.

Practice the 'Relational Paradigm'

Korean churches, in general, should embrace the 'relational paradigm' for it is both culturally Korean and 'scripturally' sound. This is what missiologists call contextualization, that is, planting Christianity in the soil and soul of the native people culturally fit but scripturally sound, so that it can flourish instead of in the pot of a foreign culture. When practicing contextualization, the following five-step paradigm is found to be helpful.

The five-step approach of Figure 3 is a systematic and sequential process but the acronym 'STARS' may be used in reference to the key elements to remember easily.

Figure 3: 'Wan's Way of Integrative Research'[26] ('STARS')

CRITERIA (STARS)	EXPLANATION
Scripturally sound (S)	Not proof-text; but the 'whole counsel of God' (Acts 20:26-27)
Theologically Supported (S)	Not just pragmatism/expedience; but sound theology
Theoretically coherent (T)	Not to be self-contradictory; but to be coherent

[26] For detailed discussion on 'biblical' and 'scriptural' see Enoch Wan, 'Core values of mission organization in the cultural context of the 21st Century' (www. GlobalMissiology.org, January 2009).

Contextually Relevant (R)	Not to be out of place; but fitting for the context
Practically Applicable (A)	Not only good in theory; but can be put into practice

A simple explanation of the items in Figure 3 is provided first, followed by illustrations of the importance of being systematic and sequential.

1) Scripturally sound: As evangelical, scripture is to be the basis and guide of Christian faith and practice. It is axiomatic for evangelical Protestants based on the conviction of '*sola scriptura*'.

2) Theologically supported: Just based on pragmatism/expedience is insufficient but sound theology is essential and required.

3) Theoretically coherent: Not to be self-contradictory but to be both consistent and coherent.

4) Contextually relevant: Not to be out of place but it is to be fitting for the context.

5) Practically applicable: It is good to have scriptural/theological support with coherent theory and cultural relevance but it can be put into practice in reality.

As presented in the ethnographic description of Korean culture, the emphasis on the nurturing and maintaining 'relationship' is a strong characteristic of Korean culture. The 'relational paradigm' meets all five criteria of Figure 3, for it is both 'scripturally sound', and 'theologically supported', and 'contextually fit' for Koreans. Therefore, it should be embraced and practiced by Koreans in their homeland and among members of KDC. It is also very practical, for its emphasis on first the 'vertical dimension' to God and the Scriptures, then the 'horizontal dimension' within both Korean culture and among the Korean community. This will correct the problem of the fragmentation of the Korean community and church schism. So in this sense, it is also 'practically applicable' – the fifth criterion of Figure 3.

Diaspora Missions: Ministering to, through and/beyond Them

The Korean churches are to reach diaspora Koreans who have geographically moved to foreign lands and have been moved by the Holy Spirit to be receptive to the gospel. KDC (Korean diaspora congregations) are to minister to their own kinsmen abroad, i.e. be engaged in 'ministering to the Korean diaspora'.

If Korean Christians allowed their cultural and linguistic homogeneity of the past to deter them from learning foreign languages or to adjust to the host culture, then they will forever stay within 'the cocoon of the Hermit Kingdom'. Instead, they should embrace a kingdom-orientation, embark on the path of cross-cultural competency, and be engaged in kingdom ministry. They should play the role of a 'bridge' for the gospel, reaching out to the non-Christian members in the host society, or other diaspora groups in close proximity, or folks back in their homeland of Korea. This is what is meant by 'ministering through and beyond the diaspora'.

There is the global trend of migrant populations moving from South to North, and from East to West.[27] Among them are many from the 10/40 windows that were previously presumed to be 'unreached' and are now accessible. Congregations, in the receiving countries (the old Christian West of industrial nations), can easily practice 'mission on our doorstep' [28] without crossing borders geographically, linguistically and culturally.[29] This is ministering *to* the diaspora aspect of practicing diaspora missions as discussed earlier in this study.

Ministering *through* and *beyond* diaspora have two other aspects of practicing diaspora missions. These two approaches are to be employed in order to seize new opportunities created by the phenomenon of diaspora. Diaspora congregations are to be mobilized for the Great Commission when individual Christians are motivated and empowered to carry out their missionary duties. This is what is meant by minister *through* the diaspora. When members of the diaspora groups have acquired the language and are adjusted to the culture of the host society, they are the natural bridges for minister *beyond* them to reach others of host societies and countries.

From the research findings of Philip Jenkins,[30] we learned that the centre of gravity of the Christian world had shifted from Europe and the United States to the Southern hemisphere. From this factual data, we see that, based on the Christian principle of stewardship, the Church is to use valuable resources (e.g. manpower, finance, sound and effective strategy, ministry opportunity, etc.) wisely and responsibly. Ministering to receptive people among the diaspora strategically (i.e. ministering *to* the diaspora) and mobilizing diaspora congregations for missions (i.e. minister *through* the diaspora) are also a matter of good Christian stewardship.

Members within the thriving diaspora churches in foreign land are to be challenged to practice 'reverse mission' (i.e. doing mission work in the post-Christian West by members from the Global South and sending members of the diaspora groups back to their homeland to engage in missions). The growing and maturing congregations in the Global South are to be collaboratively working with mission entities from the West in partnership. The

[27] Enoch Wan, 'Diaspora Missiology and Missions in the Context of the 21st Century', *Torch Trinity Journal* 13:1 (May 2010), 46.

[28] Enoch Wan, 'Diapora Missiology', *Occasional Bulletin of EMS*, Spring 2007, 9.

[29] See figure 6 'The "yes" and "no" of Mission at Our Doorstep', in Enoch Wan, 'Global People and Diaspora Missiology' (Plenary Presentation at Tokyo 2010 Global Mission Consultation, May 2010, 11.

[30] Philip Jenkins, *The Next Christendom: The Coming of Global Christianity* (Oxford: Oxford University Press, 2001)

synergy from such partnerships will enhance Christian stewardship and advance the kingdom ministry.

Relational Stewardship Based on Relational Accountability

The Great Commandment (of 'love your neighbor' is powerful in pre-evangelistic efforts and can be easily combined with the Great Commission (of making disciples of all nations) is a trademark of diaspora missions in action. There is relational accountability vertically to God and horizontally to sending agencies. When practicing diaspora missions, both 'ministering through and beyond diaspora will be done through the multi-layers of networks, that form an accountability structure to avoid the wasteful use of resources and the abuse of power.

Synergetic Partnerships

Korean diaspora congregations in many countries are to be natural partners, working closely with Korean vocational missionaries and mission agencies. In addition to Korean diaspora congregations, there are many thriving non-Korean diaspora congregations to partner with, such as the ubiquitous Chinese congregations in all continents, supported by the extensive network of 'Chinese Coordination Center of World Evangelism (CCCOWE).[31]

Thriving diaspora congregations in many lands are not to be ignored by traditional Western sending agencies. Instead, there is synergy in collaborative partnerships for the Korean diaspora with others at various levels: international (such as International Conference on Diaspora for Development,[32] Lausanne Movement,[33] Evangelical Fellowship,[34] and FIN)[35] and national (such as Korea Evangelical Fellowship,[36] the Korean Diaspora, Berlin)[37]. Genuine partnership is best practiced along with kingdom orientation that permeates all facets of Christian mission.

The paternalistic missionary practice of the past should be replaced with a synergetic partnership, such as the Korean Diaspora Forum held in May, 2010 in Seoul, Korea is attempting to nurture. The Lausanne Diasporas Leadership

---

[31] http://www.cccowe.org/eng/.

[32] http://siteresources.worldbank.org/INTPROSPECTS/Resources/334934-1110315015165/conferenceAgenda.pdf

[33] http://www.lausanne.org/

[34] http://www.worldevangelicals.org

[35] http://www.fin-online.org/

[36] http://trn.sagepub.com/content/3/4/28.2.full.pdf+html

[37] http://discoveringkorea.com/2009/03/13/the-korean-diaspora-berlin

Team has ongoing activities. There are opportunities and activities when Korean Christians can join hands with others.[38]

Conclusion

In this study, an ethnographic description of Korean diaspora has been presented. The goal is to encourage Korean Christians to break out from the 'Hermit Kingdom' orientation and launch out to embrace a kingdom orientation for the fulfillment of the Great Commission. Providentially, there are so many Korean diaspora congregations mushrooming everywhere to partner with others for the kingdom ministry and if they embrace a kingdom orientation they can break loose from the bondage of ethnocentrism and a self-reliant mentality.

Two new paradigms have been proposed to respond to the new demographic reality of the massive movement of people in the twenty-first century, including the Korean diaspora. Diaspora missiology has been explained as a new paradigm in mission studies for the new century. Based on this new diaspora missiology paradigm, diaspora missions is a new mission strategy. Likewise, the relational paradigm has been proposed to accompany the relational oriented Korean culture for practical implementation.

Several missiological implications from this study can be derived. For example, the study of diaspora missiology should be pursued and its education should be promoted. We should also seize the new opportunities created by the new demographic trends of the twenty-first century. When practicing stewardship and partnership, we shall be able to harness the synergy of the old West and the new Global South. If we embrace a kingdom orientation, we can combine the Great Commandment of 'loving our neighbor' in pre-evangelism with the Great Commission in mission. This is a practical way to demonstrate Christian faith through holistic action, when facing the new demographic trends of the new century.

[38] See the LDLT leadership team website at: http://www.gatheredscattered.com/press.

The Diaspora Experience of the Korean Church and its Implications for World Missions

Minho Song

Just before the disintegration of the Soviet Union, a retired Korean pastor[1] from Toronto, Canada, traveled to Leningrad (now St. Petersburg) to see if he could plant churches there. At 67 years of age and without the Russian language, Rev. Kim was desperate for divine guidance. He had been in the city for more than a week, moving from place to place. Tired of traveling, he went down to a path near the bank of Neva River in St. Petersburg and watched the mighty river flow. Then, he remembered the prayers of his mother spoken long ago—that one day, her son would become a missionary. He prayed for a sign that the Lord would show him whether he should stay there. Just as he finished a short prayer and headed to the hotel he was staying in, a man came up to him and asked if he was lost: a Korean Russian by the name of Ki-um Kim. Until that moment, Rev. Kim had never seen a Korean face before in Leningrad. Surprised but very thankful, Rev. Kim received the much-needed contact he had been waiting and praying for, and the rest is history. Rev. Kim's mission work in St. Petersburg grew to several churches planted for the Korean diaspora and Russians. He also founded a Presbyterian seminary.

Ki-um Kim's parents had migrated to Sakhalin Island in 1930s during the Japanese colonial era, looking for a better life. Kim was born and raised on the island. After high school, he moved to Leningrad for university, where he excelled in his studies and went on to become a successful banker. Not all Korean immigrants enjoyed the similar blessings life had to offer, especially those who went to Vladivostok for a better life. The world of Irina Kim's parents turned upside down in 1937. Suspecting that Japan was plotting destruction against the Soviet Union and that the Korean community in Vladivostok would become a breeding ground for Japanese spies, Stalin relocated all Koreans living in that region. Every Korean was ordered to board a train at short notice—for some, as short as one day—and 200,000 of them were shipped like cargo, bound for Central Asia. Forty days into their travel and suffering from hunger, bitter cold, and even death, they were mercilessly thrown out of the train in Ushtobe, Kazhakstan. There, in the middle of a vast Central Asian plain, the survivors made underground shelters for temporary

[1] Rev. Jae Kwang Kim (1923-2008) was the founding pastor of Youngnak Korean Church of Toronto. Upon retiring from the church, he served as missionary in St. Petersburg, Russia, from 1990 to 2006.

lodgings to escape the harsh winter. These victims and their descendents came to be known as Kareskys ('Koreans' in Russian), who, to this day, are spread throughout Central Asian countries and Russia, and consider themselves ethnic Koreans.

Koreans have migrated to major cities around the world. Wherever they go, they open up Taekwon-do schools, Korean restaurants, and Korean churches. This trend of migration is a relatively new development, given that the first Koreans to leave the country were thirteen poverty-stricken families who went to Russia in 1863 in order to escape a severe famine back home.[2] These families found a new home in the maritime territory of Russia, known as Primorskiy Kray.[3] Even though emigration was against Korean law at that time, the population of Koreans in Primorskiy Kray swelled to 200,000 in just two generations. In addition to Primorskiy Kray, Manchuria was a destination for many. Today, approximately seven million Koreans (or ten percent of North and South Koreans combined) live outside of the Korean peninsula, scattered in 175 countries around the world including China, Russia, Japan, and America.[4]

The Meaning of 'Diaspora' in the Bible

If we truly believe that the Spirit of Jesus guides missions (Acts 16:6-7), then we should not be surprised to see God's placement of people at strategic points in mission work. Undeniably, the 'Kareskys' are one great example of such a placement: their presence in the former Soviet Union was helpful to Korean missionaries in evangelizing the Russians and other groups of people in the Commonwealth of Independent States (CIS). Stalin's actions, toward the Koreans of Primorskiy Kray, were horrific and inhuman, but in his sovereignty, God allowed the tragic event of 1937 to be part of his plan to bring the good news to the Russians, the Kyrgyz, and the Uzbek people, as well as scores of other ethnic groups living in the former Soviet Union.[5] Who would have imagined that these communities of displaced Koreans would one day serve as 'base camps' for Korean missionaries?

---

[2] For various views on the history of Korean migration, including the view that the earliest Korean 'migrants' were the war captives taken to Japan and China, as many 100,000 Koreans each, in the seventeenth century, see Yoon-soo Chang, *Korean Diaspora and Its Cultural Network* [in Korean] (Seoul: Book Korea, 2010).

[3] Primorskiy Kray once belonged to China, but the Beijing Treaty of 1858 relinquished full control over the region to Russia.

[4] According to the 2009 figure by Overseas Korean Foundation, there are 6.8 million Koreans living abroad, of which the majority are found in China (2.3 million), CIS (0.5 million), Japan (0.9 million), and USA (2.1 million). See http://www.korean.net/morgue/status_1.jsp?tCode=status&dCode=0101 (accessed on July 30, 2010).

[5] For more information on the Korean migrants to Russia and CIS, see In-jin Yoon, *Korean Diaspora: Migration, Adaptation and Self-Identity of Overseas Koreans* [in Korean] (Seoul: Korean University Press, 2004), 87-148.

This brings us to the discussion of the role and the place of diaspora in the divine scheme of things. The word 'diaspora' refers to those people who have migrated from their homeland—either by their own will or by force—to begin new lives elsewhere. Some have called this period the 'age of migration' as millions have moved from south to north and east to west. Currently, the phenomenon of diaspora is the experience of millions. All around the world, migrants have found new homes and shaped the contours of their new societies. Turks in Germany, Filipinos in the Middle East, and Mexicans in the United States have all been drawn by the employment opportunities available to them and the hope for a better future.

However, there are many reasons why people leave their homeland, as Hanciles gives a helpful summary of the various theories of migration—the neo-classical economic perspective, the historical-structural approach, the network approach based on social capital, and the migration systems theory - all to show that migration is a complex issue to understand.[6] Geo-political or socio-linguistic points of view aside, from a spiritual perspective, we can also appreciate God's sovereign plan behind the relocation of people. Understandably, migrants often face more difficult times than those who have never left their homes. Yet, it is precisely in this difficulty that we should strive to understand the plan of God. As a result of leaving familiarity and known comforts behind, migrants also tend to be open to new possibilities. In other words, they are open to change. God works with those who have left their homes to follow him. Abraham is a prime example of this because God began the new work of building a nation through him when he obeyed the call and left his father's country (Gen. 12:1-3).

The Greek word *diaspora* was first used in the Septuagint and its use is mostly limited to Jewish and Christian literature. In the Old Testament (LXX), the word describes the scattering of the Jews (Deut. 28:25; Jer. 34:17) or the Jewish communities among the nations (Ps. 147:2; Isa. 49:6).[7] Notable examples of the diaspora communities in the Old Testament are those to which Daniel and Esther and belonged. Similarly, the term is found three times in the New Testament, referring to the Jews living among the Greeks (John 7:35) or the Christian communities scattered throughout Asia Minor or (1 Pet. 1:1) or among unbelievers (Jam. 1:1). In the epistles of James and Peter, its intended meaning is clear: it refers to the scattering of God's people, just as seeds are scattered for harvest. In other words, the act of scattering has a divine purpose. Acts 8:1 shows how great persecution against the Jerusalem church resulted in the scattering of God's people. The word 'scattered' in Acts 8:1 and 8:4 is from

---

[6] Jehu Hanciles, 'Migration and Mission: Some Implications for the Twenty-first-Century Church', *International Bulletin of Missionary Research* 27:4 (2003), 146.

[7] Verlyn Verbrugge, 'διασπορά', *New International Dictionary of New Testament Theology*, abridged edition (Grand Rapids: Zondervan, 2000), 139.

the same root word as *diaspora* (with its verb form *dia-speiro*, which means 'to scatter seeds' among the nations). Hence, the biblical meaning of diaspora is loaded with the connotation of sowing seeds or bearing witness everywhere with the expectation of a harvest.

Those who planted the Antioch church may be regarded as the first diaspora people 'in action'. Following Stephen's martyrdom, 'a great persecution broke out against the church at Jerusalem and all except the apostles were scattered throughout Judea and Samaria' (Acts 8:1). Some went as far North as Syrian Antioch and shared the good news with the Greeks, which was a clear departure from the pattern of witnessing to Jews only (Acts 11:19-20). The result was that 'the Lord's hand was with them, and a great number of people believed and turned to the Lord' (Acts 11:21). Antioch proved to be most fertile ground for cross-cultural evangelism, as testified by the successful outreach to Hellenistic Jews and God-fearing Gentiles (Acts 11:19-26).[8] The Antioch church marks the first Christian diaspora community in the Bible. The five leaders of the Antioch church mentioned in Acts 13:1 reflected the multi-cultural character of the church and 'symbolized the ethnic and cultural diversity of Antioch'.[9] From the start the Antioch church had a strong outward focus and its members readily heard the Spirit's specific call to engage in world missions (Acts 13:2).[10]

Diaspora Community and the Beginning of the Korean Church

The first Korean believers in the nineteenth century, like those believers who planted the Antioch church, were eager to share the gospel with others. In 1884, one year before the first two Protestant missionaries brought the gospel to the Korean soil,[11] the first Korean church was established in Sorae village in Hwang-hae Province by the native believers who were trained in Manchuria.[12] These believers returned to Korea from China a few years ahead of the first missionaries and preached the gospel in several parts of the country. At that time, evangelism was done in secrecy due to the government ban on any foreign religion from entering Korea. The Catholic mission to Korea, which is traced back to 1784, when Seung-hoon Lee was baptized in Beijing by the French Jesuit priest Louis de Grammont, also operated in secrecy. Lee returned

---

[8] Michael Green, *Evangelism in the Early Church* (Grand Rapids: Eerdmans, 1970), 113.

[9] John Stott, *The Spirit, the Church and the World: the Message of Acts* (Downers Grove: IVP, 1990), 216.

[10] Despite the command in Acts 1:8, the Jerusalem church was slow to act upon it.

[11] The first Protestant missionaries to Korea were Horace Underwood and Henry Appenzeller. They landed at Jaemul-po (today's Incheon) Port in 1885 with the understanding that the country was not yet officially open to the gospel.

[12] Insoo Kim, *A History of Christianity in Korea* [in Korean] (Seoul: Publishing House of the Presbyterian Church of Korea, 1994), 81-82.

to Seoul and held a class on Catholic doctrines in 1785. The 'class' grew to more than 23,000 by 1865. But the persecution was intense. During those eighty years (from 1784 to 1865), the Catholic Church suffered wave after wave of persecution, and thousands were martyred.[13]

When the Scottish missionary John Ross arrived in Manchuria in 1872, he discovered a thriving Korean diaspora community of several hundred families. He also found Korean merchants who traveled to and from Korea, and who were well versed in the Chinese and Korean languages. At a time when people looked with suspicion upon those who associated with foreigners, it was difficult to find a suitable language helper. Ross finally found one, but his joy quickly vanished when the Korean disappeared in fear:

> His [the language helper] fear had magnified itself into terror, and between Sunday night and Monday morning he disappeared, to find his way back to his native home. Having seen his terror visibly increase daily, I was not unprepared, though bitterly disappointed, at this destruction of my hopes. Several other attempts made to secure a Corean able to aid me in acquiring their language, resulted only in the disappearance of some money.[14]

Ross' first break came when he met a ginseng seller Ung-chan Yi, in 1875, who became Ross' translator and language helper. Moreover, Yi brought his three friends Hong-jun Paik, Sung-ha Yi, and Jin-ki Kim, to Ross and John MacIntyre, Ross' brother-in-law and ministry partner. Like Lee, his friends also worked as translators for other foreigners. By 1879, the first Korean Christian community was formed at MacIntyre's house in Mukden (Shenyang), the capital of Manchuria, as these four language helpers were thoroughly taught in the word and baptized.[15] This was a remarkable feat, considering the fact that Christianity was outlawed in Korea, 'the Hermit Kingdom'. Had it not been for their 'diaspora' status, they would not have received the same discipleship training back home.

Two years later, another key disciple emerged. Sang-yun Suh, also a ginseng merchant, became gravely ill and was nursed back to life by McIntyre. In gratitude for the efforts of the missionary, Suh listened intently to the gospel presentation and received it wholeheartedly. He eventually became a great evangelist. He brought the translated gospel of Luke to his home village of Sorae and starting the first church in Korea.[16]

---

[13] Insoo Kim, *A History of Christianity in Korea*, 34-64.

[14] John Ross, 'The Corean Version of the New Testament: How I Came to Make It. Part II', *United Presbyterian Magazine*, May 1883, 208.

[15] Peter Anho Bae, 'The Three-Self Principle and the Mission Method of John Ross: A Study on the Formation of the Early Korean Presbyterian Church (1874-1893)' (Ph.D. dissertation, University of Aberdeen, 2001), 73, 85, 139.

[16] Samuel H. Moffett, *A History of Christianity in Asia* (Maryknoll, NY: Orbis, 2005), II, 531.

In hindsight, one can conclude that the Korean church owes its beginning to the work of the diaspora community in Mokdum, Manchuria. That community, indeed, was the cradle of the Korean church, where the first few converts were disciple and, with their help, the New Testament was translated into Korean so that ordinary, uneducated Koreans could read the word of God:

> The importance of this work can be understood from the facts that Corean is the language of about twelve millions of people, subject to only slight and unimportant provincial differences, and that all the people, because of the remarkable simplicity of its phonetic alphabet, can read. If, therefore, this translation is to the Corean literary man what the Chinese version cannot be, it goes to the women of that country, and to the lowliest and illiterate poor, to speak to them plainly, in language which all understand and employ in daily life, of the wondrous love of him who is the Saviour of the world.[17]

While Korea was officially closed to the gospel in the nineteenth century, the work of the gospel for Koreans began and continued outside Korea. In God's plan, there is no such a thing as a 'closed door'. Men may block the road, but God opens it in his sovereign way.

From a Diaspora Christian Community to a Diaspora Missional Community

As mentioned earlier, the first Korean Christian community was formed in Mukden (Shenyang) in 1879. Today, some 130 years later, Korean churches are everywhere, even in seemingly unlikely places like Tehran (Iran), Quito (Ecuador), Bishkek (Kyrgyzstan), Abidjan (Côte d'Ivoire), and Dhaka (Bangladesh), just to name a few. In North America, over 3,000 Korean churches serve as both spiritual and social hubs for Korean immigrants. Moving beyond meeting the needs of the Korean immigrants, the diaspora churches are in a strategic position to engage in world missions. These Korean churches have unprecedented opportunities to minister to peoples around them with the gospel because they can engage in missions to their adopted country as well as to other countries.

One example will sufficiently illuminate this point. Morocco has recently become a graveyard of missionaries as government officials identified and expelled the majority of the missionaries from Morocco in early 2010.[18] The

[17] Ross, 'The Corean Version of the New Testament', 209.

[18] For example, a Christian orphanage called the 'Village of Hope' on the slopes of Morocco's Middle Atlas Mountains was shut down abruptly on March 8, 2010, when police falsely charged the group that they had 'exploited some families' poverty and targeted their minor children'. All 16 missionaries were immediately deported and the orphanage was dissolved in a matter of hours, after ten years of lawful operation in Morocco. Solana Pyne, 'Morocco expels Christian evangelists', Global Post, March 12,

Moroccan government is determined to keep out all Christian influence. The evangelistic efforts in Morocco have been significantly curtailed as a result of the expulsion of the missionaries and the arrest and imprisonment of Moroccan believers. Will this be the end of Christianity in Morocco or does God have a different plan to reach the Moroccans? In light of such intense hardship in Morocco, it would seem strategic to evangelize to the Moroccan diaspora, particularly those who live in nearby countries such as Spain and France. The Korean churches in Spain, for example, can play a key role in reaching Moroccans. Madrid is an important urban centre in Europe bustling with migrant workers. At present, it is home to the majority of some 700,000 Moroccans who live in Spain. Just as the first Korean converts were discipled and trained as evangelists outside Korea (in Manchuria) and then sent back to Korea to establish their first church, the Moroccans in Spain can be trained and return to Morocco to evangelize the whole country.

In an increasingly borderless world, 'transmigration' is a way of life for many. To use Hanciles' words, 'transmigrants are often bilingual, can lead dual lives, move easily between cultures, frequently maintain homes in two countries, and are incorporated as social actors in both'.[19] Migrants can freely travel between their newly adopted country and their country of origin as the concept of 'permanent residency' is becoming outdated. They send back not only remittances but also ideas. Therefore, since these 'closed' countries are unsafe for evangelism, it would be logical to establish training centres outside them. If the Korean churches in Spain, though only a few in number, can see the value of engaging in such a mission, the implication for the evangelization of Moroccans is significant.

However, reaching the Moroccans in Morocco through returning Moroccans, as insightful and logical as it may sound, remains solely a good idea until a congregation becomes aware of the sovereign hand of God in dispersing people and acts upon it. History has shown numerous examples of how God closes one door only to open another. It is in this light that one can truly appreciate the foresight and dedication of John Ross during the time when Korea, the 'Hermit Kingdom', was tightly sealed off from any foreign influence. Ross and his co-worker MacIntyre captured the opportunity to evangelize to the Korean merchants working in Manchuria, discipling them, getting them to translate parts of the Bible, and eventually sending key disciples back to evangelize to the Koreans in the 'closed' country.

The extent to which diaspora Christians can be used for world missions depends upon their understanding of the people of God that they exist to fulfil God's agenda in the world. No other place in the scriptures do we find this theme more clearly presented than in 1 Pet. 2:9. Peter writes that they are 'the

---

2010. See www.globalpost.com/dispatch/morocco/100311/ morocco-expels-christian-missionaries (accessed August 11, 2010).

[19] Hanciles, 'Migration and Mission', 148.

chosen people, royal priesthood, the holy nation and people belonging to God' (identity), that they may 'declare the praises of him who called you out of darkness into his glorious light' (mission). The problem with most churches is that they do not understand what Johannes Blauw once expressed as 'the missionary nature of the church'.[20] Most Korean diaspora churches are no different. Foremost on the agenda of these churches is the well-being of their own members. Unless these congregations experience the true 'conversion' from being self-serving to being missional, the great opportunities on their doorstep will be lost.

Diaspora churches face the danger of growing inwardly and catering solely to their own members' needs. Sociologist Pyung-gap Min conducted an interesting study on two hundred Korean immigrant churches in the Queens area of New York. When asked why they come to the church, the respondents gave various social reasons such as: 1) having intimate fellowship with other Koreans, 2) keeping up the Korean culture, 3) receiving help as new immigrants, and 4) gaining social status in leadership opportunities.[21] These may be necessary functions that an immigrant church is expected to perform; however, when fulfilling these needs becomes the primary call of the church, the diaspora community fails to uphold the biblical mandate to live as an apostolic and incarnational community.

According to a more recent study by a team of researchers at Massey University, 90% of some 30,000 Korean immigrants in New Zealand attended church, even though many of them did not attend church in Korea (only one out of five persons is a Christian in Korea). The overwhelming need for networking in a new country encouraged them to attend church. One Korean church, for example, offered a seminar on how to set up a small business in New Zealand.[22] Meeting the needs of the recent immigrants comes with a price: the church may end up losing the clarity of the gospel and instead gain a myopic and limiting view of catering to the needs of the immigrants only. At some point, immigrant churches must regain the true nature of the church: from a self-serving church which meets their own needs only to a truly missional church that meets the needs of the peoples around them.[23]

Of course, the problem of being inward-looking is not just confined to diaspora churches. In the West, the topic of how to transform a stagnant and

---

[20] Johannes Blaw, *The Missionary Nature of the Church* (New York: McGraw-Hill, 1962).

[21] Pyung-gap Min, 'Structural and Social Functions of Korean Immigrant Churches in the United States', *International Migration Review* 26:4 (1992), 1370-94.

[22] Lincoln Tan, 'Religion gives salvation for immigrants', *The New Zealand Herald*, August 9, 2010. See http://www.nzherald.co.nz/nz/news/article. cfm?c_id=1&objectid=10664624 (accessed August 11, 2010).

[23] For a discussion on what a missional church actually looks like, see Milfred Minetrea, *Shaped by God's Heart: The Passion and Practices of Missional Churches* (San Francisco: Jossey-Bass, 2004).

dying church into a missional and living church has been rigorously discussed for the past twenty years.[24] In the case of diaspora churches, as well, meeting the needs of their members is justified as both an urgent task of the church and the legitimate goal of their ministry. Hence, when the church does not move beyond its four walls, most members are content to maintain the status quo. At stake is the challenge of how to equip and empower the diaspora churches so that they may live out their true calling in the world as missional communities.

For a Successful Transition into a Missional Community

For a successful transition into a missional community, there are at least three factors one must consider: 1) re-examining one's ecclesiology, 2) developing transcultural mediators and 3) strategically engaging with a target group. The first step required for a successful transition into a missional community is the re-examination of one's ecclesiology. In the Apostles' Creed, we read, 'I believe in the Holy Spirit, the [one] holy catholic church, and the communion of the saints'. It speaks of unity ('one'), purity ('holy') and universality ('catholic') as gifts to the church, and at the same time as a call the church should follow. However, the Nicean Creed, formulated in the fourth century, takes its step further by including the word 'apostolic'. Thus, the Nicean Creed reads, 'We believe in one holy catholic and apostolic Church'. Therefore, a truly biblical church strives for unity, holiness, universality and apostolicity. An apostolic church lives out its calling as one being sent into the world, neither in isolation nor in accommodation, but in purposeful engagement with the world in order to expand the kingdom of God and declare God's reign upon all souls.[25] Charles van Engen calls for these four words to be regarded 'not as adjectives which modify an entity we know as the church, but as verbals which describe the missionary action of the church's essential life in the world'.[26] Transitioning into a missional church requires, then, a fresh look at the church—the church that is both committed to gathering and scattering.

In most diaspora Korean churches, the *apostolic* dimension of the church is either weak or missing. Finding themselves aliens and sojourners in a new setting, diaspora Christians have the natural tendency to stay amongst themselves because they find comfort and a sense of belonging to their own kind. This homogeneous pull brings and binds them together, but ultimately bans them from meaningfully participating in the lives of those who are outside

---

[24] Reflecting on the state of the Western churches in general, Darell Guder writes passionately about their need for continuing conversion of turning to mission. See *The Continuing Conversion of the Church* (Grand Rapids: Eerdmans, 2000), 145-180.

[25] The church engaging with the world was the theme carefully developed in the *Lausanne Covenant* (1974).

[26] Charles van Engen, *Mission on the Way: Issues in Mission Theology* (Grand Rapids: Baker, 1996), 122.

of the group. Unseen boundaries are drawn between the diaspora church and the people outside the church, and the church forfeits the opportunities of ministering to them. However, the biblical mandate for the church to go into the world is undeniable:

- 'Peace be with you! As the Father has sent me, I am sending you' (John 20:21).
- 'But you are a chosen people, a royal priesthood, a holy nation, a people belonging to God, that you may declare the praises of him who called you out of darkness into his wonderful light' (1 Peter 2:9).

The weak or missing dimension of the apostolic nature of the diaspora church must somehow be recovered. This is easier said than done because the need to belong to one's own kind is always pressing and at times overwhelming for diaspora believers. However, it is ultimately an existential decision that must be made for the sake of the kingdom and the cost must be accepted, if the church is going to obey the biblical mandate to be missional.

The second step required for a successful transition into a missional community is the development of key leaders who will bridge the gap between two or more cultures. In order for diaspora churches to engage with the world outside their own four walls, they need to raise up, in Paul Hiebert's words, 'transcultural mediators'. Transcultural mediators are those who have the capabilities to go beyond their cultural group and form bonds with outsiders, like those 'men from Cyprus and Cyrene [who] went to Antioch and began to speak to Greeks also' (Acts 11:20). Transcultural mediators are, then, those who are able to transcend national and cultural boundaries and bring two or more worlds together. To become such people, Hiebert suggests that they develop 'a metacultural mental framework that enables [them] to live in different worlds' while they keep their core identity secure.[27] For diaspora churches to become missional diaspora churches, they need more transcultural mediators. Churches must be intentional in developing such leaders. Education and training are essential.

Along with the re-examination of the doctrine of the church and the development of transcultural mediators, the third step is locating a target group and developing a strategy to engage with the group. It requires the crossing of cultures into that of the people living next door or across an ocean. The following are some examples of what being a missional diaspora church is about:

- Abidjang Korean Church in Cộte d'Ivoire was started in 1980 with three families. From its inception, the members believed in a missional church. In the past 30 years, it has planted 11 urban churches, through which 45 rural churches were further planted. Moreover, the church

---

[27] Paul Hiebert, *The Gospel in Human Contexts* (Grand Rapids: Baker Academic, 2009), 198.

was instrumental in founding a Presbyterian seminary in Cŏte d'Ivoire.[28]

- In Quito, Ecuador, the Full Gospel Korean Antioch Church with only 20 members planted 15 churches throughout the country. These churches average 150 to 200 members each, and are not only financially independent but also contribute to the mother church so that the funds collected may be used for missions and aid relief elsewhere.[29]
- Youngnak Korean Presbyterian Church of Toronto helped a Thai couple plant a Thai church in Toronto. Through English as a Second Language (ESL) classes, Thai immigrants and migrant workers were invited to participate in a home Bible study. The first Thai congregation in Canada was born and it has grown to more than 30 members. The Korean church also took in a small group of Myanmar believers and helped them become a strong church. The Myanmar church has grown to more than 70 members and planted another Myanmar church across the city.[30]

In all three cases above, each diaspora church had a clear target and a strategy. These churches were not content to serve the needs of Koreans only. Instead, they turned their focus outward and served the people outside their community.

Conclusion

The story of a poverty-stricken family finding a new home in Vladivostock, then, suddenly being subjected to a merciless train ride to Central Asia, and eventually settling in the city of Leningrad, is an incredible record of human survival. But when the family comes in contact with the gospel through a servant who lives out his missional calling, the incredible story takes on a divine meaning: God moves people for a purpose. In St. Petersburg, Rev. Kim found a group of Koreans like Ki-um Kim from Sakhalin Island, and Irina Kim from Central Asia whose roots could be traced to Vladivostok. We can only conclude that Rev. Kim's mission to Russia had been ordained, and that God saw the strategic role and place of diaspora Koreans in Russia for reaching out to the Russians.

There are seven million Koreans living in 175 countries around the world. If we truly believe that God moves people for a purpose, then Koreans will need

[28] http://ny.christianitydaily.com/view.htm?code=mw&id=183963 (accessed August 11, 2010).

[29] http://www.deulsoritimes.co.kr/?var=news_view&page=1&code=202&no=21606 (accessed August 11, 2010).

[30] Charlene De Haan, 'Youngnak Church Toronto', *Faith Today*, March/April 2010, 45-46.

to ask why so many of them have been scattered to so many different places. Incidentally, all of this movement happened in the past 150 years, a time period roughly equivalent to the reception and development of Christianity in Korea. The rapid and powerful growth of Christianity in Korea, from a mission field to a sending country, is unparalleled in mission history. One wonders at the involvement of the hand of God in all this. For a nation that has suffered from numerous foreign invasions and has never colonized others, Korea is now in the reverse position: rather than constantly being influenced by foreign ideas and powers, Korea can impact other nations with the gospel of Jesus Christ. Wherever they go, Koreans start churches. Initially, these churches meet the social functions of immigrants and migrant workers. However, there comes a point when they must choose between transforming themselves to become missional or remain within the confines of their cultural ghetto. Only history will tell whether the Korean diaspora churches maximized their God-given opportunities for the kingdom business or whether they squandered them altogether.

Part 2

Setting the Stage

A Critical Appraisal of Korean Missionary Work

Julie C. Ma

Introduction

When we read the Bible through the eye of mission, it soon becomes evident that God established his mission in a unique way. The fundamental element of mission was accomplished by God himself through the death of his Son Jesus on the cross. Thus, the author of mission is God and the history and the entire world are the theater of his mission, where He selects actors and sets the whole plot. But this mission was to be wrought jointly by God and his people, so God raised various Christian communities of men and women to fulfil his mission. It has flourished over two millennia through the work of the Holy Spirit.

We can safely say that the Lord of mission has used, in particular, the Western church in the last millennium. If Western missionaries had not come to our land to share the precious word of God, there is little likelihood that any of us would have heard the good news of God's salvation message. Therefore, I want to acknowledge the critical missionary contribution of the Western church not only in Korea, but also in other Asian countries.

It is observed that in the last quarter of the twentieth century, God granted his spiritual and physical blessings in a great measure upon the Korean church. It is also encouraging to observe that Korean Christians received them with a missionary consciousness. Since the late 1970s, the Korean missionary movement has grown rapidly. After a generation, Korean leaders of the church and mission communities began to critically reflect on various aspects of the Korean missionary movement. In this study, I plan to outline the scope of the Korean mission movement, study the key features of Korean missionaries' engagement and evaluate their strengths and weaknesses. I will keep my eyes open to the Western missionary movement for any mutual benefits to be learned.

Korean Mission Today

An annual report of the Korean World Mission Association (KWMA) reveals that in 2008, 58 denominations and 217 mission organizations sent 19,413 missionaries to 168 countries.[1] Each year of the previous four years, about

[1] Sungsam Kang, 'Basic Missionary Training: Bible and Disciple' [in Korean], *Korean Mission Quarterly* 8 (2009), 29-40.

2,000 new missionaries were added. Thus, if this trend continues, by 2030, the total number of Korean missionaries is expected to reach the 100,000 mark. These statistics make the Korean church the second largest missionary-sending church in the world. It is also revealed that the highest concentration of Korean missionaries is in Asia, with close to 12,000 (or 56.2%). Within Asia, Northeast Asia (5,353) and Southeast Asia (5,337) receive the most missionaries.[2]

In the rapid expansion of the Korean missionary force, questions have been raised as to whether their effectiveness corresponds to their quantitative growth. There are many positive and creative cases of mission engagement by Korean missionaries, but also an equally good number of cases with cause for concern. Naturally, questions have been raised in the areas of missionary motivation, missiological orientation, cultural adaptability and sensitivity, and so on.

Distribution of Korean Missionaries[3]

Continent	Area	Number of countries	Number of Missionaries	Percentage
Asia	South Asia	4	1,069	5.2%
	Northeast Asia	7	5,353	26.1%
	Southeast Asia	11	3.377	16.5%
	Central Asia	10	1,730	8.4%
	Sub-total	32	11,529	56.2%
Europe	Western Europe	20	992	4.8%
	Eastern Europe	23	996	4.9%
	Sub-total	43	1,988	9.7%
America	Latin America	17	807	3.9%
	North America	6	2,317	11.3%
	Sub-total	23	3,124	15.2%
Africa/Middle East	East-South Africa	20	823	4.0%
	West-Central	21	355	1.7%
	North African/ Middle East	18	729	3.6%
	Sub-total	59	1,907	9.3%
Oceania	South-Oceania	11	713	3.5%
	Sub-total	11	713	3.5%
Others	Itinerant Missionary		140	0.7%

[2] S. Kang, 'Basic Missionary Training', 29-40.

[3] S. Kang, 'Basic Missionary Training', 29-40.

	Under Care & Furlough		279	1.4%
	Headquarters Staff		823	
	Sub-total		1,242	6.1%
Total		168	20,503	100%

Key Features of Missionary Engagement of Korean Missionaries

Evangelism and Church Planting

According to statistics, 53.3% of Korean missionaries (or 6,589) are involved in church planting. Presently, there are 6,585 churches in existence, due to the efforts of Korean missionaries. Church planting naturally includes evangelism, thereby contributing significantly to the winning of souls.

This is not to deny the importance of church planting; it is not only the preferred work among Korean missionaries, but also Western missionaries, according to historical reports. I have seen quite a number of non-Korean missionaries, including Asian missionaries, who are passionately involved in planting churches. In fact, prior to coming to England, one of our primary works was establishing churches in Northern Luzon in the Philippines, in addition to leadership development and teaching in a graduate school. We witnessed encouraging effects through this work. Below is a short extract of my article regarding church planting that reflects much of our own experiences:

> They laid rather a heavy emphasis on church planting. For various reasons, a church dedication becomes an important opportunity to encourage the local congregation to replicate the efforts. In this special and joyous occasion, the service rightly consists of lively praises, thanksgiving and a long chain of testimonies. However, in the midst of this celebration, we make it a regular habit to challenge the church to open daughter churches in neighboring communities. In fact, our covenant with the congregation is that only through the reproducing work, will our partnership continue. This is our commitment to assist or work with them in developing new churches. Such a covenant frequently serves to motivate them to start a new house church in a nearby village where there is no established Bible-believing church. In fact, some churches, expecting our strong emphasis on reproduction, have already started new works before their church building is dedicated.[4]

[4] Julie Ma, 'Church Planting: Pentecostal Strategy for Mission', in Kay Fountain (ed), *Reflections on Developing Asian Pentecostal Leaders: Essays in Honor of Harold Kohl* (Baguio, Philippines: APTS Press, 2004), 323-55.

However, this mission priority is not without its problems. A heavy emphasis on this ministry, both among sending churches and organizations, as well as missionaries, may be driven, in part, by a too-narrow focus on the theology of the church. First, considering the highly local-congregation oriented ecclesiology of Korean Christianity, this may be in viewed as an aspect of 'church growth' of the sending church. In many cases, church planting is carried out in communities where there have been viable congregations. Sadly, we also witnessed some rural churches in the Philippines, named after the missionary-sending church, where the Korean name is completely meaningless to the congregation. Second, it is also possible that church planting produces a visible sign of a church's missionary accomplishment. Often church dedications become a celebration for the visitors from the sponsoring church, rather than for the congregation. Such an emphasis further reinforces the building-oriented ecclesiology of many Korean Christians.

Theological Education

Many are involved in training national leaders in Bible colleges or seminaries, often by establishing new schools, with only a small number in existing schools. Some of them undertake further studies to qualify for such ministries. This is one of the mission patterns that early Western missionaries did quite successfully in Korea, both in general education and ministry formation. Current reports note that about 1,415 missionaries from 867 denominations, that is, 11.5% of the total missionary force, are involved in this ministry. This is an indication of a generally agreed notion that a good supply of qualified workers is essential in missionary work.[5]

A focus on theological education[6] is not restricted to Korean missionaries, as the presence of numerous Bible schools, in mission fields, proves. As understood, theological training is closely linked to the emphasis on church planting. Also increasing are schools for general education. In many places where quality primary and secondary education is not readily available, this is an important contribution to society and, often, although not intended as the primary goal, such ministry contributes to evangelism and church planting.

---

[5] S. Kang, 'Basic Missionary Training', 29-40.

[6] See 'Theme Three: Mission and Postmodernities', in Daryl Balia and Kirsteen Kim (eds), *Edinburgh 2010: Witnessing to Christ Today* (Oxford: Regnum, 2010), 80. It notes, 'the radical change in the way of thinking and of looking at life represented by postmodernity cannot but influence theological reflection and education. The key question for churches to answer may not be so much 'where can I find a graceful God', but rather 'where do I find an authentic spirituality'? To address this need, it appears that theological education should be conversational rather than authoritarian, focusing more on encouraging students to reflect on their own experiences…'.

Some schools, established by Korean missionaries, have attained recognition by theological associations, but the majority remains struggling to survive. Their effectiveness is often questioned, especially where there had been other similar schools in operation. Lack of cooperation is a significant problem as some schools are staffed mainly by Korean missionaries, even after decades of operation. Running a school requires a lot of detailed work for the administration, and staff management and needs financial security. This work necessitates careful guidance from professional educators and administrators to prevent any hazards.

Social Work

Social work has been relatively less popular among Korean missionaries in the past, but recently has become valued. Perhaps, it is due to a change in mission trends and its influence upon them. Moreover, it is out of necessity, in order to meet the immediate felt-needs of people, who suffer from hunger and sickness. There are 703 Korean missionaries, who are involved in social ministries. This number amounts to 5.3% of the total missionaries. The urgent needs cause them to build hospitals, clinics, orphanages, child-care centres, and retirement homes. Community service also expands to HIV-AIDS ministry, skills training and agricultural development. I have seen dentists and doctors among short term mission groups, who voluntarily offer their services.

In fact, Western missionaries were enthusiastically involved in social work. A case in point is William Carey's work with the Indian government on critical social problems, like stopping the burning of widows on the funeral pyre of their husbands. Another example is drawn from Hudson Taylor, who, being a medical doctor, attempted to seek to do what he could to lessen the suffering of people. Through his influence, the China Inland Mission founded twelve hospitals within the first fifty years of mission work in China.

Others Ministries

There are 1) discipleship (1,845 missionaries or 14.9 %), 2) Bible translation (144 or 1.4%), 3) literature (139 or 1.1%), 4) ministry for missionary children (104 or 0.8%), 5) ministry for foreign workers (83 or 0.7%), 6) broadcasting work (41 or 0.3%), 7) children's ministry and other works (652 or 5.2%). This also includes those who are in the preparative process for missionary deployment (52 or 0.4%).[7]

[7] S. Kang Sungsam, 'Basic Missionary Training', 29-40.

Staff of Mission Agencies

There are 343 or 2.9% who are working in mission agencies. As staff of missionary sending bodies, their contribution to the mission movement is essential, while their accumulated experience becomes an important asset. The numbers of other staff members working together are 1,296. Ministries include publication (96 people, 7.4%), continuing education (55 people, 4.2%), communication with missionaries (80 people, 6.2%), mission administration (229 people, 17.7%), missionary training programme (296 people, 22.8%), handling mission finance (106 people, 8.2%) and others (434 people, 33.5%).[8]

Types of Missionary Work

Mission Works	Number of Missionaries	Percentage
Church planting	6,589	53.3%
Discipleship	1,845	14.9%
Education	1,415	11.5%
Social Work	703	5.6%
Medical Service	248	2.0%
Translation	144	1.1%
Ministry for MK	104	0.8%
Publication	139	1.1%
Visitation	52	0.4%
Broadcasting	41	0.3%
Ministry for Foreign Workers	83	0.7%
Others	652	5.2%
Headquarters Staff	343	2.7%
Total	12,358	100%

Evaluation

Strengths

BUILDING RELATIONSHIP WITH NATIONALS

A relationship between Korean missionaries and local people is surprisingly well-developed according to research work by Sang-cheol Moon.[9] This indicates that they consider building good relationships important as partners in God's kingdom. In fact, this is the foundation for every aspect of mission work because local church leaders are essential co-workers and they have to work

---

[8] S. Kang Sungsam, 'Basic Missionary Training', 29-40.

[9] Moonjang Lee, 'Change of Mission Paradigm', in *Issues of Korean Mission in the 21st Century: Sorak Forum, 1-4 Nov. 2005* (conference compendium, 2005), 14-31.

together. However, some unfortunately have experienced broken relationships and have suffered internally for many years.

Language Learning

They are eager to learn local languages, even if the level of proficiency may not be adequate. Often it is neither conversationally satisfactory, nor up to the level of preaching and evangelizing. However, there are a handful of missionaries who speak local languages almost perfectly. On the other hand, quite a few of them tend to stand back and never get passionate about achieving these critical skills.[10]

Keeping Good Contact with the Sending Body

Maintaining good communication with the sending church or mission agency is one of their strengths. There is a sense of flexibility against a sense of bureaucracy that is often felt from some Western mission organizations. At the same time, this may also indicate instability and lack of organizational strength among many mission organizations and denominational mission boards in Korea. This is attested by the fact that quite a number of missionaries have not secured an adequate level of financial and administrative support from their sending bodies, and it is all left to individual missionaries to maintain direct contact with supporting congregations and individual donors. (This may explain why missionaries are diligent in communication.)

Cultural Adaptation

Those, who come from a mono-cultural setting like Korea, find it difficult to adapt and adjust to a new culture. One can conjecture that their firm commitment to mission enables them to overcome cultural differences and daily challenges. In fact, without going through this process of enculturation, one cannot adequately accomplish God's mission because mission is always performed in the context of a culture. It does not mean that all Korean missionaries have successfully adapted to the recipient culture. It is expected that many have made countless innocent and unintentional mistakes. It is also true that, in spite of enculturation, a deep sense of cultural superiority still remains from the home culture.

[10] See Stephen A. Grunlan and Marvin K. Mayers, *Cultural Anthropology* (Grand Rapids, MI: Zondervan, 1988), 90. It notes that language serves the social group by providing a vital avenue of communication among the members, establishing and perpetuating such institutions. Communication is far more than simple language usage.

Spiritual Life and Prayer

Many of them are firmly committed to prayer,[11] as a hallmark of Korean Christian spirituality. Crucially, this is one of their strengths and a critical element in their missionary achievement. This emphasis is seen both in private and church life. Some missionaries even dare to enter a long-term fasting prayer, for as long as forty days, which in some cases results in a critical health condition. This influences local churches to commit themselves to prayer more seriously. Most congregations established by Korean missionaries have a substantial proportion dedicated to prayer, such as daily dawn prayer meetings. I have seen one mega-church in the Philippines, which established a Prayer Mountain, and its daily programme includes prayer and fasting, as well as Bible studies and worship in the morning and evening. This is almost identical to the Korean Prayer Mountains.

Spirituality

Korea's primary religions are Buddhism and Confucianism. However, the underlying religious force for all has been Shamanism, a Northeast Asian form of animism. History reveals that along the way, the religions were mixed with practices and beliefs of Shamanism and animism. Such a religious background explains the unique spiritual orientation of Korean Christianity. Everyone begins with a keen consciousness of the spiritual world, and this contributes to the spiritual dynamic of Korean Christianity. This also significantly helps Korean missionaries to more effectively engage in the various spiritual issues of people in the mission field.

Weaknesses

Missionary Motivation

Supposedly, a missionary's firm sense of calling[12] and commitment to mission is his/her foundation for missionary life and work. Indeed, there are

[11] See Stephen B. Bevans & Roger P. Schroeder, *Constants in Context: A Theology of Mission for Today* (Maryknoll, NY: Orbis, 2006), 367 on 'Mission as Prophetic Dialogue': '…the life of prayer of anyone can be a truly missionary act, whether a lay person fully engaged in a profession, an ordained minister or religious involved in pastoral or teaching ministry of whatever kind, a retired person with some leisure, or a person suffering or recuperating from an illness.… Prayer of those engaged in the church's work of crossing boundaries, for peoples struggling with injustice and poverty, for fragile communities of faith, for victims of human-caused or natural disasters—this is a valid way of being caught up in the saving and redeeming mission of God in the world'.

[12] See Julie Ma, *When the Spirit Meets the Spirits: Pentecostal Ministry among the Kankana-ey Tribe in the Philippines* by (Frankfurt: Peter Lang, 2000), 74-75. It notes, 'The speaker invited church members who wanted to give their lives for the lost. Her

missionaries who are deeply dedicated to giving their life to the people they have adopted as their own. On the other hand, mission provides a context where daily ministry demands are significantly reduced in comparison with the Korean setting. The daily routine of an average pastor in Korea begins with an early morning prayers, numerous house visitations, and sermon preparations. Many missionaries find their missionary life filled with a sudden 'freedom' and some have abused this, as well as the absence of a supervisory monitoring system. This, in turn, affects their ministries and their relationships with national partners. When a missionary fails to be a model Christian, it is difficult to persuade others to follow Jesus. This leads one to the question of the very motive of their missionary life. Although a call is private in nature, it is important for mission agencies to develop a process to ascertain one's genuine missionary calling.

MONO-CULTURAL ORIENTATION

Normally those who come from a monolithic culture tend to view and evaluate other cultures by the standard of their own. This immediately causes some missionaries to push their values, practices and lifestyle onto the host culture. Although there is a fine line between adopting certain positive elements of the home culture and blindly insisting on it, many congregations, established by Korean missionaries, have adopted some elements of Korean worship.[13] For instance, some churches use a portable bell on the pulpit to signal the beginning of a time for worship. Even Korean Christians do not know where it began, and yet such a practice has been uncritically 'imported' into their mission setting.

However, a more serious challenge is the grave difficulty for the average Korean missionaries to break out of their cultural shell and get out of the comfort zone of their own culture. This is clearly seen in the common practice of Korean missionaries associating with fellow Korean missionaries, regardless of their denominational orientations, while their interaction with other nationals is far less, even if they are from the same denominational tradition. A tendency is that the more they get together, the more they want to be just among themselves. Such a close relationship among themselves frequently causes conflicts, comparisons, and competition, thus, creating another form of a cultural 'missionary compound'.

---

heart was broken as she sensed the presence of God. Vanderbout was one of the first to answer. She almost ran to the altar, put her hands up in a gesture of total surrender and prayed, 'give myself to You! I will do what You ask me to do! I will go where You ask me to go! Oh God'.

[13] See Charles H. Kraft, *Anthropology for Christian Witness* by (Maryknoll, NY: Orbis, 1996), 70-71. It notes, 'Such condemnation stems from the monocultural habit of *always evaluating other people's customs and perspectives in terms of one's own culturally learned assumptions and values (worldview)*'.

Moral laxity

Moral laxity is not a unique problem among Korean missionaries. Lack of a close organizational monitoring system may contribute to this, while a new social and cultural context may make missionaries more vulnerable to temptations. Moral laxity ranges from ministerial attitudes and financial accountability to sexual issues.

This is particularly relevant to Korean missionaries as their traditional ethics are guided by who see you rather than what you do. This 'face' (or 'shame') cultural orientation can 'release' some from cultural 'restrictions' and give them courage to behave badly. Furthermore, the 'shame' culture worsens the situation when an incident occurs, as there is a strong tendency to cover up or quietly resolve the problem, instead of correcting the real issue. This is what a concerned observer of Korean missionaries sternly warned:

> This [sexual incidents among Korean missionaries] is seldom discussed openly among Koreans. The result can be immense ignorance and naivety remaining as well as immorality. Some who come to Europe perceive 'the West' as a playground of immorality and a few have indulged themselves. Not reading social signs accurately has led to immense discomfort among Western women missionaries who have received unwanted attention from Korean men on the team. In some cases this has led to actual sexual assault.[14]

Although it may be true more among short-term missionaries than long-term ones, nonetheless the observation is alarming. This definitely requires all Korean missionaries to be culturally and personally sensitive. Moreover, this calls for a system of accountability both from the sending body and the closely knitted Korean missionary communities. However, more fundamentally, a good dose of cultural learning should be a part of missionary orientation.

Aggressiveness

Koreans in general are focused and dedicated workers. This explains the economic feat of the country in less than a generation from the rubble of the Korean War. Their movement is swift and decision-making is often impulsive. Positively, some attribute Korean leadership in the IT industry to this instinct. However, such aggressive behavior, particularly coupled with poor language and communication skills, can produce gravely negative effects. National partners can perceive Korean missionaries as domineering, insensitive, and even 'imperialistic'. It is with mixed emotions that I heard a comment, 'The first words that national co-workers learn from Koreans are ppali ppali or 'quick, quick'. This, no doubt, contributes to impressive missionary achievements in many places, but this has the potential to undermine the

---

[14] Howard Norrish, 'An Evaluation of the Performance of Korean Missionaries', in *Issues of Korean Mission in the 21st Century*, 132-51.

long-term effects of missionary work, the relationships with national leadership, and more seriously, to engender an obsession for visible accomplishments as the goal of ministry.

The Next Step Forward

Having discussed various spiritual, cultural and contemporary resources as well as shady areas of Korean missionaries, how can their experiences also be a resource for other emerging missionary churches in the Global South, as well as the old (that is, Western) missionary churches? Also, what can the Korean missionary movement learn from the long experiences of the Western churches and appropriate their resources? Then, how does the Korean experience form the shaping of our own missiology? Some responses to these questions are listed below.

Lessons to Learn and to Be Learned

COMMITMENT AND HARD WORK

Although there are a good number of less-than-qualified Korean missionaries who may cause more problems than establishing a viable mission work, it is true that another good number are committed and dedicated to God's work, bearing marvelous fruits. I assume such is generally true regardless of the ethnic origin of a missionary group, including the Western entities. However, one thing I have noticed from the church growth movement in Korea is the sheer dedication of Koreans in general and Korean Christians in particular, and this is expressed not only in their actions but also in their prayer lives. In a way, Koreans are singly goal-oriented against a general cultural assumption that they are relation-oriented. In fact, they are both goal- and relationally oriented.

CULTURAL ADAPTATION

As mentioned previously, those who grew up in a mono-cultural setting find it additionally challenging to adapt to another culture and cultural behavior. Thus, it not only takes more time, but also more effort to adjust to the host culture. At the same time, Korean missionaries, like those emerging from churches from the Global South, have shared cultural traits that can be readily identified in the host cultures, unless they go to the West for their missionary vocation. This proximity is found also in their economic levels, so that the Korean missionaries find it easier to associate with nationals in their own homes and communities with much adjustment, even if there is considerable poverty. The Korean missionaries' experience during the economic difficulties can be another important source of identification with the nationals. They can easily sit with locals and enjoy unfamiliar food offered with less trouble and hesitation, use their primitive toilets, and sleep on the floors offered by local members.

Considering the adjustments that Western missionaries have to make to establish a meaningful relationship through such participations, it is understandable to see how some Korean missionaries have been successful. The same is applied to most non-Western missionaries. Also, an important resource is the divided state of the two Koreas and its continuing tensions. As many mission contexts include racial and religious conflicts, Koreans can empathise more realistically, with those to whom they communicate God's message of reconciliation.

Spiritual Life and Prayer

As a Korean Christian, I am truly grateful for this unique heritage. Korean Christians have learned that prayer is the most powerful resource they have, when they have no one to turn to in personal and national crises. This applies to the harsh period of the Japanese annexation of the country, the fierce Korean War, when Christians were a priority target along with public servants, and the ensuing conflict across the border between the two Koreas. This also applies to personal and family settings during the economic hardships after the war and during the recovery from the devastation. Hardships and struggle reinforced and strengthened the Korean Christians' commitment to a life of prayer. The presence of countless prayer mountains and prayer houses, throughout the country and among immigrant Korean communities, attests to this. It is assumed that most missionaries continue this deep spiritual tradition in their personal and church lives.

Generosity

Korean churches are, by and large, giving churches. Korean culture in general stresses hospitality and generosity as an important virtue. Christian teaching reinforces this cultural trait and, as a result, Korean Christians are known for their sacrificial giving and hospitality. Furthermore, this orientation has also been characteristic of Korean mission. However, this also requires cultural sensitivity and has missionary implications. Dependency[15] has been, from the very beginning of the modern mission, the most pressing practical issue. There are many cases of impulsive giving among Korean Christians. For example, when they are impressed by the Holy Spirit or by the presentation of a need, their inner urge to give is so strong, they just give, only to occasionally regret it later. In spite of related problems, generosity, without a doubt, is an important

[15] See a comment on dependency in Stanley E. Jones, *Christian Maturity* (Nashville, TN: Abingdon, 1957), 211. He notes, '…the relationship of many pioneer missionaries to their converts should go through several stages. At first it is one of *dependency*. The missionary, in fact, has been the parent of the church, and as such bears much of the responsibility for its growth. In time, the new Christians must stand on their own feet and learn *independency*'.

gift of the Korean church. I firmly believe that God blesses generous hearts, and that is what Korean Christianity practices and experiences.

Missiological Implications

Several issues are raised in the form of questions to both the traditional and new missionary-sending churches. First, the very fundamental issue of definition still remains as the most important question in mission: what is mission? Without going into details, the Crusades model of mission seems to have remained consistent in mission forces, past and present. This model also assumes a definition that mission is 'from the have's to the have not's'. In practical terms, the object of the 'haves' is far more than the Christian gospel: economy and civilization frequently precedes the gospel. That is, a missionary from a Christian-rich African nation working in Korea, for example, is not viewed as normal. This imperialistic model of mission is dangerously widespread among the people in the pew, which the new mission churches in the Global South have unfortunately repeated. There is no doubt that such a fundamental problem in turn affects almost every aspect of missionary activities including a hierarchical relationship between the missionary and national workers. The missionaries, partly because of their relatively rich resources and, more importantly, because of a wrong perception of mission itself, forget that they are to be guests to the host culture. If this is a critical issue, then what has motivated the sending bodies and individual missionaries to commit themselves to mission?

Second, what is the level of cultural adaptation that is genuine and desirable for missionaries? Do they feel comfortable with the people and culture of the host country? When they use their hands to eat, do we also use our hands or look for a spoon? Do we always bring toilet paper or bottled water, when we visit mountain villages? And how does one feel about tricky cultural negotiations? More fundamentally, how do we practise an incarnational lifestyle in bringing God's good news, knowing that the messenger is the most important part of his or her message?

Third, are you a good listener to the voice of God and that of newly adopted people? What is a right missionary attitude, one who is there to minister, or also ready to be ministered to? An effective missionary work requires a good two-way communication. A common tendency is to talk rather than to listen. In the same vein, the tendency is teach rather than to be taught. Do we impose our cultural practices and values? That is, does Korean missionary engagement smell of Kimchi? Do they approach the nationals with a Big Brother attitude? It is then critical to closely examine a 'partnership' between a missionary and nationals. Is it based on a mutual respect and appreciation of each other's gifts, resources and commitments, or a patronizing or even a hierarchical relationship? The latter two are not called 'partnership'.

Fourth, in a lived-out setting of our Christian and missionary convictions, what is the guiding principle? Ultimately, what motivates missionaries to leave their familiar environment and move to an unknown place to live among people other than their own? With no hesitation, that is love. Let me cite a South African Pioneer Missionary's Translation of 1 Corinthians 13[16]:

If I have the language perfectly and speak like a native and have not his love,
I am nothing.
If I have diplomas and degrees and know all the up-to-date methods, and have not his touch of understanding love,
I am nothing.
If I am able to argue successfully against the religions of the people and make fools of them and have not his wooing of love,
I am nothing.
If I have all faiths and great ideals and magnificent plans and not his love that sweats and bleeds and weeps and prays and pleads,
I am nothing.
If I give my clothes and money to them and have not love for them,
I am nothing.
If I surrender all prospects, leave home and friends and make the sacrifices of a missionary career and then turn sour and selfish amid the daily annoyances and slights of the missionary life,
then I am nothing.
If I can heal all manner of sickness and disease but wound hearts and hurt feelings for want of his love that is kind,
I am nothing.
If I can write articles and publish books that win applause but fail to transcribe the word of the cross into the language of his love,
I am nothing.

Fifth, what will then make it possible for missionaries from old and new mission churches (e.g., Western and Asian churches) to work together? There are several areas of collaboration, and some of them are: 1) Being together for fellowship, networking and cooperation; 2) Sharing information and experiences, as the older partner comes with a rich deposit of experience, both positive and negative, while the new churches have new dynamics; 3) Bringing each other's needs, especially in mission operation, so that each other's gifts can complement each other, and ultimately the kingdom's work; and 4) Creating spaces and occasions for both mission forces to come together for sharing with and learning from each other's experiences and traditions.

---

[16] Paul G. Hiebert, *Anthropological Insights for Missionaries* (Grand Rapids, MI: Baker Book House), 270.

Conclusion

I have attempted to briefly present Korean mission with its strengths and weaknesses. However, because of its relatively short history, my observations and analysis are tentative. At the same time, the process of deep reflection is essential as the 'mid-course adjustment' should be done sooner rather than later. The list of strengths and weaknesses can continue further. Out of such an evaluative process, I have become deeply aware of God's 'risky' plan to use far-from-perfect people like Koreans and the Korean church. In humility, Korean mission communities, like many newer mission churches, have much to learn from the history of Western Christian missions. Even if Christianity, in general, and the missionary movement, in particular, has consistently decreased in the West, the Western church has much to offer in preparing the new churches for mission. If everyone is honest enough, the sharing of the West's missionary mistakes will be especially useful, so that the new mission churches will not have to repeat them. The emerging missionary churches can assist the weakening West by bringing their spiritual dynamics to its churches. To this end, the immigrant communities in the West have the potential to play a critical role in the re-shaping of global Christianity. With varying sets of gifts, both the West and the 'rest' are called to closely partner for God's mission. We are acutely reminded that mission is not ours but God's, and we are simply his partners.

Although there is a good place in Christian life and mission for military rhetoric, Jesus' incarnational mission is our ultimate model, not the infamous Crusade. Jesus 'won' the adversaries, not through his heavenly power, but through giving himself for others. His power was closely restricted to his love and humility. 'Mission in humility and hope' is a phrase used in a seminal document of *Towards 2010* in the centenary celebration of the Edinburgh Missionary Conference.[17] It is important to note that this is the reflective confession of a missionary leader of the Church of Scotland, which hosted the 1910 conference. If our mission is to conquer the land and bring a victory with our own strengths and strategies, I am afraid we may never stop the unfortunate historical cycle that will haunt the church with its self-crusading and self-glorifying goals.

May our Lord continue to use new missionary churches such as the Korean, as well as the old ones, for his kingdom. Yes, mission belongs neither to the new nor to the old church, neither to the West nor the 'rest'. It is God's. *Missio Dei.*

[17] 'Mission and Postmodernities', in *Edinburgh 2010: Witnessing to Christ Today*, 61-85.

Migrant Workers and 'Reverse Mission' in the West

S. Hun Kim

Introduction

'Receiving mission' and 'reverse mission' are terms that are controversial in the modern mission era, mainly because there are variations on the terminology and their meaning. In this article, after over-viewing the background history on receiving mission, I will review current debates on its definition, whether termed as 'receiving mission', 'reverse mission', or 'mission in reverse'. Further, I will examine what are the implications of 'reverse mission' and some selective illustrations related to this mission trend.

It is my intention that, through the overview of this contemporary issue, there may be a greater awareness of the shift away from a traditional view of mission because of the 'radical dislocation' of God's people that makes them, as a consequence, join together in his 'new work'.

Background History

'Diaspora' has become a critical factor in modern mission. According to Jehu J. Hanciles, 'Since the 1960s in the post-colonial era, migrant movement has been predominantly from areas with weak economic and political systems to the centres of global dominance and advanced industrial growth'.[1] In this migration, Christians and Christian workers have played a significant part. Afe Adogame notes that, 'the reverse-mission agenda is becoming a very popular feature among African churches'.[2] An example is the Tanzanian pastors commissioned in Lutheran parishes in Germany in the early 1980s. This has also been true for Korean Christians, who migrated to North America and Europe after the Korean War, whether spontaneously, through invitation or by forced displacement. As they settled in American and European communities, they began to thrive, which impacted local churches in their regions. According

[1] J. Hanciles, 'Migration and Mission: The Religious Significance of the North-South Divide', in A. Walls and C. Darton Ross (eds), *Mission in the 21st Century* (London: Longman and Todd, 2008), 123.

[2] A. Adogame, 'The Rhetoric of Reverse Mission: African Christianity and the Changing Dynamics of Religious Expansion in Europe' (Lecture presented at the Conference, 'South moving North: revised mission and its implications', Protestant Landelijk Dienstencentrum, Utrecht, September 2007).

to statistics, estimates record more than 4500 Korean churches in North America and Europe at present.[3] This 'reverse mission' has turned the 'West (into) a site of new religious interactions which portend long-term transformations of Western societies'.[4]

Echoing the religious implications asserted by Hanciles, one notes the affirmative movements related to 'reverse mission' launched in Western churches. For example, the Mission in Western Culture Project[5] (MiWCP) noted that Western society had turned into a mission field. And in 1996, the United Evangelical Mission (UEM)[6] conducted a programme for the cooperation of German and immigrant congregations, in order to 'help German churches to understand and appreciate the movement of reverse mission'.[7] Recently, many institutional churches, such as the Anglican, Lutheran or United Reformed Churches in Europe, have made great efforts to establish relevant policies related to 'reverse mission' with their counterparts in the non-Western world. Examples of this amongst Korean churches will be articulated in a separate section below.

Indeed, reverse mission, in the 20th century, is part and parcel of the transfer of initiatives in mission to the non-Western world as non-Western churches are at the forefront of missionary work around the world. In turn, the contribution to reverse mission is a result of incidental mission by non-Western missionaries and ministers or migrant lay people through their diaspora networks.

The Issue of Definition

Certainly, the term "receiving mission" is rhetoric from a Western point of view. Accordingly, the idea, 'foster(s)…welcome of non-European mission workers into Europe to join with us in our mandate to evangelistic vision'.[8] Furthermore, the term 'receiving mission', has become synonymous with 'reverse mission', and refers not simply to 'mission in reverse', but to its

---

[3] Refer to www.kreanchurchyp.com. The total numbers of Korean churches worldwide are 5174 in 2009.

[4] Hanciles, 'Migration and Mission', 127.

[5] The Mission in Western Culture Project is a global initiative to address the question of a missional engagement in Western culture from the perspective of the local church, in order to understand the critical issues facing leadership development, discipleship, formation and witness in modern Western culture.

[6] UEM was formerly the joint mission board of six German mainline churches (Landeskirchen) and the von Bodelschwingh Institutions Bethel. It was restructured to become a communion of 33 churches in three continents engaged in a common mission.

[7] (UEM, 2000)

[8] European Evangelical Missionary Alliance, 'Receiving Mission Workers to Europe: What Every Church Should Know' (www.europeanema.org on July 2009), accessed: July, 2009.

nature, which is 'multi-lateral rather than unilateral'.[9] Reverse mission is when non-Western churches return with the gospel to societies that initially brought the gospel to them. This flows from a true sense of debt for the gospel and for the purpose of building a capacity for working in world mission together.

It has been my observation that, while receiving mission has been received by Western societies, the phenomena, of 'reverse mission' is spontaneous amongst Christians in the non-Western world, whether from Africa, Asia, or Latin America. There remains, however, a gap between Western and the non-Western points of view regarding 'receiving mission': while Western churches see reverse mission producing a greater efficiency through partnership in their mission, Non-Western missionaries view 'receiving mission' or 'reverse mission' as the mandate to bring the gospel to the whole world including Western society.

Grace Davie notes, 'how "mission in reverse" turns the traditional relationship between Africa and Europe on its head', though she admits that 'this has not happened yet'.[10] C.M. Barbour holds the view that, 'mission-in-reverse' is not teaching but learning from people previously ministered to.[11] Accordingly, 'a reverse mission approach…instead of teaching, preaching, and trying to convert others, emphasizes learning, consciousness-raising, and advocating for changes…'.[12]

One notes that, in the diverging perspectives above, 'receiving mission' can only be understood in the light of differing missional perspectives and contexts.

Implications for 'Reverse Mission'

The reverse wave of migration and the waning of Christianity in Western society have had far-reaching social, political, human and Christian historical significance. Just as in Scripture, God's radical dislocation of his people had significant global missional implications, so also the missionary influx of Christian migrants into Western society.[13]

First, the new Christian immigrants and their descendants come from the centre of vibrant Christian growth and embody a brand of Christianity that is strongly evangelistic or conversionist. Many, from outside the West, see

---

[9] Adogame, 'The Rhetoric of Reverse Mission'.

[10] G. Davie, *Europe, the Exceptional Case: Parameters for Faith in the Modern World* (London: Darton, Longman and Todd, 2002), 110. Recited from R. Catto, 'Non-Western Christian missionaries in England: Has mission been reversed?' in *Mission and Migration.*

[11] C.M. Barbour, 'Seeking Justice and Shalom in the City', *International Review of Mission* 73 (1984), 303-309.

[12] The quotation is excerpted from http://isw.sagepub.com/content/abstract/.

[13] For more information, see Hanciles and Adogame.

themselves as 'missionaries' as their growth and witness serve as a stark contrast to declining Western churches.

Second, the new immigrant congregations are more attuned to religious plurality than their Western counterparts. This enhances their missionary capacity to maintain effective Christian witness in the face of religious pluralism.

Third, this, in turn, has led to a changing definition of traditional mission in terms of what constitutes the 'mission field' as mission bases are established to re-evangelize the secularized societies of Europe and North America.

Fourth, global migration serves missionary mobilization and the call for structural reform of the Church to grapple with the challenges of migration.

Fifth, reverse missions bring a major shift in mission understanding, and provide greater sensibility to and appreciation of the multi-cultural nature of Christianity in the twenty-first century.

Sixth, the reverse trend in missions offers the 'old heartlands' of Christianity a model for renewal.

Illustrations Related to 'Reverse Mission'

In terms of 'reverse mission', three illustrations illuminate the relationship between Western and non-Western churches in Europe. First, the case of the European Evangelical Missionary Alliance (EEMA) illustrates how Western churches can prepare themselves to receive non-Western Christians. Second, the Korean churches in Europe and make their impact on local churches in their regions through local partnership. Finally, ethnic churches that fulfil the mandate of the gospel among diaspora groups in Europe are in close cooperation with local churches.

The Case of EEMA

I have observed that there are two opposite attitudes on migrant churches held by local churches in Europe: a reluctant attitude or a cooperative attitude. In many cases a healthy relationship is not established between local churches and migrant churches because state churches lack a policy regarding migrant churches.

In contrast, EEMA introduced the guide-lines, 'Receiving Mission Workers to Europe: What Every Church Should Know'[14] to improve the situation. This proactive approach engaged migrant Christian workers in Europe through:

1) Collecting background information on their sending country, national culture, church culture, theology of mission/evangelism, family; expectation, ministry gifts, financial support etc.

[14] EEMA, 'Receiving Mission Workers to Europe: What Every Church Should Know' (www.welcomeproject.net).

2) Asking useful questions about their origin, church experience, expectations of the sending churches, financial provision, and who had cross-cultural experience in their church etc.

3) Supporting mission workers in transition, cultural mentors, family support, fellowship, links to home churches, partnership in ministry, and bureaucratic support.

4) Responding to culture shock by addressing issues of culture, culture shock, cultural transition, the implications of culture shock, coping with transition and financial advice.

5) Preparing the mission workers for a return to their homeland by saying goodbye, processing the experience, preparing children, realistic expectations and links to their home church.

Along with these measures proposed by EEMA, the European Evangelical Alliance (EEA) also formulated a call for awareness of cultural diversity and a warm welcome for 'the foreigner in our midst as well as addressing hopes and fears for Europe.[15]

Korean Churches in Europe

In the 1970s, immigration into Europe from the former colonies accelerated. A significant amount of these immigrants were Christians. They planted ethnic migrant churches in Europe and have become a driving force of revival among local churches.

Korean churches were planted in Germany and the UK in the early 1970s, for the first time. Since then, they have multiplied to around 200 churches in major cities in Germany, the UK, and France.

Historically, migrant churches begin as mono-ethnic congregations and gradually become multi-ethnic churches. This progress has allowed Korean migrant churches to contribute to mission in Europe as partners with local churches.

One of the outstanding examples is the Korean church partnership with the International Presbyterian Church (IPC) in the UK in the 1980s. The two now comprise two Presbyteries (groups of churches): the IPC First European Presbytery and the Korean Presbytery. The Korean Presbytery is made up of six Korean-speaking churches in Ealing, Kingston-upon-Thames, Reading, Kings Cross and Oxford. Each June, the European and Korean Presbyteries meet together for a Synod. Because of their strong bond, the European Presbytery has been supported by the Korean Presbytery in the UK as well as in Korea.

Though not aimed at Korean churches alone, a partnership between German and immigrant congregations was developed by the United Evangelical Mission (UEM) in Germany in 1998. Seventeen Korean churches in North

[15] The article was excerpted from EEA's Authorization Team in Spring, 2007 on www.europeanea.org.

Rhein-Westphalia province were made members in 2008. Through this official relationship, Korean churches are making many positive contributions to local partner churches both financially and spiritually. Korean churches in Germany are a model for how ethnic/migrant churches can progress from locally dependent communities into self-sufficient and self-generative Christian churches by fervent worship, prayer, fellowship and theological education.

Expansion of Diaspora Ministry among Ethnic Groups

Migrant churches can be a place for incubating other ethnic churches in the diaspora environment. For example, one of the largest Korean churches in London, with a congregation of 500 members, is facilitating the birth of other Asian ethnic churches. They believe that they have been given a mandate for church planting, fervent intercession and the financial means necessary to carry out mission. The translation of the New Testament into Azeri was a result of assistance from Azeri diaspora Christians in Europe through the support of Korean churches and a local Baptist church in London.[16]

These sorts of partnerships provide opportunities for European churches and mission organizations to get involved in world mission in their own backyard, when mutual understanding on the significance of missional migration in Europe exists between Western churches and migrant churches.[17] Indeed, this invisible and incidental mission movement was driven by migrant workers this century. They are living examples of what Samuel Escobar calls, 'another missionary force' or the 'missionary from below'.

Conclusion

So far, I have discussed the current issues related to 'reverse mission' back to Western society by non-Western Christian workers. In this discussion, I attempted to magnify the significance of missional migration to Europe by 'people on the move' with various motivations. Also, I tried to articulate the multi-lateral issues around its definitions and illustrate some examples. But due to the vast nature of the recent debate on 'reverse mission', I noticed that it could not accommodate all the issues with satisfaction. However, briefly, I would like to list the following issues as the residue for further discussion:

---

[16] The Bible translation for Southern Azerbaijani in Iran began in 1991 and completed in 2003, with the publication of the New Testament in June, 2009. Now the translation of the Old Testament is in progress in partnership with many constituents in London.

[17] If we need to deal with issues of partnership between South and North particularly in the context of Europe, please refer to Kang-San Tan, 'Who Is in the Driver's Seat? A critique of mission partnership models between Western missions and East Asian mission movements' (Excerpt from www.redcliffe.org/encounters).

1) What is the relationship between Western churches/organizations and migrant churches in terms of power? Does this represent an incarnational partnership?

2) The issue of control and mission in terms of finance and authority in the Western nations, as compared to the Global South with less power, less authority and less money.

3) Who is the key driver in 'reverse mission', the migrant worker/church or local church?

4) In what ways are ethno-centrism and neo-colonialism obstacles for reverse mission?

Thus, to quote Catto, 'So, even though I do not see mission as having been reversed as yet…the notion of "reverse mission" is not completely invalidated: it captures an observable and growing trend'.[18]

Then ultimately we need to continue to probe the following question: how do we (both Western churches and migrant churches) understand 'reverse mission', if it is God's new paradigm for world evangelization, as well as the revival of Western society by 'people on the move (diaspora)' for the next mission century?

[18] Catto, 'Non-Western Christian Missionaries in England', 177.

Korean Evangelicals' Responses to Muslim Neighbours

Matthew Keung-Chul Jeong

There are an estimated seven million Koreans in the worldwide diaspora today. They live alongside many other national communities, including the Muslim community. According to a Korean government source, (the Ministry of Justice), there are also about 110,000 Muslims in South Korea in 2007. The population of Muslims in Korea is expected to increase in the future.

The purpose of this paper is to offer recommendations concerning Korean Evangelicals' (hereafter KEs) responses to their Muslim neighbours, in partnership with the global church, especially from a non-Western perspective. I hope that this paper will maximize the contribution of Korean Diaspora Evangelicals, serving in about 5,000 Diaspora Korean Churches around the world and KEs in Korea, fulfilling God's mission to their Muslim neighbours.

It is essential to view the issue through a biblical lens, and learn from history. Only then can a meaningful set of suggestions be made as appropriate responses from Korean Evangelicals to Muslims abroad and in Korea.

Biblical Lens

In order to chart a new approach, and a meaningful relationship, for Korean Evangelicals with Muslims, Koreans must develop a biblical re-interpretation of the Old and New Testaments and the Qur'an. It is important for Korean Evangelicals to discuss amongst themselves these new opportunities and challenges, so they may have biblical and constructive ways in responding to their Muslim neighbours.

The first is to discern whether or not their current fears of Muslims and Islam are legitimate. Twelve representatives of Israel were sent out to explore the location and people in the land of Canaan. Their reports are found in Num. 13:1-33, 14:1-38, and Deu. 1:19-33. Out of these, ten leaders were afraid of the Canaanites but two were not. Is it legitimate for some Korean Evangelicals to take a confrontational response to the new presence of Muslims through fear?

The second is to examine whether their perspective about Muslims comes from themselves, on a personal level, or from God (Jer. 23:16-32). God spoke to Jeremiah to ask the prophets whether they 'stood in the council of the Lord' (Jer. 23:18), and whether they received 'the visions and messages which the Lord gave to them', or whether they 'ran with their messages though God did not speak to them with the same message', (Jer. 23:21). So, have Korean

Evangelicals 'stood in the council of the Lord' (Jer. 23:18), regarding the Muslims 'with the visions and messages which the Lord has given to them?' Or, are they are running with their own thoughts about Muslims and Islam?

The third is to have an open and constructive discussion amongst the Korean Evangelical leadership about how to approach Muslims. In Acts 15, the leaders in Jerusalem discussed and debated what God had done in the midst of the Gentiles and decided what the Lord wanted them to do. (Acts 15:1-33) Are Korean Evangelical leaders ready to discuss seriously amongst themselves what is going on between Muslims and Christians and decide what God wants them to do?

Here are a few biblical examples for Korean Evangelicals to explore as ways to learn about Muslims and Islam.

1) Abraham knew very well the religions of his time.

2) Moses spent forty years in an Egyptian palace, and forty years in the wilderness, where he learned the languages, traditions and politics of Egypt and his community (Ex. 1-4).

3) When Peter became more mature, he changed his attitude from speaking to listening (1 Pet. 3:15), and enduring suffering (1 Pet. 2:18-25; 3:14). His earnest appeal was to pray for us to love each other deeply and offer hospitality to one another (1 Pet. 4:7-9).

4) Paul knew three languages in his contemporary world, Greek, Hebrew and Aramaic. He was a Jew with Roman citizenship, who had tent-making skills (Acts 18:1-3; 22:25-28). He was of the tribe of Israel, of the tribe of Benjamin, a Hebrew of Hebrews, and in regard to the law, a Pharisee (Phil. 3:5-6). He was thoroughly trained in the law of the Jewish fathers under Gamaliel and was just as zealous for God as any of the Jews (Acts 22:3).

5) In Luke 2:46-47, we see Jesus at the age of twelve, before starting his ministry, sitting among the teachers, listening to them, asking them questions, understanding the issues of the theological schools in his time, and answering them. It is critically important for Korean Evangelicals to perform this kind of exercise before taking any action or giving any response to Muslims that would be a false witness.

Korean Evangelicals must be challenged and encouraged to look at the following questions from the biblical perspective in the light of the examples mentioned above:

1) How can you fairly treat your Muslims neighbours and their leaders today, just as Jesus treated the ordinary Jews and their leaders in his time?

2) How do you deal with the characteristic of Islam that is anti-Christ (1 John 2:22-23; 4:1-3), in comparison with other religions, which deny Jesus as the Son of God, just as Islam does? Does only Islam deny Jesus' Sonship of God as Messiah? And what is the right attitude towards those who are anti-Christ (1 John 4:4-21)?

3) Have you ever appreciated Muslim festivals and prayers?

It is astonishing to know how often God commanded Israel to 'Love your strangers', in connection with their relationship toward their neighbours. It is known that the command to 'love your strangers' appears more often than simply 'love your neighbours' (e.g., Ex. 22:21; 23:9, Lev. 19:10, 33, 34).

When the people of faith in Israel were a minority as monotheists in the midst of a majority of people of other religions, how did they act? What was the response of Abraham and his family, Isaac, Jacob and the people of Israel towards the majority of the people of other religions around them?

On the other hand, how could Ruth (a Moabite) and Rahab (a prostitute in Josh. 2:1-24) as pagan women live among the majority in believing communities and become ancestors of Jesus (Mat. 1:5)? Job from the land of Uz, with no connection to Israel, was known as a man who feared God and shunned evil (Job 1:1-8). The Recabites (Jer. 35:12-19) were accepted by God and became priests to serve God before the Israelites. Even though they were pagans, they obeyed their father's (Jonadab, son of Recab) commandments and his instructions, for example, not to drink wine, and to obey faithfully.

Historical Lens

A historical study of encounters and clashes between Muslims and Christians for the last fourteen centuries will definitely shed an important light on Korean responses to Muslims.[1] However, this section will only list lessons we can learn from the history of encounters.

The first is the importance of the imitation of Christ. Muslims highly respected godly men, who reflected the character of Jesus Christ in their lives as imitators of Jesus. These men of God were very different from Muslim leaders in character and attitude toward their fellow human beings. These men of God had an important impact upon the people, whom they served.

The second is 'discipleship' as demonstrated by Christians holistically. Discipleship, that is relevant to Muslims through the genuine 'friendship,' in holistic ways, is very much needed today.

The third is the need to learn the local languages, as well as Qur'anic Arabic. All of the great missionaries in the Muslim world learned the local languages. Even Charles de Foucauld (1858-1916), a French monk and missionary in North Africa, especially in Algeria, learned Arabic and Hebrew.[2] He became an authority on their history and collected and transcribed their proverbs, poetry, and traditional folklore.[3] I believe that while most Diaspora Koreans have

---

[1] We can learn a great deal in this area from Jean-Marie Gaudeul, *Encounters and Clashes: Islam and Christianity in History*, vols. 1 and 2 (Rome: Pontificio Istituto di Studi Arabi e Islamici, 1990), and from Hugh Goddard, *A History of Christian-Muslim Relations* (Edinburgh, UK: Edinburgh University Press, 2000).

[2] Merad, *Christian Hermit in an Islamic World*, 48.

[3] Merad, *Christian Hermit in an Islamic World*, 6.

learned the local languages well where they live, they may not have learned Arabic. So, some of them need to learn Qur'anic Arabic to understand Islam.

The fourth is global cooperation and partnership. My survey (2002-2009) shows that both Westerners and nationals have had their most positive experiences with Koreans in terms of the sacrificial dedication of the Koreans.[4] One clear indication is that the first three 'positive experiences' – dedication/ commitment, prayer, and zeal (enthusiasm or passion) for evangelism – are strongly related to each other in terms of ministry. Westerners and nationals have given the highest marks to Koreans in these categories.[5]

'A Common Word between Us and You'[6]

On 11 October 2007, a large group of 138 Muslim scholars, clerics, and intellectuals sent an open letter entitled, 'A Common Word between Us and You to Pope Benedict and the Leaders of Other Christian Denominations':

> …in obedience to the Holy Qur'an, we as Muslims invite Christians to come together with us on the basis of what is common to us, which is also what is most essential to our faith and practice: the Two Commandments of love.

This Common Word document has received many responses from individuals and institutions. The most highly-publicised response was written by a group of four academics from Yale University, entitled *Loving God and Neighbours Together* and has been endorsed by over 300 Christian leaders from around the world. This document accepts the basic propositions of the Common Word and, in places, goes beyond them. The Yale Response attributes the title 'Prophet' to Mohammed and explicitly apologises for the Crusades – neither of which was called for in the original wording of the Common Word.[7]

How can Korean Evangelicals find positive ways to respond to 'A Common Word between Us and You'? In new and biblical ways, Korean Evangelicals should make contributions to this invitation, not for doctrinal debate, but for world peace. These are diplomatic and political suggestions for the common good between the peoples of the two religions in conflict, as they consist of more than half of the world's population.

---

[4] Matthew Keung-Chul Jeong, *Toward Best Practice Concerning Partnership between Koreans and Other Nationalities: A Model for Interserve* (Pasadena, CA: Fuller Theological Seminary, 2009), 87; my dissertation for the Doctor of Ministry at Fuller Theological Seminary.

[5] Jeong, *Toward Best Practice,* 87.

[6] For the full contents, please see http://www.acommonword.com/index.] php?lang=en&page=option1, accessed on 20 December 2009.

[7] Sam Solomon and Al-Maqdisi, *The Truth about 'A Common Word'* (2008) 11-12.

Korean Evangelicals

Before we consider a Korean Evangelicals' response to Muslims, it is firstly worth noting the important role of Korean Evangelicals in the 21st century. Secondly, current problems and strengths that the Koreans have today in relation to this topic need to be examined. Then, finally, I will make some recommendations to Korean Evangelicals about how Koreans can and should respond to the challenges of their Muslim neighbours.

With the emergence of globalization and a new age of mission, the ways in which Korean Evangelicals have been doing things must change.[8] Korean missiology to Muslims has been influenced by various Western schools, especially the Americans. Now is the time, before it is too late, for Korean Evangelical leaders, in particular, to think about and to radically and appropriately change their missiological and theological framework that has been adopted from the West. They must bring new insights from their reviews and reflections on God's Word, as well as what Korean missions have done and where they have gone wrong in the field, in terms of serving Muslims.

The Korean government and Korean Christians do not have a negative history or negative relationships with Muslims or Muslim countries so far.[9] Some Muslim countries have some suspicions and reservations about Koreans in political-diplomatic areas because Korea has been an ally of the USA and the UK, and Israel, but the Muslim countries do not yet view Korea as a Christian country.

Therefore, this current period is a pivotal and historical 'kairos' for Koreans to play vital roles in relationships with Muslims around the world. In God's mercy, Koreans can and should begin to develop new relationships with Muslims, from a tabula rasa, as reconcilers in the triangular relationship between Muslims, the East, and the West, avoiding the same mistakes that 'Muslims and the West' have already made for the past fourteen centuries.

To develop a new history, a new relationship, and a new role for Koreans with Muslims, and to reconcile everyone involved, from non-Western perspectives, we need to examine some issues and strengths in Korea.

Issues, which Korean evangelicals face, regarding their response to the Muslim presence, include the following:

Firstly, the theological issues, which include a pre-millennium approach to Muslims, and Evangelical Christians' Zionism, giving favor to Israel against Palestine (Muslims), allying with the USA, and an eschatology centred around the Euphrates and the Tigris rivers in Iraq, a Muslim country.

Secondly, the missiological problems, which include Koreans' ethnocentricity, Kim-Chi missiology with the Korean national flag and denominationalism, ignorance about the Qur'an and Islamic concepts, and

---

[8] Stephen B. Bevans and Roger P. Schroeder, *Constants in Context: A Theology of Mission for Today* (Maryknoll, NY: Orbis, 2000), 397.

[9] Merad, *Christian Hermit in an Islamic World*, 93.

providing the wrong information about Islam and Muslims through secondary and one-sided sources, rather than authentic, balanced and objective ones from the open and friendly discussion between Muslim-Christian scholars.

Thirdly, the Koreans' fear of Islam stops Muslims from hearing the Good News of Jesus. Korean Evangelicals are losing golden opportunities to share Jesus with their Muslim neighbours on their doorsteps. Out of fear, they just do not meet their Muslim neighbours!

Nevertheless, the writer's research (2002-2009) shows Korean Christians have many advantages with regard to mission. These are listed below, according to the order of the strongest:[10] 1) Sacrificial commitment to mission; 2) Prayer life; 3) Zeal for evangelism, church planting, and discipling ministry; 4) Friendliness; 5) Hospitality; 6) Respect for authority; 7) Koreans' relational and community-based nature, not Korean ethnicity or Koreans sticking to themselves; 8) Cultural affinity to Muslim people and countries as Asians; and 9) No historical attachment of Koreans with the Crusades and the colonialism of the West.

These strengths are very relevant and important in their new roles to their Muslims and need to be maximized.

Korean Evangelicals' Responses to Muslims Abroad and in Korea

How should Koreans abroad respond to Muslims? Historically, there has been a spectrum of responses to the challenges of Islam, such as a 'polemic response' on the one hand, and a 'liberal and universal response' on the other hand. In the middle, there has been a way of 'promoting faithful witness to the gospel and constructive engagement with Muslims for peaceful co-existence'.[11] Korean Evangelicals should take the last option as a 'Faithful Response to Muslims' or 'engaged orthodoxy'.

In general, most Korean churches are considered as conservative evangelicals. So, the Korean Evangelicals' approach to Muslims has been an ironic one. But in the last five years, a polemical approach has been introduced into the Korean church, and has had a negative impact on Korean Evangelicals. Opinions about what Islam is and who Muslims are (enemies, terrorists, or friends) have been divided.

In fact, the theology and missiology of Korean leaders in Korea, in connection with Muslims, have influenced Diaspora Korean Evangelicals abroad and are still influencing them. So, generally, it is well understood that they are more conservative than Korean Evangelicals in Korea, having made less changes in their theology and missiology because they have been influenced by and learnt from Western theological schools, and have emigrated

[10] Jeong, *Toward Best Practice*, 86-90.

[11] "Programme for Christian-Muslim Relations in Africa," 50th Anniversary Celebrations Programme, 19-24 November 2009, 13.

to a new country and kept within a Korean (Kim-Chi) ghetto society. However, the theology and missiology of one and half (1.5), and second Diaspora Korean generations, who have known the culture and language of the country well, where they were born and educated, are much better and hopeful towards their Muslim neighbours. So, these young Diaspora Christians firstly need to be encouraged to have new perspectives on their Muslim neighbours, whereas the first generation of Diaspora Korean Evangelicals need to be re-educated and changed by non-Western perspectives.

With a basic understanding of the background of Muslims, gained through the basic survey in the previous section, I want to discuss how Korean Evangelicals can learn from the West, and then make two recommendations: firstly, inter-relations with Muslims (between Koreans and Muslims), and secondly, intra-relations amongst Koreans.

Lessons to Learn from the Western Experience

We acknowledge the fact that there are a number of limitations because of the differences between Korea and the Western countries in history, culture, and socio-political background, such as colonial Christendom in Britain, for example, when Korean Evangelicals try to apply in their own context what they should (not) learn from the West.

What Korean evangelicals should *not* learn from Western responses to Muslims:

1) Western (British, for example) colonial history and attitudes;

2) Selling church buildings to Muslims and restaurants and pubs especially, or guest houses or houses for games;

3) Losing the evangelistic zeal to reach out to Muslims, as in Britain today.

When the first Muslims immigrants came to Britain in the 1960s, British churches should have proclaimed 'Firm Friendship and Faithful Witness' to their Muslim neighbours, but they this lost golden opportunity. If the first priority of local churches' had been for 'mission' rather than for 'maintaining a worshipping Christian presence', the present situation in the Church of England would have been better, as the report of 'Presence and Engagement' of the Church of England in 2005 has clearly indicated.[12]

4) Accepting the fallibility of the Bible, from German liberal theological schools, weakened their evangelical theological foundations.

On the other hand, there are lessons to be learned from the West:

1) Openness toward Muslims and Islam in a multi-cultural environment for greater integration;

2) Open discussions in intellectual and academic circles, as well as ordinary debates;

---

[12] Mission and Public Affairs Council, '"Presence and Engagement": The Churches' Task in a Multi Faith Society' (London: General Synod of the Church of England, 2005), 74.

3) Meetings with Muslim leaders in politics and with scholars in educational institutions;

4) Humane attitudes in treating Muslims;

5) United efforts among different Christian leaders, from different theological backgrounds, to tackle issues of concern to their Muslim neighbours;

7) Genuine efforts to care for their Muslim neighbours in need;

8) Efforts made to know Muslims and Islam both academically and practically;

9) Efforts made against terrorism in conjunction with government authorities;

10) Huge resources and materials and books written in these fields in the West (for example, Britain as well as in Europe) can and should be used by Koreans. These historical treasures accumulated over fourteen centuries are very useful and helpful resources for current intellectual scholarship and debates and for practical purposes, and Koreans can and should make unique contributions to the Koreans and their Muslim friends, and the West in general, after they study some of the relevant materials.

Inter-relations with Muslims or 'between Muslims and Koreans'

Inter-relations with Muslims or 'between Muslims and Koreans' refer to Korean Evangelicals' responses to Muslims in Korea and abroad. Korean Evangelical Christians must care in the workplace for Muslims, who have been injured or discriminated against in their jobs by Koreans or other nationalities abroad. This is important because Muslims, in general, work in 3D situations (difficult, dangerous and dirty work).

Firstly, Korean Christians, and, moreover, Christian leaders, must reflect the image of Jesus and treat their Muslim neighbours as genuine friends. Islam admires this kind of friendship highly (Q 5:82) as 'the nearest friend'.[13]

To be a friend is to know and to care about what truly matters to the other person. 'Greater love has no one than this, that he lay down his life for his friends' (John 15:13-14). Deuteronomy 10:12-22 and Luke 10:25-37 clearly show the very nature of God and the purpose of God's people by loving strangers. Most of the Muslims abroad today need a true friend because they are threatened and lonely. It is common sense to look after any human being in need, regardless of whether we are Christians or not. In this case, as people of hospitality and friendship, from an eastern culture and tradition, (non-Western perspective), Koreans can make true friendships with their Muslim neighbours, by their care and support.

Secondly, for conversations or dialogue between Muslim leaders and Christian leaders, open space and forums need to be created, so that both

[13] Merad, *Christian Hermit in an Islamic World*, 41, 84.

leaders and Korean Christians and Muslims, in general, can seek to live in peace and harmony, by understanding the similarities and differences between the two religions. They can support each other in freedom of religion and freedom of conscience and speech, clarifying how much freedom needs to be given and the kind of boundaries.

So, we need to have clear criteria for genuine and biblical dialogue to avoid the two extreme models – one that is too compromising and the other that is too narrow in their own views. Both leaders should not compromise on their own doctrines, but respect the people and religion of the other faith. KEs can do this well because they are relational and people-oriented and this culture needs to be encouraged, such as listening and talking to Muslims, by drinking a cup of tea together.

Thirdly, we need to stand together against potential terrorist activities and Muslim crimes. Romans 13:1-5 shows the role of government against evil. Regardless of religion, all governments and civil authorities must take their responsibilities seriously with respect to the criminal actions of terrorists or global Muslim radicals.

It is a very challenging issue for governments to make proper policies to prevent Muslim terrorist activities, without a pre-judgmental attitude towards Muslims, as we have seen in Britain and the USA today. If KEs collaborate with their government authorities wherever they live, they can reduce radical Muslim crimes in advance, by making sincere friendships and relationships.

Fourthly, we need to share the salvation message with Muslims. The Korean church has had tremendous blessings from the Lord and has experienced a world mission for the last thirty years. We have learned and identified some Korean strengths and weaknesses through recent evaluations. Now, it is time for the Korean church to lead her people around the world into a new direction to 'boldly share the Good News with Muslims'.[14]

Maximizing Korean strengths like sacrifice, prayer, community, holistic discipleship, and minimizing Korean weaknesses like cross-cultural communication skills, personality clashes, due to immaturity, and so on,[15] they should share the Good News with Muslims in a 'bold humility'.[16] Korean Evangelicals should not lose the golden opportunity to share the Good News of Jesus with their Muslim neighbours on their doorsteps because of the excuse of Islamphobia from 9/11 in New York and 7/7 in London.

Korean Evangelicals also need to be aware of Islamic Da'wah (mission). When both peoples from the major religions try to convert people to their own

---

[14] *The Moslem World,* vol. 28 (Hartford, CT: The Moslem World, 1938), 'with all boldness', no. 2 (April 1938), 109-113.

[15] Jeong, *Toward Best Practice*.

[16] Bevans & Schroeder, *Constants in Context*, 348; David J. Bosch, *Transforming Mission: Paradigm Shift in Theology of Mission* (Maryknoll, NY: Orbis Books, 1991), 489.

religion, there is a clash between the two religions, socially and politically. So, Britain has made an important statement for mutual agreement on mission between Muslims and Christians in the '10 Guidelines for Ethical Witness'. Koreans should learn the important lessons from this publication.[17]

Intra-relations amongst Korean themselves: Practicalities

I would like to recommend the following to Korean Evangelicals to faithfully help them in intra-relations with one another:

Firstly, we need prayer and fasting, relying on the work of the Holy Spirit. We must pray earnestly to God together just as Christians in the first century in sharing the Gospel with Jews and non-Jews, through the four Ws (words, wonders, works, and weaknesses) in holistic ways, relying on the Holy Spirit. Prayer movements for Muslim neighbours should be organized wherever Koreans live for this strategically important ministry.

Secondly, we need to work together in partnership as Korean Evangelicals: Korean Evangelicals must be united for this ministry in evangelical teams in Korea and abroad.

Thirdly, we need to know the whole gospel: there is an urgent need to help the Korean Church everywhere understand the meaning of the whole gospel for a holistic ministry with kingdom values, not just a soul-saving gospel or a prosperity gospel. Koreans need a serious review of the biblical gospel message and repentance within themselves to meet the cultural needs of Muslims.

Fourthly, a holistic discipleship is needed by a review of what holistic Christian discipleship really means for Muslims through the examples (the life and stories) of Francis of Assisi, Charles de Foucauld, Temple Gairdner, Thomas Valpy French, etc. These provide good role models for Koreans in the relationships between Muslims and Christians. In the light of understanding the whole gospel, KEs need to engage with poverty, global warming, environmental issues, community development, and human rights in Muslim communities, in more holistic ways, not just for church-planting.

Fifthly, we need to be community-oriented for reconciliation. Muslims have a community culture, 'Umma' and Koreans have a 'We' culture too, which they have lost at the expense of economic development and modernization. Though Korea is becoming more of an 'I' culture, it is not too late for KEs to restore the losing culture, ('we' culture), for relationships with their Muslim neighbours. This is a powerful and relevant perspective and a non-Western one toward Muslims in the dehumanizing world of today. This requires a long- term investment through a lifelong commitment, not through short-term gain. Through this relationship, two religious peoples need to be reconciled with

[17] See http://www.christianmuslimforum.org/downloads/Ethical_Guidelines_for_Witness.pdf for the full details about it.

each other and to God. The issue of a persecuted church in Muslim countries must be dealt with accordingly.

Sixthly, we need a centre for mutual research and publication, for clarity and genuine dialogue and to learn from one another. Through this centre, consultations, seminars, training, course development with proper materials and publications can be arranged by team work. For example, consultations and seminars between Korean leaders and non-Koreans, such as 'Building Bridges,' can be held. This needs an intellectual and godly exercise between Muslim scholars and Korean Evangelicals through dialogue, as already suggested. The publication of books is required with healthy, balanced and objective perspectives about Islam and the Qur'an, and books about a history of Muslim-Christian relations, and about mission history toward Muslims, Bible study materials with a good theology, and a relevant missiology, so that non-Western perspectives on the Muslim community are developed and introduced for the world today for ministry amongst Muslims. Therefore, KEs have to recruit Korean Islam scholars urgently. KEs need scholarship to study Islam at an advanced level. These future scholars must research seriously into what kind of new perspectives and contributions KEs can/should make in relationship with Muslims in the world from non-Western perspectives.

Seventhly, we need to develop training courses for ordinary Christians, Christian leaders and pastors such as a Korean version of 'Friendship First' course, so that pastors and leaders of churches abroad and in Korea are equipped with the appropriate knowledge about Islam and Muslims and the power of the Holy Spirit, especially the love for Muslims, without fear (1 John 4:1-21). Appropriate training courses are urgently needed for Korean mission workers, who serve Muslims, giving a new orientation for Korean leaders with a new curriculum.

In conclusion, everything that is done by Korean Evangelicals, in response to their Muslim neighbours, should be done with hospitality and love. 'Do not forget to show hospitality to strangers (*philoxenia*), for by doing that some entertaining angels without knowing it' (Heb. 13:2). 'Whoever does not love does not know God, because God is love' (1 John 4:8).

Mission Korea: The Contribution of Global Youth Mobilization

Chulho Han

World Missions and Young Adults Mission Mobilization

Throughout the history of world missions, at the heart of every Protestant mission's movement was a large-scale voluntary commitment and the participation of young adults and students. This is very natural. Generally speaking, a nation's mission movement begins when its young adults and college students are mobilized as missionaries. The United Kingdom's mission movement, in the late nineteenth century, was a result of the college student mission movement began by the Cambridge Seven in 1885. America's aggressive sending of missionaries, since the early 1900s, was also a result of the Student Volunteer Movement (SVM) that began in 1888. However, the centre of Christianity in the world shifted from the global North to the Global South, as is evident in the increasing number of missionaries sent from the Southern countries and by the acceleration of young adults and students' mission mobilization movements in those countries. One early account of such movements was the Mission Korea Student Mission conference, a young adults and college students' mission mobilization movement in Korea, which ran in parallel to the sudden surge of missionaries from the Korean church since the late 1980s.

Mission Korea began in 1988 as a joint student mission mobilization conference, organized by various campus mission organizations and overseas mission organizations and was supported by churches throughout Korea. It is currently run by 35 mission organizations. Since it was established as a full-scale joint movement in 1990, the Mission Korea Student Mission conference has been held biennially over 22 years. It has had a cumulative total of 53,700 participants, 31,800 of whom had indicated their decision to be involved directly in missions, such as long-term missionaries. Mission Korea has become a great inspiration for the Korean church's mission mobilization.

Mission Korea's vision is six-fold. First, Mission Korea aims to teach and share with college students and young adults the calling for world evangelization in their generation through a spiritual awakening. Second, Mission Korea aims to produce missionary candidates for world missions through its conference and other ministries. Third, Mission Korea aims to produce mission mobilizers by sharing the urgency of mission mobilization.

Fourth, Mission Korea aims to set a platform for Korea's young people to grow as strategic and dynamic missionaries, by having the nation's churches, student organizations and overseas missions organizations work together in unity and humility. Fifth, Mission Korea aims to encourage the young adults and students to start prayer movements, mission collaboration movements, mission mobilization movements and so on, in their own churches and communities to transform their churches as missional churches and contribute to a revival of the Korean church. Sixth, acknowledging that God's mission work always involves young adults and students' mission movements, Mission Korea aims to share its vision with the young adults, students and church leaders of Asia and of the world and help start similar students' mission mobilization movements around the world.

Mission Korea Conference's Background and Results

The Mission Korea conference began with the revival of the campus missions organizations. Many college mission organizations in Korea were founded around the late 1950s, when the Korean church began to experience a revival. Well into the 1980s, those organizations began to experience a rapid growth with many members committed to the gospel. Those committed began to offer themselves as missionaries for the nations and many were indeed turning their eyes to the world. Korea was then going through a social transformation. The democratization movement in 1987, and the Seoul Olympic Games in 1988, both forced Korea to open up to the world. As limits on overseas travel lifted, the young people were now able to visit the mission field and embrace a wider vision for world evangelization. As the Korean church's role and ministry in world missions rapidly increased since 1990, the Mission Korea movement received much attention, both inside and outside the country. Today, the Mission Korea conference plays a crucial role for young adults and students' mission movement in Asia, comparable to Urbana in North America.

The Mission Korea conference bore many fruits for the Korean church in its 22 years' history. First, the Mission Korea conference mobilized a huge number of young people for missions. The first Mission Korea conference in 1988 was attended by over 500 people. The second conference in 1990 was attended by 1,500 people and Mission Korea 1992 was attended by about 3,000. The conference is now attended by about 5,000 to 6,000 people. Cumulatively, over 53,700 people have participated in the Mission Korea conferences and about 31,800 of them have decided to serve as missionaries for 1 year or longer. They make up a big portion of the missionaries sent from Korea since the mid-1990s.

Second, the Mission Korea conference made a great impact on the Korean church's mission movement. The young people who participated in the conferences took the mission movements and prayer movements to their churches and communities, and so contributed greatly to the whole development of the Korean church's missions.

Third, the Mission Korea conference greatly influenced the mission strategies of the Korean church. The mission strategy for a frontier mission movement and to unreached people groups were first introduced to Korea through the Mission Korea conference. Similarly, other important mission concepts for a laymen's mission movement, tentmakers' mission movement, mission trips, short-term missionaries, etc. were either introduced or developed through the conferences.

Fourth, the Mission Korea conference acted as a stimulant for unity. The conference, being a joint effort of many organizations, caused other joint movements, not only in the field of missions, but also in many other ministries such as the youth ministry. The model of unity seen in Mission Korea had a great influence over campus evangelization, resulting in the formation of the Campus Evangelism Association. There was much synergy for joint works by young adults and in youth evangelism. There was also a lot of coming together between overseas missions organizations and campus organizations and between campus organizations and churches.

Fifth, the Mission Korea conference introduced a new model for worldwide mission mobilization. Young adults and students mission mobilization movements are now seen, not only in North America and Europe, but also in Asia, Latin America and Africa, where Mission Korea's model of unity is becoming an important benchmark. For instance, the new mission mobilization movements currently taking place in Indonesia, Nagaland (India), Bangladesh, and the Philippines are joint movements modelled on Mission Korea.

The Changing Environment of Young People's Mission Mobilization

Looking into the future of the Mission Korea conference, one needs to carefully observe the changes in the entire world, the global mission movement, the Korean church, and the youth movement. First of all, the new term 'glocalization' is perhaps the best word to describe the world today, where globalization and localization are taking place at the same time. There is an increasing uniformity in the global culture and yet regional uniqueness is stressed more than at any other time in history. Openness and control co-exist. In general, things are opening up economically and culturally, but religious and philosophical elements are becoming highly individualized or regionalized. This will make missions even more difficult. Creativity is no long an option in this fast changing world. From the global perspective, it is clear that world mission is no longer dominated by the global North. The Global South has grown enormously and the universal Church must work in partnership and unity for missions. From the strategic perspective, the mission movement no longer follows the from-here-to-there pattern but it is a from-everywhere-to-everywhere movement, going in all directions. At the same time, we must continue our efforts to reach the unreached people groups that still remain. In other words, the whole church must work together to accomplish her mission in the twenty-first century, and the Korean church's role is ever increasing. This calls for a future development of the Mission Korea movement, which will play a key role in expanding the Korean church's missions and in producing missionary forces.

On the other hand, the lack of a strategic approach for Korean missionaries, as seen symbolically in the 2007 Afghan abduction of Korean mission trip goers, and the worsening image of Christianity within Korea, calls for a serious reflection and a new paradigm for the Korean church's missionary works. Currently highlighted by the Mission Korea conference, mission mobilization of young Korean adults also requires a new paradigm. The Korean church's growth is now reaching a plateau. Considering the fact that growth in missions and church revival go in tandem, the slowing down of the Korean church's growth will certainly have detrimental effects on her mission movement. We are now faced with a great challenge in the revival of the Korean church and the evangelization of the young Koreans.

Looking at the entire spectrum of ethnic Koreans around the world, the missional passion saturated within Korea is now spreading over to the eight million Koreans scattered throughout the world. In this globalized world, many Korean young adults now constitute a big portion of the Korean diaspora church community, as they go abroad studying, training or migrating. Mobilizing such young people for missions is becoming an important agenda. The stage is set before us to mobilize the Korean Christian community, both in Korea and outside Korea, to bring about a new breakthrough in world missions. Also, the number of international students in Korea is rapidly increasing. Mobilizing them for missions is yet another challenge.

The Future Vision and Task of Mission Korea

Let us consider Mission Korea's future direction and vision as rapid changes take place in missions and in the church.

First, Mission Korea must light the fire of spiritual awakening among the young people, so that the mobilization of young Christians for missions can be accelerated. Revival always precedes missions. This fact has been proven again and again through the history of missions and the history of the student movement. In other words, the success of the Mission Korea movement depends on the revival of the young people. This calls for another true revival and awakening within the campus evangelism organizations and young adults departments of churches. And this is a mutual responsibility to be borne both by Mission Korea and by the Korean church.

Second, the young people's cultural, philosophical and environmental changes must be well understood and mission mobilization strategies must be formed according to the analysis. Each generation sees a new breed of young people. New strategies and new approaches are required for mobilizing them. Especially in Korea, the major changes the country went through were very closely related to the changes its young people went through. The young people, today, are in a completely different situation than those in the 1980s and 1990s. But they are also beneficiaries of the economic development, achieved in the last 20 years, and they too have participated in the democratization process of the country. Compared to the previous generation, the young people now are living in a relatively wealthier society, experiencing the fruits of the preceding generation's sacrifices. In this aspect, the previous generation's participation in missions was a means of mutual satisfaction and pride as they worked together for the grand mission of accomplishing the kingdom of God. On the other hand, the generation after 2000 has been enjoying a relatively wealthier culture, but has not yet realized the full economic benefits. This makes the new generation highly individualistic. Therefore, they are looking for the means of personal accomplishment and satisfaction when participating in missions. We should not dismiss such an attitude as negative, but must develop appropriate approaches for mission mobilization. The very characteristics of this generation must be utilized for better mission mobilization. For instance, as short mission trips are losing their attraction, short-term missions programmes, that run anywhere between one year and two years, should be developed to accommodate the new demands of the young people.

Fourth, our challenge is to educate and motivate the young people of Korea in the global reputation and responsibility of the Korean church in world missions today. God gives each nation and each generation a Godly assignment. And it is more than obvious that God has given the Korean church of this generation the assignment of world missions. We must actively help the young adults of Korea to participate in this calling. The mission mobilization movement must continue to grow. There are still many more young people to be mobilized for missions. The young people today are exposed to missions in many ways. Compared to the days when the Mission Korea conference first began 22 years ago, the young people are given many more chances to participate in missions. Nonetheless, a huge number of them are yet to come in full contact with missions. The Mission Korea conference has become well-known, but it still remains unknown to many. The number of churches that have sent their young adults to Mission Korea is less than 1,500. The opportunity must open up for those who have never been on missions. At least, every committed young believer should be given the opportunity to participate in the biennial Mission Korea conference. Despite the changes in time and culture, large-scale mobilizations continue to take place at large-scale gatherings. This is seen in North America's Urbana and Europe's Mission-Net. Therefore, systematic implementation and the churches' support are necessary to make the Mission Korea conference even more effective.

Fifth, carefully orchestrated mobilization ministry efforts are required. While many young people have been mobilized through the Mission Korea conference, there remains the quest to assist them through adequate training and commissioning. The young people, mobilized through the Mission Korea conference, must be trained and assisted by their campus organizations and churches. Mission Korea's primary role is in initial large-scale mobilization. History has shown that a large-scale mobilization movement is indeed necessary in any nation. However, any mobilization must be followed by careful and detailed training and equipping of those mobilized and Mission Korea is required to play a part in this process. There is a serious bottleneck between large-scale mission mobilization movement and the actual number of missionaries sent out. The biggest reason for this is the lack of an infrastructure for missions. This was inevitable as the large-scale mission mobilization rose in Korea before any adequate infrastructure was established. Despite the past, we must now look forward. It is not right to limit the extent of the large-scale mobilization, or just wait for the infrastructure to be set up in its natural course of time. Post-mobilization training programmes and tools must be researched and developed, so that those mobilized can be guided into the mission fields. For this reason, recently, Mission Korea had to undergo a major restructuring. The ministry now has two main parts: Mission Korea conference, with a focus on mobilizing young people through conferences, and Mission Korea partners, with a focus on developing tools and an infrastructure for providing practical help to those committed to be missionaries.

Sixth, young members of the Korean diaspora church must be mobilized for missions. Mission Korea formed the Korean Student Mission Mobilizers Network in 1993 and has been working with Korean young adults mission mobilizers in North America. Mission Korea is also concentrating in mobilizing Korean Christians around the world as a member of the KODIMNET (Korean Diaspora Missions Network) since 2002. Mission is a shared task. The commitment to missions, felt by the young people in Korea, must be shared out with the young Korean people around the world and also the young people of different nationalities worldwide. A truly global mission mobilization movement must take place. Commemorating the 20th anniversary of Mission Korea, the Mission Korea 2008 Conference (August 4 - 11, 2010) incorporated the Student Mission Mobilization Roundtable (SMMR), which was attended by 97 student mission mobilizers from 22 Asian nations. The participants were given first-hand experience of the Mission Korea conference, the largest and the longest-running mission mobilization movement in Asia, and a series of practical discussion and prayer sessions were held with the intention of replicating Mission Korea elsewhere in Asia. To date, Bangladesh, the Philippines, Indonesia, Malaysia, Nagaland, and Kazakhstan saw mission mobilization movements newly emerging, which were the results of the commitments made at the SMMR to follow the Mission Korea model.

Conclusion

Mission Korea has played an important role in mobilizing young Korean people for missions in the past two decades. This has many implications in the history of mission mobilization. There are two important fruits of the Mission Korea ministry. Firstly, it directly contributed to increasing the number of Korean missionaries by staging an intentional and organized young adults' mission mobilization movement. Secondly, the Mission Korea movement became an excellent example of people coming together in humility and unity for the kingdom of God.

For Mission Korea to continue its calling, it now needs more efforts to adjust to the fast changing environment of world missions. It must make adjustments to better mobilize the young people in Korea, to mobilize the young members of the Korean diaspora church, and to help mission mobilization movements of young people in other nations.

New Missional Avenues for Asian Churches

Byung Yoon Kim

With the rapid growth of churches and missionaries in the Global South, the Asian church has begun to assume a greater responsibility for world missions[1] and contemporary mission is from everywhere to everywhere. Steve Hoke and Bill Taylor, therefore, have predicted that, 'as we move into the third millennium, the church of Jesus Christ has become truly globalized, and missions are now from all nations to all nations',[2] while Paul Pierson notes the rapid growth of the non-Western Christian missionary movement as, 'the greatest new fact of our time'.[3] In this brief article, I will discuss the role of Asian churches in missions and my personal involvement through Asia Vision Short-Term Missions project (AVSTM), and the Global Connections for Advancement project, which I have recently launched to multiply missions for Asian churches.[4]

The Importance of Mission Planting in the Field

As a missionary, I have struggled with the chronic problem of 'dependency' in national Christian leaders, which leaves Asian churches weak and missions are considered as 'high costs with low efficiency' enterprises. Evangelical missionaries and local pastors in the Philippines, for instance, planted a great number of churches between 1975 and 2000, but most of these churches are still weak and even dying. They struggle with both financial shortages and leadership problems. With 51,625 evangelical churches in the Philippines as the result of the Disciple A Whole Nation (DAWN) 2000 project, not many pastors are being paid enough to survive.[5] Furthermore, the average attendance of each church is only about thirty-five people. I also have planted several churches

[1] David Harley, *Preparing to Serve: Training for Cross-Cultural Missions* (Pasadena, CA: William Carey Library, 1995), 4.

[2] Stephen T. Hoke, 'Paradigm Shifts and Trends in Missions Training - A Call to Servant-Teaching, A Ministry of Humility', *Evangelical Review of Theology* 23 (October 1999), 19.

[3] Paul Pierson, 'Non-Western Missions: The Great New Fact of Our Time', in Patrick Sookhdeo (ed), *New Frontiers in Mission* (Exeter, UK: Paternoster Press, 1987), 9.

[4] Global Connections for Advancement is the follow-up project of the AVSTM which aims to multiply missions throughout Asia and beyond.

[5] According to the Philippine Council of Evangelical Churches' survey in 2000, about 80% of pastors in Luzon received about $18 a month as honorarium from their churches.

among the Igorots in northern Philippines and see those churches struggle in similar ways to survive. Therefore, it was obvious that Filipino churches could not send missionaries out to the world because of their financial shortages and the mind-set of dependency.

Reflecting on this gloomy picture of national churches, in places like the Philippines, I have re-read the Bible and tried to find reasons why the Asian churches (especially Filipino churches) remain 'so dependent' for many years. In the past, the Western churches and agencies were seen as the torch-bearers who led and funded missions. Non-Western churches were considered 'dependent' entities, not adequately developed or resourced for the task of cross-cultural missions. It became obvious to me, that mission planting rather than church planting is the end goal of missions. I believe that the local church will be healthier when she takes ownership of the gospel and shares the good news to the world. In reality, it is not a matter of a shortage of money or strategies because the early churches even took the initiative of missions though they were not affluent in finance.

A Missions Planting Model: The Asia Vision Short-Term Missions Project

In 2002, after visiting the Tuol Sleng Genocide Museum and one of the Cambodian 'killing fields', I wanted to move my mission station from the Philippines to Cambodia. Somehow, my mission field became my comfort zone and I was thinking that the Lord is challenging me to re-dedicate myself to him in a new field. So, I decided to move to Cambodia to plant churches among the poor and I brought my family there to see the country prior to moving there. However, we could not find a school, where we could send our second child. It bothered me because it meant that I was not quite committed to the Lord. One day, when I shared this in one of my mission classes, some of my students said, 'If you cannot go there, can you not send us instead?' At first, I laughed by myself because that is impossible, since the economic situation of the Philippines is weak, and many churches struggle with a lack of finances.

As a teaching missionary, I was thinking that I just need to train Filipinos as good Christian workers but never thought of sending them as missionaries. The Lord, however, continuously touched my heart whenever I prayed to him. Without confidence, therefore, I asked students, 'Who would love to go to Cambodia?' and some raised their hands. I asked them to submit application forms if they were willing to serve as short-term missionaries (STMers), and thirty-four applications were turned in! With these in my hands, I had to make a trip to Cambodia and other countries in Indochina, in order to arrange fields for those applicants. I spent a month there for the preparatory work.

Many seminarians, in reality, were not able eat three times a day due to a lack of financial support. Just as I thought, only nine out of the thirty-four applicants could pay US$10 on time as an application fee, when we launched the AVSTM project for the year 2003. Some Filipino faculty members said that not more than half of the STM applicants could join the mission trip due to financial shortages. It was troublesome for me because I already completed the line up travel to Cambodia and other countries in Indochina where we could assign all thirty-four STMers to work, and if they could not raise enough support, what would happen to the hosts in Cambodia and countries in Indochina?

I had challenged the STM applicants to proactively attempt great things for God, rather than passively waiting great things from God. I also encouraged them to put their faith in God and prove that our God is a living God. The STM applicants, mostly Filipinos, started to form a dawn prayer meeting and cried out to God. I invited Ms. Ched Arzadon, a Filipina who had over 20 years of supporting raising ministry, to share how to develop partners in missions for the STM applicants. Indeed, it was a big challenge for the STM applicants but the Lord graciously and faithfully answered their prayers. They experienced God's miraculous provisions for their plane tickets and expenses for their missions. All thirty-four STM applicants were able to leave for Cambodia and countries in Indochina, and served the Lord with great joy. There was a breakthrough in their lives and ministries. Kevin Daugherty, a faculty member of the seminary, described the AVSTM project as a blessing to the seminary that brought a 'transformation of the seminary'.

The STMers successfully served the people in the mission field with the word of God and some evangelistic tools because they identified with their hosts. The Lord blessed and used Filipino STMers when they eagerly offered their tears and sweat for his people. It has been said that, 'it is not great men who change the world, but weak men in the hands of a great God!' and the Lord greatly used Filipinos as effective missionaries. It was not in the seminary classrooms but in the mission field and among the locals, that STMers have changed their perspectives on Christianity and their role in missions. Since then, I have served as a mission catalyst to encourage, not only seminarians, but also local church members, to join the Great Commission. By sending these Filipino and Asian STMers out to the mission field, we could correct their long time 'dependency' and foster a new 'ownership of the gospel' among Filipino and Asian Christians.

From these humble beginnings has emerged the Asia Vision Short-term Missions Project (AVSTM). From thirty-four STMers in 2003, the AVSTM (with its mission partners) grew to about 1,200 STMers in 2010. The project has a vision of sending 3,000 STMers from Asia to Asia by the year 2015, so that more people in Asia can hear the Good News and enjoy salvation through the work of committed Asian missionaries. In addition to that, all STMers and their mission partners have ownership of the gospel and create a new image of Christianity among Asian countries.

Though leaders have tended to view Filipino Christians as weak and dependent, I have found that they possess some strategic strength for missions through sending them as STMers. Filipinos are:

1) Multi-lingual: Most Filipinos speak Tagalog, English, and one or two additional languages. Thus, they can easily learn a new language or teach a language (such as English) to others.

2) Multi-cultural: Centuries of colonial rule and their country's multi-racial composition helps them to adapt easily to a new culture.

3) Versatile: They easily blend into other Asian cultures without being noticed. One of the most important values in Filipino culture is SIR (Smooth Interpersonal Relationships).

4) Resilient: They have been made strong by hardship and are able to adjust without complaint to contexts without electricity or sufficient water.

5) Highly educated: Most have an opportunity to study in colleges and they can teach effectively in various mission fields.

6) Non-threatening: Since the Philippines have no history of aggression, they are welcomed in many Asian countries. Even visas are waived, especially among ASEAN countries in Southeast Asia.

7) They have experienced rapid church growth in the last 35 yeas. The evangelical churches have grown from 5,000 in 1975 to 51,625 churches in 2000 and even try to double the numbers of the Church by this year, 2010. This sort of church growth experience can be shared and applied to many Asian countries.

These particular advantages do not make Filipino Christians better suited to mission than members of other Asian churches. What they illustrate, however, is that the supposedly 'weak' members of the Global South churches are often equipped with unique strengths of their own.

Also, I have challenged the underground Chinese churches to give their people and finance for missions. The Chinese churches started to send their missionary candidates to me and deployed them to various countries in Asia as missionaries, after a year of missionary training. The Chinese churches formed their own mission agency and do fully support their own missionaries. The Chinese church is new to missions, so I am helping them in lining up mission fields, selecting and supplying selected missionary trainers, and mission consulting. Also, I am closely working with churches in Nagaland (India), Indonesia, Japan, Papua New Guinea, among others in the area of missions.

Paradigm Shift 1: New Missional Avenue for Asian Churches

The right relationship with the local people has to be anchored in identification with them (cf. 1 Cor. 9:20-22). A genuine love for the local people is what makes this identification possible.[6] This kind of deep relationship with the

[6] Paul G. Hiebert, *Anthropological Insights for Missionaries* (Grand Rapids, MI: Baker Book House, 1993), 110.

people can be called 'incarnational ministry'.[7] Just as 'the Word became flesh and dwelt among us' (John 1:14), so missionaries must identify themselves with the people they serve. Jesus' own missionary work included entering into the culture of the Galilean people. He lived with the inconveniences they experienced, even traveling all over the land of Israel on foot to preach the gospel. As a good shepherd, he even laid down his life for the sheep (John 10:11). Jesus' incarnational model (Phil. 2:4-8) has to be the basic principle of cross-cultural missions. Modern missions, however, omitted the incarnational missional approach in the field. Throughout mission history, most missionaries tried to identify with the locals but still there were big gaps between the missionary and the locals. They must fully bond with the people in the target culture, experiencing a sense of belonging with the local people.[8]

The AVSTM's little success was possible because of her workers' incarnational approach among the people in their respective fields. One challenge facing the AVSTM, however, has been poor financial support. Since Asian churches are still financially weak, it is hard to support their missionaries on the high-cost Western missions system. It was obvious to me that Filipino churches could not afford $1,000 to $2,000 a month to support their missionaries. On the other hand, the affluence of such financing might be a hindrance in the missionaries' relationships with the local people.

To meet that standard, I developed a new approach to funding missions. I line up work for each STMer in the host country. I also arrange for the STMers to stay in the houses of local people and encourage the hosts to cover board and lodging for the STMers while they work. In most areas of Asia, this allows STMers to serve for no more than $100 a month. Besides lowering costs, though, this system is very effective in helping the STMers to identify with the host people in the field. Almost all of our STMers enjoy life-changing experiences through living with the local people, and on their return, STMers find themselves missing the people whom they served. Many decide to return to serve as long-term missionaries. Many churches have been planted across Asia through the incarnational ministry of these STMers, and they have helped to create a new image of Christianity as a religion for all, not just for Westerners.

Since the STMers live in the areas where the people are, I have challenged them to minister for at least 8 hours a day. Most laborers work 8 hours a day but it seems that the average evangelical missionary does not work that much in the field while the Mormon missionaries work 8 hours or more a day. Hence, the Mormons experienced 173 times of remarkable growth between 1960 and 1990 while the evangelicals enjoyed only 11 to 25 times of church growth in

---

[7] E. Thomas Brewster and Elizabeth S. Brewster, *Bonding and the Missionary Task* (Pasadena, CA: Lingua House, 1992), 6; William D. Reyburn, 'Identification in the Missionary Task', in W.A. Smalley (ed), *Readings in Missionary Anthropology II* (Pasadena, CA: William Carey Library, 1978), 746-60.

[8] Brewster & Brewster, *Bonding and the Missionary Task*, 6.

the Philippines. The Mormons were known and characterized by their zeal and an admirable missionary spirit. Tens of thousands Mormon missionaries (mostly, short-termers) actively work today. For instance, they visit every prospect (and church members) at least twice a week, and meet about 20 people a day and thus they have a very strong relationship with the locals.

Paradigm Shift 2: A New Missional Partnership between the Global North and South

If we are to foster ownership of the gospel among the churches in the global South, the role played by missionaries from the West in these partnerships also has to change. Since most non-Western missionaries are in need of proper training and care, Western missionaries can often contribute best by equipping them as trainers, coaches, consultants, and encouragers in their fields. Western missionaries also need to prepare for multi-cultural and multi-lingual teamwork. The individualistic missionary of the colonial era is no longer viable. An ability to work with, and under, the leadership of other nationalities is essential.[9] The ideas of interdependency (in contrast to independency) and accountability must be central to the emerging paradigm for contemporary missions.

Mission agencies are already responding by becoming more pragmatic about whom they will accept as missionaries from the global South. Many show an increasing interest in the actual competence of their candidates, rather than in their formal credentials or degrees. The key question asked is: 'can they do the ministry they will be assigned to do?' This means, in some cases, requiring less formal theological education before the first term and providing more practical, mentored, on-the-job training.[10] Individuals, previously excluded from missions, can then be valued for the unique life experiences which may prepare them for reaching out to growing segments of the population.

Missiology is responding with several trends that promise to re-shape the discipline. An attempt is being made to capture a more global perspective, acknowledging the dynamic and potential of the churches in the global South. An increasing emphasis is also being placed in theological and missions training on a more holistic approach to ministry, one that highlights the interlocking causes of poverty, oppression, and hopelessness. Perhaps most significant is the emergence of a global South missiology and the willingness of Western thinkers to take seriously the perspective of their non-Western brothers and sisters.

There may still be a role to be played at times for financial support from Western churches, provided it is re-thought in ways that are less paternalistic

---

[9] Patrick Johnstone and Jason Mandryk, *Operation World*, 21st century ed. (Waynesboro, GA: Paternoster Lifestyle, 2001), 12.

[10] Hoke, 'Paradigm Shifts and Trends in Missions Training', 336.

and do not foster dependence. Steve Murdock, for example, suggests that, 'if the support is seen as 'seed money' and not as a perpetual lifeline, and there is an exit strategy that is viable and realistic, then monetary support can be healthy'.[11] He then exhorts Western missionaries: '[D]o not create a ministry or structure that is not duplicable within the cultural or social context in which you are working; do not begin funding a work with no growth strategy plan or exit plan; and do not do all the work yourself'.[12]

Most important, though, is the basic shift that is taking place in the way Western missions agencies understand their relationship with their Global South counterparts. The buzzword in missions today is 'partnership', as opposed to 'sponsorship' which suggests an unequal relationship. Western churches and mission agencies are recognizing how, if they are willing to work closely with their non-Western counterparts, resources can flow in both directions. Sponsorship and paternalism can be replaced by mutual recognition of selfhood and cooperation as equals.[13]

Conclusion

We are facing increasing challenges and hostility from Muslims, Hindus, Buddhists and many other groups in the various mission fields, thus we need to find new avenues in missions and bring more mission forces into the field. The AVSTM proved that Asian churches could spread the gospel throughout Asia with their own people and finances. The Asian churches' humble involvement in missions creates new images of Christianity and brings transformation even to their own churches, but this does not mean an end to Western involvement in cross-cultural missions. Instead, we need to maximize our mission forces for the sake of the world because the remaining task is too great.

Whenever I meet and share the missions with Asian church leaders, I have learned that they also would like to be involved in missions but their role model or mind-set in missions is of the Western churches, so they would not able to partake in the Great Commission. Through the AVSTM project ministry, I have developed new avenues in missions which fit the context of Asian churches and even dying European churches, so I am trying to multiply missions through a 'low costs with high efficiency' principle in both the global North and South.

---

[11] Steve Murdock, 'Cuttings the Purse Strings: How to Avoid and Overcome Paternalism', *Evangelical Missions Quarterly* 45:1 (January 2009), 66-71.

[12] Murdock, 'Cuttings the purse strings', 66-71.

[13] Pierson, 'Non-Western missions', 9.

Part 3

Korean Diaspora in Mission

History of the Korean Diaspora Movement

Doug K. Oh

God uses various nations and people for his glory. As God chose the Jews to give and maintain the Law, he has raised various people for the gospel movement. He establishes churches in many places and has done his work through them. When a nation works out his will, He uses another nation to lead his great mission (Rev. 1:20; 2:5). The gospel movement will continue in history and will lead the glorious Church era at the end of age.

The Gospel's Course in History

Among the theories, that God works through different nations and peoples in church history, is the theory that the gospel movement is bound for the West. This was first brought up by Richard Sibbes (1577-1635), an English Puritan preacher. In his sermon in 1630, 'The Bruised Reed', he encouraged the Puritans who were immigrating to the New World, by the following: 'The gospel's course hath hitherto been as that of the sun, from East to West, and so in God's time may proceed yet further West'.[1] According to Sibbes, the gospel movement has moved from Judah to Rome, from Rome to the European continent, and from the European continent to England. And after the seventeenth century, Sibbes foresaw it would actively move to the New World, to North America.

As in Sibbes' preaching, the New England Puritans had opened the glorious church age in the seventeenth and the eighteenth centuries. They refused the sophist teachings and sought Bible Commonwealth, building a constitutionalism country and pursuing the 'city on a hill' which all European nations could see and admire. They also established a Holy Commonwealth in which the visible saints were reigning. By the eighteenth century, there was the Great Awakening, when approximately 250,000 out of the 300,000 population of New England experienced conversion and the movement to evangelize native Americans started in earnest. In the early nineteenth century, the gospel moved westward to evangelize the frontier areas of America. As the United States became the centre of evangelism in the world, the gospel movement traveled west again, this time crossing the Pacific Ocean.

As Kenneth S. Latourrette pointed out, due to the world mission movement led by the English missionary William Carey (1761-1834), the nineteenth

[1] Richard Sibbes, *Works of Richard Sibbes*, ed. Alexander B. Grossart, reprint ed. (Edinburgh: Banner of Truth Trust, 1982), 1:100.

century became 'the greatest century in church history'. It was in this century when Christ's great commission, 'go and make disciples of all nations' (Mat. 28:19), began to be fulfilled. Missionaries were sent to Africa, India, Persia, and Indochina and finally to Korea, the country considered as the world's end. In this hermit nation, missionaries bore abundant fruit.

The Korean mission has been most fruitful. During the 120 years of mission history, over 25 percent of the population became familiar with the gospel. Today, the president, the prime minister, government officials, one-third of the members of the national assembly and the head of the Supreme Court confess their belief in God. Not only does Korea have the largest church in the world, it has the largest Presbyterian church and the largest Methodist church. Promising young leaders study at the nation's theological schools. From more than 40 theological colleges and seminaries, over 100,000 church workers are annually produced. Students come from all over the world to Korea for theological training. Numerous missionaries, the world's second largest in number, are sent throughout the world from Korea.

The once known edge of the gospel movement has now become the centre of it. Moreover, Korea also achieved remarkable economic progress. Half a century ago, Korea was one of the poorest countries in the world, but, today, Korea's trade volume is the ninth largest, and its economic power is the thirteenth strongest in the world. According to a report from Goldman Sachs, it will be the second richest country in the world by 2050. The candlestick moved to Korea, and now the gospel era of this nation has begun.

For the evangelization of Korea, God sent many missionaries to Korea and also dispersed many Koreans all over the world. It was in the mid-nineteenth century when a Welsh missionary named Robert Jermain Thomas (1842-1866) arrived at the Daedong River thus opening a new chapter of the Korean gospel movement. As Thomas arrived in 1866 by an American ship the General Sherman, he was instantly martyred, but he sowed a seed in this barren land of the gospel. At this point, as God sent his people to this country, He simultaneously dispersed Koreans all over the world, making use of the Koreans' nomadic nature.

The history of Korean emigration can be divided into four periods. The first period is in the late Chosun Dynasty, the kingdom of Korea. Due to natural disasters, many people began to depart for survival. The second period is when King Gojong of the Chosun Dynasty changed the country's name to Daehan (the Great Korea) Empire and proclaimed modernization. In this time some Koreans left for Hawaii and Mexico. The third period is the Korea-Japan annexation, when massive emigration took place to avoid Japan's oppression. The last period starts from 1945, after Japan was defeated in World War II and Korea was liberated. Koreans then moved actively abroad to other countries such as the United States and Germany.

Emigration at the End of the Chosun Dynasty (1858-1897)

Before Korea became modernized, migration was strictly prohibited. The population of a country was a symbol of power, so only diplomats could travel out of the country and those who even planned on migrating for any reason were sentenced to extreme punishment. However, at the end of the Chosun Dynasty, because of political turmoil and famine caused by natural disaster, farmers began to seek ways to move abroad. In this situation, as the border control between Korea and China weakened in the mid-nineteenth century, many Koreans escaped out of the country beginning the era of mass exodus.

The number of emigrants rose in 1858, when Russia started developing the Maritime Province of Siberia (Yunhaeju) and encouraged people to move in and develop the region. In the winter of 1865, thirteen farmer families crossed the frozen Dooman River seeking refuge near the Ussuri River in Russia. By 1869, over 4,500 farmers had left for the Maritime Province and Manchuria. This was mainly due to the great famine of the 1860s which threatened to put their livelihoods at risk. By 1870, over 2,000 settlers formed 30 Korean villages in West Gando in Manchuria.[2]

As China permitted immigration to Manchuria in 1881, Korean emigration accelerated. They settled down at Korean-gate near Bongwhang castle, and cultivated West Gando. In 1899, when Yakyeon Kim moved to Longjing in North Gando reclaiming its wasteland, 142 people followed. As time passed, the number of immigrants increased. 'During the eight months from September of 1909 to April of 1910, the number Korean families that emigrated to North Gando reached 1,304 households'.[3]

Koreans who went to Manchuria and the Maritime Province lived diligently fostering the habit of thrift and saving. Many lived in affluence, having great influence on their community. Especially, Koreans in the Maritime Province succeeded in growing rice so pushing up the Northern limit of rice growing. They voted for a leader to manage the Korean community and established self-government. Koreans who had visited the settlers were eager to enforce the settlers' governing system back home.

However, the most monumental achievement of the Korean diaspora was translating the Bible into Korean. This took place in Manchuria and Japan simultaneously. Among the people, who emigrated to Manchuria, Eungchan Lee and Kyungjo Soe accepted the gospel by the Scottish missionary, John Ross, in 1880, and with his help they translated the Books of John and Luke in 1882. By 1887, they had translated all the New Testament and had published *Yesu-shungkyo-junsoe*, the first Korean Bible. In Japan, Soojung Lee, a member of the *Shinsa Youramdan*, the visitors from Korea to Japan, received help from an American missionary, Henry Loomis, and translated the Book of Mark into Korean in 1883. The Bible translation from Manchuria was

[2] Heonchang Lee, 'Emigration Era Is Opened', *Chosun Daily News*, Feb. 3, 2010.

[3] Lee, 'Emigration Era Is Opened'.

distributed in Hwanghae Province by Sangyune Suh. It was Suh, who built the very first Korean church, in Sorae in Hwanghae Province, before the Western missionaries arrived in Korea. The Bible from Soojung Lee was presented to Koreans by one of the first missionaries, Horace Underwood. Likewise, the Korean diaspora in the late Chosun laid the foundations for the evangelization of Korea.

Emigration during the Korean Empire (1897-1910)

Though immigration in the late Chosun was illegal, immigration in the Korea Empire was legal. In 1897, King Gojong accepted the public opinion from within and without and proclaimed Chosun as the Korean Empire and called himself the Emperor. In 1901, to aggrandize the newly proclaimed nation's wealth, the Emperor sent five Koreans to a Hawaiian sugarcane farm, the first modern immigration, characteristised by labor.

On December 22, 1902, in Incheon, one-hundred and two people embarked on a Japanese ship, the Genkaymaru, to emigrate. After stopping at Nagasaki, Japan for physical check-ups, these Korean passengers made a transit to an American liner, the Garlic, and crossed the Pacific Ocean to Honolulu on January 1, 1903. Afterwards, ships arrived one after another and the number of Koreans, 'became 7,226 in 1905' and there were '6,200 men, 640 women, 550 children'.[4] Even though immigration ceased with Japan's interference, around 860 more Koreans, including approximately 800 picture brides, arrived during 1910 and 1924.[5]

During this period, around 40% of the 7,000 immigrants were Christian. Six months after their arrival, the Koreans founded a church on July 4, 1903 at Mokulreyiah, Oahu Island. Socializing within the boundaries of their church, they sought comfort from their lonesome daily lives. Wherever the immigrants went, a church was built and the number of churches rose to thirty-nine.

To Koreans, a church was the only place for them to gather. It was a place to worship God, a school for education and a centre for social gathering. Where a church was built, so was a school because the chapel for weekends was used as a school on weekdays. Schools were the place for the people to gather and were used for education and unity.[6] Thus, church activities and Korean diaspora activities were inseparable.

By 1905, the emigration of Koreans spread to Mexico. Immigration in Mexico was in fact a result of a Japanese broker's fraudulence. As overseas migration gained popularity, a Japanese broker took commissions, promising

---

[4] Injin Yune, 'Korean Diaspora: Immigration, Accommodation, Identity of Overseas Koreans' [in Korean], *The Society of Social Study in Korea* 6 (2003), 127.

[5] Overseas Koreans Foundation, *Contribution of Koreans in Hawaii to Korean Society* [in Korean] (Incheon: Inha University Press, 2009), 25.

[6] *Contribution of Koreans in Hawaii*, 71.

Koreans to take them to Mexico, 'the land of dreams'. However, they were dragged off to Yucatan in East Mexico and worked like slaves on an agave plantation. 'We were beaten if the owner disliked our work. Those who escaped are usually got caught and sent to jail. We were whipped 25 times when caught, and 50 times when caught again. Some even escaped leaving their wives while others hung themselves on Indian mallows to die'.[7] The immigrants in Mexico had no churches or leaders to confide in and the absence of the church led to a thorough localization of the Koreans.

Emigration to the mainland of America started in 1903 when a small number of migrants moved from Hawaii to San Francisco. The number gradually increased and by 1907, the number reached 1,037. In 1903, the San Francisco Korean Methodist Church, and in 1906 the San Francisco Korean Presbyterian Church were founded. The zeal for education was high, more than those of the Japanese, the Chinese or the Americans. They also had great interest in the independence of their home country.

Some of the nation's pioneers tried to gather the Korean diaspora to build a religious and ethnical community in America. One of the most well known was Dosan An Changho. He went to the States to study pedagogy in 1902. He gathered Koreans and established the San Francisco Korean Methodist Church in San Francisco in 1903. Under his leadership, the church fought for the rights and unity of Korean immigrants and struggled to improve their living conditions in the States. It also served as a refuge for those who were worn out. After returning from a short trip to Korea, Dosan formed a coalition with *Gonglip Hyubhoe* (Public Association) which he had organized and *Hanin Hapseong Hyubhoe* (Korean Association). It eventually developed into the *Daehanin Kookminhoe* (Assembly of the Great Korean). The Assembly of the Great Korean spoke for immigrants' rights, and became one of the most active organizations to participate in the country's independence movement.

Korean-American churches in this period supported the modernization and independence of their mother country. Despite their economic difficulties, they supported the Assembly of the Great Korean by raising funds for the independence of Korea, actively participating in the independence movement, and created political organizations to ensure the rights of Koreans. The churches were especially enthusiastic about the education of their children because they believed that better education was a means of recovering the country's political and economic power. Also, Korean women's organizations of the diaspora churches were also eager to raise funds to send to their home country. Persistently interacting with Koreans, they fostered their identity as Koreans[8] and preached the gospel. They also mediated jobs and gave scholarships to the Korean students in the States.

---

[7] Lee, 'Emigration Era Is Opened'.

[8] *Contribution of Koreans in Hawaii*, 20.

Meanwhile, Koreans in North Gando, in Manchuria, tried to build a model society in the hope of contributing to the mother country becoming civilized and independent. Yakyeon Kim, who conducted immigration to Gando, and his company, believed that the only hope for Korea was Christ, therefore, they all converted to Christianity in 1909. With the vision to 'enlighten their country of the east', they created a village called Myungdong. They considered education and a religious movement based on Christianity as their top priority and on this ground they actively supported the independence movement of Korea. When Junggeun Ahn, a Korean patriot, was rejected by a Korean Roman Catholic church in Gando, when asking for space for a gunnery exercise to assassinate Ito Hirobumi – the Prime minister of Japan who annexed Korea to Japan by force – it was the Myungdong Church that made the mission possible with church members' support.

Emigration in the Japanese Occupation Period (1910-1945)

After Japan deprived Korea of its national power by force, the Japanese established many colonization companies in Korea. The companies plundered the farmland. The majority of farmers who lost their land went to Manchuria, Russia and Japan to avoid Japanese oppression and to escape from poverty, thus leading to the increase of emigrants. At the time of Japanese annexation in 1910, the population of Koreans was 17 million. 1.7% of the population, which is around 300,000, was in the diaspora. Around 220,000 went to China, 60,000 to Russia, 6,000 to Hawaii, 1,000 to the mainland of America, 2,527 to Japan, and 974 to Mexico.[9]

Mass emigration of Koreans to Manchuria began when Japan started to develop the area to build the Kingdom of Manchuria in 1932. There were more than 500,000 Koreans in Manchuria in the late 1930s. Among the population, 250,000 had settled in Manchuria to escape from poverty.[10] Many were Christians. According to one of the statistics, in 1932 there were 122 Korean churches with 16,200 believers. However this statistic is known to be incorrect because the number is fewer than the statistics of the Japanese Government General of Korea from 1925.[11]

During this period, emigration to Japan also started in earnest. Because of the 1st World War Japan was economically booming, so many Koreans went to Japan as workers. In 1937, Japan started the Sino-Japanese War and, in 1941,

[9] Lee, 'Emigration Era Is Opened'.

[10] Taewhan Kwon, *Koreans in the World - China* [in Korean] (Seoul: Ministry of Unification, 1996).

[11] According to the statistics of the Japanese Government General of Korea, in Gando there were 116 churches and 17,538 church members in 1925. Youngjae Kim, *History of Korean Church* [in Korean] (Suwon: Hapdong Theological Seminary Press, 2004), 180. However, there were more Korean churches and church members in China.

the Pacific War, and drafted Koreans into the military by force and dragged them into Japan, so increasing the Korean diaspora. When Korea was liberated from Japanese colonial rule in 1945, more than 2,300,000 people were in Japan, but most of them came back to Korea and in 1947 only 598,508 remained.[12]

During Japan's colonial occupation, as refugees, Koreans suffered more than their share. The sufferings of Koreans in the Maritime Province in Russia were especially indescribable. However, they introduced rice farming and thrived economically. They managed to train the military, built a base for the country's independence and established *Shinhan* (New Korea) village. Their leaders, such as Jaehyung Choi and Sangsul Lee, founded the Gunup organization, built a Korean school and a Korea theater, all serving for the liberation of Korea. This movement also led to the construction of an autonomies province. However, all was suspended by Russia that proclaimed for the greater Russia. In 1937, Stalin forced 36,442 Korean families, a sum of 171,781 people, to move to central Asia, such as Kazakhstan, Ukraine, Uzbekistan, Turkmenistan, Tajikistan, and Kyrgyzstan. Many of them died during the trip and many more suffered after the settlement.

As many Koreans went overseas, native churches sent pastors for the Korean immigrants and help them to preserve their beliefs. In 1907, the Presbyterian Church of Korea formed the first presbytery and established a bureau for the diaspora Koreans and sent several evangelists to take care of the immigrants. Pastor Kwanhol Choi was sent to Vladivostok, Russia in 1909. As the Korean immigrants grew in number, the presbytery sent Pastor Huyngchan Kim in 1918.

To Japan, the presbytery sent Sukjin Han, one of the first Korean pastors. He went to Tokyo and preached the gospel to students from Korea for 3 months and returned in 1909. The following year, elder Younggil Park went to the church that Sukjin Han founded and took care of the students. When the church became stable, in 1911, elder Jongsoon Im went to help the students and the next year, they started the United Church with the Methodists.[13]

The Presbyterian Church of Korea sent pastors to Manchuria. Pastor Youngjae Kim was sent to North Gando and Jingeun Kim was sent to West Gando by delegates of Pyungan-Bukdo in 1910. Also, to look after Koreans and evangelize the Chinese, the Presbyterian Church sent three pastors, Younghoon Kim, Taero Park and Byungsoon Sa to Sandong province in China

---

[12] Moonwoong Lee, *Koreans in the World - Japan* [in Korean] (Seoul: Ministry of Unification, 1997), 66-70. In spite of their situation, the Korean diaspora in Japan donated the buildings of the Korean Embassy and General Consul in Japan to the Korean government in 1945 when Korea was in difficulties. In fact, they donated more than 4000,000 dollars to the motherland when Korea was so poor that the government could not pay the money for the embassy buildings. *Contribution of Koreans in Hawaii*, 16.

[13] Y.J. Kim, *History of Korean Church*, 174.

in 1913. After they returned to Korea, the church sent Hyowon Bang, Seungmo Hong in 1917, and Sangsoon Park the following year.[14] As time went by, the number of immigrants grew and the number of churches grew as well.

The Methodist Church of Korea also sent pastors for the immigrants and built churches. The church sent Pastor Hwachoon Lee to Longjing in China in September, 1909. In 1910, Pastors Hyungsik Bae and Jungdo Son were each sent to the southern and northern parts of Manchuria. By 1920, the Council of South Manchuria Methodist Church was organized. From 1920, the church also sent pastors to Russia to take care of the Korean settlers.[15] The Korean diaspora was able to settle down successfully in foreign countries because of the keen interest and support shown by the churches and they were able to maintain ethnic identity and beliefs within the boundaries of the churches.

Meanwhile, under Japanese imperialism, the Korean diaspora churches made great efforts towards the country's independence. The independence movement was developed from the churches so naturally, that the churches served as the base camp and also the sanctuary for patriots. The Korean diaspora, in Manchuria, covertly supported the churches, and church members in Japan took care of those studying abroad, the potential leaders of the country and likewise the churches in the United States.

The Korean churches in America, 'cried together, prayed for the suffering and were with them' and they became 'the centre of the independence movement'.[16] The Korean church was always the centre of Korean society and had a great influence on the lives of immigrants religiously, socially, culturally and psychologically. It was the only shelter for many where they could relax. Standing on the churches' grounds, various social groups arose and led the independence movement. The church stood not only for religious goals but for social and cultural purposes and it performed accordingly.

The biggest role it played was fund-raising for Korea's independence. The performance of the Hawaii Assembly of the Great Korean is one of the many examples. The organization was run like a church and collected 'the independent movement fund, population tax, patriotism fund, independent bond, special tax for the mother country, and many kinds of special funds'.[17] In December, 1937, they also opened a temporary Board of Representatives and 'decided to fully sponsor military exercise in China; they stopped all business except for business to cover operating expenses and collected population tax, patriotism fund and sent it to the Provisional Government of Republic of Korea in Shanghai'. The Assembly of the Great Korean raised more than three million

---

[14] Y.J. Kim, *History of Korean Church*, 177.

[15] Y.J. Kim, *History of Korean Church*, 179.

[16] Hongki Kim, *Theology for the Lay Persons* [in Korean] (Seoul: Ewha Women's University Press), 218.

[17] *Contribution of Koreans in Hawaii*, 33.

dollars from 1909 to 1920 and 'most of them were sent to the Provisional Government of Republic of Korea'.[18]

In addition, Korean churches in America played an important role as a cultural centre for the settlement in the United States. For example, early Hawaii immigrant churches established schools within the churches and created a space where all Koreans could gather. Churches opened English-speaking classes and American culture programmes, to help Koreans to adjust to American society.

It was in September 1904, when the Korean Methodist Church rented a small building, and built the first Korean school also using it as a church. After awhile, in Hawaii, 24 Korean schools were established within the churches.[19] These were places for worship and education. These Korean churches also started Korean language schools for the second generation to learn about Korean nationality. In 1913, Methodist Church Mission found Korean Central Agency (School) and actively worked for women education.[20] Thus, everywhere the Korean diaspora spread, they built churches, and churches established Korean schools in which Hangul (Korean characters) and Korean history were taught. Therefore, Korean schools helped immigrants to carry on their national identity and to have identities as Christians.

Emigration Movement after the Liberation from Japan

Korea was liberated from Japan on August 15, 1945 when Japan was defeated in World War II. People who had left to avoid Japanese oppression returned from Japan, China and Russia. However, because of Chinese communism, restrictions were imposed on those who were willing to return to Korea, so many had to settle involuntarily and acquire Chinese nationalities. These people became the Chosun tribe in China. Those living in the Soviet Union, who also could not return, settled in Central Asia and were called Koreiski. However, with the independence, many came back to Korea and the number of immigrants reduced.

In 1950, the Korean War occurred and through this event, the history of Korean emigration started anew. Between 1950 and 1964, 6,000 women married American soldiers and crossed over to the United States.[21] After the Korean War, around 5,000 war orphans were accepted in the United States. In 1953, the US government implemented the policy for Korean War orphans

[18] *Contribution of Koreans in Hawaii*, 35.

[19] *Contribution of Koreans in Hawaii*, 79.

[20] *Contribution of Koreans in Hawaii*, 75.

[21] From 1950 to 2000, women married to US soldiers who went abroad numbered around 100,000. Injin Yune, 'Korean Diaspora: Immigration, Accommodation, Identity of Overseas Korean' [in Korean], *The Society of Social Study in Korea* 6 (2003), 127.

permitting numerous orphaned children to be adopted in the States.[22] Also, many students who were studying in the States decided not to return. There were about 15,000 Koreans in the States by the mid-1960s and the majority was internationally married people.

Until 1960, emigration was limited. The new era of emigration began in the mid-1960s, when the Korean government fully allowed emigration. The Korean government tried to send the surplus population to foreign countries to reduce the population pressure and earn foreign currency. The government made contracts with South America, Western Europe, the Middle East, and North America to send Korean laborers. Under the guidance of the government, in the mid-1960s, agricultural emigration began to Paraguay, Argentina, and Brazil. From 1960, nurses and miners left for Germany.[23] Koreans spread to the United States, China, and Japan and also various parts of Asia, Europe and South America.

In 1965, as the United States amended the law prohibiting Asian immigration (PL 89-236), emigration to America began in earnest. When the United States proclaimed to accept Korean immigration in 1968, hundreds of thousands of Koreans moved abroad searching for economic prosperity and political freedom. Most of the immigrants were highly qualified: 70% of them were highly educated or skilled technicians. According to US census data, 'Koreans over the age of 25 with a bachelor's degree or more education were 34.5% while those with the same level of education among Americans were 20%'.[24]

The immigrants in America settled in urban areas. Unlike other Asian immigrants who settled in Hawaii or Western farmlands, Koreans went to the major cities of the United States such as Los Angeles, New York, Chicago and Philadelphia, in search of better economic opportunities. They laid the foundations of immigration, lived thriftily, received recognition from natives and achieved financial wealth. In addition, wherever they went, they built a church to maintain their ethnic identity as Koreans and to keep their faith as Christians. Wherever Koreans went, Korean churches were built. Korean churches still functioned as the foundation of the Korean community.

The advent of new immigrants meant that the reasons for emigration also varied. Before the liberation from Japan, the emigration group consisted mostly of poor farmers and their reasons were to temporarily escape from famine, oppression and colonial rule. However, after the 1960s, new emigrants migrated to pursue higher living standards and educational opportunities in advanced countries and they preferred to settle permanently.

---

[22] 156,951 people were adopted by the United States from 1953 to 2005. Yunesoo Jang, 'Korean Diaspora and Overseas Adoption', 237-38.

[23] 18,993 nurses and miners were sent to Germany until 1977, according to Truth and Reconciliation Commission of Republic of Korea.

[24] I. Yune, 'Korean Diaspora', 142.

Since 1980, new reasons for emigration emerged. With the Billy Graham Crusade in 1973, Explo '74, and the National Crusade for Evangelization in 1977, churches in Korea grew significantly, thus opening the era of the missionary movement. Many emigrated with the purpose of spreading the good news and emigration increased publicly and personally.

Migrating to 'the Bamboo curtain' of China showed other reasons for emigration. In 1986, the Asian Games were held in Beijing, and in 1992, South Korea established diplomatic ties with China. Koreans expanded their businesses and for employment purposes, they moved to China. These people were called *Sinseonjok* (New Chosun Tribe in China). They migrated to the capital city Beijing, the commercial city Shanghai, Tianjin, Qingdao, Yantai and more. Many of the *Sinseonjok* were Christians and they worshiped in secret and were eager to evangelize the Chinese. After awhile, under the permission of the Chinese government, Korean worship services were held and churches were established all over China. Churches were started in Beijing in 1991, Qingdao in 1992 and Shanghai in 1993. Over the years, the settlement of Korean Christians increased and, today, the number of Korean churches has reached over 300 throughout China.

After the economic crisis that occurred in 1997, many people migrated for economic reasons. However, that was not all. From this decade, many began to migrate for their children's education. Most of them went to English-speaking countries such as the United States, Canada, Australia, New Zealand and the Philippines. Recently, people went to China to learn Chinese.[25] Parents wanted to provide a better environment to raise their children and thus, many families migrated in pursuit of a better education. However, there were those who could not migrate as a whole family. Usually the fathers had to remain in Korea to financially support their families abroad, and they were called 'goose fathers' because they could only meet with their family occasionally like migratory birds.

So far, I have briefly looked over the history of Korean emigration. In spite of its short history, there are Korean immigrants in almost every place in the world. According to the statistics of the Ministry of Foreign Affairs, in 1991, overseas Koreans numbered 4,832,414 and in 2001, 5,653,809 were living in 151 countries. In 2009, 6,822,606 people are residing in 176 countries. During the 10 years from 1991 to 2001, around 800,000 people migrated. In the 21st century, migration accelerated; from 2001 to 2009 the number of migrants

---

[25] However, migration is not increasing in all parts. Migration due to international marriage is decreasing steadily. In the year 1981, 6187 people went, but by 2005 only 445 migrated. See the website of Overseas Koreans Foundation, http://www.korean.net/morgue/status_2.jsp?tCode=status&dCode.

increased by 1,620,000 and the number of countries Koreans emigrated to increased by 25.[26]

Table 1: The Overseas Koreans Foundation, 2009 Statistics[27]

Regions	Country	2005	2007	2009	Percentage	Growth Rate
Asia	Total	3,590,441	4,040,376	3,710,553	54.39	-8.16
	Japan	901,284 (284,840)	893,740 (296,168)	912,655 (320,657)	13.38	2.12
	China	2,439,395	2,762,160	2,336,771 (1,923,329)	34.25	-15.40
	Others	249,732	384,476	461,127	6.76	19.94
America	Total	2,392,828	2,341,163	2,432,634	35.65	3.91
	U.S.A.	2,087,496	2,016,911	2,102,283	30.81	4.23
	Canada	198,170	216,628	223,322	3.27	3.09
	South America	107,162	107,624	107,029	1.57	-0.55
Europe	Total	640,276	645,252	655,843	9.61	1.64
	CIS	532,697	533,976	537,889	7.88	0.73
	Europe	107,579	111,276	117,954	1.73	6.00
East Asia	Total	6,923	9,440	13,999	0.20	48.29
Africa	Total	7,900	8,485	9,577	0.14	12.87
Total Sum		6,638,338	7,044,716	6,822,606	100	-3.15

(Notes)

1) Total number of Koreans who took Japanese citizenship in 1952-2004 (including the Chosun tribe);
2) Total number of Koreans who took Japanese citizenship in 1952-2005 (including the Chosun tribe);
3) Total number of Koreans who took Japanese citizenship in 1952-2008 (including the Chosun tribe);
4) China national census in 2000 on the Chinese (Chinese nationals), the total number of Korean Chinese.

The Korean emigration movement is in some way unique. First, considering the short period of time of the emigration, Koreans spread very extensively.

---

[26] Statistics of Foreign Affairs of Overseas Koreans are less accurate. In the case of Korean Americans, even if they are US citizens, they are included as Koreans being classified by ethnicity. However, in the case of Japanese Koreans, they are not counted as Koreans. I. Yune, 'Korean Diaspora', 125.

[27] See Overseas Koreans Foundation at http://www.korean.net/morgue/status_2.jsp?tCode=status&dCode=0103

The Jews, though having the longest history of diaspora, only went to dozens of countries, while the Koreans in two centuries went to 176 countries. Also, the rate of the migrant population divided by the total population is higher than other countries. Compared to the Chinese, the nation with the world's biggest population, Korea has a much higher percentage of emigrants. While the Chinese have 13 billion people, with 36 million people abroad,[28] a ratio of 0.28%, the Koreans have a ration of 10%. Using the Koreans' nomadic nature, we believe God has a good purpose in spreading Koreans all over the world.

Secondly, the Korean diaspora has maintained its national identity. From the beginning, a large portion of emigration was purposeful, as it desired the country's independence. This was the reason why Koreans could unify and maintain ethnicity. This interest did not change even after the liberation of the country in 1945. The migrants sponsored the democratization and economic development of their mother country. It is not an exaggeration that the achievement of the democratization and economic development of South Korea today, cannot be thought of without the support of the Korean diaspora. Koreans had the tendency to focus on the Korean language and culture, rather than the local culture and formed Korean towns, so they could maintain their national identity. This phenomenon is shown not only in under-developed countries, but also in highly developed countries. Though Christianity emphasizes cosmopolitanism, the Korean diaspora showed a strong ethnic identity. Examples are the Bible and hymns they used. Unlike many other ethnic groups, the Korean diaspora only tended to use the Bible and hymns that were published in Korean. This goes for not only the United States, but also for China and Russia.

Thirdly, the Korean diaspora is church-centred. Korean churches sent missionaries and took care of immigrants and so they naturally became the centre of the immigrants' life. In addition, missionaries were granted a missionary vision, so wherever Korean people went, they established churches so that, today, over 5,500 churches in 176 countries have been built. Through this phenomenon, many say 'Chinese open restaurants wherever they go, Japanese open offices for business, and Koreans start churches'.

Churches became the centre of the Korean diaspora and church life played the most important role in overseas Korean communities. Church attendance became a way of life to the Korean Americans and nowadays approximately 65-70% of Koreans attend church two or three times a week, and around 80-90% go to church at least once a week.[29] For the Korean diaspora, church is inseparable from their lives.

---

[28] Lawrence Tong, 'Mission Potential of China Diaspora and Partnership with NEAN'.

[29] Kyeho Kim, '100 Years of Korean Diaspora Church in America: Retrospect and Prospective, with Special References to Religious-Sociological point of View' [in Korean].

Conclusion

From the beginning of the emigration movement until now, the Korean diaspora churches have grown up with a close relationship with their mother country. At the end of the Chosun Dynasty and the Korea Empire period, the Korean diaspora churches devoted all their strength to the country's modernization and evangelization. During the Japanese colonial period, they fought for Korea's independence. After the liberation from Japan, they prayed for and participated in the revival of Korean churches, economic development, democratization and national reunification. As the Korean diaspora fulfilled the given mission in each period, the country has made progress in church and society.

The Korean diaspora churches preserved their cultural heritage and did their best to nurture immigrants in faith. The diaspora Christians believed in the Bible as the word of God, and were acknowledged by people outside of the church by living in the word. They preached the gospel to those who did not know the good news and led many to church. As a result, among the people who were not believers about 40% became Christian after emigration.[30] Approximately 25% of the Korean church members have church offices, and the majority of them are proud to hold church offices. This shows how important church life is to the Korean diaspora.

The Korean diaspora churches fulfil their duty as a social shelter for immigrants. This has served well those in the United States, a multi-cultural society, where Koreans are an ethnic minority. Though the society seems to be tolerant of cultural differences superficially, multi-culturalism in the United States is considered lop-sided. The mainstream culture is based on the WASP (White Anglo-Saxons Protestant) culture and others that originate from other foreign countries are somewhat down-graded.[31] Because of these discrimination, cultural differences and language barriers, the immigrants' frustrations mounted but the Korean churches were devoted to reduce the stress and fought to establish the Koreans' social status. They opened Korean schools, kept Korean culture alive to preserve ethnic kinship and connections, and also created a social network to help Koreans find jobs. They also created a family-like atmosphere for the peace of mind of the immigrants so they could achieve social cohesion in the Korean community.[32]

---

[30] Kim, '100 Years of Korean Diaspora Church in America'.

[31] Joonkyu Park, 'Identity of Korean in America as Diaspora' [in Korean].

[32] The evidence was found in 2008 edition of *Christianity Today*, which was launch of 11th anniversary, and carried 'the Korean American Church Status' for pastors' survey. According to the survey, most of Korean pastors pointed out that the most important elements of church growth are 'hardship of immigration life' (23.3%) and fundamental role of Church to immigration society (18.8%). This stands for the Korean churches have been positive attitudes to the Korean.

However, the Korean diaspora should not be satisfied with these achievements. Koreans have to understand that it was God's great will to spread them to 176 countries and to allow them to build over 5,500 Korean diaspora churches in the world within only a century. As pointed out in the early part of the text, to spread the gospel to Korea, God raised the world missionary movement in the nineteenth century. As God used other nations and people to fulfil his work in Korea, He will also use the Koreans to fulfil his works in other countries. Moreover, the Korean pop culture, also known as the 'Korean Wave', is now spreading all around the world, and this can activate a new means to boost the evangelization of nations that accept Korean culture. As missionary Minyoung Jung pointed out, 'The hidden reason for God waking up people of the hermit nation from its long hibernation and spreading them all over the world is for a missionary purpose'.[33] Jung's point is well-timed, for to use Korean churches as a tool of mission for today, God has made Koreans travel and settle all over the world.

The Korean diaspora does in fact have a great understanding of the local history and language, and are well prepared workers. Especially, the second generation of the Korean diaspora, the people with the knowledge of the local language and culture, should accomplish world mission. If we take advantage of these resources in mission, our achievements will be fruitful. Such an example can be found in Brazil and Chile where Koreans are evangelizing the locals and recently sharing a time of harvest.[34] Moreover, Korean churches are ready to unite in an evangelical faith by sending the second generation as missionaries to adjacent countries to accomplish the commission.[35] If the Korean diaspora churches, Korean missions and Korean churches strengthen their solidarity, Korea will be able to bear fruit enormously.

To achieve the great commission, the diaspora churches must become healthy. Pastors should teach and deliver the words of the Bible with all their heart and take care of the believers. The saints should live as the light and salt of the world and by evangelization they should build a healthy church. Furthermore, the Korean churches should endeavor to fulfil their historical mission given to their people, such as the unification of Korea. Also they should avoid individualism and form the unification between local churches to execute God's work.[36] Based on these unities, they should develop wholesome

---

[33] Minyoung Jung, 'Mobilize the Korean Diaspora for the Mission Resources as Strategy' [in Korean] (Presented at the Baltimore Forum, 2004), 3.

[34] Kwongsoon Lee, 'Direction of Korea Presbyterian Mission' [in Korean], 163.

[35] 'Singapore Korean Churches are now sending missionaries to Indonesia, Malaysia, and to India'. Union Church and Youngnack Church in Sao Paulo, Brazil are also sending missionaries worldwide. K. Lee, 'Direction of Korea Presbyterian Mission', 163.

[36] For this, there was the first Korean diaspora forum in Baltimore by Rev. Soongeun Lee in 2004. The second was in New York (2005), the third in Beijing, China (2006),

pastor leadership and education programmes to inspire the next generation so they can work out and fulfil the world mission.

---

the fourth in Tokyo, Japan (2007), the fifth in Kuala Lumpur, Malaysia (2008) and the sixth in Shanghai, China (2009) and the seventh in Sokcho, Korea (2000).

The Founding and Development of the Korean Diaspora Forum

Soon Keun Lee

This article is intended to introduce the founding and development of the Korean Diaspora Forum which took place at the seventh Korean Diaspora Forum in 2010. For a better understanding of the forum, I begin with a brief history of the Korean diaspora.

History of Korean Diaspora

According to 2005 statistics, 6.6 million Koreans are estimated to live in 160 different countries around the world.[1] About 10% of the total population of the Korean Peninsula, including North Koreans, are scattered all over the world. The majority are regionally settled in China (2.43 million), the United States (2.08 million), Japan (900,000) and the Commonwealth of Independent States (530,000). Although the history of the Korean diaspora was an unintentional consequence of the unfortunate modern history of Korea, this diaspora has become an invaluable human resource with respect to globalization.

Historically, there are four periods of the Korean diaspora.[2] The first period is from the 1860s to 1910, when farmers and labourers emigrated to China, Russia, and Hawaii to escape famine, poverty, and oppression by the ruling class. The second period is between 1910 and 1945, when Koreans moved to Japan to fill a labour shortage during the war. In this period a group of political refugees and activists also migrated to China, Russia, and the United States to carry out independent resistance against the Japanese colonization. The third period is from 1945 to 1962, the year when the South Korean government established an emigration policy. The fourth period is from 1962 to the present. In 1962 the South Korean government promoted emigration widely to Latin America, Western Europe, the Middle East, and North America.

In China, in the 1860s, Koreans were forced to move to the northern border due to severe famine and poverty. Since then, the majority of the Korean population in China have settled in the northeast parts of China until now. Its

---

[1] Statistics by the Ministry of Foreign Affairs and Trade, Korea (2005).

[2] In-Jin Yoon, 'Understanding the Korean Diaspora from Comparative Perspectives, Transformation and Prospect toward Multiethnic, Multiracial and Multicultural Society: Enhancing Intercultural Communication' (Presentation at the Asia Culture Forum, 2006), 1.

population in 1990 was 1,865,000 (Chinese census 1990). But in the late 1980s, they began to scatter to the big cities in China and the migration extended overseas: first to Russia, then to South Korea and Japan, and finally to the United States and Canada. They are called Korean Chinese.

In the former Soviet Union (CIS), there are 521,694 Koreans, according to statistics by the Ministry of Foreign Affairs and Trade of South Korea in 2001. A large scale of migration began to Russia due to the famine in 1863. Additional waves of migration to Russia have been made because of the Japanese annexation between 1910 and 1923. 120,000 Koreans had settled in the Far East in 1925.[3] But in 1937 by an order from Stalin, the entire population of 171,781 Koreans was relocated to Central Asia, particularly to Kazakhstan and Uzbekistan.

In Japan, Korean migration took place during the annexation of Korea to Japan. As of May 2000, 636,548 Koreans had Korean nationality as compared to 160,000 Koreans who became naturalized Japanese citizens. Korean migration to Japan has occurred several times due to its historical proximity. There is a clear distinction between those who migrated to Japan during the annexation period, and those who migrated after independence. The first generation formed ethnic enclaves isolated from the Japanese in large industrial cities. Later generations assimilated into Japanese culture and society.

In America, early Korean migration was initiated by Hawaii's sugar planters. American missionaries such as Dr. Horace Allen played a crucial role in linking the demand for cheap labour with migrants from Korea. Between the liberation of the nation and the post-war era (1945-1965), there were a sizable number of intermarriages and many Korean students came to America. Since 1965 when America opened its door to all immigrants, many Koreans began to emigrate in search of better economic and educational opportunities. In 2000, the U.S. census showed the Korean American population to be 1,076,872. Ninety-six percent of Koreans live in large cities.

In Canada, Canadian missionaries took the very important role of bringing prospective Korean students to Canada in the 1900s, by way of the missionary scholarship programme. The early Korean immigrants before the 1960s consisted of church pastors, medical doctors, and scholars. In 1966, as the change of immigration policy allowed 'people of colour' to enter into Canada, Korean immigrants also increased gradually. During the last four decades, 88,957 Koreans entered Canada for permanent residence.

In Europe, Korean immigration began with students and employees of companies in the 1960s. The first group of coal miners and nurses arrived in Germany in 1963 as part of a labour export programme agreed upon between South Korea and West Germany. As many European countries insisted on a policy of non-immigration, most Korean immigrants could not settle in the

---

[3] H.Y. Kwon, *The Koreans in the World: The Commonwealth of Independent States* [in Korean] (Seoul: Korean Ministry of National Unification, 1996).

region as permanent residents after completing their studies or contracts. According to recent statistics in 2005,[4] about 500,000 Koreans were living within 48 European countries.

In addition to the above regions, as early as the 1960s, Koreans also began to scatter to South America, Africa, Australia, the Middle East and South East Asia.

Korean Diaspora Churches Worldwide[5]

The history of the Korean diaspora in most areas is very closely linked to the history of Korean churches in the different regions. It is clear that the Korean church has historically been the centre of the migrant society.[6] It has greatly affected many lives of migrants, not only religiously but also socially, culturally, and emotionally. For example, during the Japanese colonization, the early Korean churches in America set up a political campaign for independence from Japan.

In general, many academic observations[7] show there has been a significant change in Korean churches between the early and later migrant stages. The church began with a strong political and social agenda, but became privatized and personal. At the same time, Korean churches were often observed to be an ethnic community that reinforced a tendency of sectarianization and ghettorization[8], separated from the society where they lived. This phenomenon has resulted from an increasing religious faith and a personalized commitment to the religion. Furthermore, many Korean diaspora Christians, like other immigrants, took refuge in the church as they believed it gave them practical incentives for life.

---

[4] The number was prepared by the Ministry of Foreign Affairs and Trade in Korea. 48 countries include countries in Central Asia and Russia as well as CIS countries in Europe.

[5] According to *Directory of World Korean Diaspora Churches* (Korean Christian Newspaper in America, 2010), there are 3,882 churches in America, 254 in Canada, 206 in Japan, 150 in Australia, 67 in Germany, 56 in the UK, 54 in Brazil, 54 in Argentina, and 205 in other areas. The total number of churches in 2009 was 4,928.

[6] Nancy Abelmann and John Lie, *Blue Dreams: Korean Americans and the Los Angeles Riots* (Cambridge: Harvard University Press, 1995), 69.

[7] Refer to Kye Ho, Kim, *A Review of 100 Years of the USA Korean Churches and Looking to the Future, Diaspora Britain* [in Korean] (London: KCA, 2004), 176-178.

[8] According to Kim, *A Review of 100 Years*, Korean diaspora churches have been characterized as an ethnic community by fostering the micro-level functions for the immigrants. Meanwhile, Korean diaspora churches have shown a tendency not to be involved in social issues of the host countries. He conceptualized this phenomenon as secterianization or ghettorization.

Even though the KDC took a very significant role in Korean migrant societies in past times, it is apparent that Korean diaspora churches have been losing their intrinsic commitment to mission as part of the nature of church.[9]

To analyze the mission performance of the KDC and find its implications for Korean mission, it is necessary to scrutinize both internal factors and external influences in the formation of the KDC, to provide a context for the research. The KDC has been marked by quite distinctive features. These distinctive features have resulted not only from the influence of distinctive Christian practice of the home country, [10] but also from social-cultural factors[11] in the host country.

It was observed that the key function of the KDC was to provide for the practical and urgent needs of church members. This implies that the KDC merely took on cultural, social, and psychological roles. The KDC can facilitate ethnic fellowship for the members as they use the same language and share the same culture. In this respect, the church provides an atmosphere where members can find identity, solidarity, and security.

Viewed from a social perspective, most Koreans of the diaspora of the first generation are marginalized in society in terms of economy and social status, due to language barriers and cultural differences. Therefore, they tend to withdraw from the host society. Viewed from a psychological perspective, the KDC is the place where Korean immigrants attempt to get rid of their frustration and sufferings of their tough immigrant lives by relying on God. This kind of religious fervour often enhances their commitment to attend religious meetings more frequently in order to get inner peace and experience God's presence. The KDC, in this respect, stimulates their religious fervour by

---

[9] As David J. Bosch signifies in *Transforming Mission: Paradigm Shifts in Theology of Mission* (Maryknoll, NY: Orbis Books, 1991), 370, the church is the mission. He quoted the summary of Newbigin for three categories: 1) 'the church is the mission'; 2) 'the home base is everywhere', and 3) 'mission in partnership'.

[10] These practices by Korean immigrants were influenced by the Korean church tradition in the home country. Thus, the Christian practice has to be reflected by the home culture and tradition. Korean Christians tend to be particularly religiously fervent, doctrinally fundamental in faith, highly committed to authority, externally isolated to the world, and strongly privatized in their religion. Refer to the following lists for more conceptualizations about the distinction between religion and sect. Ernst Troeltsch, *The Social Teaching of the Christian Churches* (New York: Macmillan, 1932), 331-41; Bryan Wilson, *Religion in Sociological Perspective* (New York: Oxford University Press, 1982); Meredith B. McGuire, *Religion: The Social Context* (Belmont, CA: Wadsworth Publishing, 1992), 133-148.

[11] Yoon, 'Understanding the Korean Diaspora', 6, under 'A Model of Social-cultural Adaptation of Overseas Koreans'. According to Yoon, there are four modes of social-cultural adaptation: 1) integration (accommodation), 2) assimilation, 3) isolation, and 4) marginality.

inspiring and encouraging them. Thus the church became sectarianized, and privatized.

Although there are as many as 5,000 Korean diaspora churches, and there are a variety of different mission activities that they are involved in, it seems difficult to evaluate the effectiveness of their mission work. Could it be that the KDC has a lack of understanding of the importance of the mission due to an unawareness of the crucial role of the church?

The Origins of the Korean Diaspora Forum

This forum came into existence with the hopes of addressing three main issues that the immigrant Korean churches face: ministry, education, and mission. These three issues can be summarized into the following questions. First, how can these churches be healthy in ministry? Second, how can they raise up the second generation as godly people? Lastly, how can they contribute to world missions? The forum originated in order to address these issues as a Korean diaspora community, and what follows is a discussion of these three key questions.

Ministry

Ministry in the Korean immigrant churches does not differ too much from the ministry of Korean churches in Korea. Nonetheless, certain conflicts arise in the ministry to Korean immigrant churches precisely because they are immigrant or bicultural and cross-cultural settings. Therefore it becomes important to prevent or minimize these conflicts. The Korean immigrant church is often the social centre of a local Korean immigrant community. This means that the immigrant church is not only a faith community but also a social hub of the Korean community. Therefore, various problems that may arise in any small society are often found within the church. This is a unique trait of ministry to immigrant churches, and there is a need to directly address these problems in ministry.

Education

The second generation Koreans growing up in the immigrant churches go through an identity crisis, not only on the level of psychological development, but also on the social, cultural, and racial levels as well. Somewhere in their identity formation they must ask the question: 'Am I an American or a Korean?' or 'Am I a Brazilian or a Korean?' etc. Whereas the Korean churches in the U.S. tended to instill in the youth, 'You are a Korean-American' in the past, nowadays they tend to say to them, 'You are a United States citizen of Korean heritage'. These youth tend to view themselves as Americans but often experience that the mainstream society views them as Koreans, especially in college. Korean churches in North America try to prevent this crisis of identity by running Korean schools where they teach Korean culture, history, and even Taekwon-do in addition to the Korean language.

The Korean immigrant churches of Southeast Asia face a different situation in educating the second generation. The majority of the youth growing up in Korean churches in China, the Philippines, Malaysia, Thailand, Indonesia, and Vietnam have strong identities as Koreans. The question on the table for them is not identity formation but college destination. They must choose if they want to attend college in their resident country, in Korea, or in a third country such as the USA, UK, or Canada. Attending college in Korea is not a simple matter because although they tend to speak Korean more fluently than their counterparts in North America, they are often incapable of reading and writing Korean at the university level. Furthermore, attending college in their resident country is also difficult because unlike many of their counterparts in North America, often they are citizens not of their respective resident countries but of Korea. Therefore, the second generation youth in Southeast Asian countries are often expected to attend university in Korea. But as aforementioned, in reality the language barrier makes such expectations nearly impossible to fulfil. Lastly, attending college in an English-speaking country such as the USA, UK, or Canada is also not easy because of the comparably high cost, worsened by their international student status at the financial aid office.

In terms of Christian education, in the case of Korean youth in North America, many attend church regularly throughout high school but leave the church after college matriculation. Currently, churches in North America are struggling with this issue. It must also be noted that in North America currently many second generation youth are leaving Korean churches and starting independent congregations of not only second-generation Koreans but also Chinese, Japanese, and Southeast Asians as well. Multi-ethnic or pan-Asian churches are being planted by second-generation Koreans who are leaving their home churches. While such a phenomenon is beneficial in some ways, it points to the fact that the Korean immigrant churches in North America are facing some serious issues in trying to relate to and connect with the next generation.

Mission

From a mission perspective, North America, where the majority of diaspora Korean churches are, forms a large sending bloc as the USA and Canada are high-sending countries. On the flipside, Korean churches in China must focus on being a missional church rather than on sending missionaries elsewhere as they are in a primarily receiving country. Further, most Korean immigrant churches outside of North America find themselves in the mission field. In that sense, mission is more of a reality for the Korean diaspora churches than for the Korean churches located in Korea. From the studies previously found through this forum, the churches abroad tend to use more resources, both human and financial, on missions than the churches in Korea. Whereas the churches of Korea are sending the missionaries to the field, the Korean churches abroad are working together with the missionaries in the field.

The mission potential of the Korean churches abroad is immense in that that they can serve the local churches of their regional mission field. An important mission strategy for them will be to partner with the local churches and organizations to help the indigenous church grow and to keep it healthy in addition to evangelizing the local people directly. Such a ministry, in cooperating with the local churches in the mission field, will also help in constructing a missional partnership between the Korean churches abroad and the ones in Korea. The Korean churches in Korea can pass on their certified ministry strategies and resources to the ones abroad, while the Korean churches abroad can share them with the local churches in order to strengthening their ministry, and the healthy local churches can evangelize the local non-Christians to ultimately bear fruit in missions. The multi-directional partnership among the privileged Korean churches in Korea, the diaspora Korean churches, and the local churches in the mission field can be an effective strategy for missions.

The Founding and Development of the Korean Diaspora Forum (Previously the Baltimore Forum)

In 2004, Bethel Korean Church in greater Baltimore in Maryland, USA, celebrated its 24th anniversary. Rev. Soon Keun Lee, the senior pastor of Bethel Church at the time, invited Korean ministers from many major cities by continent to the 'Invitational Open Forum for Korean Pastors' for the church's 24th anniversary. Ministers from North and South America, Asia, Europe, Oceania and Africa gathered together for four days to earnestly discuss and pray for the Korean churches abroad and their ministry, education and mission. The major questions were: 'How can these Korean churches be healthy?' 'How can we raise the second generation Koreans to be Godly people?' and 'How can we specifically contribute to world missions?' On the last day of the forum, the attending pastors decided to continue on with such gatherings and to call it the Baltimore Forum. They left Baltimore with an agreement to meet and discuss the three major questions over the next two consecutive years. As Rev. Jae Yeol Kim of the Korean Central Presbyterian Church of New York volunteered to host the second forum and Tae Yoon Park of the 21st Century Church of Beijing offered to host the third forum, everyone departed with high hopes for the next year's meeting. For many of these Korean diaspora pastors, the forum had been a time when they could break away from the lonely immigrant ministry field and come together with other pastors in similar situations. It was a time of comfort, rest, and fellowship with other pastors in the context of a greater vision for Korean diaspora churches.

As planned, in May of 2005 Rev. Jae Yeol Kim of the Korean Central Presbyterian Church of New York hosted the second forum. This year happened to be the church's 25th anniversary, and the forum again became a part of an anniversary celebration. Although the second forum's participation level was a bit lower than hoped because many events were going on in New York at the time, it acted as a crucial bridge for the continuation of the Korean Diaspora Forum as a whole. During that time, the name 'Baltimore Forum' rose as an issue, although its appropriateness was questioned as the meeting was held in New York. At the end, to preserve the history of the forum, the name was kept and the term 'Baltimore Forum in New York' was used.

In 2006, the third forum congregated in Beijing as scheduled, and this time around 'Teacher' Tae Yoon Park's active networking provided for a very vibrant forum. New participants were gathered, including not only Korean ministers in China but also ones in other regions from around the world. A broader networking pool was established, and the Korean immigrant pastors continued to discuss the prominent issues at the forum's founding. A ministry team of the 21st Century Church called *Jeephyun-jun* (after the house of scholars in the Chosun Dynasty who served the king) served throughout the forum to help it run smoothly, and the participants enjoyed walking around the busy night markets of Beijing together. During the final general assembly of the third forum, the participants decided to continue the forum annually rather than finish with the three consecutive years as had been planned. And so on the last day's session of the third forum, the next few years' hosts and schedules were tentatively scheduled. The fourth forum would take place at the Yohan (John) Tokyo Church and be hosted by Rev. Gyu Dong Kim despite the short notice, and the fifth one by Rev. Gi Hong Kim in Kuala Lumpur, Malaysia. The sixth host and venue went to Rev. Chul Bum Shin in Dubai, and the seventh went to Rev. Eun Il Jung in South Africa.

The fourth forum, held in Tokyo, provided the participants with a closer look not only at Rev. Gyu Dong Kim's ministry at Yohan Church but also the current state of missions in Japan as well as the important role of Korean churches in Japan. This also was a time of blessed fellowship as many new ministers were invited by Rev. Kim and joined the forum for the first time. On the last day each participant received a CD of all the meetings of the conference and the discussion content, with much credit to the Yohan Church's support and manpower! The participants also had a grand tour of the Fuji Mountain and enjoyed a natural spring spa experience together.

The Open Church in Kuala Lumpur hosted the fifth forum. Rev. Gi Hong Kim, the senior pastor of this church, is known for his 'free-spirited, laughter-filled, and Spirit-filled ministry'. Fittingly, the general atmosphere of this forum was natural, casual, and relaxed like the climate of Kuala Lumpur. The hotel was famous for once having hosted the G7, and the interior was decorated with all sorts of horse decorations due the owner's love for them! One important item on the agenda was changing the name from the 'Baltimore Forum' to the 'Korean Diaspora Forum'. As the forum had started settling down into an annual structure and becoming more well-known, it was concluded that Baltimore was a small region and the name was hard to remember. So for better communication with the general public and for its appropriateness to the character of the forum, the name was permanently changed to the Korean Diaspora Forum.

The location for the sixth forum was originally Dubai, but due to the decline of the world economy, it would have cost substantially more than usual to host it there. After an urgent discussion, Rev. Gi Young Um offered to host the sixth forum in Shanghai. This forum in Shanghai was significant in several ways. First, a major ministry of the forum which had been developing in the past forums – BAM (Business as Mission) – found its place during this forum. Second, it was meaningful that the forum took place for the first time with the new name, the Korean Diaspora Forum. Third, a committee was officially formed to put on the World Korean Pastors United Forum to take place in Seoul in May 2010. Fourth, Rev. Gi Hwan Jung of Manila was officially designated the secretary general of the Korean Diaspora Forum. Lastly, it was a time of valuable discussion regarding the establishment of the Korean Diaspora Research Center, which is being pursued in collaboration with KODIMNET.

Due to the World Cup, the seventh Korean Diaspora Forum took place in the motherland of South Korea instead of South Africa on May 18-21, 2010. It was hosted by Rev. Soon Keun Lee of All Love Church and took place at the Kensington Star Hotel located in the Seol-Ak Mountain. This particular hotel is owned by E-Land, a major company in Korea that is intentionally Christian, and it is also a place where various mission conferences have taken place. It was very exciting to host the KDF at such a place with E-Land's cooperation. The scenery around the hotel was spectacular since it was located just below a Budhist temple Shin Heung Sa. A total of about 160 to 170 participants gathered together: immigrant church pastors and wives, Korean church pastors and wives, and missionaries. Also attending were some members of the diaspora team of the Lausanne Movement and a few non-Korean Christian diaspora leaders. The main purpose of the seventh forum was to form a strong network between the immigrant churches abroad and the churches in Korea. Of course, this collaboration was for the purpose of world mission. Also it was important to form a strong network between the Korean diaspora churches and Lausanne as well as with the various diaspora churches from other ethnic groups around the world.

The Prospects of the Korean Diaspora Forum

Looking at Jesus' command to go beyond borders ('therefore, go') and beyond race ('make disciples of all nations') to share the gospel, it is important to note that the Korean diaspora churches have already gone beyond the borders. The fact that currently Koreans have scattered to approximately 180 countries all over the world means that they have gone beyond borders. However, the mission to go beyond race in making disciples is far from being fully realized among the Korean diaspora churches. There are, of course, some churches abroad that have already gone beyond racial barriers for missions. Some of these churches are Yohan Tokyo Church, where Rev. Gyo Dong Kim is the senior pastor, the 21st Century Beijing Church with 'Teacher' Tae Yoon Park, and the Thailand Korean churches of Bangkok led by Rev. Yong Sup Kim.

I believe that if Korean immigrant churches can come together to go 'beyond race', then this would go down as a celebratory record in world mission history. However, this cannot be done with the efforts of the Korean churches alone. It will be impossible to accomplish this without the networking between the Korean churches in Korea, the churches of other races, and the local churches of the resident countries. I pray that through this forum, the Korean diaspora churches will intentionally network with those churches and with one another in order to overcome racial barriers for the sake of world missions.

I personally like Ephesians 3:20-21 and find it appropriate for praying for KDF at this time: 'Now to him who is able to do immeasurably more than all we ask or imagine, according to his power that is at work within us, to him be glory in the church and in Christ Jesus throughout all generations, forever and ever! Amen'.

As this passage states I believe our God will accomplish things beyond our wildest imagination through the Korean Diaspora Forum!

A South Korean Case Study of Migrant Ministries

David Chul Han Jun

Introduction

According to the *Korea Herald* newspaper, we are living in a global nomadic age, where one out of seven people is a migrant in today's world population.[1] The United Nations Development Program (UNDP) in its regular publication stated, 'Migration contributes to human development and it is a motive power, and it increases individuals' finance, health, and education'.[2] For this reason, people move from country to city, and similarly we have many migrant workers, which we now call 'new nomadic people'.

If we visit any mega-city in the world, we will see many different groups of ethnic people living together. I view this phenomenon as a God-given opportunity for world mission. God has also given this opportunity to the Republic of Korea through the immigration of foreign workers and students, and multicultural families. We must seize this unprecedented opportunity for world mission on our doorstep.

The nickname of the Israelites of the Bible is 'the diaspora'. The meaning of the term comes from a Greek word that indicates 'scattering'. The diaspora originally meant the Jews relocated from Palestine. They had to endure their fate as the diaspora. Through the prophets, God reminded them of their identity as God's chosen people. When the Israelites lost their identity as God's missionaries, God dispersed them to restore their mission.

After Jesus was resurrected, his disciples were filled with the Holy Spirit on the day of Pentecost in Jerusalem. God-fearing Jews and converts to Judaism were visiting Jerusalem at that time. There were Parthians, Medes and Elamites; residents of Mesopotamia, Judea and Cappadocia, Pontus and Asia, Phrygia and Pamphylia, Egypt and the parts of Libya near Cyrene; and visitors from Rome. Among the Gentiles, Cretans and Arabs heard the gospel of Jesus, and some of them believed and returned to their countries (Acts 2:9-11). The Apostle James started his letter 'To the twelve tribes scattered among the nations'. The Apostle Peter also begins his letter: 'To God's elect scattered in the world'.

[1] 'New Nomadic Era,' *Korea Herald*, 5 Oct, 2009.

[2] UNDP, 'Human Development Report' (http://hdr.undp.org/en/reports/global/hdr2009/papers/HDRP_2009_02_rev.pdf, 5 Oct, 2009).

Scattering itself is a painful event in history, and yet there is always God's sovereign will in that history. In Acts chapter 8, there was a great persecution in Jerusalem, and all Christians left there to go to Judah, Samaria, and to the ends of the world. Through their scattering they began to preach the gospel in Judah, Samaria, and to the ends of the world.

The experience of diaspora is not only limited to the Jewish people, but also to the people of many other nations. For instance, the Chinese now live all over the world, as do Spaniards, Portuguese, British, and Germans. This is due to economic, political, and military reasons. Lately, Koreans are also living in over 200 different Nations. When I traveled to the west corner of Africa, I visited the Benin Republic and the Republic of the Gambia, and I was surprised to meet Koreans there. Wherever Koreans emigrate, many of them start Christian churches, and these churches become the centre of their migrant life.

God is now using the Korean diaspora as a missionary tool. During the Japanese occupation of Korea, Japan forcefully sent many Koreans to Sakhalin and Central Asia; nevertheless, the descendants of these Koreans have helped Christian missionaries in the Soviet Union, especially with translation. Some of the Korean diaspora in mainland China have themselves also become useful missionary resources. I believe over seven million Koreans who are now living as diaspora are potentially extremely important for mission in the twenty-first century. The recognition of the Korean diaspora mission is one of the most important strategies in recent Korean Christian mission.[3]

On December 2009, the Korea World Missions Association (KWMA) held the nineth Korea mission leader forum and its memorandum declared that world mission should be developed by the diaspora:

> We need to notice the significance of world mission through diasporas, and especially the Korean diaspora because of their church development through the 'three-self formula': self-supporting, self-propagating, and self-governing. This Korean diaspora church development should become a model to other nations' diaspora church establishment. All diaspora churches should become self-supporting, self-propagating, and self-governing, so that they will become missional churches wherever they are.
>
> 1) Development of Korean Diaspora Church: We are paying our attention to the Korean diaspora churches. They were dispersed all over the world due to historical, economical, and military reasons. Wherever they have gone, they have voluntarily established churches and have become missionary sending stations. The Korean diaspora churches have been approved by missionaries for their great contribution to world mission. Korean diaspora churches and missionaries should co-operate with each other; in other words, lay leaders in the Korean diaspora

[3] C.H. Jun, 'World Christian Mission through Migrant Workers in South Korea and through the Korean Diaspora' (A presentation at Tokyo 2010 Global Mission Consultation and Celebration, Tokyo, May 2010).

churches and missionaries should support each other by taking different roles to fulfil world mission.

2) Development of Diaspora Mission within the Republic of Korea: We have to take notice of Korean and other diasporas in the world, and we should use diasporas within the Republic of Korea for world mission. We have to take a careful look at various types of diasporas within Korea in order to develop appropriate training programmes for them. Our goals for diaspora mission in South Korea are witnessing, discipleship, and missionary training because the people reached represent potential future missionaries for their own countries. We need to continuously develop worship services for diasporas in S. Korea according to their major tribal groups and languages. Korean mission societies should provide workers for this ministry. For this migrant mission we also need to have various networks to have more effective ministries.[4]

The above shows the diaspora mission process in South Korea, and its direction and strategy. The development of diaspora mission in South Korea upgrades world mission evangelism. When the Korean churches see 1.2 million foreigners as future co-workers in mission rather than as an object of witness a new window will open for mission. For this kind of diaspora mission, all Korean churches and world churches must participate together for success.

Since the late 1980s, a new group has formed in Korean society. They are the migrant workers who work in factories where Koreans do not want to work because of low salaries and poor working conditions. When migrant workers come into Korean society, they bring their culture but we are not ready to receive them. Therefore, we experience cultural conflict, and it causes new problems in our society. We need to know each other's cultures and use this wonderful opportunity for God's kingdom. According to the Ministry of Justice statistics, the national total number of foreigners is more than 1.2 million.[5] This figure corresponds to 2% of the total resident population in South Korea, and in 2020 we are expecting it to increase to 5%.

Predicaments of Migrant Workers

Although the foreign workers' institutional status is getting better, factory owners still have more advantages than the migrant workers. For instance, when foreign workers want to move to better factories, they have to have their factory owners' permission. They also experience the fear of living in a new society. It happens to everyone although it may differ from person to person.

[4] 'A Statement of the 9th Korean Mission Leaders Forum' [in Korean], in *Memorandum of the Nineth Korean Mission Leaders' Forum* (http://www.kwma.org, 2009).

[5] Ministry of Justice, '2009 Annual Statistics of Ministry of Justice' [in Korean] (31 Dec, 2009).

There was a case in Inchon in 2006 involving Mr. H from Indonesia. Even though he never started working in the factory, after a week he went to an organization for foreign workers and asked them to help him to go back to his country. The factory owner said that he could not understand why the foreign worker could not work although he never started working. The owner said if he came to work, he must work even if it might be hard for him. Fear of living in a new society and loneliness happen to all migrants, and yet we do not understand them.

The Korea Labor Institute and Korea Women's Policy Institute corporately studied the Koreans' perspective on foreign workers. They asked Korean workers how they communicated with foreign workers in their factories: Korean language is 63.2% and body language is about 30%.[6] From this study we assume that their communication is not efficient. This ratio would not change regardless of the Korean workers' work experiences with migrant workers whether it is long or short.

Means of Communication with Foreign Workers[7]

Work experience with foreign workers	Korean (%)	English (%)	through Inter-preter (%)	body language (%)	Etc (%)	Total
Less than 1 yr.	59.7	5.2	0.0	33.8	1.3	100
1-2 yrs.	66.4	3.6	0.7	28.6	0.7	100
2-4 yrs.	57.5	7.5	1.4	30.8	2.7	100
More than 4 yrs.	67.9	5.2	3.0	23.9	0.0	100
Average	63.2	5.4	1.4	28.8	1.2	100

In other words, most Korean workers mainly communicate with their foreign workers in Korean and body language, so if migrant workers cannot understand Korean, they would not be able to communicate. Before entering South Korea, a migrant workers' ability to communicate in the Korean language determines the success of his work experience. Although migrant workers have Korean language training both prior to and after arrival in South Korea, their training is rather short, and it may not practically help them to communicate with their Korean workers. For this reason, foreign workers often have accidents in their work places.

---

[6] Korea Labor Institute and Korea Women's Policy Institute, 'Percepntion of Korean General Public towards Foreign Laborors' [in Korean] (2007).

[7] G.T. Oh, 'Korean Perspective on Migrant Workers: Focus on Work Places' [in Korean] (A study presented at the Shinchon Forum 22, 2007), 83.

At the Ansan Immigrants Center, Rev. Chon Eung Pak notes that the four most frequent foreign workers' human rights violations are discrimination (27.7%), withholding identification (26.7%), violence (15.5%), and forced labour (14.3%). If violations continue migrant workers do not enjoy their life in South Korea. Moreover, when they leave South Korea, foreign workers do not have a good impression.[8]

The biggest obstacle for foreign workers to adjust to, in Korean society, is our prejudice toward them. As Pak's study points out, Korean workers' prejudice against fellow foreign workers is the highest percentage. This reflects the Korean society's lack of experience in living with foreigners. Most Koreans are not ready to live with foreigners, who have a different language, culture, religion, and are of a different race. Furthermore, most Koreans do not have an opportunity to experience life with foreign workers because they usually reside in different areas.

In addition to the foreign workers' fear of living in a new society, prejudice and poor working conditions, migrant workers also have a high level of stress. In addition, their lack of good communication with fellow Korean workers may increase their desire to give up their Korean life all together. If they experience violence, unpaid wages, withholding identification, and prejudice, they will resent or hate Koreans. Although migrant workers still work in our factories, they will only work for their wages. They are going to seek revenge for their poor treatment in South Korea when they have their chance. This is a great loss for our nation.

Therefore, churches and missionary organizations are taking care of migrant workers by helping to improve their difficult life in South Korea, so that they open their hearts to the gospel message and have a good impression of this country.

Mission Status of Foreign Workers: Features and Challenges

Since the 1990s, many churches and missionary organizations have been ministering to foreign workers. Churches and missionary organizations have been working with foreign workers to solve various human rights' violations for them because they have become our social problems. Rev. Haesung Kim, who is the pastor at a missionary organization for Chinese Koreans, started his organization as a counseling place for migrant workers, mainly focusing on their human rights. On the other hand, evangelical churches and missionary organizations focus their ministry on the gospel to foreign workers because their ultimate goal is to make them disciples of Christ. We now have around 500 churches and missionary organizations in South Korea ministering to foreign workers.

[8] C.E. Park, 'The Present Reality of Foreign Workers and Multicultural Policy Agenda' [in Korean] (A paper presented at the Shinchon Forum 22, 2006), 36-37.

Many more Korean churches should be involved with the foreign workers' mission, yet most Korean churches either do not have a proper knowledge about or are ignorant of the foreign workers' mission. Rev. Changsun Moon, of the Withee missionary organization, points out that some ministries to foreign workers are not effective due to their focus on human rights, rather than on the gospel. He also points out that there is a lack of expertise and cooperation between migrant workers' missionary organizations and churches.

However, some foreign workers' mission organizations have become more effective because they are meeting both of the migrant workers' needs: physical (human rights) and spiritual (the gospel). Certain mission organizations for foreign workers realize the importance of a holistic ministry: their focus should include their personal and spiritual needs. The migrant workers' mission bridges local missions and world missions, which adds a new dynamic to both missions. For instance, churches and mission organizations train committed foreign workers, and send them as missionaries to their own people when they return to their countries. They are the best equipped missionaries because they are natives, so they will most effectively expand the kingdom of God.

When we go to the world's mega cities, we will see all peoples of the world living together. This phenomenon, from a Christian mission perspective, is God's purposeful work for mission. Migrant workers, multicultural families, and foreign students are God's gift to Korean Christians. We have to use all of our resources to make them missionaries to their own countries.

Status of Children in Multi-cultural Families

According to the Ministry of Government Administration and Home Affairs' statistics, there are 44,258 children from international marriages nationwide. Children from international marriage families are 6.1% in the total number of foreigners in South Korea. The number increased from 25,000 in 2006 to 44,000 in 2007, a 75.3% increase. Among them 59.8% are less than 6 years old and 32.5% are between the ages of 7 to 12. Therefore, 92.3% are less than 12 years old. The total number of school children from international marriages who attend elementary to high school is 13,445.[9]

A multi-cultural family children's mission takes place in alternative schools. Alternative schools are established in many parts of South Korea. Sae Nal alternative school, established in Gwangju in Jeolla Namdo province, hold a worship service at the beginning. The educational goals of the school are instilling the fear of God, practicing serving and sharing, and embracing multi-culturalism.

The school was established for children of international marriages, foreign students and workers, and North Koreans, in order to educate them in the

---

[9] Korean Ministry of Education, Science and Technology, 'A Study of Students of Multi-cultural Families' [in Korean] (July, 2007).

Christian perspective to live as citizens in South Korea and to be leaders of the world. Thus, the school's purpose for students is that they will deeply value their life and live purposefully, be neighbours of the poor and at the same time become international leaders. To live as foreigners in South Korean society is not easy because Korean society has been proud of its single culture and race.

Domestic Ministry Model of Migrant Workers

When we look at the 20 years of domestic migrant workers ministry, we have two main types: human rights oriented and mission oriented ministries. Within mission oriented ministry, there are several models. Medium to large size Korean churches usually have a migrant workers' mission department for ministry.

Initially, foreign workers are invited to participate in Korean church worship services aided by interpreters. Following the service Korean churches usually have fellowship with them through meals and assist them with medical, physical and legal needs in order to open their hearts to the gospel message. Moreover, some other churches hire foreign pastors to minister to their own foreign workers with separate worship services. In Incheon, they are Juan Presbyterian Church, Sungeui Church, Jay Church, Gesan Presbyterian Church, and Sujeong Church. In Seoul, they are Myungsung Church and Onnuri Church M centre. In the southern area, Jeonju Antioch Church ministers to foreign workers.

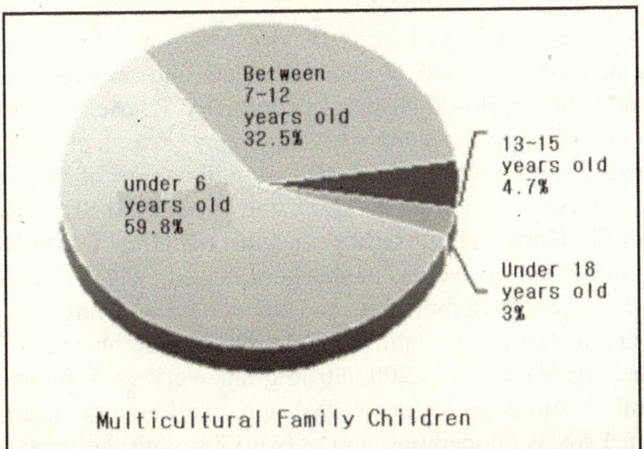

There are also specified ministries according to language groups: Chinese, Vietnamese, Thai, Indonesian, etc. They usually have native ministers to help them to become disciples of Christ, and they also have special retreats during Korean national holidays. Some migrant missionary organizations do their ministries in several languages and have branches in different parts of South Korea: Antioch International Mission, Nasom Community, Withee Mission,

Jubililee Mission, Friends of All Nations, etc. Some other migrant ministries include several ethnic groups together using English. All of these different foreign ministries need native ministers to make foreigners disciples of Christ.

I myself started a migrant workers' mission centre in Incheon City at Namdong National Industrial Complex using two container boxes on a factory site. Classes were opened for computers, Korean language and culture. This is the most economical and effective way to minister unto them. If one cannot find a space in an industrial complex, a room can be rented about the size of a container. Ministries need to find inexpensive spaces to rent so that the cost does not interfere with the migrant workers' ministry and one can easily find sponsors.

In the early years of the Friends of All Nations (FAN) ministry, a female elder offered forty million won for migrant workers' ministry to commemorate her deceased husband, so FAN established 4 branches located near industrial complexes. A foreign workers' ministry can be established if an individual or a church donates ten million won. In this way, FAN built twenty branches near industrial complexes throughout South Korea. FAN branch leaders are former missionaries, pastors, and Christians.

Migrant Workers' Ministry of Friends of All Nations

Ministry and Goal of FAN

FAN is composed of a board of trustees, which is made up of inter-denominational Evangelical church leaders and an executive committee which oversees the day-to-day aspects of ministry. Those, who work at FAN, have been committed to missions work for many years and have experienced different cross-cultural involvement. Following the words of Jesus to 'love your neighbor as yourself', we want to share the love of Christ with the foreign workers living in Korea. Thus, we hope to fulfil the Great Commission to make disciples of all nations, as well as to shepherd these believers. Thus, when these foreign workers return home, they can be the ones acting as missionaries, sharing the Good News and establishing churches in their home countries.

1) In reaching out to the 1,200,000 migrant workers, foreign students and multi-cultural families here in Korea and working to fulfill the Great Commission, FAN is cooperating and networking with the local churches and ministries in the area.

2) Through one-to-one discipleship, FAN is shepherding and maturing new believers in their faith. For them to desire to grow and learn more spiritually at a higher level of education, FAN also makes available the necessary provisions for them to attend a seminary to receive formal Bible Training.

3) FAN is also running various programmes and volunteer opportunities to involve college students and young adults in the different ministries. Through

these, volunteers can receive practical training in mission as well as have the opportunity to develop their foreign language skills. By these interactions with the foreign workers, volunteers can be exposed to different cross-cultural situations, as well as learning about different religions that will prepare them for future work in missions.

4) FAN partners with overseas missionaries who have returned to Korea permanently, or are on furlough. These missionaries, with overseas experience, can reach out to the foreign workers from the country where they were previously missionaries. In this way, these missionaries continue to have an active ministry with the people from the country they once worked in while being a valuable bridge in linking FAN with different peoples.

5) FAN also connects foreign believers who are studying in Korea with foreign workers from the same country. This allows the gospel to be shared by foreign workers and native believers from their home country.

6) With the support of local churches, FAN also sends out discipled foreign workers with FAN trained missionaries to plant churches overseas.

By reaching out to the foreign workers already here in Korea, we are able to take advantage of a new type of harvest field. There is a greater openness and responsiveness from these foreign workers who are no longer held by the cultural and religious pressures from back home. This is especially true among those of a Muslim background, where there is the greatest need of evangelism. By drawing together the resources of the local churches, missionaries and laymen are able to make the most of this new strategy of evangelism.

FAN currently has 20 branches throughout South Korea. The headquarters have five different language worship services: Filipino, Vietnamese, Thai, Indonesian, and English, with between 100 to 150 foreign workers usually in attendance. The Filipino community has a Wednesday night prayer meeting, a Friday all-night prayer meeting, a Saturday Bible study, and a Sunday night discipleship training. Besides these meetings, 8 cell churches meet in different factories or dormitories during weekdays and they use various training materials: One to One (6 to 9 months), Train & Multiply (2 years), and Omega Course (2 years). When migrant workers finish these courses, our intention is to have them return to their countries as missionaries.

Mobilizing Volunteers for Foreign Workers' Mission

For a foreign workers' mission, we need a lot of volunteers and sponsors for financial and spiritual support, so returned or retired missionaries and retired senior Christians are good candidates for this ministry. They do not usually have a financial burden and their children are already grown up and independent. Returned or retired missionaries have migrant experience, so they can understand migrant workers. Retired senior Christians usually have special skills and experiences, which they can use in their ministry, and they also have many human contacts who can become their sponsors and volunteers. Senior

Christians easily devote themselves totally to this ministry as their last opportunity to serve the Lord; as a result, they have a better chance to succeed in this ministry.

Characteristics of Migrant Mission: Holistic Ministry and Discipleship

The foreign workers' mission has to be a holistic ministry by meeting all their needs: physical (medical) and spiritual (counseling and worship). Jesus commands us to treat our visitors well. They are more than visitors; they are our neighbors. Since Jesus was a friend of strangers, outcasts, and sinners, we also ought to treat our migrant brothers and sisters as friends and share the gospel with them. Mark 12:31a says, 'The second is this; 'Love your neighbor as yourself'. Therefore, we must love our foreign workers as ourselves, and meet all their needs. Secondly, we must also obey our Lord's great commission in Matthew 28, 'Make disciples of all nations'. When our migrant brothers and sisters open their hearts through our love, we must make them Christ's disciples, so we can bring Christ's second coming sooner thus fulfilling our Christian duty. These two verses are the key verses for FAN. Our goal is to make migrant workers become missionaries in their own countries. When migrant workers' ministries bear this fruit, they will not give up their ministries.

Who is a disciple of Christ? According to Luke 9:23, Jesus requires: 'If anyone would come after me, he must deny himself and take up his cross daily and follow me'. This simple verse teaches us the meaning of being a disciple. A disciple is an individual who hears Christ's calling and denies his own desires daily to follow Jesus. This invitation is not limited to Jesus' twelve disciples, but 'anyone' who hears Christ's voice and makes a decision. Therefore, discipleship training is not just a programme, but is a commitment and a changing of one's direction of life. We have to teach this truth to our migrant brothers and sisters who make a commitment to follow Jesus.

Church Planting through Migrant Workers' Mission

In May 2008, we examined the outcome of the domestic foreign workers' mission by checking church planting in their native lands. This event took place through a seminar hosted by GMA a Korea indigenous mission groups, consisting of eight different migrant worker reports. All of the eight ministries have more than a ten-year history and yet the church planting by their native missionaries is in the beginning stage.

Out of eight migrant worker mission groups, the Filipino group in Sujeong church planted seven churches in the Philippines. The Sujeong Church had their first worship service for Filipino migrant workers in May of 1993. For fifteen years the church has been motivating their church members for mission. Their goals for the migrant workers mission were helping Filipinos become disciples of Christ and missionaries to their own people. Because of these clear objectives, Sujeong Church has a successful ministry for the migrant workers' mission.

In their early foreign workers' ministry, Sujeong Church invited a Filipino pastor to start a worship service. Moreover, they also established four to five Filipino community ministries in South Korea. Those Filipino Christians, who were trained in these groups, went back to the Philippines with support from Sujeong Church and established churches there. The church made a special department to support this migrant workers' mission project.[10]

Rev. Gosu Choi, of Gongchon Foreign Workers' Mission, has been undertaking several Mongolian ministries for over ten years. He planted a church in Mongolia. One couple and thirteen students trained at the mission centre and returned to Mongolia and established a church. The Gongchon Mongolian Community also collected an offering with which they purchased land in Mongolia to begin places of worship. Meanwhile, deacon Ohryona entered Monglia United Theological Seminary and became a seminary student. With additional collections (thirty million won) from South Korea, they built a two- storey church building. They also bought a piece of farm land to support themselves financially. They bought cows, sheep, goats and pigs to breed, and also planted many trees. Moreover, they made a scholarship fund for young people who have a vision. Currently, they support three seminary students and two university students.[11]

Antioch International Mission has been ministering to Indonesians in the Bupyung, Ansan, Suwon, and Pyungtack areas for fifteen years. During 2007, the average attendance of Sunday worship service was more than 200. Financially they are 40% self-supporting while relying on external support for the rest. They are grateful that God allowed them to experience a conversion of Muslim workers during the last thirteen years of ministry. The staff at Antioch prepare for a deeper ministry for Indonesian Muslims through prayer, because they want to support the converted Muslims when they return to their country. They said that they have not been able to minister to those who returned, but they want to do so in the near future.[12]

Rev. Yoonwoo Lee has been ministering to the Vietnamese in South Korea for twenty years at Saejungang and Saemunan Churches. At first he invited Vietnamese workers to the fourth Korean Sunday worship service at Saemunan Church and provided a simultaneous interpretation. After the worship service, he led a Bible study for Vietnamese migrant workers so that he could train them in the Christian faith. Whenever he thought they needed worship service

[10] G.S. Choi, I.L. Jo, and E.J. Lee, 'Migrant Worker Ministry Network: Migrant Worker Ministry Models in South Korea' [in Korean], *Global Mission Alliance* (2008), 1-11, 21-30, 57-64, 57-64.

[11] Choi, Jo, & Lee, 'Migrant Worker Ministry Network', 1-11.

[12] Choi, Jo, & Lee, 'Migrant Worker Ministry Network', 21-30.

training, he had a separate Vietnamese worship service. Rev. Lee also had seasonal joint retreats on New Year's Day (two days) and on Thanksgiving Day (three days) and through them some Vietnamese Christians made a commitment to become pastors and missionaries. Rev. Lee promised support to those who would start churches in Vietnam. As a result of this promise, nine churches were established in eight different regions. Amongst them, five churches have twenty to thirty in their congregation; two churches have thirty to fifty; two churches have sixty to seventy. This is a good model for a migrant workers' mission in South Korea because it achieves the most advanced stage of migrant mission, training migrant workers as missionaries in their own countries. Rev. Lee, in his interview, said that the migrant workers' mission's goal has to be making them become missionaries to their own people, otherwise, foreign workers' ministry becomes just a mercy ministry, for when the workers return, all the ministry efforts become in vain.[13]

Migrant Mission Network in Korea (MMNK)

The Migrant Mission Network in Korea (MMNK) is a network for migrant missions in South Korea, of which I am directly involved. I want to explain the development of the diaspora mission within South Korea by introducing MMNK. At the end of 2008, several mission organizations got together and formed the MMNK network. After forming the network, they had their first large meeting, '2009 Korean Migrant Mission Expo'. This mass meeting consisted of migrant missionaries and exhibitions of migrant mission ministries. Through this meeting we were introduced to many migrant ministries, and shared our knowledge and experiences of these various ministries. It also clarified our vision for migrant ministry in South Korea. During the mornings, we presented various migrant mission ministries and during the afternoons about 200 migrant mission organizations and around 7,000 foreign workers gathered together for mission festival meetings. Through these meetings we are able to communicate to the Korean churches that migrant mission is a rice-bed for world mission.

Until now, it has been very difficult to continuously train foreign workers' faith due to their frequent moving of their locations. However, through MMNK we can tell them where they can go and continue their training when they move to other jobs. The chart below shows the different migrant workers' mission organizations.

---

[13] C.H. Jun, 'World Mission through Korean Migrant Worker Mission' [in Korean] (Presentation at the Forum for Korean Mission Leaders 9, 2009).

Table 1 Mission Organizations by Nationalities

Nation	No. of groups	Region					Major Network
		Seoul	Gyeong-gi	Young-nam	Ho-nam	Chung-cheong	
Nongo-lia	44	23	14	4	1	2	Monggol Diaspora Network
China	88	9	27	28	9	15	Han Jung Mission
Viet-nam	42	5	21	11	3	2	Vietnam United Mission
Nepal	7	1	3	1		2	Nepali worship
Thai-land	21	2	18		1		Global Thai Mission Network
Indo-nesia	20	2	9	7		2	Antioch Inter-nation al Mission
Cam-bodia	9	1	5	2	1		Cambodia Mission
Sri Lanka	10	1	6	2	1		
Bangla-desh	8	2	6				Bangladesh Mission
Russia	31	10	12	5		4	Russia Mission
Philip-pines	16	5	10	1			
Eng-lish	43	6	17	12	5	3	

This chart shows the migrant workers' mission organizations according to nations, so this network chart can help foreign workers as well as returned missionaries for their domestic mission ministries. Besides this network chart, MMNK has a specialized network for foreign students, multicultural families and their youth and shelter ministries.

Table 2 MMNK Special Mission Organizations

Expertise	Number	Region					Main Network
		Seoul	Gyeong-gi	Young-nam	Ho-nam	Chung-cheong	
Foreign students	9	1	2	3	3		International Student Fellow; Hang Jung Mission
Multi-cultural family	18	2	6	5	4	1	Together Multi-cultural Network
Educational mission	8	1	5	1	1		Computer, auto-mechanics, sightseeing, Taekwondo
Shelter Ministry	28	2	13	5	4	4	
Muslim	31	2	18	8	1	2	

Until now, all mission organizations and church missions remained within their framework of ministries. For this reason, their resources easily dried up and they experienced a burn-out. However, they now can exchange their experiences and resources to create a good synergy. Most important matters in this networking are sharing each other's training and necessary resources for church planting. This network should not stop here in South Korea, but it also needs to network in the migrant workers' countries, so that they can plant churches more efficiently.

I have been ministering to several ethnic groups of migrant workers for the last nine years. Amongst them the Filipino group has become the most prominent community. When a Filipino wants to become a Christian, our Filipino pastor teaches him: first, spiritual blessings in Christ while learning assurance of salvation in Christ for a couple of weeks; and then Christian community life through our shelter, while practicing daily devotion and self-denial for a couple of weeks. We use 'One to One Discipleship Training' for six months to a year, and its contents include: 1) Assurance of Salvation; 2) Characters of God; 3) The Bible; 4) Prayer; 5) Spirit filled Life; 6) Fellowship in Christ; 7) Witness; 8) Test; and 9) Obedience. After finishing this book, we teach them about the church and baptism, and then we baptize them. Many who have returned are actively participating at local churches and some of them began house churches in the Philippines. Some have led family members to salvation.[14]

[14] A. Broom and L. Broom, *One to One Discipling* (Vista, CA: Multiplication Ministries, 1999).

About six years ago an American mission organization, One Mission Society (OMS) invited me to become their shepherd for Every Community for Christ (ECC) programme, so I visit the OMS headquarters once a year to participate in their seminar. They have a specially designed curriculum for church planting called 'Train & Multiply'. This material trains local Christians to plant their own churches, and it is very practical. This programme first started in South America. The content of this training includes: 1) prayer and devotional life; 2) evangelism and church multiplication; 3) teaching and discipleship; 4) organization, leadership and spiritual gifts; 5) corporate worship and communion; 6) giving and serving the needy; 7) fellowship and church life; 8) pastoral care, relationship and counseling; 9) pastoral leadership training; 10) discipling the nations; and 11) evaluation of Activities. Local Christians can select any part of this training that fits their needs, so its nature is very practical. This curriculum has three stages: 1) planting; 2) developing; and 3) increasing. When a local Christian finishes this course, he can train others.[15]

Only one who starts a small group can receive this training. The training can be done while he/she is working. This training is done every other week for two years. This training also has two intensive trainings a year. Train and multiply encourages local Christians to plant a church while they are working, so the church will not have a financial burden in supporting a pastor.

Therefore, if we want to make an impact through our migrant workers' mission, we have to train migrant Christian workers to become missionaries to their own people and train them to work with other missionaries already serving in their countries. We have to network with them in their native countries by supporting their church planting efforts. The domestic migrant worker mission goal has to be training them to become missionaries to their own people when they return. We have to train them to establish house churches.

Continually nurturing the faith of migrant workers within South Korea has been a problem due to their frequent change of jobs. MMNK can solve this problem because through this network we can provide information for all the migrant ministries in South Korea. This network can also provide ministries for returning missionaries from overseas. Recently migrant ministries have expanded their focus from migrant workers from different countries to include ministries for foreign students, multicultural families and youth. Such ministry groups can continually nurture their members' faith, and can network with the other existing migrant mission groups.

Up until now, each migrant mission organization and church has worked only within their own resources. For this reason the organizations and churches can easily lose their passion and resources and become burned-out. Networking, among the organizations and churches with migrant ministry,

---

[15] Train & Multiply, *Student Activity Guide: For the Trainer to use with each Student* (Surrey, Canada: Project WorldReach, 2001)

enables them to exchange their experiences, information, and resources, and to benefit from a synergy effect and mutual encouragement. The most important things in this networking are training migrant Christian workers and sharing resources for planting churches. Migrant mission networking involves networking among migrant missionaries as well as local churches, which will help trained Christian migrant workers for mission to establish churches when they return to their own countries.

International Evangelical Student Mission Movement: UBF Case Study

Peter Chang

Introduction

At the beginning of the twenty-first century, God is in haste to preach the gospel to the ends of the earth. According to Ralph Winter, mission work now calls missionaries to evangelize all people of all nations, especially the tribes beyond the coastal borders and those in remote areas. Thus, mission now focuses on evangelizing 7000 unreached peoples, especially in Muslim countries and North Korea. In response to this call, the University Bible Fellowship (UBF) student mission movement was introduced as a Korean model, similar to the Moravian Mission, at the fifth meeting of NCOWE (National Consultation of World Evangelization) in Seoul and Pusan in June 2010.[1]

However, the Korean diaspora mission work of the UBF through self-supporting professional lay missionaries was not based on a specific mission model or theological theory. This ministry has developed naturally from a student gospel movement to a mission ministry. It cannot but be explained as the work of the Holy Spirit.[2]

Two main characteristics of the Korean diaspora mission of the UBF are: firstly, a burning desire for world mission, and secondly, world mission through self-supporting professional lay missionaries. The work of the Holy Spirit through the Korean diaspora mission of UBF has been a remarkable one.

In July 2008, 3,500 students from 80 nations of the world attended the UBF International Bible Conference at Purdue University in the U.S.A. During this conference, about 500 students and second-generation youths, made a pledge to go out as missionaries, whenever and wherever God may send them.[3] In 2009 almost 1,200 people from 45 nations attended the UBF European International Bible Conference in Eringerfeld, Germany. Among them, around 200 students

---

[1] Samuel H. Lee, 'Korean Moravian Mission Model' [in Korean] (A Presentation at the Fifth National Consultation of World Evangelization Conference, Seoul, 2010).

[2] Hyoung Chong Kim, *God's Mission Ministry: European UBF Mission History* [in Korean] (Bonn: UBF Press, 2009), 731-37.

[3] John Jun, 'World Missions UBF Newsletter: 2008 UBF International Conference at Purdue' (Private Newsletter, 2008), 3.

and second generation youths from Europe came up on the stage as they made the decision to live as missionaries.[4]

Nowadays, the mission paradigm is changing drastically. Consequently, new strategies are required, especially to meet the strong challenge of aggressive Muslim expansion. The Korean diaspora mission work of the UBF through self- supporting professional lay missionaries is regarded as a good model for the world mission movement.

University Bible Fellowship

Campus Mission Movement

The UBF campus mission movement is similar to that of the Holy Club Movement at Oxford University; college students grow spiritually as they earnestly study the Bible and obey its teachings.[5] The UBF ministry also resembles Hudson Taylor's China Inland Mission (CIM) and the Student Volunteer Movement (SVM) during their most active times, in that it equips people to carry out the world mission task regardless of race, sex, denomination, or educational background, and it trains students who are spiritually reborn to devote themselves fully to God by realising Jesus' world mission vision.

Moreover, this mission movement can be better understood in the context of the Pietist movement in Germany, (which elicits the characteristic of 'church within a church') in that it focuses on raising a few leaders through discipleship training, instead of evangelizing the masses. In addition, the UBF's common life and church-centred spiritual life share similarities with the monasteries of early Christians and of the Middle Ages.[6] Also, the emphases on a mission-centred life, Christian marriage, and ministry through self-supporting professional lay missionaries- on the strong foundation of the saving grace of Jesus- are comparable to the Moravian Church shaped by Zinzendorf.[7]

University Bible Fellowship (UBF) movement was founded by Rev. Samuel C. Lee and Rev. Sarah Barry, in the fall of 1961, in a period of turmoil in Korean history, after the military coup d'etat of May 16th, 1961 and nationwide

---

[4] *The Hope of God: European Summer Bible Conference 2009* (Bonn: Europe UBF, 2009), 5, 84.

[5] Jun Ki Chung, *A Short History of University Bible Fellowship* [in Korean] (Kwangju-City, Korea: Gospel Culture Publishing, 1992), 28.

[6] Moses Jung, *UBF 40th Anniversary Missionary Seminar* [in Korean] (Chicago: UBF Press, 2001), 26, 27.

[7] Samuel H. Lee, 'The Direction of UBF Ministries', in Peter Chang (ed), *Five Loaves and Two Fish: The 40-year History of UBF European Campus Mission Compilation* (Bonn: UBF, 2009), 60; Peter Chang, 'A History of the Student Evangelical Movement', in *Five Loaves and Two Fish*, 234.

demonstrations on April 19.[8] Rev. Samuel Lee and Rev. Sarah Barry, who was sent as a missionary from the USA by the Southern Presbyterian Church, shared Jesus' compassion with young students in the rural city of Kwangju, Korea. From small beginnings, the movement grew into what it is today: 10,000 students and graduates from almost all universities in Korea, as well as 1,750 Korean diaspora UBF missionaries who are serving campus mission ministry in 92 nations of the world under the motto 'Bible Korea, World Mission'.

The University Bible Fellowship is a non-denominational, evangelistic campus mission organization focused on raising disciples of Jesus who live sacrificial lives for the gospel and contribute to society and their nation by preaching the gospel of Jesus Christ to college students and young people.[9] The UBF serves world campus evangelism by raising professional self-supporting lay missionaries among campus students and sending them throughout the world. For this purpose, the UBF teaches the Bible to college students and young people and helps them to live according to the teachings of the Scriptures and to practically obey Jesus' world mission command (Acts 1:8).

The Philosophy of UBF World Campus Mission Movement

MANGER SPIRIT

Jesus is God himself and has the power and glory of the almighty Creator God. Nevertheless, in order to serve sick and suffering people, Jesus gave up all his privileges and honor and humbled himself by being born as a baby in a manger. It is the expression of God's greatest love and humbleness and the Good News of salvation for all those who are dying because of their sins.

The UBF movement began with this manger spirit. Learning Jesus' humility and sacrifice, UBF shepherds lived together with sin-sick souls on campus and served them. Lay missionary families opened their houses and humbly served new students. Through a common life, in small and humble apartments, student leaders learned Jesus' life-serving spirit as they ministered to younger students.[10]

While many churches of today are focusing on attracting the masses and having many church members, the UBF world campus mission movement—which is deeply rooted in Jesus' manger spirit—has grown into a living and inwardly strong church. God has used the UBF ministry because

[8] Joshua Lee, 'UBF Ancestors' Gospel Faith and Missionary Spirit', in *Five Loaves and Two Fish*, 15, 16.

[9] UBF, 'Origin and Purpose of UBF (University Bible Fellowship)', in Pter Chang (ed), *Preach the Good News to All Creation* (Bonn: Europe UBF Press, 2008), 146, 147.

[10] Sarah Barry, 'History of UBF Ministry' in Peter Chang (ed), *Preach the Good News to All Creation*, 168-170.

Jesus' manger spirit of humility and sacrifice were reproduced in each member's life. The power that came from the manger spirit has ignited the fire of the gospel in the souls of the young people in Korea, as well as in other nations, and raised numerous professional lay missionaries. This manger spirit has conquered campuses all over the world with the gospel of Jesus and is propelling the evangelization of nationals in each country.

Giving Spirit

In the 1960s, Korean churches were divided into different denominations, through the influence of missionaries from Western countries. Korean churches were not only influenced theologically, but were also dependent on the financial support of Western mission organizations. In this situation, the UBF established itself to be independent financially and administratively through a biblical faith in God. The UBF put the giving spirit of God into practice. The UBF helped students to live a life of giving and planted giving spirit in their hearts.

Through a giving spirit, the UBF first supported nursing homes and orphanages in Korea during every Christmas season, and later sent relief offerings to Bangladesh, Ethiopia, Mexico, Somalia and North Korea. God's word, 'You give them something to eat' (Mk 6:37) inspired the UBF to serve the world campus mission movement beyond evangelizing Korean campus students. Accepting the prayer and sacrifice of the UBF members as their 'five loaves and two fish', God is working mightily, already having sent out 3,000 UBF professional self-supporting lay missionaries to more than 90 countries around the world.[11]

Raising disciples of Jesus through one-to-one Bible Study

God took 25 years to raise one man, Abraham. Jesus also focused on raising the twelve disciples rather than gathering a huge crowd. The most important prayer topic of the UBF campus mission ministry is to raise one person of faith as a disciple of Jesus. This prayer topic is based on the belief that, through raising one person as a disciple of Jesus, one nation, a whole generation, and even the whole world, can be saved. The mission model that is used to raise one person as a disciple of Jesus is one-to-one Bible study and a common life. This is most effective in helping one person to grow spiritually when practiced with sincere love for each person and deep concern for their spiritual problems.[12] Loving and considering one person very precious, and caring for them one-to-one, through Bible study, became a core mission model for the UBF ministry and the driving force in fulfilling the vision of Bible Korea and World Campus Mission.

---

[11] University Bible Fellowship, *Early Pioneers of UBF: Their Faith and Spirit* (Chicago: UBF, 2005), 33-36.

[12] S.H. Lee, 'Korean Moravian Mission Model', 11.

MISSION SPIRIT AND FAITH

When the UBF was being established as a university evangelist movement, leaders studied the gospels intensively. At the end of each gospel, they were challenged by Jesus' world mission command. But at that time, in war-torn Korea, nobody imagined that Koreans would go out as missionaries and carry out world mission. So the UBF leaders were left in a quandary. Anyway, they accepted Jesus' world mission command by faith and prayed for it with burning hearts.

While praying for Southeast Asia, the UBF sent one woman missionary to the Jeju Island in 1964 as a fruit of their prayer.[13] It was not a different country but it was 'overseas' and an expression of their faith and obedience towards Jesus' world mission command despite the impossible situation. This was the starting point for the world campus mission movement through the UBF. The evangelization work through the UBF spread to West Germany in 1969 and to the USA in 1971.[14]

Evangelism through Korean UBF Missionaries[15]

Europe

In September 1969, the UBF sent out three nurses, who were on their way to West Germany to earn money, as self-supporting lay missionaries. This was the way that God opened for Koreans to go out as self-supporting lay missionaries to West Germany. With this event, the UBF Korean diaspora mission work in West Germany began.[16] Since then, many nurse missionaries have been sent out to various cities in West Germany every year. During the day they worked as nurses, and at night they gathered in their dormitory rooms, read the Bible and prayed together wholeheartedly. In this way they overcame their loneliness and tiredness due to hard work, which was not easy for them to bear as young women in a foreign country. At the same time they learned the German language with a sense of mission. Adjusting to the German lifestyle, they went out to campuses and preached the gospel to German students. As a result of their mission work, there was a great work of God. Five years after they had been sent out, 165 people (40 Korean missionaries) attended the first West Germany UBF Conference in Switzerland, in 1974.[17]

---

[13] J. Lee, 'UBF Ancestors' Gospel Faith and Missionary Spirit', 97-98.

[14] *Early Pioneers of UBF*, 97-98, 100.

[15] Samuel H. Lee, *Calling as UBF Missionaries* [in Korean] (Seoul: Sungkwang Munhwasa, 1999), 35-44.

[16] Samuel C. Lee, *The Light of People: West Germany UBF Conference in Switzerland and Life Testimony Symposium* (Seoul: UBF Press, 1974).18.

[17] *Early Pioneers of UBF*, 99.

In the 1980s, campus evangelization through nurses developed into evangelization through self-supporting student missionaries. Despite many hardships in mastering the language and studying, student missionaries served disciple-making ministry, holding on to the word of God and preaching the word of God through one-to-one Bible study. Through their labour of faith and prayer and sacrificial life, many influential national shepherds were raised among German students. In the 1990s, campus evangelization spread to many universities in Germany, and also actively to European universities. From 1990 to 1999, 250 self-supporting student missionaries from Korea were sent to Germany and Europe, and began evangelizing university students in European countries, branching out the ministry.[18] Evangelization in developed countries, which seemed impossible, also began through Korean diaspora self-supporting student missionaries. Through the spiritual co-working of European national shepherds with missionaries, a new productive stage of disciple-making began. In the 1990s, ancestor house churches were established among national shepherds, and, in the 2000s, many national shepherds were raised as leaders, who now serve campus evangelization in Germany and Europe as responsible Sunday messengers and stewards of the UBF ministries.

In addition to their cross of study and self-support, Korean diaspora student missionaries also carried three or even more crosses: raising their children; serving campus mission; Sunday message preparation; serving coworkers. They held on to Mark 11:22 and challenged the impossible by faith. They also moved the mountains of work and visa permits, self-support and citizenship by faith. They were victorious in their university studies by faith, and more than 300 student missionaries were able to obtain Ph.D degrees.

UBF self-supporting lay missionaries laid the foundation of the campus mission ministry in Europe through much prayer, one-to-one Bible study, and sacrifice—even opening their homes. They faced rejection and misunderstanding of highly intellectual and proud native campus students in the developed countries. But through obeying Mark 11:22 and Mark 6:37 Korean UBF diaspora self-supporting lay missionaries served national students faithfully with one-to-one Bible study, overcoming various barriers, and raised them as disciples of Jesus. They could experience the power of God's word and the great work of the Holy Spirit and render glory to God.

The missionaries in the pioneering stage not only raised nationals as disciples but also helped their own children to learn gospel faith and to grow spiritually through one-to-one Bible study so that they could overcome challenges of the postmodern environment and grow as bible teachers and spiritual coworkers for the ministry.[19] Nowadays, there are more than 300

---

[18] Stephanus Park, 'The Growth of Germany UBF Mission (1990-1999)', in *Five Loaves and Two Fish*, 143.

[19] Mark Yoon, 'Education of Second Generation Missionaries', in *UBF 40th Anniversary Missionary Seminar, May 2001, Chicago* (Chicago: UBF, 2001), 122-32.

second generation missionaries (SGMs) in Germany and Europe, who co-work with their parents with a clear spiritual identity as second generation missionaries. Some of them also established house churches based on the biblical values of marriage and now even third generation missionaries are being born and are growing.[20] These days, 160 missionaries in 20 UBF ministries in Germany, as well as 120 missionaries in 48 UBF ministries in 22 European countries (excluding Germany) and Israel, are preaching the gospel to more than 3,000 European campus students every week through one-to-one Bible study, co-working with 60 national leaders and second generation missionaries.[21]

Due to the great diversity of languages and cultures in Europe, it is not easy to serve Europe campus missions as a whole. In many UBF ministries, or even in one nation, just one or two UBF missionary families serve the ministry. They often faced loneliness. Since 2007, they could overcome this problem through co-working in regions, which were formed according to related languages and cultures.[22] After the European International Bible Conference in August 2009, commemorating the 40th year of campus mission in Europe, a new flame of prayer for the spiritual revival and the work of the Holy Spirit through Bible study has been ignited and grows stronger day by day.

In the English-speaking region (UK and Ireland), UK national leaders are currently serving disciple-making ministries and co-working with Ireland UBF to serve the ministry. The Francophone region, (France, Switzerland, Belgium), has a joint conference each summer and many French-speaking young people have been raised as disciples of Jesus. Several house churches have been established. Northern Europe, (Denmark, Sweden, Norway), prays to raise one ancestor of faith in each country and for Northern European countries to become strong nations of the gospel, which can send out self-supporting lay missionaries. In the Central European region, (Poland, Czech Republic, Hungary, Slovakia, Austria, and Croatia), missionaries and house churches are raising national shepherds for their respective countries and this year also they are holding a historical first joint conference for second generation missionaries in Europe and Israel. In the Iberian Peninsula, (Portugal and Spain), missionary house churches pray for laying the foundation of campus evangelization. The UBF ministries in the Balkan area, (Serbia, Greece, Romania, Bulgaria, and Macedonia), have a regional conference every two years. They challenge slumbering orthodox believers and Islam through one-to-one Bible study, and are raising national disciples in Greece and Bulgaria for their disciple-making ministry is very fruitful.

---

20 S.H. Lee, 'Korean Moravian Mission Model', 13.

21 Markus Kum, 'Endurance and Advancement of Germany UBF Mission (2000-2009)', in *Five Loaves and Two Fish*, 160-61.

22 M. Kum, 'Endurance and Advancement', 165.

In conclusion, the Korean UBF diaspora self-supporting lay missionaries, who were sent out to Europe, knelt down in prayer and served campus mission ministry by faith, believing only in the promise of Almighty God. Through their struggles and prayers, many European nationals came back to God and devoted their lives to Jesus. In Germany / Europe UBF there are now 10 national staff members and 60 dedicated national leaders, who serve campus mission sacrificially just as well as the missionaries.

North America

In 1971, the door to the USA was opened for Korean diaspora missionaries. Doctors, nurses, textile workers, and others were sent as self-supporting missionaries.[23] After the summer conference in Korea in 1971, Rev. Samuel Lee gave a prayer topic to hold a future summer conference at Niagara Falls within ten years, with 200 American attendants. At that time, when only three UBF missionaries were in the USA, it seemed to be an impossible prayer topic. Nevertheless, UBF co-workers prayed wholeheartedly with this prayer topic. And the Lord God Almighty answered. In 1981 the first UBF International Conference at Niagara Falls was held with 203 American student attendants.[24]

In 1977, Rev. Samuel Lee went to the USA as a missionary with his entire family.[25] Shortly thereafter Rev. Sarah Barry joined him. Later many Korean diaspora missionaries followed their example and went to the USA as missionaries. At present there are more than 700 UBF Korean diaspora missionaries working in the USA. In the pioneering stage they put much effort to overcome the language as well as cultural barriers in order to serve American students with the word of God. Especially, Rev. Lee studied the Bible diligently and devoted himself to prepare and deliver Sunday messages in English. The word of God penetrated the hearts of young American students with the power of the Holy Spirit and gave them spiritual rebirth. Many who had despaired over their sins of sexual immorality found forgiveness and new hope in Jesus. Many, who were wounded by their parents' divorce, found healing and unconditional love in Jesus, their everlasting Father. The diaspora missionaries had the vision to raise 561 American staff members according to the number of the American college campuses.

As the UBF ministry prospered in America, there were many misunderstandings due to cultural differences among members. Those, who remained throughout this time, deepened in their commitment as Jesus' disciples and carried out the world mission command continuously. The main Bible verse, the missionaries held on to, was 1 Peter 2:9. With this word they

---

[23] J.K. Chung, *A Short History of University Bible Fellowship*, 52

[24] Samuel C. Lee, 'A Decision of Faith', *The Campus Mission*, issue 103 (Summer, 1981), 1.

[25] *Early Pioneers of UBF*, 103.

prayed for America to be a kingdom of priests and a holy nation.[26] Their further prayer topics were to establish God and mission centred house churches and to raise Ph.D. students as the main leaders in the ministry. Since then, more than 200 house churches have been established and about 50 Americans with Ph.D.s are serving the ministry.

The number of Bible teachers, in Chicago UBF, increased from a few missionaries to more than 500, with 60% being American. At present, there are 90 UBF ministries in America serving more than 130 colleges and universities. Since 1986, Chicago UBF, world mission UBF headquarters and leading UBF ministries such as Toledo, Cincinnati, New York, Washington D.C., and Los Angeles UBF have been hosting UBF international conferences. They were held on the campuses of Michigan State University from 1986 to 1998 every two years. From 1998 until 2004 they were held every three years, after 2004 every four years, due to the growth of the work of God in other continents through Korean diaspora missionaries. In 2001 Rev. Dr. Lee passed away and Mother Sarah Barry took over the general leadership of the UBF. Rev. Dr. John Jun is now the general director of UBF since 2006. Under his leadership the 2008 UBF international summer Bible conference was held on the campus of Purdue State University surpassing 3,500 people.[27] Currently, the international conferences take place every five years.

In the early 1980s, 23 missionaries worked as sewing-machine operators for pioneering campus mission in Canada. When the application for sewing-machine operators was advertised through the Canadian Human Resources Development Center, 100 UBF members applied. Among them, the UBF chose 30 persons and trained them intensively for three months, even buying them 20 sewing-machines. Most of them were college graduates but there was even one sister with a master's degree. Through intensive training, they could earn their certificates as sewing-machine operators and were sent out as missionaries. Some of them also applied to be chicken butchers. Nobody could understand this. Nobody would do such a thing in obedience to a man's command, but they did so in order to obey Jesus' world mission command. During the day, they worked as sewing-machine operators and in the evening they studied English. On campus they preached the gospel. Later, they received better jobs and integrated well into Canadian society.[28] In a similar way, many pioneering missionaries were also sent to South America.

---

[26] Moses Jung, 'UBF's Gospel Ministry in context of the Students' Evangelization Movement History' (A Study Presented at the UBF 40th Anniversary Missionary Seminar, Illinois State University, Normal, July-Aug, 2001), 35.

[27] John Jun, 'World Missions UBF Newsletter' (a private newsletter, 2008), 3.

[28] Sarah Lee, 'From a Sewing Machine Operator to a CPA Manager Missionary', in *World Mission Report 2006* (Seoul, UBF Press, 2006), 9-11.

Asia

Mr. Lee was sent out as a self-supporting lay missionary while an employee of a big Korean company to India. There, he was able to invite many campus students to Bible study and bore much fruit, raising them as disciples of Jesus. Among them, three nationals even became missionaries. Now, four chapters in India have been established through four national leaders, who serve the ministry working as professors, at the same time. Among them, there are many, who were converted from Hinduism to Christianity. Missionaries were also sent out to Indonesia and Hong Kong as company employees and to Mongolia as teachers, as well as to Central Asia as businessmen serving world campus mission. The ministries, in those nations, saw amazing growth, during the past few years.

Most pioneering missionaries, in Japan, were student missionaries. They supported themselves by delivering newspapers early in the morning and working as janitors at night, while studying during the day. Twenty years have passed. Now there are more than ten Ph.D. students among them and some are serving campus mission as professors, assistant professors, researchers and counsellors.

CIS, China and Muslim Countries

At the 8th World Mission Report, in Korea, in 1985, Rev. Dr. Lee announced the prayer topic to send out missionaries to Russia, the leading communist country, in the next ten years. Everybody prayed persistently even though that seemed to be an impossible prayer topic. As a result, in 1990, the first missionary went to Moscow with a 3-day visa through Hungary.[29] This was even before South Korea and Russia established friendly diplomatic relations. When the Iron Curtain fell, 30 lay missionaries were sent out to Moscow, in 1991. In August 1991, the first Russian UBF conference took place in St. Petersburg with 120 Russian students attending. In 1992, the first lay missionary was sent out to China. Besides, many missionaries went out to Muslim nations. Hence, in 1994, the UBF held the mission report in Seoul, commemorating having sent out 1,000 missionaries (actually 1,003 were sent out to 72 countries).

Comparison between the UBF Diaspora Mission and the Moravian Church

First, whereas the Moravian Church was focused on the conversion of one person through evangelization, the UBF ministry is focused on raising disciples of Jesus among national campus students through intensive one-to-one Bible study.[30]

---

[29] Y.K. Lee, *Bible Study Model for Establishing a Community of Faith*, 5-16.

[30] J. Lee, 'UBF Ancestors' Gospel Faith and Missionary Spirit', 35-38.

Second, the Moravian Church sought to evangelize all people. The UBF ministry focuses on national campus students in the mission field. The UBF raises them as leaders and helps them evangelize campus students themselves. The UBF's focus on evangelizing the intellectuals and raising leaders is the main difference.[31]

Third, the Moravian Church raised missionary candidates by the training of believers. The UBF evangelizes unbelievers and raises them as disciples of Jesus and as missionaries through ten years of discipleship training. With the motto of 'raising all members as disciples of Jesus' and 'changing all members into missionaries', the UBF serves campus mission. Therefore, all the UBF members are missionary candidates.

Fourth, the goal of the UBF is to raise national leaders in each country. Now, many national leaders and Bible teachers have been raised in Germany, America, Canada, India, Mongolia, China, South America and Africa. Also, many national Bible teachers have been raised.

Fifth, the UBF not only raises national students as disciples, but also sends them out as self-supporting missionaries to developing countries. National shepherds who received missionary calling were sent to developing countries. Now there are around thirty missionaries who were raised among national campus students. Through this, we can see the vision that many national missionaries will be sent out to other nations and begin the next stage of world evangelization ministry by the UBF. For example, in Mexico, brother Efrain accepted the gospel through Korean diaspora self-supporting missionaries, received discipleship training and was sent out as a missionary to Peru. Brother Vladimir from Ukraine accepted the gospel through Korean missionaries, received discipleship training and was sent out as a missionary to Turkey.[32] In Sudan, Moses O., who accepted the gospel through Korean missionaries and received discipleship training, was sent out to Egypt.[33] Don Kuper could have enjoyed his life in America but he decided to go out for God's mission in Argentina.[34] John and Maria Peace, from the USA, serve the ministry in Ukraine as missionaries. Matthew Singh from India, who received the gospel through a Korean missionary, now serves the ministry in Portugal as a responsible staff member.

Sixth, in the Moravian Church, the proportion of church members to missionaries is about 12:1. In 200 years, 3,000 missionaries were sent out to 14 countries. In the UBF the proportion of church members to missionaries is 2:1. The small UBF ministries also sent out missionaries. For example, even small

---

[31] S.H. Lee, 'Campus Mission and Disciple-making Ministry' [in Korean], in *Mission Strategy Research Report* (Seoul: UBF Press, 2005), 9-12.

[32] P. Vladimir, *A Holy Nation People III* [in Korean] (Seoul, UBF Press), 309-315.

[33] O. Moses, 'I Hate Muslims, I Love Muslims', in *World Mission Report 2008* (Bonn, Europe UBF, 2008), 124-131.

[34] Don Kuper, 'World Missions: UBF Newsletter' (Private newsletter, Sept, 2007), 26.

ministries with only 30 members sent out 10 missionaries. Sending this many missionaries is possible through the self-supporting professional lay missionary model.[35] In the past 40 years, the UBF sent out 3,000 missionaries. 2,000 trained members are waiting to be sent out as missionaries, whenever and wherever the door for self-support is opened. All the UBF members, throughout the whole world, are praying to send out 100,000 self-supporting professional missionaries worldwide.

In the 1980s, when the self-supporting professional lay missionary-sending mission model was still unknown and sending clerical missionaries was the common mission model, the UBF had already sent several hundreds of self-supporting professional lay missionaries to 30 countries and now sees the fruit of disciple-making ministries among nationals. By the end of 2009, the UBF had sent 3,092 self-supporting missionaries to 92 countries. Among them, in 1976, one group split off and formed 'SBF' (later called ESF). In 2001, several members split off and formed another group called CMI.[36] Presently, 1,750 self-supporting missionaries are serving world mission as UBF members. They are working in 300 different kinds of professions and occupations in 92 nations, supporting themselves in the mission field and serving campus mission and disciple-making ministries through one-to-one Bible study. Their jobs vary from professors and computer programmers to even dog hairdressers, and various other jobs.

99.9% of the UBF missionaries are self-supporting lay missionaries. However, the UBF supports them, whenever necessary. For example, the UBF supports missionaries in third world countries with school tuition fees for their children, money for medical treatment, etc. especially in remote and under-developed areas. When necessary, UBF builds a base camp for supporting these missionaries. Support is provided by a UBF collective mission fund, not by interest from bank deposits because it is too little.[37]

Examples of UBF Professional Self-supporting Lay Missionaries

Medical Profession

Mr. Yoo met Jesus in the first semester of his medical studies and received discipleship training. He was a medical doctor and even became a professor in Korea. However, he gave up his job and his security and was sent to Uganda, in Africa, in 1992, as a missionary and as an employee of KOICA (Korea

[35] Tae-chul Yang, 'GMI's World Mission and the Professional Self-supporting Mission Ministry' (A Study Presented at the Guatemala Professional Tentmaker Missionary Conference, Guatemala City, Guatemala, Oct, 2007), 51, 52.
[36] S. Lee, 'Korean Moravian Mission model', 5.
[37] S. Lee, 'Korean Moravian Mission model', 6.

International Cooperation Agency). He suffered a lot as a foreigner, especially because of AIDS and the prevelant malaria, and due to the lack of public systems and security. However, in 2002, he opened a mission clinic and provided free medical treatment for two orphanages in Kampala and for children of poor families. Apart from that, he dedicated himself to campus mission and disciple- making among students who are the hope of this nation. Each week he holds a worship service together with national student disciples, delivers a message, and does his best to raise disciples. The hospital there is also used as a base camp for UBF mission journey teams from Korea, which consists of doctors and nurses, to provide free medical support and to preach the gospel.[38]

Student Missionaries

In 1970, in his first semester of his economics studies at Yonsei University in Korea, Mr. Hong studied the Bible and accepted Jesus personally and also received discipleship training. In 1977, when he was 25 years old, he accepted Jesus' world mission command and was sent to America as a student missionary. While pursuing his master's and Ph.D studies in Bowling Green and Toledo, he served the pioneering ministry. Now, each Sunday, about 80 national students are attending Sunday worship service. Moreover, Mr. Hong became academically successful and currently serves as a tenured professor and supervises several Ph.D students.[39]

Corporate Employees

Mr. Lee was sent out by a large Korean company to India as an employee. There he preached God's word to many students and bore much fruit and raised many disciples of Jesus. Putting his effort into leading a pious life, praying and serving his fellow workers, he earned a good reputation and achievement in his work and renewed his residency three times. However, as he was promoted, he was pressurised to return to Korea. Instead, he quit his job and stayed in India. Indian students were encouraged through his sacrificial life to devote their lives to serve God. Missionary Lee established a factory and hired dozens of employees. He was also head of a Korean association and was rewarded with the President's medal for bringing honor to the nation of Korea. In India, four student UBF churches have been established and four national student leaders

---

[38] Samuel Yoo, 'A Kernel of Wheat That Falls on the Ground' (A Study Presented at the Guatemala Professional Tentmaker Missionary Conference, Guatemala City, Guatemala, Oct., 2007), 103-111.

[39] Paul Hong, *Laymen Are Called* [in Korean] (Seoul: Sunggwang Moonhwasa, 1999), 45-48

are serving the ministry as professor shepherds. There are many who have been converted from Hinduism. [40]

Embassy Officers

Mr. Shin encountered Jesus during his college years and accepted the calling for world mission. In 1991, he and his wife went out as an assistant officer and domestic help for the ambassadors' family. In that way, they could preach the gospel in Mongolia as self-supporting missionaries. At that time, in Mongolia, only the New Testament had been translated. After work, Mr. Shin studied Mongolian at the University. In order to teach the Bible to national students, he and Mr. Lim began to translate the Old Testament into Mongolian. Later he established a Bible translation team together with other churches which translated the whole Bible into Mongolian. Now, about 200 Mongolian students are serving God in three ministries. They study the Bible in Mongolian and hold Sunday worship services in Mongolian as well. Six Korean lay missionaries are also working there.[41]

Immigration Mission

Mr. Lee accepted God's missionary calling in 1988 and went to Paraguay as an immigrant, giving up a secure job in Korea. He studied the language in a local school. At the beginning of his ministry, he lived on savings he had brought from Korea. While taking language courses at the university, he began preaching the gospel to students. After one year he opened a business in order to support himself. At first, he sold clothes and other merchandise articles, using his car as a mobile shopping mall. Later, he opened a business for electronic devices. He now runs a farm. He preaches the gospel to students, and currently some of them are growing as disciples of Jesus.[42]

Developmental Aid Mission

Mr. Ahn accepted Jesus during his college studies. He looked for an opportunity to be sent out as a missionary. Finally he found a way to go to Sri Lanka as a missionary through KOICA (Korea International Cooperation Agency) as an agricultural engineer. The main task for the aid organization was to work for the developing country for free. While working as an agriculture engineer, he established contacts with Sri Lanka students at the same time. Due

---

[40] Jimmy Lee, 'For India to Be the Kingdom of Priests', in *Thy Kingdom Come: 2004 World Mission Report* (Seoul, UBF Press, 2004), 188-195.

[41] Matthew Lim, *A Holy Nation People III* [in Korean] (Seoul: UBF Press, 2006), 231-35.

[42] John Lee, *A Holy Nation People II* [in Korean] (Seoul, UBF Press, 2006), 94-98.

to his developmental aid service he had been well accepted by national people and was a good influence on them. His good influence enabled him to establish a trusting relationship with national students and to start Bible study with them. In this way many of them accepted Jesus and decided to live as disciples of Jesus.

Business Mission

Mr. Kim runs a wig manufacturing business and is a CEO of a large company of around 200 workers. He started by hand-making wigs at home. Mr. Lee in Mexico runs a sock manufacturing company and has 200 employees. In the beginning, he started with a small shop, but his business became very successful. Since he now has many managers under him, he is able to serve the discipleship ministry with no constraints. He has raised 100 Mexicans as committed disciples of Jesus. Through his business he made enough profit to build a conference centre. This conference centre is now being used for Bible conferences in UBF and also by other organizations on a rental basis.

Educational Mission

Mrs. Lee works as a primary school teacher in a Korean school in Moscow. When she arrived in Moscow, she first began to teach her students the gospel. After work and on the weekends, she goes on campus and where she is bearing much fruit among university students.

Musical Mission

Mr. Jeong was a voice major in Han-Yang University in Korea. After graduation he went to Germany as a student missionary. During his mission life he pursued a master's degree from the university in Dortmund. Later he was accepted as a member of the opera in Dortmund. In this way he solved his visa and self-supporting problems.

Silver Missionaries

Mr. J. worked as a primary school teacher in Korea throughout his lifetime. He prayed to be a missionary at some time. When he was about to become head of his school, he quit his job and went to R. as a so-called 'silver missionary'. He went there only by faith in God's calling. By God's grace, the university had just opened the language department and he became the first language professor. Even though he and his wife are almost 60 years old, they are full of spirit and vision like young people, preaching the gospel to students, raising disciples, and also studying Russian.

Thus far, some examples of professional lay self-supporting missionaries have been introduced. These are only a few of many examples. Currently, numerous lay self-supporting missionaries in hundreds of professions and occupations are serving the world mission ministry around the globe.[43]

How UBF Raised Korean Diaspora Missionaries

Disciple-Making

The key for raising missionaries is to raise sacrificial and devoted disciples of Jesus. Therefore, many church organizations are very interested in making disciples. But the problem is 'how' or, in other words, the methodology. The methods of raising disciples in the UBF will be introduced briefly.

DEEP BIBLE STUDY

In the UBF, all members study the Bible text deeply. They begin by inviting unbelievers among college students and helping them to study the Bible using the inductive Bible study method (i.e. Genesis, Exodus, etc., by books, chapters, and verses). Mostly, this Bible study is on a one-to-one basis, and each Bible study takes around one and a half hours. In addition, leaders study the Bible in groups. All members study a common passage every week with leaders, at least once a week, on a one-to-one basis. In addition, they study other books of the Bible in a systematic manner. Without interruption, such Bible study goes on for 4, 10, or 20 years, and even longer, for a lifetime. This Bible study is not just to accumulate theoretical Bible knowledge, but to challenge and help Bible students to practically obey the word of God. Furthermore, deep one-to-one Bible study is the basis of the trusting relationship and spiritual foundation for living and co-working together between Bible teacher and Bible students based on the word of God.[44]

TESTIMONY WRITING AND SHARING

After Bible study, Bible students hear the Sunday message based on the Bible text that they studied. Then they write testimonies every week based on the Bible study and the message, having been provided with a written manuscript. This facilitates the process of accepting God's word into their hearts. Through writing testimonies, the word of God is planted in their hearts and practically applied in their lives.[45] They share their testimonies one-to-one or in groups. They also memorize important Bible verses. Through writing and sharing testimonies, they begin to repent and to have faith in God's word. Then, they

---

[43] S.H. Lee, 'Professional Self-supporting Lay Mission Cooperation of UBF', 31, 32.
[44] Y.K. Lee, *Bible Study Model*, 35-41; 114-16.
[45] Brian M. Abshire, *Get More from Your Bible* (London: Scripture Union, 1988), 84.

learn to obey the word of God. Through sincere Bible study and testimony writing, a biblical view towards life and the world and a spiritual value system are established.[46] In other words, Bible study in the UBF changes the inner being of a person. The focus of Bible study in the UBF is to change one person to resemble the character of Jesus. Therefore, they grow into sacrificial persons who do everything for Christ. To help and raise one person up to this level takes 10 years at least. Through such Bible study college students receive a missionary spirit and also a world mission vision. They grow as disciples of Jesus and Bible teachers themselves. UBF missionaries are those who received this kind of training during the 4 years of their college years and for 5-6 years after their graduation. One missionary said, 'I studied the Bible for ten years in the UBF and now I have become a self-supporting lay missionary'.

Common Life

Just as Jesus shared a common life with his disciples, once Bible students make a decision to devote their lives to Jesus, they are invited to live a common life.[47] Through a common life, they begin to learn the spirit of their brothers and sisters in Christ and can encourage each other. They are also protected from worldly influences and can dwell in an environment that fosters receiving spiritual training. Through a common life, they also learn how to deny themselves and to love and serve each other.

Shepherd and Leadership Training

Those who accept Jesus and become disciples, begin to preach the gospel to other students and teach the Bible one-to-one by themselves. They receive training to feed sheep. Through shepherd training they grow into Bible teachers who can reproduce believers. Also, the UBF raises them as messengers for Bible conferences. After graduation, the UBF trains them to get a professional job and be an expert in their career as well.

Early Morning Prayer

Early in the morning, leaders gather at each ministry for prayer. They meditate on the word of God with a small booklet called *Daily Bread*, which is designed to cover the whole Bible every four years. They meditate on the respective day's bible passage and write a short personal testimony according to the guideline with application in their practical lives. Through daily bread training, the UBF trains leaders to grow in spirit and to live a spiritual life based on the word of God day-by-day.[48]

---

46 Dietrich Bonhoeffer, *Life Together* (New York, Harper & Row, 1954).

47 Y.K. Lee, *Bible Study Model*, 29-35.

48 Samuel H. Lee, *Meditation, Confession and Healing in Writing Testimonies* (Longwood, FL: Xulon Press, 2008), 100-105.

MISSIONARY TRAINING

Once the mission field is decided, they receive intensive training at the UBF headquarters in each continent. Around 80% of the missionary training consists of Bible study. Through *Daily Bread* training, the factual study of Acts and other important Bible passages, the UBF instils a missionary identity, vision and faith into the hearts of missionary candidates. Besides, they receive a basic training to prepare themselves for adjusting to the culture and the theological background of the mission field.[49]

Raising Second Generation Missionaries and Children

RAISING SECOND GENERATION MISSIONARIES (SGM)

In the UBF, the children of Korean diaspora missionaries are called 'SGM' or 'Second Generation missionaries' from a young age. By calling them SGM, the UBF plants a spiritual identity in them as God's people, a kingdom of priests and a holy nation (1 Pet. 2:9) into their hearts. Most parents teach their children the Bible one-to-one every week. The UBF encourages children to take part in their parents' ministry.[50] Upon college graduation, the UBF helps them to devote their lives as responsible co-workers, Bible teachers and missionaries. The UBF headquarters in Korea, and also continental headquarters, develop various programmes for SGMs appropriate for the mission field's culture. By doing this, they overcome their identity crisis and grow as excellent mission co-workers. Since they have neither a language nor a cultural barrier, they are better equipped for serving the campus mission ministry than their parents' generation. As the number of missionaries grows, the number of their children is also growing. It means that the number of SGMs, who can speak a native language and who have no cultural barrier, is growing, and they constitute a core foundation for expanding the future world campus mission ministry.[51]

As they are being trained to hear the word of God from an early age, they are also able to concentrate on their school studies. Being trained, through Bible studies and writing personal testimonies, helps them to write school papers. Through testimony sharing training, they are also able to improve their public speaking skills and deliver good presentations at school. Moreover, through mastering a musical instrument, they learn a discipline and endurance to overcome hardships in higher-level studies such as in pursuing Ph.D. studies.

---

[49] John Shin and Chul-Dae Kim, 'Missionary-candidate and missionary education' [in Korean], in *Mission Strategy Research Report* (Seoul, UBF Press, 2005), 97-112.

[50] Moses Yoon and Spurgeon Lee, 'Second Generation Education That Will Span for the Next 100 Years' [in Korean], in *Mission Strategy Research Report* (Seoul: UBF Press, 2005), 135, 136.

[51] Peter Chang, 'Interview: The Coming of God's Kingdom through Cooperative Mission', *Christian Today Europe*, Nov 14, 2009.

Most SGMs receive good grades at school and are admitted to prestigious universities. Upon their graduation, they reap double harvest in their spiritual and their professional lives as they are able to enter directly into the mainstream of the society as leaders, both spiritually and in their professions.

EDUCATING CHILDREN OF THE KOREAN DIASPORA MISSIONARIES

The UBF teaches SGMs the Bible and trains them spiritually from kindergarten. SGMs are divided according to their age group and are trained step-by-step through CBF (Children Bible Fellowship), JBF (Junior High School Bible Fellowship), and HBF (High School Bible Fellowship). Throughout these steps, they learn and inherit the spiritual legacy of their parents and are raised to participate in the campus and the world mission as capable and responsible co-workers and to grow as excellent bible teachers and global leaders (Ezra 7:10).[52]

Conclusion

The mission work paradigm, in the twenty-first century, is changing drastically. Firstly, the ratio of the number of the missionaries being sent out is not growing according to the ratio of the population growth. Secondly, the number of countries and regions which ban traditional missionaries is rapidly increasing. Thirdly, cultural and ethnical barriers are growing, as each country intentionally protects their own religion and culture. Lastly, the fund-raising problem for supporting traditional missionary work, the education of missionary children, the health care of missionaries and their future security, is getting more and more serious.

In light of these huge challenges, the sending of traditional missionaries alone is an insufficient response. These challenges can be overcome through the mobilization of self-supporting lay missionaries. In addition to sending out traditional missionaries, churches must also put into practice the mission strategy of 'self-supporting professional lay missionary mission. This mission model, which is at present exemplified by the UBF world campus mission, seems to be an effective response, which can propel world mission ministry forward in our postmodern times, and even prepare the environment of the twenty-first century for a new spiritual awakening, as well as coping with the challenge of an aggressive Muslim expansion.[53]

---

[52] S.H. Lee, 'Moravian Mission Model', 14.

[53] Stephen Neil, *A History of Christian Missions* [in Korean], trans. Chi-mo Hong and Man-kyu Oh (Seoul: Sung-kwang Munhwasa, 2006), 718-22.

Kingdom-Centred Identity:
The Case of Bicultural Korean-Brazilians

Do Myung Chun

Introduction

Korean immigrant churches in Sao Paulo, Brazil, where I come from, have been living a unique situation during these last few years. In the same ecclesiastical locus, we encounter at least five distinct groupings forming a particular faith community: the first Korean generation; the 1.5 Korean generation; the second Korean generation; non-Koreans (Brazilian, Japanese, Chinese); and cross-cultural marriage people.

Each of these five cultural entities presents its own aspirations, customs, values, and ways of expressing its Christian faith. Particularly, in my home church, which is a Presbyterian one, conflicts among these cultural groupings have emerged as the main problem since a Portuguese-speaking worship service was instituted within the church twelve years ago. An uncomfortable state of tension was inevitably established between the Korean-speaking old generation and the Portuguese-speaking younger generation. Despite their commitment to the same Jesus Christ, cultural differences between them seemed to cause an impact much more powerful than their Christian faith on both of them.

In view of these circumstances, I have sensed a need for an appropriate contextual theology able to overcome whatever cultural barriers may exist, and bring these all five groupings together under the Lord's transcendent authority. Therefore, by means of this project, I will attempt to focus on the issues related to Korean inter-generational conflicts, and find out a contextual theology able to give them a strong sense of oneness in Christ, which effectively transcends any cultural and generational differences in any place and at any time. This is, by no means, an approach to homogenize all culturally different groupings into a universal mould of Christian faith. On the contrary, my proposal is to offer a biblically consistent way of seeking unity in diversity, where each one's peculiar cultural values are highly respected for what they are. Simultaneously, I will try to seek a transcultural (or transcendental in a broader sense) model that might establish a common basis where culturally different peoples can express their Christian faith more freely.

First of all, I will describe briefly my faith community, which I am serving in Sao Paulo, Brazil, and its demographic make up from an anthropological point of view. How similarities and differences of these three distinct Korean generations in Brazil interact with each other will be analyzed with more details.

In order to support the solution of Korean inter-generational problems, I will introduce the concept of 'cultural symbiosis'. The core idea of this concept is that all three distinct Korean generations are inevitably bicultural from the very moment they stepped onto Brazilian land. Thus, an individual's capacity of cultural assimilation and personal preference for both Brazilian and Korean cultures, or predominantly for either one, must be respected and encouraged. Since culture itself does not have any power, only people have power, it is a human task to establish creatively an environment for mutually beneficial relationships between different peoples, who are part of the same momentum. Once this culturally symbiotic relationship is built up among three distinct Korean generations, the next step is the elevation of their cultural oneness to a higher level of purpose of human existence, or in other words, the spiritual dimension of human beings for the sake of fulfilling God's original purpose of creation. For this, I employ some of the assumptions of the Transcendental Model of Contextual Theology, by pointing out the supremacy of human ontological identity, centred on the kingdom of God, over any human identity, based on cultural or ethnic assumptions. Moses' call from God is presented as a biblical model for my theological reflection on how one's struggle with his/her own faith and identity crisis was and still is handled by God.

The last two cultural sub-groups (non-Koreans and cross-cultural marriage people) will be treated on another occasion, not because they are of less importance, but because they deserve closer attention and more accurate analysis in order to formulate a consistent contextual theology.

Context

Brazil is a country built basically by immigrants. Besides its racial miscegenation between many peoples, and nations which constitute the so-called Brasileiro (Brazilian people), every single people brought its own traditions that, after mixing with others, ended up forming an unique multi-cultural or multi-ethnic society.

Following the Europeans, predominantly, Portuguese, Italians, and Germans, the Asian peoples entered and occupied this huge continental sized country at the beginning of this century. Among Asians, the Japanese were the first to come to this tropical country already occupied by Caucasians, Africans, and Indians. The first generation and a large percentage of the subsequent generations of Japanese immigrants have predominantly dedicated their lives to develop agriculture in Brazil.

In the 1970s, Korean immigrants commenced arriving in Brazil in massive numbers. After working for a short time in agricultural fields like the Japanese immigrants, the majority of the Koreans concentrated their settlements in large urban cities like Sao Paulo in search of better social conditions. As soon as they started to set up their businesses in the city, an incipient Korean social community emerged around the evangelical churches. As newcomers arrived, they gathered in churches in search of companionship. Even those who never had stepped into an evangelical church before coming to this new land did not hesitate to participate in Sunday morning services.[1]

This large and voluntary mobilization of Korean immigrants into their community churches was motivated in part by Christian faith, but the majority of the church seekers were there due to their need for emotional support, information, and a sense of security. Desperately, they sought help to meet their need for reaffirming their national and ethnic identities, and a sense of belonging to a homogeneous social group where they could maintain their traditional values and customs in the midst of a new, strange, adverse, hostile, and huge Brazilian society.

In this way, the first evangelical church built for the Korean community in Brazil, before any other kind of non-Christian Korean association had been organized, was the Korean United Presbyterian Church, in Sao Paulo, in 1965. Since the congregation was exclusively made up of Korean immigrants, all religious services, programmes and activities were performed in the Korean language. In doing so, the contact with the Brazilian Church was virtually out of the question, at least in its early stages of establishment. Its Sunday school served not only as a precious source of Christian education, but also as an institutional organization responsible for providing Korean immigrants' children with the cultural forms and meanings of their parents. However, this Christian educational system's imposition of Korean values on young people caused some side-effects. Sometimes religious values and cultures forms were mixed up in such a way that those who could not speak Korean fluently, or

---

[1] Eun C. Hwang, 'The Mission of God's Pilgrim People: Toward a Contextual Ministry for Korean Churches in Brazil' (Doctor of Missiology dissertation, Fuller Theological Seminary, 1993), 122-23, writes, 'Korean immigrant to Brazil began in 1918 when twelve people, who were identified as fourth-generation Korean immigrants to Japan, moved to Brazil along with another 120 Japanese immigrants. In 1956, fifty former North Korean prisoners of war settled in Brazil, having spent in South Korean prison camps. A few of them became evangelical pastors and almost all of them had missionary zeal. Official Korean immigrant took its first step in 1961 when the agricultural immigration policy of Brazil was instituted. Since then, a large number of people have immigrated to Brazil from Korea. This full-scale immigration was inaugurated when the first letter of invitation was issued by the Brazilian Immigration Bureau'. However, Koreans who were supposed to settle down in rural areas and work in agricultural activities, left plantations for a series of reasons (inadequacy of agricultural techniques, low degree of receptivity on the part of native people, precarious work conditions, lack of adequate educational infrastructures for their children, etc). Upon leaving a rural environment, Koreans settled mainly in Sao Paulo State because of its better job opportunities, a good educational system, and favorable climatic conditions.

were not very familiar with Korean tradition were viewed with suspicion. Some elders accused those who appeared to act more as Brazilians than Koreans of bringing 'undesirable' elements of native culture into the Korean church contaminating it with secular influences.[2] As a result, Korean young Christians who had to live out simultaneously these two cultures had their minds always impregnated with a constant state of tension and identity instability.

As the Korean immigration history in Brazil completed almost 45 years of its existence, this two-cultural-setting demographic composition of the Korean Christian community brought some progressive changes. For instance, there was a significant inversion in terms of power of the one over the other, between those who regarded themselves as culturally Koreans and the people who preferentially adopted a Brazilian lifestyle. The latter came to outnumber the former[3] and a new wave of social and religious adaptations gained impetus in Korean local community churches.

In order to respond to an increasing influx of Korean–Brazilian members, whose first language was no more Korean but Portuguese, Korean immigrant churches in general, began to institute a new worship service held in Portuguese. In reality, this provision was taken due to a conscious decision of opening the doors of Korean churches to welcome non-Korean peoples, as well as those couples married cross-culturally and their relatives.

Cultural contrasts between the first and the second generations of Korean immigrant churches in Brazil are now more openly discussed and both sides are seeking a creative solution to maintain their unity.

---

[2] 'Socially, they are strongly tied to their homogeneous unit, which is often so exclusive that they cannot interrelate with other homogeneous units. Koreans are socially quite isolated from the Brazilian community. This is caused by a narrow-minded and ethno-centric nationalism. There is no room for a transcultural exchange of ideas. Even though they are living in a Brazilian context, they maintain a definitively Korean style of living and ways of thinking'. Hwang, 'The Mission of God's Pilgrim People', 125. Korean church in Brazil is not only a religious entity, but sociologically it is also a functional source of Korean cultural products both material and non-material. In reality, these two elements interact so deeply with each other that often the observance of certain Korean rituals or customs are improperly regarded as an expression of Christian faith.

[3] According to Hwang, 'The Mission of God's Pilgrim People', 122-23, 'Since then, the number of immigrants has continued at a steadily increasing rate. This active emigration from Korea was accelerated even more by the Korean government in the 1970s. Initially their principal expertise was in administration, however, they worked at manual labor instead, particularly in garment manufacturing. Since the mid 70s there has been a significant influx of immigrants, and they have achieved rapid economic growth. The Brazilian government decided not to admit any more Korean immigrants due to the dissolution of their immigration contract in which they were contracted to work for agricultural development in Brazil. In actuality, Koreans still continue to enter Brazil'.

Anthropological Model: Cultural Symbiosis

In the Korean immigrant church in Brazil, there are three distinct generations of immigrants. Each of them has its own aspirations, expectations, and lives according to its own social and religious context. Here, I will describe briefly some of the characteristics of each generation.

First Generation

Korean adults, who immigrated to Brazil, constitute the first generation. This generation is under a tremendous pressure and stress to succeed in the new land. Every day is a new battle to survive in a society that treats them as aliens and outsiders. They passionately want to play an active part in the local community life, but cultural and language barriers inhibit them from thrusting themselves into local society more aggressively. Due to these difficulties, they adopt a centripetal orientation, gathering around their immigrant churches, where they can freely express and share their frustrations and hopes, as well as worship God in their way and encourage one another spiritually. They tend to preserve the Korean language, heritage, and hierarchical power structure, and are willing to transmit them to their younger generations. Their number is decreasing day by day because the influx of new Korean immigrants to Brazil has been interdicted since the first years of the 1980s. Therefore, while Brazilian immigration policy toward Korean immigration continues to be antagonist, the chances for this unique 'sub-community' becoming extinct in the next few decades is a socially predictably phenomenon. However, despite their gradual withdrawal from the economic market, due to their numerical reduction from the ageing process, the economic power, that maintains the Korean community in Brazil, in the midst of a competitive national market, is still in their hands.[4]

---

[4] Hwang, 'The Mission of God's Pilgrim People', 124, 'Almost all of the Korean immigrants live in Sao Paulo. Clothing factories and retail outlets are their main sources of income. Almost ninety-five percent work in this industry. A wide variety of jobs were created in order to develop a network among Koreans. Some have shops to sell the clothes and others produce them. The rest of them work in sales. The textile industry was primarily introduced by those Koreans who had sufficient financial resources. The whole system promotes full-scale interaction among Korean businesses. Because of this, other working areas are very weak. There are few who are working in the areas of medicine, law or politics'. This massive concentration on clothing factories and retail outlets located specifically in two main market areas called 'Oriente' and 'Bom Retiro', formerly occupied by Jews and Palestinians, ended up creating a kind of 'Korea Town' in the central part of Sao Paulo city. It serves as a supporting base and a source of information for fellow compatriots who venture to enter the market. Nowadays, there is increasingly a positive self-awareness of Koreans and a favorable public recognition on the part of the Brazilian population in general regarding this socially unique adjustment that Korean immigrants have developed in the process of adaptation to a new

The 1.5 Generation[5]

This group includes those who immigrated to Brazil with their parents from Korea when they were young children. They have brought with them to Brazil a Korean cultural identity and a good command of the Korean language. They are bilingual and 'bicultural'. They are truly a half-and-half generation, neither 100% Korean nor 100% Brazilian. In their process of cultural and social assimilation, they face serious problems, because both first and second Korean generations can reject this 'sandwich' generation as aliens. The first generation can reject them because they are too 'Brazilianized', while the second may reject them because they still are too Korean. They tend to play on both sides according to their interests and capabilities, without really becoming part of either one. However, it is also true that they can play a crucial role as an effective bridge in the community between the Korean and American cultures.

Second Generation

The second generation refers to Korean Brazilians, who were either born in Brazil, or who came to this country at an early age, that Korea has little place in their psychological identity. Portuguese is their primary language. They are Brazilians in every sense, except for their oriental appearance. Like the 1.5 generation, they are not fully accepted by either Korean or Brazilian societies. Because of the short period of Korean immigration to Brazil (not more than 45 years), most of them are still single and live along with their 1.5 generation parents, and receive a reasonable amount of Korean cultural education from

---

environment. This social phenomenon certainly led Korean immigrants in Brazil toward a strong sense of participation in the development of national economics and a sort of corporate contribution to Brazilian society in general. For, in the midst of a high unemployment rate that is devastating the whole country, the percentage of participation of Korean businessmen in offering job opportunities to Brazilians cannot ever be despised. Moreover, their ongoing efforts in increasing the quality of Brazilian garment products launched predominantly into the national market to meet the need of the population with a low earning power deserves a closer appreciation. If they failed to contribute agriculturally in the past, the present moment is a time to concretize once and for all the Korean immigrants' position within Brazilian society as an active and beneficial community for the sake of national well-being.

[5] Moo H. Won, 'Korean American Pluralism: The "1.5" Generation', in Sang Hyun Lee and John V. Moore (eds), *Korean American Ministry* (Louisville, KY: PC USA, 2006), 215-216: 'Since the term 1.5 generation has only recently been coined in the Korean community, one cannot turn to a dictionary or the literature on immigration for a definition. Although the terms in Japanese for first, second, and third generation immigrants, *is-sei, ni-sei,* and *san-sei,* are found in standard English dictionaries, no such term as 1.5 generation has been ever used with reference to other immigrant groups'.

them. Thus, a significant percentage of them are still bilingual an 'bicultural'. Their inter-generational struggle, especially with the first generation, is intense.

Personal expectations and aspirations of these three sub-groups are different from each other. By the way, none of the three Korean generations mentioned here are 100% Korean or 100% Brazilian, since all of them are living integrated into a bicultural environment. What really distinguish these three groups are not their birthplaces, but the variation of degrees with which each of them assimilates itself into a bicultural structure.

Even though the division of Korean immigrants to Brazil into three distinct generational categories has helped them understand who they are from an anthropological standpoint, its application to a local Korean Christian church seemed to have caused more complications than benefits, in terms of corporate cohesion. In view of this reality, we need to be aware that our goal is not to learn how to just label people. The anthropological description of generations should not be used to typecast or label others or, conversely, to excuse ourselves for negative behavior. If a categorization or labeling helps to clarify differences, then it is useful, but if it is used to create barriers to communication, it is confining. My intent is to clarify, rather than to confine, and to seek a creative way of preserving the wholeness. For to preserve uniqueness of a particular part, at the expense of the disintegration of the whole, goes against the biblical principle of 'one in Christ' in Eph. 2:11-22, 'For he [Jesus Christ] himself is our peace, who has made the two one and has destroyed the barrier, the dividing wall of hostility' (Eph. 2:14).

Therefore, instead of exploring dissimilarities to justify why they cannot be incorporated into a common cultural entity, a creative and integrative mind-set toward a self-awareness of their oneness is mandatory.

A conscious step to transform their cultural diversity into a means of seeking a genuine and a totally new cultural identity must be taken. Within this context the concept of cultural symbiosis takes its due place. The word 'symbiosis' is a term, borrowed from ecology, which originally indicates an association of two plants, or of a plant and an animal, or of two animals, in which both dissimilar organisms maintain a mutually beneficial relationship.

As matter of fact, this cultural symbiosis occurs inside every single individual, who is integrated into a bicultural setting, regardless of his or her generational identity. What determines the status of a bicultural person's cultural assimilation is not necessarily his/her biological age or his/her position within a descendant ramification of generations of a given family or ethnicity.

For many years, the terms 'cultural conflict' or 'culture shock' have been used to describe a state of tension, when psychological instability, generated by the interaction of cultural patterns due to their differences, ends up by breaking one's life balance. Although the term 'conflict' or 'shock' does not carry with it a necessarily pejorative meaning, the break-up of harmony and balance of a living structure certainly cannot be freed from its negative connotations. Cultural symbiosis may be understood as another anthropologically creative way of approaching the interaction between two different cultural settings in such a way that, for instance, both Brazilian and Korean parts of a bicultural personality can benefit mutually without generating antagonistic forces between them. Here, what really matters is an individual's selective capacity of assimilating what both cultures have to offer to contribute to the formation of one's cultural identity. Therefore, one is to develop this capacity to select from the contact with both cultures in everyday situations, those habits, values, patterns, behaviors, and religious practices that he/she judges to be helpful to incorporate into his/her individual bicultural formation.

Cultural symbiosis may seem to be too idealistic, theoretical, and purely cognitive at first glance. However, it is exactly this kind of cognitive process of self-awareness of what really is going on, that Korean generations in Korean-Brazilian churches need to work on, in order to move forward in consistently practical steps toward oneness in Christ. In other words, it is a time to introduce into the Christian education agenda a programme dealing with bicultural issues more directly. Cultural symbiosis theory guarantees us a common denominator for the different generations, or even for various segments inside of a same generation, upon which we can build a unified sense of a corporate identity. As all the immigrants, either the first or the subsequent generations, are bicultural by definition, their cultural pointers[6] are located more or less to the right or to the left along the cultural symbiosis Continuum (Table 1). All use, in some way, both cultural forms, Korean and Brazilian, in the resolution of problems that emerge in their routine activities, in the accomplishment of their objectives, dreams and aspirations, and in the release of their anxieties, or in the satisfaction of their basic needs.

---

[6] A cultural pointer determines one's cultural status along the cultural symbiosis continuum, indicating his/her position in relation to a certain bicultural structuring. Throughout the wide spectrum of cultural symbiosis, the cultural pointer of a bicultural person could be located in any position. Just as the position of the pointer of a thermometer varies in agreement with the atmospheric temperature, an individual's cultural pointer along the spectrum of cultural symbiosis can also vary according to some factors, such as: 1) Extrinsic factors (social) including a) Time period of contact with the two cultures, respectively; b) Degree of interaction with the two cultures, respectively; c) Positive or negative experiences in the past with the two cultures; and d) Cultural subsystem in question (religion, art, economical, politics, technology, etc), and 2) Intrinsic factors (individual), which include a) Degree of cultural absorptivity: pre-disposition or capacity to absorb everything that a given society has to offer as their cultural forms and meanings to meet one's individual needs, b) Degree of cultural selectivity: pre-disposition or capacity to choose selectively certain cultural forms or meanings that a given society has to offer in order to meet one's individual needs. The position of a cultural pointer is unique for each person, and for a specific momentum of his/her life. Therefore, any attempt to attribute a generic cultural status for an entire group of individuals, or an ethnic community, or a certain generation, is not feasible as well as being indicative of an anti-ethical attitude.

Based on the diagram below, the following mathematical equation may be formulated:

K' + B' = S

K' = portion of Korean Culture that one assimilates into the formation of his/her bicultural identity

B' = portion of Brazilian Culture that one assimilates into the formation of his/her bicultural identity

S = Cultural Status of a bicultural person

Letters C, J, or P along the Cultural Symbiosis Continuum line arbitrarily represents Cultural Status of a given Korean-Brazilian bicultural person. 'C' could represent, for instance, a first Korean generation with his/her predominant affinity with Korean culture. 'P' may symbolize a second Korean generation's cultural self-awareness, while 'J' would characterize a 1.5 generation's cultural preference.

Table 1 Cultural Symbiosis Continuum

K________C_______J________P_______B
100% 100%

K = Original Korean Culture (100%)
B = Original Brazilian Culture (100%)

Instead of wasting time and energy in only describing discrepancies and differences between one generation and the other, or simply letting the generations be alienated from each other, our effort should be driven in the direction of maximizing a strategic way of constructing a framework in which we can help mutually to achieve common goals. It is clear that in this model, there is no oppressive attempt to impel one's cultural pointer to either of the two poles. That is, nobody is forced to turn into a 100% Korean, or a 100% Brazilian. What is sought in this scheme is that each individual feels comfortable where he/she is, and that his/her cultural pointer positioned in his/her due equilibrium point indicates his/her real cultural status at a given moment. And as such, it needs to be valued and respected. For instance, one's cultural pointer could be located in a point that represents 30% Korean to the left and 70% Brazilian to the right, or 80% Korean to the left and 20% Brazilian to the right, and so on. The challenge is for a bicultural person to become conscious of his/her actual cultural status and to work on it in the best way possible to cope with the circumstances of life and to become synergistically cooperative with other members of the same community.[7]

[7] Here, I am talking about 'cultural synergy' which only exists in relation to a practical set of circumstances and mutual understanding, and it takes place by necessity when two bicultural persons with wide differences between them in terms of cultural status come

Now, in order to attain this kind of cultural integration, it is mandatory that all of the members of a given bicultural setting be engaged in passing through an ongoing process of mutual agreement. A consensus in establishing an atmosphere of recognition and mutual respect for various possible cultural status that exist throughout the Cultural Symbiosis Continuum is an indispensable prerequisite for the success of this model.

Once one can stand for his/her individual cultural status confidently, and be respected the way he/she is, I believe that a sense of human dignity and a strong desire to maintain the harmony of a structure that inspires confidence and security will emerge naturally among people.

So as not to be too theoretical, let me give an example. One of the practical issues every day in the church that we face, as Korean-Brazilian bicultural people, is about language. A 1.5 generation person wants to express himself/herself interchangeably in Portuguese or in Korean. A first-generation elder wants to communicate predominantly in Korean, while a second-generation adolescent prefers to communicate in Portuguese. What is important here is that we need to understand that every language is, like any other cultural form, an instrument or a means to be used for the sake of communication within a given community. It is so sad to see that one's linguistic preference turns out to be a splitting or discriminating factor among the members of the same community. I believe that a person's preference for a certain cultural or linguistic form, at best, should be respected and encouraged, at worst, recognized as a valid and appropriate option for the person. Therefore, when it comes to a relatively small bicultural setting like the Korean-Brazilian church, it is advisable that all of the participating members in that community set up an inclusive and multi-cultural atmosphere to amplify the extent of acceptance of other cultures. In doing so, a given speaker's grammatical mistakes or lapses in pronunciation, can be perfectly tolerated by the entire faith community as far as there is an acceptable degree of mutual comprehension. If that is not possible, the community chooses among its members those who can play an interpreter's role. Besides, this three-person setting of communication, sender-intermediary-receiver, is another form of lifting up a spirit of corporate unity among the members, since instead of two people, there are now three people's participation in the conversation on a given topic.

Kraft rightly points out that, 'people have the right to reconstruct their cultural life in any way they choose'.[8] This means that the Korean immigrants in Brazil, including all three generations above cited, have the right to adopt customs and ways of thinking that they assimilate from both Korean and

---

to the mutual conclusion that they need to unite their efforts in order to achieve their respective and corporate goals.

[8] Charles H. Kraft, *Anthropology for Christian Witness* (Maryknoll, NY: Orbis Books, 1996), 340.

Brazilian sources, by either adding or replacing their previous customs. The resulting bicultural structuring can be called a 'third culture' where cultural symbiosis constitutes its basic principle in the mechanism of action. It is made up of partly Brazilian culture as well as traditional Korean culture and as a distinct, new, and creatively emerging cultural entity, this 'third culture' should be respected and taken seriously.[9]

Between being 100% Brazilian as Brazilian society forces Korean-Brazilian bicultural persons to be, on the one hand, and being 100% Korean to which the traditional segment of the Korean immigrant society in Brazil tends to push its young generations,[10] on the other hand, I suggest that an authentic Korean-Brazilian bicultural person should be neither 100% Brazilian, nor 100% Korean. Instead, each of the bicultural persons should be 100% who he/she is

---

[9] Kraft rightly states, 'When working with people who have effectively mixed traditional and Western assumptions and practices, the resulting cultural structuring needs to be taken just as seriously as either of the source cultures. The new structures are the appropriate way of life for those who practice them'. The 'Third Culture' as a new emerging cultural setting with its own patterns, which in turn, is neither wholly Korean not Brazilian, must be appreciated as an another authentic way of life for those who deliberately have chosen it. Kraft continues and points out that, 'Traditional parents need to be helped to understand the validity of their children's approach to life and to encourage structures, within or apart from their own churches, that work with their cultural and linguistic preferences. Young people need to be helped to understand and appreciate where their parents are coming from and to make decisions that are as considerate as possible of their understandings and practices'. Kraft, *Anthropology for Christian Witness*, 311-12.

[10] There have been some attempts to compromise the two cultures: 1) 'Korean-Brazilian bicultural people should strive to be 100% Korean and 100% Brazilian simultaneously!' My response: It is a fictitious proposal once human beings are limited in time and space, it is unlikely to experience the two realities at the same time. It is like an animal that wants to fly in the air and swim in the sea at the same time. Only Jesus was able to do that because he was 100% God and 100% human. 2) 'Korean-Brazilian bicultural people should be '50% Korean and 50% Brazilian!' My response: This proposal assumes that being a half Korean and half Brazilian would be an ideal status for any bicultural people regardless of his/her uniqueness. Those who fail to fulfill this ideal certainly will suffer serious psychological consequences. But what is verified empirically is that there is a great range of variations of cultural blending between the two cultural extremes. 3) 'The first generation are more 'Koreanized' while the second generation are more 'Brazilianized', and the 1.5 generation are in-betweens'. My response: This is not true, because in practice, among the first generation, there are some with their mentality more oriented toward Brazilian culture than Korean culture. Conversely, among the second generation there are those who hold Korean tradition and live up in agreement with the patterns of Korean culture with more flexibility than many of the former generation do. Therefore, depending on social and cultural interactions in which one is involved and consequent degree of satisfaction of personal and social interests that he/she experiences, the preference for one culture or for the other, or for both, varies a lot.

with his/her own cultural status positioned in some point between the two cultural polarities that give him/her a sense of cultural stability.

However, the cultural symbiosis concept, like any other anthropological approach to a reconciliation of inter-generational conflict, is essentially a descriptive model, that is it helps to define and localize a bicultural person's cultural status at a given time. The self-awareness of their authentic 'biculturality' is not by itself sufficiently motivational and persuasive to thrust them toward a more sublime purpose God has entrusted them to carry out for the sake of his kingdom. That is why a transcendental approach must be included in their search for their true identity, because it complements their sense of oneness in Christ, their primordial motivation for human existence on the earth, and finally gives them consistent guidelines to express their faithful allegiance to the Lord.

Transcendental Model:[11] Kingdom-Centered Identity

Based on this model, Moses' call experience, that is, an intimate encounter between God and a human being, is analyzed from personal and psychological perspectives. By understanding Moses as a person of faith, involved in his individual experience with God at a particular historical, cultural, and psychological momentum of his personal life, I intend to offer insightful foundations for a contextual theology for those who are within a similar historical and cultural setting. As a bicultural person struggling with my own cultural identity, and now, more than ever, as a church leader, I feel obligated to provide my fellow Korean-Brazilian sisters and brothers with an adequate and practical contextual theology that restores or redefines their true identity. For such a purpose, there is no better example in the Bible than Moses, who also wrestled with himself because of his identity crisis, after being alienated from all of his significant individual people and communities.

In this model, I also assume that 'the only place God can reveal 'Godself' truly and effectively is within human experience, as a human person is open to the words of scripture as read or proclaimed, open to events in daily life, and

---

[11] Stephen B. Bevans, *Models of Contextual Theology* (Maryknoll, NY: Orbis Books, 1992), 98, argues, 'A fundamental presupposition of the transcendental model is that one begins to theologize contextually not by focusing on the essence of the gospel message or of tradition as such… Rather, the starting point is transcendental, concerned with one's own religious experience and own experience of oneself… However, it is important to understand that one does not and cannot start in a vacuum… I am precisely who I am because I exist at this particular point in time, because I am a recipient of a particular national and cultural heritage, because I have a particular set of parents and have received a particular amount and quality of education, and so forth. What might seem at first glance to be a very personal and even individualistic starting point is really extremely contextual and communal'.

open to the values embodied in a cultural tradition'.[12] God's revelation is an event, and as such, it is inserted into a time, place, and person framework with a divine purpose as the motivator of its process. In other words, if God seeks someone, there is a good reason for the person being sought, and secondarily, biblical meanings extracted from his personal experience with God assumes a historical character, whose values can be reproduced at a later time. Regarding this assumption, Bevans points out that, 'while every person is truly historically and culturally conditioned in terms of the content of thought, the human mind operates in identical ways in all cultures and all periods of history'.[13]

This conviction allows me to identify myself with Moses, by the time he was called after forty years of his life in the wilderness.

Human lives are centred on relationships with relatives, friends, colleagues at work, etc. Through these inter-relationships we gain our identity within a society and an image of ourselves. Therefore, the search for a community is one of the fundamental searches that are decisive in this life's pilgrimage, especially for bicultural people who are very sensitive to issues related to their identity and sense of belonging. Here, the case of Moses arises to give a sort of orientation to deal with this profound matter, which in turn has to do with the meaning of our own existence.

Genesis closes with Jacob's family of seventy people moving to Egypt. But, in the opening scene of Exodus, 350 years later, hundreds of thousands of their ancestors are toiling on Pharaoh's huge construction projects - not as guests but as slaves. Adopted into the palace, Moses gets the benefit of a superb classical education. His Egyptian upbringing is balanced by his Israelite nurture. Later on, God takes the initiative to come to Moses and commences a love relationship with him at the burning bush. Many texts throughout Exodus, Leviticus, Numbers, and Deuteronomy illustrate how God pursues a continuing love relationship with Moses. Whenever God gets ready to do something, He always reveals to a person or his people what He is going to do (Amos 3:7). However, Moses tries to take matters about the children of Israel into his own hands. In Ex. 2:11-15, Moses begins to assert himself on behalf of his own people. That costs him forty years of exile in working as a shepherd.

The focus of the Bible is on God. The essence of sin is a shift from a God-centredness to self-centredness. The essence of salvation is a denial of self, not an affirming of self. Yet it does not mean the loss of one's identity. On the contrary, by confirming who one is, he/she can go forward onto next step, which is faith and action.

Interestingly enough was Moses' response to God's calling in Ex. 3:11, 'WHO AM I?' I am inclined to believe that it was not only a crisis of belief but also a crisis of identity that Moses had been experiencing during forty years in the Median desert. Moses was not sure about his individual and collective

---

[12] Bevans, *Models of Contextual Theology*, 99.

[13] Bevans, *Models of Contextual Theology*, 99.

identity as a member of a group, and as a part of a nation. For, in the same verse, three significant entities with which he had identified himself are mentioned:

'Who am I that I should go to Pharaoh, and bring the Israelites out of Egypt?' Moses' personal relationship to Pharaoh as his daughter's son represented Moses' royal identity, the highest relationship that any human being would want to have in his days. However, this identity was lost when he killed an Egyptian and Pharaoh 'tried to kill Moses' (Ex. 2:15). As for the Israelites, to whom Moses undoubtedly believed that he belonged, they did not accept Moses as one of them (Ex. 2:14). Moses' ethnic identity as a member of the Hebrew clan or tribe was also gone. Finally, his nationality as an Egyptian was also lost when he intentionally murdered an Egyptian on behalf of a Hebrew and became a criminal fugitive. Sarna comments that:

> The opening words of the divine address mentioning of Moses' ancestors, 'I am the God of your father, the God of Abraham, the God of Isaac, and the God of Jacob', must have had a tremendous impact on Moses, jolting him into renewed consciousness of his Israelite heritage and into the sudden realization of his true and inescapable identity.[14]

Certainly, out of these three different levels of identity that Moses possessed, the most significant to him would have probably been the ethnic identity related to his Hebrew cultural background, with which he felt more kinship affinity than the other communities. This assumption is based on Ex. 2:11, where Moses refers to Hebrews as 'his own people'. There is another reference in the New Testament that shows his identification with Hebrews, 'By faith Moses, when he had grown up, refused to be known as the son of Pharaoh's daughter. He chose to be mistreated along with the people of God rather than to enjoy the pleasures of sin for a short time' (Heb. 11:24-25). At this point, it is important to focus our attention on how Moses defined his both his individual and collective identity because it is well documented that:

> Traditional culture defines the individual's identity in the following ontological formula: Cognatus ergo sum; I belong, therefore I am. To belong is to participate in and contribute to the life and welfare of the family. This is in opposition to the individualistic dictum of Descartes: Cogito ergo sum: I think, therefore I am. It is not the individual's capacity to think which is the prime source of his or her identity formation, but rather the reality and the ability of belonging, participating, and sharing.[15]

---

[14] Nahum M. Sarna, *Exploring Exodus: The Original of Biblical Israel* (New York: Schocken Books, 1986), 42.

[15] David W. Augsburger, *Pastoral Counseling across Cultures* (Philadelphia: Westminster Press, 1986), 79.

Jacob and his family moved out into Egypt as in the times of Joseph, about 350 years earlier. Moses, as an offspring of Hebrew immigrants in Egypt, and, therefore, as an Egyptian-Hebrew bicultural person, was having a serious struggle with his own identity because with his total isolation from his beloved people, he did not know who he really was anymore.

He was neither Hebrew nor Egyptian. In the midst of the wilderness He did not belong to any significant community that had participated in the formation of his cultural and nationalistic background. According to Augsburger's comment:

> In traditional society, the society is the end and the human individual is the means. Here, the society is a people, which exists as a whole greater than the sum of its individual parts and from which each individual draws life, receives being, continues family, learns personhood, and expresses the culture's wisdom.[16]

He was now a miserable fugitive pretending to be a mere shepherd in the midst of the Midian desert. Moses' psychological aloneness and isolation during his stay in the desert can be clearly observed when Zipporah gave birth a son, and Moses named him Gershom, which meant 'I have become an alien in a foreign land' (Ex. 2:22). Sarna rightly comments on that, saying, 'it evokes Moses' unhappy personal situation as a fugitive and a man without a country'.[17]

Taking into account these considerations, now we can understand why Moses' response to God's call was a prompt question on his identity: 'WHO AM I?'

Similarly to Abraham, instead of defining who Moses was, God revealed first who He was. He answered Moses' question about his identity with a statement regarding God's own identity: 'I AM WHO I AM' (Ex. 3:14).

And when God said, 'I AM WHO I AM', He meant to say, 'I am who I am, the eternal God, and you are who you are, eternally My people'. The revelation of the identity of God once again preceded a man's search for his own identity.

It allows us to conclude that the main stream that flows throughout the entire Old Testament is God's persistent directness toward the revelation of his identity to his people. Correspondingly, our identity becomes gradually clearer as we are exposed to God's revelation and involved in a relationship with him, and afterwards with others. For 'human beings are in the image of God yet co-images of God'.[18] This means that our true identity can be found, not in our individuality, but in our relatedness, not in our separateness, but in our responsible co-humanity with each other. Moses' identity is restored, not in his autonomy, but in his responsive co-existence before God.

---

[16] Augsburger, *Pastoral Counseling across Cultures*, 81.
[17] Sarna, *Exploring Exodus*, 37.
[18] Augsburger, *Pastoral Counseling across Cultures*, 106.

Let us to see now how God dealt with the crisis of identity that Moses was facing. Interestingly enough, in Exodus 3:10, God sent Moses back to the same three communities with which Moses had no longer any connection: Pharaoh representing the royal family community, the Israelites, the Hebrew ethnic community, and Egypt, the national community. These are three different levels of humanly organized communities, to which a person normally belongs. Human beings are always, to a certain extent, in the process of developing a sense of belonging to one community and then another, whether the community is family or church or a nation, because identity and a sense of belonging are really two sides of one coin. Identity is the personal side, and a sense of belonging, the collective side. How can we know who we are if we do not belong to anywhere? It seems that God intended to show Moses that above and prior to these three different levels of human community, through which a man desperately seeks to find his identity, there was a fourth community. This community was the broadest, the most comprehensive, and the most essential for every human being. God wanted to remind Moses of something that was transcendental and eternal, in contrast to any other human reality, which was circumstantial and inconsistent.

This primary identity has to do with the fact that we are all God's creatures prior to belonging to any other human communities. We are God's people. We belong to God's kingdom. At the level of family, we are sons of God, the heavenly Father, at the ethnic level, we are Church, the faith community, and at the national level, we are his people, the citizens of the kingdom of God. As we can see, this kingdom-centred definition of one's identity gives him/her a fresh way of understanding man's ontological need for his individual and collective identity in a given historical context. Here is the rediscovery, the restoration of our very original identity as ones who belong to the beloved people of God.

I am not ignoring the pluralistic character and uniqueness of every different race and class. However, whatever divisions may exist in society, and whatever may be the right solution to them, within the body of Christ, there is 'neither Jew nor Greek, slave nor free' (1 Cor. 12:13). All are, without exception, one. For all of Christ's people are servants of the same Lord, fellow citizens of the same kingdom, and heirs of the same hope. This is the time for the emergence of a kingdom-centred identity.

Here, one question arises, as a natural result of this new understanding about our identity: is there any way of reconciling all these different aspects of identity in such a way that we preserve our traditions for the next generations, and at the same time open the door of our minds to accept other nations to live together in a multi-ethnic faith community without or with a minimum of cultural or inter-generational friction? The answer is 'YES'. However, there is an important and indispensable precondition to make this assumption viable. All of us need to be aware of our kingdom-centred identity and keep it in mind all the time. If we define ourselves, with our own existence focused on the kingdom of God, then any other identities whether cultural, national or ethnic are nothing more than mere tools, that God entrusted us to use on behalf of the expansion of the kingdom of God. I do not mean that we should no longer keep our cultural tradition or nationality or worship God in the company of those who are like-minded. As Glasser has already commented, 'this transformation should not depersonalize believing individuals by forcing all into the same 'Christian' mold. Nor should it deculturalize diverse believing communities so that all cultural distinctives are eliminated'.[19]

This assumption implies that all our previous experiences with other nations, peoples, languages, cultures, or even with other religions, may serve as precious instruments in our hands to communicate God's love to all the nations. It is a matter of God's love being expressed in different languages, cultures, traditions, customs, value systems, moralities, etc. Every single resource, that we have in hand, must be employed for the sake of the kingdom of God. In the midst of this willingness and attitude, our kingdom-centred identity takes its proper place. The Church is to exhibit before the world as the prototypical community that transcends all barriers human society has erected, so that men may see in it a reflection of God's redemptive community.

We should lay aside all our pride and prejudice and accept differences among all nations as God's blessings. We all have the same citizenship as members of the living Church. Jesus is coming and when we are to meet him face to face, I do not believe that He will call us by our cultural identity, or by our political identity, or by our generational identity, or what is most unlikely, by our ethnicity. All his attention will be focused on those who believed in his word and who fulfilled by faith and deeds God's purpose. He will ask for our kingdom-centred identity and not our earthly identity. John Bright also stresses this point of view by saying:

> There is no hope for man until he can find some citizenship higher than that which national loyalty, class interest, and political ideology can impart. The salvation of man awaits precisely hid decision whose man he is, what commands his ultimate allegiance, in what he reposes his faith. Man must find a saving community. And it is the business of the Church to declare that there is such a community, and only one: the Kingdom of God and his Christ.[20]

Our commitment to Christ implies that we also accept his sovereign ruling and action over and within all nations and peoples on the earth. The God of the Hebrews was also the God of the Gentiles. The Lord, whom Brazilian Christians worship, is the same Lord, whom Korean Christians praise. The centrality of all Christian believers must be focused on the person of Jesus Christ, to whom they dedicate their primary allegiance and lives. And this

---

[19] Arthur F. Glasser, *Kingdom and Mission* (Pasadena, CA: Fuller Theological Seminary, 1989), 17.

[20] John Bright, *The Kingdom of God: The Biblical Concept and Its Meaning for the Church* (Nashville: Abingdon Press, 1981), 257.

covenantal relationship with God transcends all the nationalities, ethnic groupings, and geographical or cultural boundaries established by human beings. Unlike secular historians, who narrate histories of different peoples and nations from a mere scientific perspective, we, who have committed ourselves to Christ, should see the whole of human history as scenery, in which God's redemptive work through Christ takes place unceasingly. This Christo-centric faith community is universal and can be experienced by everyone, even in his/her own homeland. However, immigrants are given the privilege of experiencing this cross-cultural fellowship more intimately, inasmuch as they enter a new and foreign land, and come to know people living there.

Conclusion

The 'third culture', based on the cultural symbiosis concept, was introduced into the Korean-Brazilian bicultural community to solve the conflict between its generations by a symbiotic interrelationship with mutual trust, respect, and benefits. However, the Christians' search for their identity must go beyond a mere cultural level. It must go in the direction of a transcendental reality. This transcendental entrance into God's kingdom is only possible as we become aware of our kingdom-centred identity. We need to find our kingdom-centred identity and concretize our theological positions regarding tensions created by human cultural issues. This is not an attempt to ignore the pluralistic character and uniqueness of different races and classes. However, we cannot passively accept these facts and take an attitude in favor of fatalism. Whatever divisions may exist in society, and whatever may be the right solution to them, within the body of Christ, there is 'neither Jew nor Greek, slave nor free' (1 Cor. 12:13). All are, without exception, one. For all of Christ's people are servants of the same Lord, fellow citizens of the same kingdom, the heirs of the same hope. 'It is the community of all who have heard the sound of the kingdom of God drawing near, and have said 'Yes' to its coming. It is the new Israel, the new people of God, One Holy Church Universal'.[21] In short, this is not a matter of antagonism between a kingdom-centred identity and a cultural identity of believers, nor a movement in favor of cultural homogenization or a denial of cultural relativity, but rather it is about how we, as Christians, may live accordingly to 'The Age to Come-centred identity' in This Age. This is a matter of inclusiveness of the 'kingdom-centred identity', that transcends and welcomes comprehensively the 'cultural symbiosis' of all sorts of earthly communities for the sake of the kingdom of God.

[21] Bright, *The Kingdom of God*, 256.

Mobilizing Senior Christians in Korea and Among the Korean Diaspora for Mission

See-Young Lee

Introduction

> 'The harvest is plentiful but the workers are few. Ask the Lord of the harvest, therefore, to send out workers into his harvest field' (Matthew 9:37~38)

In Korea, we face a situation where it is becoming increasingly difficult to send large numbers of young people abroad as long-term missionaries, despite the continued global need for more harvesters. This phenomenon is attributable mainly to a steady decline in the growth of the youth population in Korea over the years, with the birth-rate reaching a record low of 1.1 % last year, as well as to the general tendency of the younger generation to pursue more secular lives as Korea becomes an increasingly affluent society in terms of material wealth.

On the other hand, South Korea is known to be one of the fastest ageing societies in the world. It is expected to become a 'super-aged' society in ten years, with the number of people over 65 forecasted to reach 20.8 % of the estimated 48 million population. Koreans' average life-span will soon reach 80 years, whereas the average retirement age continues to fall to the mid-50s, which are also elements accelerating the proportionate increase of the aged population. Furthermore, the time has arrived when Korea's baby-boomer generation (i.e., those born between 1955 and 1963), which is estimated to number about 8 million, will begin to retire in the next ten years.

Needless to say, all of these trends are also manifesting themselves in the over fifty thousand churches in Korea as well as in the nearly ten thousand Korean diaspora churches abroad. If those Korean churches at home and abroad can make a serious attempt to seek and mobilize some of their retired members – those who are experienced in their respective professional fields, more mature in their faith and mission-minded – for mission related activities in a variety of ways suitable to their capabilities and circumstances, we will soon find that quite a number of hidden but able harvesters the Lord has already prepared are readily at hand with great potential to be used fruitfully in his plentiful harvest field at this crucial juncture.

Is There a Real Need for a Senior Workforce in the Mission Field?

The idea of mobilizing senior Christians for missionary work was floated by this author at the Korean Diaspora Forum held in Beijing in 2006, in a proposal dubbed the 'Caleb Initiative'. As a follow-up to this proposal, the Korea Research Institute of Mission (KRIM) conducted a survey of Korean mission agencies in December 2006, with a view to identifying the actual need for a senior mission workforce.

Twenty-six major Korean mission agencies responded to the survey. The findings of the survey are as follows:

1) The aggregate number of senior workers needed in mission fields is 648.

2) The number of senior workers needed according to the field of work is 515 serving in the mission field (abroad), with 133 serving at headquarters (home).

3) The number of senior workers needed according to the work pattern is 487 in full-time and 161 part-time services.

4) The number of senior workers needed according to the work term is 218 for short-term (less than one year), 127 for mid-term (one to two years), and 303 for long term (more than two years) service.

5) The number of vocational categories that can be assigned to senior mission workers is 19.

Initial Moves to Mobilize Senior Christians in Korea and among the Korean Diaspora for Mission

At the initiative of several mission agencies in Korea, encouraged by the results of the 2006 KRIM survey, the First National Conference for the Mobilization of Senior Christians was held in July 2007 at Halleluiah Church in Bundang, Korea, with the participation of about one thousand senior and other Christians and 40 mission agencies. The participants at the conference resolved to hold a similar national conference every two years and to establish a Secretariat.

The Second National Conference was held in May 2009 at Nam-Seoul Church and Shin-Banpo Church, co-sponsors of the event, with the participation of about one thousand senior and other Christians and 36 mission agencies. The participants decided to establish a national training course for senior Christians who volunteer as missionary candidates.

The national training courses were thus held in 2007 and 2009, with 29 participating senior candidates. Other regional missionary training courses for seniors were also initiated by several churches in Seoul, including, among others, Halleluiah Church and Nam-Seoul Grace Church, as well as those in provincial cities like Daeduck and Kwangju. There is also an increasing demand from small and medium-sized churches in Seoul and provincial cities for help in conducting missionary training courses for the growing number of senior missionary aspirants in their respective churches.

Some of the Korean diaspora churches in North America are particularly very active in taking initiatives to recruit and train retired senior church members for missionary services. For example, in Chicago and the New York area, there are two senior training schools which have been mobilizing, training and sending out senior church members into various mission fields. Also in Toronto, Canada, there is a church which has already mobilized more than a dozen senior member couples, trained them and dispatched them into the field, mainly in poor urban areas in Northeast Asia.

It is estimated that there are more than 3 million Korean diaspora Christians worshipping in approximately 10,000 churches in almost all countries of the five continents of the world. We hope and pray that they will continue to be equipped to mobilize the increasing number of their senior members for missionary service. For this purpose, we plan to further strengthen the communication and coordination networks in this area between and among such Korean and Korean diaspora churches and mission agencies and other Christian organizations based in other parts of the world.

Future Course of Action

Having identified the actual substantial demand among Korean mission agencies for a senior workforce in various mission fields, and also the huge potential supply of senior mission workers from Korean and Korean diaspora churches, we believe there is an urgent need to take concrete measures to efficiently bridge such demand and supply, as part of God's grand design to mobilize the already prepared but unreleased harvesters to fill the plentiful harvest field. Such measures include the following:

'Matchmaking' platform will soon be established with two pools: one consisting of 'supply' (i.e. available senior Christian human resources) and the other of 'demand' (i.e. available positions for senior mission workers). The platform will function as a place, either online or offline, where senior missionary aspirants can be matched with mission field job offers, based on various criteria. For that purpose, the work has started to build a website with two databases, one covering 'demand' and another 'supply'. It is hoped that the platform will be in operation by the time of the Third National Conference for the Mobilization of Senior Christians for Mission, scheduled for sometime in the middle of 2011.

To update and substantiate the information on the mission agencies' need for senior mission workers, additional research, including an updated survey of mission agencies, will take place in order to identify and collect job descriptions of mission field assignments that are deemed necessary and appropriate for senior workers. KRIM has agreed to conduct such an additional survey and research by the end of this year.

The Secretariat for senior mobilization envisages establishing an independent unit which will be in charge of establishing and operating the 'match-making' platform described above. A mechanism will also be created therein to strengthen and facilitate communication and coordination between mission agencies involved and churches sponsoring senior mission workers.

A campaign will be launched, through various means of mass communication and individual contacts directed towards churches, para-churches and other Christian organizations and groups, with a view to heightening awareness of the importance of senior mobilization for mission work and to helping them initiate efforts to mobilize their senior members for mission-related services.

A Call for Global Action

The harvest is plentiful and more workers are urgently needed. Since the second half of the 20th century, the Lord has in fact been preparing a large number of potential senior harvesters who are capable and available. However, such potential senior harvesters have largely been neglected and have not been identified as such, and thus remain uninvited to join younger harvesters currently in his harvest field.

Such potential senior harvesters include experienced former professionals and skilled workers who are spiritually mature as well as mission-minded. These individuals possess not only qualities that complement those of younger mission workers, but also easier accessibility as professionals and workers than regular missionaries to restricted access countries in and around the 1040 window, and thus have the potential to play an indispensable role in such difficult mission fields.

The phenomenon of an increasingly aged population is not unique to Korea; it characterizes most of today's advanced industrial societies. As much as the phenomenon is global, the unique opportunities it presents are also global. We strongly hope, therefore, that the efforts recently initiated in Korea and among the Korean diaspora for the mobilization of senior Christians for mission work will be widely shared by other Christian communities around the world, to the glory of God.

Business, Diaspora and the Future of Mission: Reflections on Shanghai Korean Business Forum

Sam Cho

Shanghai Korean Business Forum (SKBF) was founded in April 2007 with the goal of integrating business and mission. My first purpose is to provide organized information on business as mission (BAM) from what has been shared over the last four years of the forum. SKBF is now considered as one of the focal points where Koreans who are interested in BAM confer. The past experience of the forum may help future BAMers and mission leaders avoid the repetition of negative past experiences and gain valuable insights.

One of the contexts of the forum is the diaspora Korean church in Shanghai, China. Many characteristics of this forum, on reflection, are deeply rooted in this diaspora background. The diaspora experience of Korean Christians may bring some insights into how current diasporization worldwide can be viewed from a kingdom perspective.

The universal experience of business and the diaspora of peoples worldwide are two children of globalization. The employment of the free market in economic systems worldwide has taken place over the last thirty years along with the rapid development and increase in the utilization of information technology. Almost all work has taken the form of a business and this new culture helps to accelerate the diaspora of peoples by providing a common ground for human relations across cultures and nations. When these two global phenomena are put together as a rise of common culture of humankind, they can bring some insights into the future direction of mission.

This paper is not a summary of all the events that have taken place during the last four years of the forum but rather it is an attempt to effectively explain the points mentioned above. With this in mind, I have tried to recount the past experience as objectively as possible to serve as a record for the forum. Attending the forum, starting from 2008 (the second one) and being in charge of planning the forum for 2009 and 2010 has helped me understand the general flow of the forums over the past few years in a more objective way.

The paper, therefore, discusses: 1) Background: the Shanghai Korean Community Church; 2) Business in the kingdom of God: a reflective summary; and 3) Business, diaspora, and the future of mission. An appendix is also included for summary statements of the three previous forums.

Background: The Shanghai Korean Community Church

BAM is now becoming a buzz word in mission circles. However, even until mid- 2000, thinking of business and mission together sounded very strange to many Korean churches. It was very rare for a local church, not a mission organization, to start this type of conference at the time. As background information, I must explain the four codes of the Shanghai Korean Community Church (SKCC).

The first code is diaspora Koreans[1] in China. It was in the year 1992 that China and South Korea resumed their formal relations, almost ninety years after Japan took away the rights of foreign relations of Chosun, the last Korean dynasty, signalling the beginning of the Japanese colonization era. Many South Koreans started to migrate to China from 1992. According to 2010 data, the number of South Koreans in China is more than a million, when short-term visitors are included in the statistics. There is another group of Koreans who had a much earlier presence in China- the Korean Chinese. They started their migration to China a hundred years ago, during the late period of the Chosun Dynasty and the beginning of the Japanese colonization of Chosun. They are Koreans with Chinese nationality and their number is close to 2.5 million.

The presence of the latter group helped the new migration of the former group to China, as they often worked together in business. With the fast immigration of South Koreans and their relatively smooth settling in, with the help of the Korean Chinese, the number of churches hosting South Koreans rapidly increased. The SKCC is one of the biggest Korean churches of this kind.

The second code is business. Shanghai is the number one business centre of China and one of the focal business hubs in the global economy and trade. Most South Korean migrants moved to China for business purpose. The SKCC's congregation mostly consists of businessmen/women and their family members. In guiding the SKCC members into faithful disciples, understanding business from a kingdom perspective is important because of this background, and the BAM conference is a result.

The third code is the Chinese Church: the fastest growing Christian community in the world. China has two aspects in terms of mission. She is both a missionary-receiving and a missionary–sending country. Though its Christian population is huge (often estimated somewhere close to 100 million), its growth comes mainly from the Han-majority Chinese. The Western area of China, where many minorities reside, still needs more outreach. When it comes to the sending part of mission, the Chinese churches are at an early stage but with a

[1] Koreans here mean descendants of the Chosun Dynasty, which perished in 1910. Koreans residing in the South Korean peninsular are the biggest group, numbering 45 million. Koreans residing in north peninsular number 25 million. Koreans residing outside of the peninsular, number more than 7 million. The biggest presence is in China, North America, the CIS countries and Japan, in that order.

huge potential. Though Chinese churches have many different colours and are not free from inter-sectional tensions, they generally share the zeal of the Back to Jerusalem vision. [2] However, their support and systems for the implementation for the vision need improvement. The Korean churches have a mission of partnering with Chinese churches to utilize the potential for the kingdom of God.

The fourth code is the leadership of the church geared toward building a missionary church. Rev. Ki-young Um is the senior pastor of the SKCC. He had served as a missionary in Japan for ten years before he started his first ministry as a pastor for Koreans. In addition to his missionary experience, Rev. Um is known for his deep understanding of the kingdom of God and his zeal for sharing it through a series of lectures within the Korean churches. His missionary background has influenced the SKCC to initiate and host various para-church movements beyond a local church ministry and move toward a missional and ecumenical church with kingdom perspective. SKBF has grown with the support of this church.

Business in the Kingdom of God: A Reflective Summary

The first SBKF started in May, 2007, in Shanghai, and held its fourth forum in June of this year. The forum has grown quickly, both externally and internally, during this time. Externally, it has become a forum representing the Korean churches in general on the BAM issue from its start as a local church event. All of the seventy attendants at the first forum were from the SKCC, except the presenters. However, by the fourth forum, the number of registered participants reached more than two hundred and they came literally from all over the world.

At the early stage of the forum, most participants were business men and women. By the fourth forum, many missionaries and related workers started to attend as participants. The two distinctive groups, business and missionary, began to acknowledge each other's talents in the kingdom of God, sharing information and resources and producing early cases of cooperation for BAM. Noticing these changes, the SKBF leadership formed a task-force team, during the fourth forum, in order to make the SKBF a hub, where these two groups meet and to prepare an organization that extends the SKBF from a local forum to an international one for Korean Christians overseas.

The forum has also grown internally, as many BAM cases have been shared, and ideas and perspectives on BAM have evolved over the years, especially the 'business in the kingdom of God'.

If I had to single out one perspective from all the past forums, that would be the holistic perspective of mission. From the start of the forum, discussions

[2] The meaning of BTJ can differ depending on whom you ask. In this paper, it simply means carrying on the great commission to Western side China and further, into mostly Muslim areas.

around BAM have been geared toward holistic mission. Starting with Dr. Kim Young-Gurl's lecture on holistic mission, from the first forum in 2007, to Mats Tunehag defining BAM for the second forum, to Dr. Tetsnao Yamamori's lecture on kingdom and business for the fourth forum, the holistic perspective has been consistent.

Holistic mission means the effort of showing all the richness of the gospel and, as a result, displaying the full power of the kingdom of God at present by comprehending and reflecting on aspects of the kingdom of God in mission works. In short, this means mission in the kingdom of God. In Picture 1,[3] three dimensions of the kingdom of God are presented and these are reflected in six different ways of mission, when the wholeness of the gospel is effective in reality without losing its richness and balance.

Picture 1. Three Dimensions of Holistic Mission

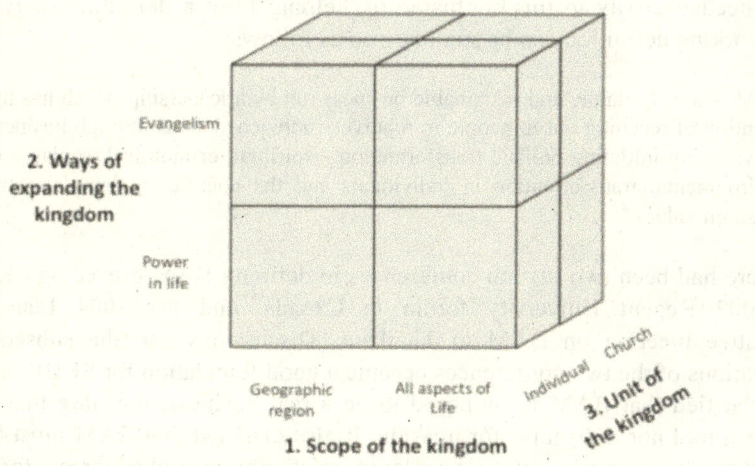

Three questions can be asked when mission works, including BAM, refer to the wholeness of the kingdom. First, what is the scope of the kingdom? i.e., what does his kingship govern? That is going to be mission filed. Second, how does his kingdom expand? That is how we participate in his mission. Third, what is the basic working unit of the kingdom? That is where our mission starts.

[3] S. Cho, 'Defining BAM' [in Korean], *Various Forms to Various Peoples; Korean Interserve Quarterly*, March, 2010.

Scope of the Kingdom

BAM stands at the cross-section of the two different worlds of business and mission. Business, as a part of human life, needs to be redeemed in the kingdom of God, and mission is the human participation in the geographical expansion of the kingdom: both are under the kingdom's governing scope. However, these two rarely went hand in hand in church history, indeed they have been juxtaposed at opposite ends of the kingdom, often with business on the downside.

Confusion was inevitable in defining BAM as an integration of the unlikely and untried match of the two. The confusion came mainly from the different ways of defining BAM. The first SKBF of 2007 was typical of this when some speakers talked about business as a platform or tool for evangelism while others discussed a case of managing a company, based on Christian values, not necessarily having the intention of extending it to restricted-access nations. Mats Tunehag's participation as the main speaker for the second forum brought much-needed clarity to this confusion by helping form a definition of BAM. This working definition can be summarized as follows:

> BAM is a real, viable, and sustainable business run by a leadership which has the intention of reaching out to people in relatively unreached areas through business activities by initiating holistic transformation - spiritual, economical, social, and environmental transformation in individuals and the community based on the kingdom values.[4]

There had been two pivotal conferences in defining BAM preceding SKBF: the 2002 Regent University forum in Canada[5] and the 2004 Lausanne committee meeting on BAM in Thailand.[6] Discussions and the subsequent publications of the two conferences became a good foundation for SKBF in that they clarified that BAM is supposed to be a real business, meaning that it is neither a tool nor a disguise for mission. It also clarified that BAM must have the intention to reach out to people in relatively-unreached areas for the Christian transformation of individuals and communities.

The first dimension of Picture 1 shows that business, as a part of human life, and mission, as an effort of expanding the kingdom geographically, have something in common; both are under the scope of the kingdom. The culture command of Gen. 1 and the great commission of Matt. 28 should be integrated

---

[4] M. Tunehag, 'God Means Mission: An Introduction to Business as Mission (BAM)' (unpublished manuscript, 2008).

[5] A summary of the Regent University meeting, later published T. Yamamori & K. Eldred (eds), *On Kingdom Business: Transforming Missions through Entrepreneurial Strategies* (Wheaton, IL: Crossways, 2003).

[6] M. Tunehag, W. McGee & J. Plummer, 'Business as Mission' (Occasional paper No. 59) (Pattaya, Thailand: Lausanne Committee for World Evangelism, 2004). This paper is available at http://www.lausanne.org/documents/2004forum/LOP59_IG30.pdf

in mission works in order to reflect the full richness of the kingdom. In fact, even in the great commission, when the 'make disciples of all nations' part of chapter 28 is properly noted, we can see that the culture command: 'making disciples' is already an integrated part of the great commission.

Over the four years of SKBF, it has become evident that people in the business world and people in the mission field have a different focus in this regard. The former are more interested in how to live kingdom values in the business world, whereas the latter are more interested in how to share the gospel with unreached people they may meet through business. However, the objectives of these two different groups should be integrated simultaneously, both in works and ministries, so that the holistic power of the kingdom is revealed in full measure. Business men/ women should be mindful of sharing the gospel with people in an unreached area by intentionally extending their business activities abroad whereas missionaries need to learn to run Christian-value-based and sustainable businesses.

Despite the stability the above definition of BAM brought to the forum, there have been lingering tensions and uneasiness about the definition too. When one reads the summary statements of SKBF of the past in the appendix of this paper, one can see different terms, similar to BAM, such as kingdom business or marketplace ministry, being used along with BAM. The definition set the boundary of BAM only for business owners or entrepreneurs, who are mostly not Christians.[7] It also has the implication that BAM is applied only to people working in restricted-access areas, especially those who are primarily missionaries. However, many Christians, whose residence is not in the area, meet unreached people and build relations with them as part of their daily business activities.

A good example is a group of Korean Christian businessmen/women in China, who meet the non-Christian Chinese and other nationals through business on a daily basis. BAM is not meant to be, nor should be, strictly for business owners or missionaries working in the Muslim areas. Lines between missionaries and non-missionaries and mission field and non-mission field have been blurred over the last thirty years of globalization. If BAM can be taken as a perspective to view life, then BAM becomes a part of everyday life for any Christian who has an involvement in any form of business activities.

A need for a more relevant definition of BAM, for the majority of Christians, emerged after the fourth forum in 2010. The limitations of the current definition come from its way of defining business. Business is an entity in this definition. When business as an entity is considered as a base of BAM, the focus of BAM lies in the ownership and leadership of business. Whether the ownership and

---

[7] Recent publications on BAM have also focus on BAM companies rather than BAM activities: Neal Johnson, *Business as Mission: A Comprehensive Guide to Theory and Practice* (Downers Grove, IL: IVP, 2010); M. Russell, *The Missional Entrepreneurs: Principles and Practices for BAM* (Birmingham, AL: New Hope Publishers, 2009).

leadership belongs to Christians, and the level of commitment they have to kingdom values, then become the agenda. However, the majority of people who experience business are neither business owners nor entrepreneurs, and their experiences are mostly about transactions, and relations in the form of a business. Business as an activity not as an entity needs to be considered as the basis in defining BAM in order to embrace people generally.[8] In this case, BAM is a perspective to view our daily activities in business from the standpoint of the kingdom.

This does not downplay the importance of BAM companies working in restricted-access areas. On the contrary, supports that are much needed for these companies can be facilitated by having a majority of Christians involved. Then again, BAM as a perspective provides the meaning of kingdom for the majority of Christians. BAM companies can be considered a specific and important area of BAM.[9] The current BAM movement, which started as a missionary movement, has reinstated the meaning of the kingdom of God in our daily lives, which cannot be contained just within some missionary circles. BAM as a perspective can break down the dichotomies between the holy and the secular and between mission and non-mission in Christian life.

Business is defined as work from this perspective. Work means the service of using physical and mental labor to satisfy the needs of creatures, including human beings, according to Genesis.[10] Work becomes business, first when the service of work has the form of an exchange or a promise of exchange to satisfy mutual needs of the parties involved, and second when it uses the means of market and money. Markets are a collection of promises and exchanges of mutual services and are one of the most common forms of human relations across cultures.[11] Money is the apparatus that makes social and legal bonds for these promises and exchanges.

Coming back to the first dimension of Picture 1, BAM is a holistic perspective, by which we view every business activity as a way of living, declaring God's love and justice and an opportunity to share the gospel with other people. This lifestyle and sharing of the kingdom of God takes place daily everywhere including business activities.

---

[8] M. Seo, 'Business Activities in the Kingdom of God' [in Korean] (unpublished manuscript, 2009). This paper reveals limitations of defining business as an entity and suggests a standpoint of viewing business as activities in order to enhance comprehensiveness and wholesomeness of kingdom in business world.

[9] S. Rundle and T. Steffen properly separate the concept of BAM from BAM companies by calling the latter the great commission companies. S. Rundle and T. Steffen, *Great Commission Companies* (Downers Grove, IL: IVP, 2003). M. Russell also properly does so by calling the latter missional entrepreneurs. Russell, *The Missional Entrepreneurs.*

[10] Y. Kim, *Ways to BAM: Collection of 1st and 2nd SKBF Lectures* [in Korean] (Shanghai: SKBF, 2009).

[11] A.P. Fiske, 'The Four Elementary Forms of Sociality: Framework for a Unified Theory of Social Relations', *Psychological Review* 99 (1992), 689-723.

Ways of Expanding the Kingdom

How does the kingdom expand? Jesus and apostles in the New Testament used both evangelism and the power of Holy Spirit in witnessing the immanence of the kingdom on earth. The second dimension of Picture 1 suggests that both ways need to be integrated in order to be holistic for our participation in the expansion of the kingdom. As SKBF progressed, I noticed that the missionary group and the business group often have different interests in this regard. The former is more oriented in evangelism through business whereas the latter is more interested in the power in business, often confused with business success.

We need both! The imperative of evangelism can never be underestimated. Salvation comes from the gospel. How holy we look, or how much trust we attain from others, or how deep are our relations with others, by themselves, cannot bring salvation to anyone; only the word of God has the power of salvation. However, evangelism cannot have that power until people have an opportunity to listen to the gospel. The power of the Holy Spirit displayed in the midst of human life brings people to the point of humbling themselves to receive the word and to listen to the truth. We need a bridge to close the gap between Christians and non- Christians for evangelism by exhibiting the power of God. Evangelism and power cannot be separated!

The theme of the third forum of 2009 was the 'Anointing of theHoly Spirit in Business'. The motivation for setting such a theme was benign and understandable in that most participants in the forum were fully aware that challenges coming from conducting business in a holistic way in this made them look idealistic, if not naive, even to themselves. We need the power of God to overcome the challenges, and to show real evidence that it is working. After all, we are in a fierce spiritual warfare!

How does the power of God affect Christian life or business then? Compared to the understanding of evangelism, it was found in the forums that there was a limitation and even confusion in understanding the power. Many different ideas on power were suggested (or discussed), their tacit assumptions were revealed, and some of them were found to be conflicting. Especially, the tendency of attributing, if not identifying with, visible business performance to the works of the Holy Spirit such as the lucrativeness or expansion of business was noted. This tendency is not much different from secularism that proves what is right only based on visible results. There was also a hint of worshipping power itself, where the use of control and manipulation are encouraged in proselytizing others, often justified by religious zeal.[12]

---

[12] In Rev. 13:11-18, an Anti-Christ figure appeared himself in the form of a lamb and spoke like a dragon. I personally interpret this as the advent of economic secularism under a disguise of religion. Integrating business and religion is not just our idea after all! This figure also exercises various kinds of miracles by using his power to prove himself and many will follow him to receive a Satanic seal. The Biblical understanding

We need to understand and clarify what the power of God and the anointing of the Holy Spirit actually mean in the business world. I personally think that the power of God working in us and others is the power of love, sacrifice, as epitomized in the death of Christ on the cross and his victory through the resurrection. More cases need to appear on how the Holy Spirit enables us to love the un-lovable in business relations, to sacrifice ourselves as atonement, and to come to see transformations taking place in individuals and communities through God's business.

Open presentations and the following discussions on the power of God in business in the third forum bore some positive fruits. Acknowledging our weakness in this spiritual warfare and the confrontation with evil forces led to recognizing the importance of intercessory prayer. In the fourth forum of 2010, an agreement on the importance of intercessory prayer became a part of the forum summary statement. I have always considered an ardent and persistent prayer as an important heritage of the Korean church, and was glad to see that intercessory prayer was recognized in SKBF. However, remember that the kingdom of God should be at the centre of our prayers, not (or rather than) the power itself or our longing for our personal advancement. We should not forget that the precious heritage of prayer works in Korean churches was often marred by the pursuit of parochial prosperity over the kingdom.

Unit of the Kingdom

What is the basic unit of the kingdom? Where does the kingdom start? Who carries on the task of expanding the kingdom with God? The answer is humankind, both as individuals and as a community. We have the mission of expanding God's kingdom and it is only when we realize this that God's governance truly takes place. The third dimension of Picture 1 shows that both individuals and churches, as God's community, need to be holistic. Just as God is in the Trinity, we, as the image of God, are both individuals and a community.

The theme for the second SKBF of 2008 was 'the church and BAM'. At this forum, the difficulties of running BAM companies in restricted-access areas were shared through various case presentations. This realistic picture helped us realize how BAM entrepreneurs call for help and that BAM requires more than a person or a couple. Picture 2[13] illustrates various resources for a BAM company to take off as a business. There are two groups of resources. The first group is about business-related ones whereas the second is about mission-related ones.

---

of power is much in need now, especially for Christians working in the business world, in order to avoid being misled by a false gospel.

[13] S. Cho, 'BAM from Church Perspective' [in Korean], *Various Forms to Various Peoples*, June, 2010.

Picture 2. Resources for a BAM Operation

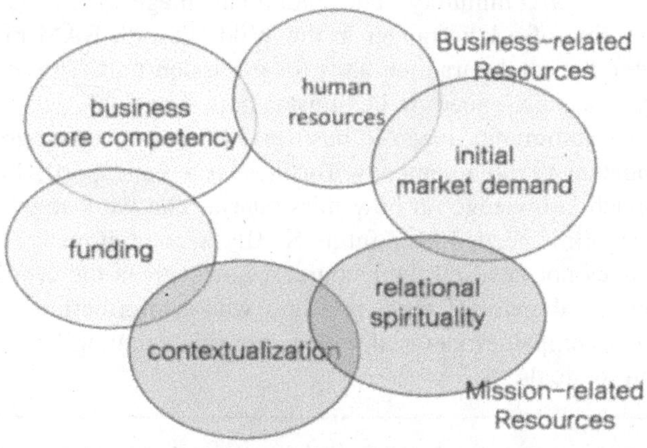

There are four resources in the first group. Funding or initial seed money is always necessary from the start of a business. Competence in business against future competitors needs to be developed for long-term sustainability. You also need a group of committed people with business experience and expertise in a chosen business area. Demand and income from sales are critical for a cash-flow turnover of a business, especially at the early stages. Even for a secular business, all these four resources are eventually needed as a business takes off and maintains its sustainability in the long run.

Extra resources in the second group are needed for a BAM company, in order to carry out mission. At a minimum level, contextualization-related knowledge and relations require the understanding of local cultures and social networks with local stakeholders. Business does not exist as a social island, but is deeply embedded in a society with human relations, expectations of various stakeholders, and cultures.[14] This is more the case in less-developed countries. The development of this resource usually starts with the learning of a local language, and always requires many years in acculturation.

Another resource is spirituality in relations, which manifests at the level of the healthiness and maturity in personal relations with God and neighbours. Getting to know God's personality, recognizing and listening to God's voice, and following the voice require effort and years of experience. Relating to other people with love and wisdom, building long-term relationships, sharing the gospel, and working with others in a church also requires years of discipleship. It is a very critical asset for mission and cannot be attained overnight.

---

[14] M. Granovetter, 'Economic Action and Social Structure: The Problem of Embeddedness', *American Journal of Sociology* 91:3 (1985), 481-510.

Now, a question: who has all these resources? Answer: realistically, a very few people. That means running a BAM company requires more than an individual or a couple. We must remind ourselves that another part of the kingdom unit is a community. The traditional image of a missionary can be compared to that of a lone ranger in the Wild West. A BAM ministry cannot survive without a total paradigm shift for a mission unit. The importance of a community or a church needs to be reinstated.

What does community mean in business? First, it means a group of talents working together to run a company. Business is a team sport! However, we do not have much knowledge on how missionaries can work together on a daily basis; homework is needed for a future SKBF. Second, it means a network. An individual does not have all the resources; however, in the cosmic church, all these resources abound! If there is a hub where information on resources is shared, BAM companies can easily carry out this daunting task of business as mission and set goals.

Picture 3. Christian Resource Networking hub

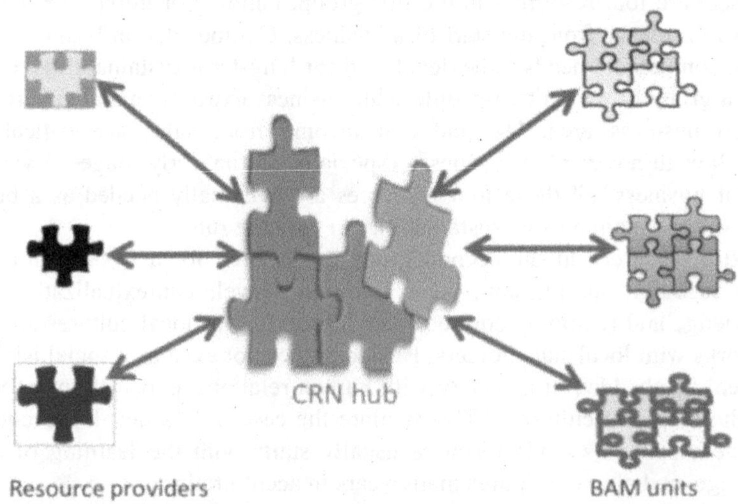

In Picture 3,[15] a network hub is illustrated. The hub's main function is to effectively distribute the information on resources. Without the hub, the information cost would be substantial for two reasons. First, languages and ways of communication in the business world and the mission world are very different; streamlining information on a commonly-agreed format is costly, especially at an individual company level. The second reason is trust. Trust is hard to build and easy to break, more so when the parties involved in communication are culturally different and geographically distant. The hub's

[15] Cho, 'BAM from Church Perspective'.

role is gathering information efficiently and providing trustworthy information so that the cost of networking becomes reasonable.

This idea of a hub was suggested in the title of Christian Resource Networking (CRN) at the second SKBF. A CRN hub connects the resource-providing group with BAM companies efficiently, by providing trustworthy information to the two groups.[16] After being proposed in the second forum, the idea of a CRN hub started as an experiment, and the three cases of CRN hubs were presented at the fourth SKBF of 2010. When cases accumulate, we may develop more organized information about CRN, especially on how to build and manage it effectively. I personally think that the biggest finding from the SKBF is a re-evaluation of the importance of community in mission, which was reflected in the CRN idea. Both individuals and the church as God's community need to be integrated as a starting point of any mission work, so that the richness and power of the kingdom of God reaches its full potential.

Business, Diaspora, and the Future of Mission

The period of the last thirty years marked the beginning of a very different era in human history. A basic community, within which a human being relates to others, has broadened beyond the traditional bonds of family, races, religions, and nations. Two driving forces for this expansion are the fast development of information technology and universal application of market economy i.e. globalization. When it is narrowly defined, globalization is often considered as a synonym of a laissez-faire economy with minimal government involvement.

However, when defined in a broad sense, globalization means a fast and global dissemination of individualism and pluralism as a belief system. The idea of accepting others as individuals and embracing differences in beliefs and religions has been rapidly passed over during the last thirty years. It is a social and cultural phenomenon. Of course, individualism and pluralism themselves are nothing new—they are traceable back to the Greco-Roman period. However, this level of sharing in terms of speed and coverage is something extraordinary compared to any time of history including that of the Roman Empire. Journalists and social scientists call this the rise of a new culture of globalization in the early 1990s. Different prospects of globalization have been presented: some rosy and others not so rosy.[17]

---

[16] The idea of networking and CRN is not new. In their book, Rundle and Steffen suggested two types of BAM companies: pioneering great commission companies, which is the equivalent of BAM companies of Picture 3, and facilitative great commission companies, which is the equivalent of resource providers. Rundle & Steffen, *Great Commission Companies*.

[17] Two exemplary books are selected for contrasting different prospects. At the rosy end, Fukuyama, in his 1992 book, envisaged the dominance of individualism as the final dominant belief system and democracy as the final dominant political system in human

What does globalization actually mean in daily life then? In this paper, two phenomena are noted. First is the prevalence of business in human relations. Traditionally, an individual human being relates him/herself with others in two ways: through family and through works. Whereas sexual and social needs are the initial motivations of human relations leading to a family, mutual gains coming from cooperation are the motivation for human relations through works. As work is increasingly taking the form of business, as market economy globally expands and the role of the extended family becomes less and less important with global urbanization, human relations through business became dominant. Thanks to this experience of business, it is now much easier for us to relate to people of different religion and cultures.

Another phenomenon is the migration of people throughout the world and in the diaspora. People are dispersed for many reasons and in different forms. Some flee from natural disasters and regional disputes whereas some voluntarily move for economic gains or for better educational opportunities. Some migrate over generations whereas some migrate just for connecting flights. The world is full of a migrating diaspora one way or the other, and meeting with different people is part of daily life for the majority of people in the world.

If we believe that God is responsible for human history, we may need to explore and examine implications for mission in the light of these two phenomena. SKBF stands at the cross-section of the two, and, this reflection on the past four years may have some implications on the future of mission. Three implications are suggested: first, we are entering the age of integration where the lines between life and mission, between missionaries and non-missionary Christians and between mission fields and non-mission fields are all blurred. When we reflect on the holistic nature of the kingdom presented in Picture 1, this is a natural regression to what was supposed to be. Both life and the geographical area are under his kingship, and thus we as Christians must live a

history based on the Hegelian idea of human instincts and motivations of self-expression. F. Fukuyama, *The End of History and the Last Man* (New York: Avon Books, 1992). At the other end of the scale, S. Huntington's initial paper in *Foreign Policy* and later his published book criticised the prevalent optimism of the late 1990s about globalization. Whereas he agreed that the relative power of individuals and business companies has drastically increased compared to traditional institutions, he did not think that this power given to individuals would necessarily lead to the rise of a universal and monolithic culture of individualism. On the contrary, he proposed that individuals would form collective groups called civilizations, beyond tribes and nations, probably based on religious beliefs and ideologies in the face of rising individualism and the consequent sense of losing communal identity, and confront other civilizations based on this new collective identity. S Huntington, *The Clash of Civilizations and the Remaking of World Order* (New York: Georges Borchardt, 1996). Now, 15 years or so after the above prospects, we see both prospects are realized, even if not completely, and ironically, that they co-exist.

missionary life no matter where we live and whatever we do for living! What is real to God has not been so real until now due to the limitations in our paradigm of reasoning, which is usually bound by our limited conditions in space and time. Just as the rapid development of the last thirty years in transportation and information technology has helped us overcome our bounded conditions in space and time, so our way of thinking becomes able to overcome the past dichotomies.

What does all this practically mean for mission? Missionary life should be a requirement for all Christians now. Without distinctions between missionary Christians and non-missionary Christians, there is only one distinction, that between missionaries and non-Christians. What was supposed to be, but once thought to be impossible, now looks real, more than ever.

Second, the warfare that we are facing ahead is now neither simple nor easy. The distinction between life and mission in the past made our Christian simpler and easier; so did those between missionaries and non missionaries and between mission fields and non-mission fields. Removing these simple dichotomies actually means more burdens and responsibilities on the shoulders of every Christian. From a macrocosmic standpoint of view, this means warfare where every confessing Christian engages in the spiritual battles against Satan in their endeavor to live a life by the kingdom standards, and at the same time, extending it to unreached peoples and places. Satan is not kept at bay in the meantime, but, knowing this change, rather employs all possible ways to make Christians incapacitated. We need the power of the Holy Spirit for the war; it is time to receive his holy anointment. Kneeling down before the throne for empowerment and interceding for others is not something extra any longer. Evangelism goes hand in hand with power in life. That is how Jesus performed his ministry for his first coming, and that will be how he is going to empower his followers to prepare for his second coming.

Third, this warfare calls for the rise of the church. As BAM was reviewed over the last four years' experience of SKBF, it became obvious that the past model of individual gladiators in the arena cannot sustain the forthcoming battles. The church is the fullness of Christ that fills everything in every way according to Ephesians. Though the past co-operation among missionaries, mission agencies, and local churches are commendable, we have not yet seen this fullness of Christ from the church. As a participant in a diaspora Christian movement in a mission field like China, I have witnessed that our parochial and minor differences in culture, nation, and denomination fade away when people realize the enormity of challenges before us. The church as the basic unit of the kingdom movement should be restored.

Concluding this reflection on SKBF, I would like to share what took place on the last night of 2010 SKBF. When selected participants were given an opportunity to share their sentiments on the forum, some confessed that they could witness after the forum that it is God himself that is now moving all the resources and people around the world at an increasing speed in order to complete the work of the kingdom. The confession instantly produced a resonance of agreement from the rest of the participants. I also agree that it is God himself behind all these rapid changes taking place now. We are coming close to the consummation of history, which signifies the coming of Jesus Christ.

Missio Dei! Yes, indeed, the Lion of Judah himself is the one who is performing mission now. We just happened to surf on this flow by his grace. I pray that others reading this paper see this and come to participate in this mission by discerning his voice and obeying it.

'He who has an ear, let him hear what the Spirit says to the churches' (Rev. 3)

Appendix: Summary Statements of the Previous Forums[18]

Second SKBF Summary Statement, May 28, 2008

We, 100 attendants of 2008 SKBF, from last four days of the forum, have found that God has granted business to us as part of his plan of completing his kingdom on earth and called us to participate in this vision through business and its related works. We came from various areas of the world including the Shanghai region, and our professions vary from business to missionaries to scholars. We together made the following statements as a summary of the forum:

1. We believe that businessmen/ women are called for the glory of God by bringing in changes in business area based on the kingdom values and holistic transformations in communities through business.
2. We acknowledge that the restoration of integrity based on kingdom values is much needed in the area of business over the world, and we believe that business as mission (BAM) should bring holistic transformations in communities such as social, environmental, economic, and spiritual transformations including new employment opportunities.
3. We believe that the gospel has the power of transforming business and communities, and that God is able to provide us with the power that enables humble ones trusting in God like us to accomplish God's kingdom and showing God's love and righteousness in the area of business.
4. We believe that BAM can be brought to its full potential in achieving the above mentioned purposes by being networked with various

[18] There was not a summary of statements for the first SKBF.

resources in the cosmic church. Local churches should be part of this networked connection.

5. We acknowledge that there is need for building networking hubs for resource sharing and cooperation between various Christians for the realization of the potential of BAM, and we commit ourselves to these goals.

Third SKBF Summary Statement, June 4, 2009

We, 200 attendants of 2009 SKBF have found that God has granted business to us as a part of his plan of completing his kingdom on earth and called us to participate in this vision through business and its related works. We came from various areas of the world including the Shanghai region, and our professions vary from business to missionaries to mission mobilizes to scholars. We together made the following statements as a summary of the last four days of the forum:

1. We confirm that BAM, kingdom business (business operation by Christian leadership), and marketplace ministry (Christian-value-based activities in a market economy) are inherently same in that all three are to establish the kingdom of God in the realms of business and market economy.
2. We confess that transformed individuals by kingdom values in business and economic activities reflect the presence of the kingdom of God and the glory of God in the daily life of human beings.
3. We believe that our transformation in business and economic activities is possible only by the anointment of Holy Spirit that sets us apart from the world, transforms us and empowers us.
4. The power of the Holy Spirit, first, enables us to acknowledge the Lordship of God in every part of business activities, second, to witness the gospel to all people met through business and, third, to seek for every possible cooperative opportunity with other Christian brothers and sisters who confess the same beliefs and to work together in diverse forms.
5. We confirm that people in business and mission are just different parts of the same body of Christ, and that they need to acknowledge others' respective talents and to cooperate together in order to magnify the presence of the kingdom of God on earth.
6. We confirm the imperative of networking that enables communication and the flow of information and resources for BAM, and promises an active participation in building networking hubs and networking itself.

Fourth SKBF Summary Statement, June 11, 2010

We, the 260 attendants of 2010 SKBF, have found that God has granted business to us as part of his plan of completing his kingdom on earth and called us to participate in this vision through business and its related works. We came from various areas of the world including the Shanghai region, and our professions vary from business to missionaries to mission mobilizers to pastors and to scholars. Together we made the following statements as a summary of the last four days of 4th forum and the last four years of SKBF:

1. We believe that the current movements of kingdom business and BAM are based on concurrent obedience of biblical commands of the culturalization commission of Genesis chapter 1 and the great commission of Matthew 28, and both the movements are under the guidance of the Holy Spirit that leads to the consummation of the kingdom of God both in every area of human life and every geographical area of the earth.
2. We confess that spiritual warfare, involved with kingdom business and BAM, is not something we can win by ourselves for only by the anointment of the Holy Spirit are we capable of winning.
3. We believe the importance of intercessory prayer in kingdom business and BAM.
4. We believe in the anointment of the Holy Spirit upon kingdom business and BAM that comes from unity and cooperation of brothers and sisters in the cosmic church that is the body of Christ, and have agreed that the Holy Spirit has already initiated networking various resources and building hubs within the church and is preceding them for kingdom business and BAM.
5. We believe that God has brought diverse talents within the cosmic church, and we commit ourselves to respect others' talents and to seek for every possible opportunity for cooperation for the glory of God and for the full consummation of the kingdom of God.

Point5: Serving the Returned Korean Diaspora

Jae Ryun Chung

Point5 is a worship community within the Onnuri Community Church in Seoul, Korea, that began to meet as a prayer group in January 2010 to address the needs of the Koreans, who, after having experienced living in other nation(s), now find themselves living in Korea as a 'Returned Korean Diaspora' (RKD hereafter). Though a majority of them understandably expected familiarity and comfort in coming back to the motherland of Korea, as strange as it may sound, many of them faced culture-shock and various difficulties in adjusting to the dynamic and rapidly-changing nature of Korean society, and hence accepted the paradoxical fate of living as 'strangers' in their homeland. It was not hard for me to relate to RKD, since I am a 1.5 generation Korean-American who had emigrated to America at the age of eleven, and had come back to minister in Korea after a quarter-century of living abroad. So to identify the needs and to plant Point5 at Onnuri Church was perhaps the most natural response to my new found circumstances.

Being a Christian community, Point5 is most concerned with the outcry of the RKD, who find it especially difficult to adjust to church life in Korea. The most common testimony is that many of them 'met God in a small Korean immigrant church' in respective foreign lands where they used to live, but they are currently 'not even going to Sunday worship on a regular basis'. Of course, there is no shortage of churches in Korea to suit every taste and theological orientation. In fact, many claim to have church-hopped for several months and yet have not 'sampled' all the churches they wanted to visit. There are also many 'English ministries' in Seoul that draw hundreds of expatriates from around the world. However, many of the RKD are not from the English-speaking parts of the world—having lived in China, Japan, Germany, etc.—and, furthermore, they long to be part of a community that could meet their needs for associating with the Korean Christian culture and communicating at times in the Korean-language, which for 1.5 generation in particular, is their 'heart-language'. With the beginning of Point5 Sunday worship at Yangjae Campus of Onnuri Community Church on July 11, 2010, and the subsequent development of small groups, team ministries, seminars and outreach programmes, specifically designed for such multi-cultural people groups, some of these needs are being met. A church community committed to the needs of RKD had been born.

Meaning Behind the Name Point5

The name 'Point5' comes from the concept of '1.5 generation', the sociological term first used among American sociologists in the 1980s to describe an emerging generation of Korean Americans who would not fit into the clear-cut mold of the first and second generations. The name, however, while denoting the spirit of 'in-between-ness' and 'bridge-building', does not have direct correlation to the sociological definition of a people group as the association may suggest. As the lead pastor of Point5, I wanted to name the community to reflect the complexity of the make up of the RKD population I befriend and serve in Korea, and the uncertainty of being a RKD, even though the name represents the infinite possibilities and hopes that the RKD possess, implied by the infinity of numbers between any two whole numbers.

Even though it is still the beginning stage of Point5, I believe that the mere fact that a church community exists in Korea for people, who are united by their affinity with Korean Christian culture and their experience of having lived part of their lives in distant lands, opens up many a constructive dialogue. My hope is that this paper, which tells the story of Point5 and the RKD community that I am part of, will give birth to a new collective imagination and action for Korean Diaspora ministries.

Proposal for Further Exploration

In this paper, I seek to explicate the need for more RKD ministries in Korea. To do so, first, I present a brief historical analysis of the rise in number of RKD in order to both define the scope of RKD and to discuss the implication of this trend for the national and global missions of Korean Churches worldwide. One will see that the study of the RKD phenomenon requires an understanding of a rather large group of people—including, increasing numbers of Korean overseas travelers, missionaries, business women and men in multi-national companies, immigrants who are migrating back to Korea, students studying abroad, the Korean Diaspora finding work in Korea due to economic downturns where they were living, RKD serving their military duties, Korean-adoptees seeking connection with Korea, children of parents who live trans-nationally due to their work assignments, 'international school' graduates, *ghee-rhu-ghee* (wild goose) families, multi-racial families, participants of language courses abroad, etc. After a glimpse into the complexity of the world of the RKD, Point5 will be discussed in detail for the remainder of my study, as an example of a pioneering attempt at addressing the needs of the RKD.

Characteristics of the Point5 Community

Multi-lingual Worship

Mainly, Korean and English are used throughout the worship, interspersed by languages through which participating members feel most comfortable expressing their spirituality. For example, a member from Germany may end her corporate prayer by praying in German or a hymn cherished from her past immigrant life in Malaysia can be translated and sung in Korean or English.

Cross-generational Worship and Mentorship

Point5 Sunday worship welcomes people of all ages. Most worshippers are in their late teens to 30s. However, 30 percent of the attendees are in their 40-70s. There is a separate bi-lingual worship for Point5's children in two different age groups—pre-schoolers and kindergarten (Jesus Rock) and elementary children (Jesus Crew). Point5 sees great value in worshipping together as families. While there is much to gain in being separated into youth, young-adult and adult Sunday worship, cross-generational aspects of spirituality gets lost when not given a regular chance to see people from other generations in a worship setting, leading to missed opportunities for understanding each other's stories and needs. Age-specific needs are partially met by small groups following the worship, which is divided along age brackets. In a context of such intermingling, cross-generational mentoring is not only possible, but also natural.

A Base or a Hub for Networking and Ministering among Korean Diaspora

First, many Korean Diaspora populations regularly visit Korea to see their families and friends. The vibrance of the Korean economy and the increasing popularity of the Korean media through growing recognition of *Hallyu*, or the 'Korean Wave', are only encouraging more visitations. In such context, it is strategically sound for Korean churches in Korea to create a hub for the Korean Diaspora populations to interact together.

Second, students studying abroad come back to Korea during summer and winter vacations and want to have a 'home-church' to come back to. Even though some of them grew up in their parents' churches, these churches no longer feel like home after years of living abroad. When there is a welcoming community for such yearly visitors from abroad, it increases the chance of spiritual growth taking place during vacation time. Summer programmes for *Gyo-Po* and study abroad students are a great way to make friendships among the Korean diaspora.

Third, the diaspora experiences of RKD differ greatly, depending on the geography and timing of the experiences. Point5 is a perfect place to share those experiences. As the ministry's motto for the year 2011 is 'Care, Share, Prayer, Dare', it encourages members to *care* enough to *share* about those different experiences so that members could be blessed by the hand of God working around the globe among His people. Genuine sharing often leads to heart-felt *prayer*. When God's people pray sincerely, heaven opens up and we are empowered to *dare* to change the world for Christ.

Outreach Opportunities

Because members of RKD populations have experienced cross-cultural and multi-cultural contexts, many of them having been in the minority groups or the 'strangers' in new places, it has been easy to discover and cultivate in the Point5 community sympathy for the marginalized and 'estranged' in the Korean society. In seeking out and serving others in Korea, often utilizing the gifts they have of being able to overcome cultural barriers and being comfortable in multiple language settings, Point5 members are discovering anew how God is able to use all that He has give us, including our cross-cultural and cross-lingual experiences. There are many outreach opportunites that Point5 has been exploring.

The first is providing language classes in Korean orphanages.

The second is supporting domestic and international missions using existing international networks.

The third is conducting youth and young adults outreach. Visiting and networking with Korean diaspora youths and young adults in Europe has taught me personally how different the experience of the European Korean diaspora is from the experience of the Korean diaspora in the United States. This only points to the richness and the diversity of the Korean diaspora experience. Coming back to Korea, I finally saw that my own prejudice and blind spots as an American have gotten in the way of seeing God's greater vision for the Korean diaspora. Point5 seeks to hold conferences for the youth and young adults in the Korean diaspora of multiple continents, designed and lead by the participants themselves.

The fourth is assisting Korean adoptees ministry. Korean adoptees visit Korea to meet their birth mothers or to simply experience Korea on their own or with their loved ones. Point5 members host these families for three nights in their homes to give the first-time visitors a home to be welcomed and a church family to lean on, at their most vulnerable time.

Seminars and Bible Studies for RKD

In order to serve the particular needs of the RKD population, the following training tools (materials for seminars, workshops, training, and Bible studies) were deemed crucial to develop and utilize.

First, LALA School (Life After Living Abroad) is a 7-week programme of Bible study, lectures, testimonies, practical tips, small group sharing and training worshops that seeks to help RKD to adjust well to their new life in Korea. It brings people in their 20 and 30s to live abundant lives in Christ by reinterpreting their past through the word of God, living the present in faith and discovering God's calling in their life's future.

Second, LBLA School (Life Before Living Abroad) is being developed tohelp to prepare those who are getting ready to depart Korea to live/study/work in another country.

Third, workshops are being designed for the parents with children who are studying overseas. There is a tremendous emotional and spiritual toll on the families with children living abroad, even if the children are living in the relative safety of residing with an extended family member or in well-renowned educational institutions.

Trans-national Koreans 'for Such a Time as This'

The paper gives particular attention to the 'trans-national' Koreans, whose early life experience of multiple national cultures before their adulthood allowed them to identify with many cultures, while not having a great level of exclusive patriotic sentiments towards any one nation or group of people. These 'trans-national' Koreans are rapidly emerging in Korean society as many global Korean companies and organizations send their employees with their families across continents, at an unprecedented rate.

The Korean diaspora ministry is a kingdom work *among* and *through* the Korean diaspora. As such, it calls for all, who are involved in it, to engage in an honest dialogue to discover all that God desires *in* us and *from* us. It certainly is amazing how God has allowed the scattering of so many Koreans among so many nations in such a short space of time. It is imperative that we take a detailed look at all forms of Korean diaspora ministries worldwide at this juncture in the history of the Korean diaspora. When we do so, we will discover that God has not scattered his seeds without a plan of harvest in mind. Serving Point5 for the past year has enabled me to see first-hand what a unique and special role the Korean diaspora might play in the kingdom of God. It is with awe and humility that I join the group and women and men, who see God's hand in the scattering and the calling together of his people. Only a God-sized vision could allow for the raising up of such a great generation of God's people 'for such a time as this…'

Postscript

Wonsuk Ma and S. Hun Kim

As this book is completed, it may afford an opportunity to offer a brief reflection on the subject matter in the context of global Christian mission.

Year 2010

The centenary year of the historic Edinburgh Missionary Conference of 1910 gave an unprecedented opportunity to look back on a century of Christian mission. After the 'great century' of missionary advancement in the nineteenth century, the twentieth century was rather a remarkably turbulent period of radical changes in Christianity, in politics and economies. To recognize the new setting for Christian mission, the year 2010 was filled with various mission gatherings, global, regional and national in scale. Several global gatherings are noted below.

Tokyo 2010

As the first of three global mission events in the year, Tokyo 2010, held in May, was intended to celebrate what God has done since 1910, to envisage the future for mission, to reflect and introduce new global models and to facilitate coordination among mission organizations for the full engagement of world evangelization. Initiated by Ralph Winter before his death, one of the distinctive factors for this consultation was an emphasis on mission organizations as the core of the Edinburgh Conference in 1910. As expected, the conference had a relatively less focus on the church as the major mission player. The gathering also highlighted the growing and critical role of the majority world Christianity as holding the key to future Christian mission. The consultation was intended to create a movement that will strengthen the mission movement in the non-Western world. Accordingly, 74% of its delegation came from the non-Western world. Though Tokyo 2010 was carefully planned to succeed Edinburgh 1910 and 1980, it has been accomplished in a way that non-Western mission leaders, networkers and agencies organized it with a minimal contribution by the Western world.

Tokyo 2010 eventually evolved from the previous gatherings in 1910 and 1980 in its contribution to global missions with a declaration of the transformational dimension of the Great Commission and the pioneer mission to Europe as a 'reverse mission' and so on. However, the consultation also pioneered a global network which facilitates inter-mission cooperation to finish the world mission through the established Global Network of Mission Structure (GNMS). According to the analytical report on Tokyo 2010, there was a general lack of global mission intelligence in multiple areas. Therefore, the future of global mission could only be promised through networking and partnership to fill the gap of global mission information between 18 coordinating task forces and GNMS. Although not directly emphasised, the significance of the diaspora in mission was expressed in various ways.

Edinburgh 2010

Although the smallest in size, the Edinburgh 2010 Conference held in June represented the broadest world churches. Its general council consisted of representatives of fifteen global Christian families and five global mission organizations. A quick glance at the church representatives proves the incredibly ecumenical nature of the conference: from Catholic, Orthodox, and Anglican, to mainline, Evangelical and Pentecostal churches. The conference, which drew 250 global delegates, was a 'working conference' around the nine mission themes. Before they arrived in Edinburgh, the delegates had received a copy of the conference book, *Edinburgh 2010: Witnessing to Christ Today*,[1] the summary of the nine study themes, and transversals. The study themes were:

1. Foundations for Mission
2. Christian Mission among Other Faiths
3. Mission and Postmodernities
4. Mission and Power
5. Forms of Missionary Engagement
6. Theological Education and Formation
7. Christian Communities in Contemporary Contexts
8. Mission and Unity: Ecclesiology and Mission
9. Mission Spirituality and Authentic Discipleship

In addition, there were at least seven transversal topics:

1. Women and Mission
2. Youth and Mission
3. Healing and Reconciliation
4. Bible and Mission: Mission in the Bible
5. Contextualization, Inculturation and Dialogue of Worldviews
6. Sualtern voices
7. Ecological Perspectives on Mission

[1] Daryl Balia and Kirsteen Kim (eds), *Edinburgh 2010: Witnessing to Christ Today* (Oxford: Regnum Books, 2010).

The conference agenda was equally diverse and the broadest of the three gatherings, obviously reflecting the mission thinking and ethos of the World Council of the Churches. It was noted in the conference that 'evangelization', the focal point of the 1910 conference, was replaced by 'witness' and whether they meant the same thing was questioned. The legacy of the conference, however, would not be the size of the gathering but the sustained influence of its documents, currently expected to reach twenty volumes. The conference adopted a Common Call, following the nine themes of the conference process. Diaspora was never discussed as a single missiology theme, but was often inbedded in various discussions, including justice issues.

The Third Lausanne Congress

The Third Lausanne Congress on World Evangelization in Cape Town, 2010 was the most diverse and the broad consultation in church history. The scale of gathering was 4000 delegates from 198 countries. Organizers extended its reach into over 650 GlobaLink sites in 91 countries and drew 100,000 unique visits to its website from 185 countries during the week of the congress.

Many evangelical issues on mission were addressed: an affirmation of the uniqueness of Christ and the truth of the biblical gospel; a clear statement on evangelism and the mission of the church rooted in Scripture. At the culmination of the congress, the Cape Town Commitment revealed the five-fold plans in the future for local church: to stay light on its feet, remaining agile in its ability to respond to new challenges and opportunities; to be strong theologically, firmly rooted in Scripture and nourished by the best reflections on how we take the word to the world; to provide a reliable and credible contribution to Christian discussion and mission; to keep a focus on identifying and developing younger leaders; to be strategic in gathering the right people at the right times in the right places.

Though the congress was in the spirit of both Lausanne I and II, and it published a promising commitment beyond Cape Town, the spirit could not be manifested fully in a movement that claimed to combine the evangelical message with radical social action. Since Lausanne II in Manila, the view of Christian mission as involving both evangelism and social responsibility gained wider acceptance in evangelical circles and Rene Padilla, who is a champion for social justice of gospel, in his article, 'From Lausanne I to Lausanne III'[2] has raised his voice that social responsibility is exercised with an evangelistic conscience because the good works are carried out in Jesus' name as visible signs of the kingdom of God that was brought into history by Jesus Christ. However, compared to the buzz at the congress with many multimedia presentations, and never-ending array of renowned speakers in the congress,

---

[2] C. Rene Padilla, 'From Lausanne I to Lausanne III', *Journal of Latin American Theology: Christian Reflections from the Latino South* 5:2 (2010), 43-50.

Lausanne III was not entirely united over the social gospel. One of the major contributions of Lausanne I and II was to change the way of thinking about 'primacy only on evangelism' in Christianity. But now it is time to act, to demonstrate the reality of the gospel in evangelism.

There was one refreshing hope presented during the congress, that is, the emergence of diaspora as a mega-trend in world mission. Diaspora has been re-assessed as a way of future mission, which God authentically intended for his mission (*missio Dei*). It is acknowledged that the gathering and scattering of people across the earth is a central part of God's mission and redemptive purpose for the world. Therefore, disapora missiology has emerged as a biblical and strategic field of missiology, defined as a framework for understanding and participating in God's redemptive mission among people living outside their place of origin. In the section on diaspora at the congress, Global Diaspora Network or GDN was formed in order to advocate 'his conspiracy' for people on the move towards the worldwide church.

Observations on the Korean Diaspora

The collection of studies in this book has illustrated the potential of diaspora studies within the framework of mission studies. First of all, reflections on diaspora from various angles are important. One biblical study, for example, may not be sufficient, while there is a huge amount of theological exploration still awaiting those involved in mission. The core of the book is in the form of case studies. They provide the examples of commited Korean Christians to respond to emerging needs, to mobilize creative resources, to experiment with various approaches, to learn from trials and errors, and to share their experiences with others.

Also evident is the pragmatic orientation of various approaches: it is often the immediate needs or mission opportunities which prompt action. In this way, it is more reactive than pro-active. What is critical is theological reflection following one's missionary response, even if it is an afterthought. Such theological exploration will enrich praxis deeply, as now action is informed and motivated by one's theological understanding and conviction. Also this level of theoretical reflection is 'universalizable', readily applicable and sharable regardless of cultural orientations or social make-ups. This is where the Korean church has a call to resource, facilitate and empower other emerging churches to appropriate diaspora communities both in their own context and their people in other locations. At present, however, this two-tier exploration is not visible in the studies.

One conspicuous absence noticed in this collection is the active role of the church among North Korean refugees. It is understandable that security issues may hamper the open discussion of issues and the sharing of various experiences. Perhaps this single theme is significant to warrant attention in a separate volume.

Another area of deficiency is learning from others. The first is between general social science and Christian mission. There is evidence that some research takes advantage of studies undertaken by government agencies and secular researchers. However, the degree of incorporation of social science research is still a token. Furthermore, Christian research on diaspora should aim at influencing the policy-making process. This will require profiling Christian research in the mainstream of the social sciences. A lively dialogue between the social science world and Christian research can be fruitful. An initial approach can be made with Christian social scientists. Equally absent is an eager attitude to learn from the experiences of others in different places. For example, Hanciles' book may prove extremely useful, although African immigrants to North America may not have a direct parallel with the immigrants we see in Korea. However, the Korean diaspora in the West may find some of Hanciles' findings quite valuable. For this matter, the Korean government may be a step ahead as it has studied cases of other countries, including Japan. This openness will work mutually as we are open to learn from others, and our experiences and reflections will flow to others through the same open channel. Furthermore, the studies reveals that we tend to maintain a one-sided perspective. Most authors working in Korea focus on how to minister to 'foreigners', while those working outside of Korea tend to focus on how the Korean communities can contribute to the host societies. Seldom do we see the other perspectives: how the 'foreigners' can contribute to the Korean church and society, and also how the host churches and socieities can strengthen the ministries of Korean diaspora communities. Unless we finally acquire the balanced perspective, we will continue our lopsidedness.

Diaspora and Modern Mission

The current book project was not unconnected with the significant global mission gatherings in 2010. In fact, the pre-publication version of the book was presented at the Lausanne Congress in Cape Town, where the diaspora multiplex (or a major parallel session) was hugely popular. As discussed in the Introduction, diaspora has been an important mission theme developed both by the evangelical (through the Lausanne movement) and ecumenical circles.

Therefore, in order to fulfil the Great Commission for the world, it is inevitable for global churches to seek networking and partnerships, biblically and practically, particularly in the diasporic contexts. Now, it is time to reflect and evaluate what we have done over the past decades and the challenging issues in the future. Globally, is it possible for diapora to become an issue adopted by Christian movements whatever their theological and ecclesiastical orientations? If so, how can it be implemented? Perhaps Korean churches could take a role to facilitate at least a pan-Asian diaspora network in cooperation with Global Diaspora Network.

However, the global dimension for networking and partnership is not linear and simple but multi-layered and complicated. Therefore, a call for unified cooperation has to be made by various ethnic initiatives like Korean Diaspora Forum for Koreans, Diaspora Network for Japanese for the Japanese, International Network of South Asian Diaspora Leaders for Indians, Filipino International Network for Filipinos, Chinese Coordination Centre of World Evangelism for the Chinese, COMIBAM for Latinos, and many more institutions for education and research, mission organizations, NGOs, Christian NGOs, government structures, UN and faith-based groups worldwide as well as Global Diaspora Network initiated by the Lausanne movement recently. Through the unified cooperation among these established networks, we may arrive at more synergistic outcomes from the major challenges in mission: the challenge of radical discipleship, the challenge of globalization and poverty and the challenge of the destruction of the ecosystem.[3] Finally, we do not limit our goal to inner issues related to churches but dare to pioneer possibilities of inter-religious cooperation.

[3] Padilla, 'From Lausanne I to Lausanne III', 43-50.

Selected Bibliography

Adogame, A. 'The Rhetoric of Reverse Mission: African Christianity and the Changing Dynamics of Religious expansion in Europe'. An Outline presented at the Conference of 'South moving North: revised mission and its implications', Protestant Landelijk Dienstencentrum, Utrecht, September 2007.

Asamoah-Gyadu, J.K. 'African Initiated Christianity in Eastern Europe: Church of the "Embassy of God" in Ukraine'. *International Bulletin of Missionary Research* 30:2 (2006), 73-75.

Augsburger, David W. *Pastoral Counseling across Cultures.* Philadelphia: Westminster Press, 1986.

Balia, Daryl and Kirsteen Kim (eds). *Edinburgh 2010: Witnessing to Christ Today*. Oxford: Regnum, 2010.

Barbour, C. M. 'Seeking Justice and Shalom in the City', *International Review of Mission* 73, no. 291 (1984).

Bevans, Stephen B. *Models of Contextual Theology.* Maryknoll, NY: Orbis Books, 1992.

Bevans, Stephen B. and Roger P. Schroeder. *Constants in Context: A Theology of Mission for Today*. Grand Rapids: Baker Book House, 2006.

Bosch, David. *Transforming Mission: Paradigm Shifts in Theology of Mission.* Maryknoll, NY: Orbis. 1993.

Brewster, E. Thomas, and Elizabeth S. Brewster. *Bonding and the Missionary Task.* Pasadena, CA: Lingua House, 1992.

Bright, J. *A History of Israel*. Rev. ed. London: SCM Press, 1972.

_____. *The Kingdom of God: The Biblical Concept and Its Meaning for the Church.* Nashville: Abingdon Press, 1981.

Broom, A. and L. Broom, (1999). *One to One Discipling.* Vista, CA: Multiplication Ministries, 1999.

Castles, S. and M.J. Miller *The Age of Migration: International Population Movements in the Modern World.* New York: Guilford Press, 1998.

Cho, S. 'BAM from Church Perspective' [in Korean]. *Various Forms to Various Peoples: Korean Interserve Quarterly*, June, 2010.

_____. 'Defining BAM' [in Korean]. *Various Forms to Various Peoples: Korean Interserve Quarterly*, March, 2010.

Choi, G.S., I.L. Jo, and, E.J. Lee. 'Migrant Worker Ministry Network: Migrant Worker Ministry Model in South Korea', *Global Mission Alliance*, 2008.

Choi, Jaeho. 'Islamic Radicalism in the UK: An inevitable or an Avoidable Phenomenon?' M.Sc. Dissertation. Cranfield University, 2007/2008.

Davie, G. *Europe, the Exceptional Case: Parameters for Faith in the Modern World.* London: Darton, Longman & Todd, 2002.

De Vaux, Ronald, *Ancient Israel: Its Life and Institutions.* Trans. John McHugh. London: Darton, Longman & Todd, 1973.

Escobar, Samuel. 'The Global Scenario at the Turn of the Century'. In William D. Taylor (ed). *Global Missiology for the 21st Century.* Grand Rapids, MI: Baker Book House, 2000.

_____. *The New Global Mission: From Everywhere to Everyone.* Downer's Grove, IL: InterVarsity Press, 2003.

Ferguson, E. *Backgrounds of Early Christianity.* 2nd ed. Grand Rapids, MI: Eerdmans, 1993.

Fiske, A. 'The Four Elementary Forms of Sociality: Framework for a Unified Theory of Social Relations'. *Psychological Review* 99 (1992), 689-723.

Frost, Michael. *Exiles: Living Missionally in a Post-Christian Culture.* Peabody, MA: Hendrickson Publishers, 2006.

Frost, Michael and Alan Hirsch. *The Shaping of Things to Come: Innovation and Mission for the 21st Century Church.* Peabody, MA: Hendrickson Publishers, 2003.

_____. *ReJesus: A wild Messiah for a Missional Church.* Peabody, MA: Hendrickson Publishers, 2009.

Fukuyama, F. *The End of History and the Last Man.* New York: Avon Books, 1992.

Glasser, Arthur F. *Kingdom and Mission.* Pasadena: Fuller Theological Seminary, School of World Mission, 1989.

Glaser, Barney G. and Anselm L. Strauss. *The Discovery of Grounded Theory: Strategies for Qualitative Research.* New York: Aldine De Gruyter, 1967.

Granovetter, M. 'Economic Action and Social Structure: The Problem of Embeddedness'. *American Journal of Sociology* 91:3 (1985), 481-510.

Griffis, William E. *Corea, the Hermit Nation.* New York: Scriber's Sons, 1894.

Grunlan, S.A and Marvin K. Mayers. *Cultural Anthropology: A Christian Perspective.* Grand Rapids: Academic Books, 1988.

Hanciles, J. 'Migration and Mission: Some Implications for the 21st Century Church. *International Bulletin of Missionary Research* 27:4 (2003), 146-153.

_____. 'Migration and Mission: The Religious Significance of the North-South Divide'. In A. Walls and C. Ross (eds). *Mission in the 21st Century: Exploring the Five Marks of Global Mission.* London: Darton, Longman & Todd, 2008.

_____. *Beyond Christendom: Globalization, African Migration and the Transformaiton of the West.* Maryknoll, NY: Orbis Books, 2008.

Harley, David. *Preparing to Serve: Training for Cross-cultural Missions.* Pasadena, CA: William Carey Library, 1995.

Hiebert, Paul G. *Anthropological Insights for Missionaries.* Grand Rapids, MI: Baker Book House, 1985.

_____. *Anthropological Reflections on Missiological Issues.* Grand Rapids, MI: Baker Book House, 1994.

_____. *Transforming Worldviews: An Anthropological Understanding of How People Change.* Grand Rapids, MI: Baker Book House, 2009.

Hofstede, Geert. *Cultures and Organizations: Software of the Mind.* Trans. Jaeho Cha and Eunyoung Nah. Seoul: Hakjisa, 1995.

Hoke, Stephen T. 'Paradigm Shifts and Trends in Missions Training - A Call to Servant-Teaching: A Ministry of Humility'. *Evangelical Review of Theology* 23 (October 1999), 329-346.

Huntington, S. *The Clash of Civilizations and the Remaking of World Order*. New York: Georges Borchardt, 1996.

Hwang, Eun C. 'The Mission of God's Pilgrim People: Toward a Contextual Ministry for Korean Churches in Brazil'. Doctor of Missiology dissertation, Fuller Theological Seminary, 1993.

Jacobson, Matthew Frye. *Whiteness of a Different Color: European Immigrants and the Alchemy of Race*. Cambridge: Harvard University Press, 1998.

Johnson, N. *Business as Mission: A Comprehensive Guide to Theory and Practice*. Downers Grove, IL: IVP, 2009.

Johnson, Scott and James D. Ludema (eds). *Partnering to Build and Measure Organizational Capacity: Lessons from NGOs around the World*. Grand Rapids, MI: Christian Reformed World Relief Committee, 1997.

Johnson, T. and K. Ross. *Atlas of Global Christianity*. Edinburgh: Edinburgh University Press, 2010.

Johnstone, Patrick and Jason Mandryk. *Operation World: 21st Century Edition*. Waynesboro, GA: Paternoster Lifestyle, 2001.

Jones, Stanley E. *Christian Maturity*. Nashville: Abingdon, 1957.

Jun, C.H. 'World Mission through Korean Migrant Worker Mission'. *Forum for Korean Mission Leaders* 9 (2009).

_____. 'World Christian Mission through Migrant Workers in South Korea and through the Korean Diaspora'. *Tokyo 2010 Global Mission: Consultation and Celebration* (2010).

Kang, Sungsam. 'Basic Missionary Training: Bible and Disciple' [in Korean]. *Korean Missions Quarterly* 8:3 (2009), 29-40.

Kang, Taewook. 'BAM and Church Community: The Compendium of the Second Shanghai Business Forum'. Uunpublished Conference Report (2008).

Kim, Hajoong. *God's Ambassador* [in Korean]. Seoul: Kyujang, 2010.

Kim, Kyudong. *My Life, My Faith*. Tokyo: Yohan Tokyo Christian Church, 2001.

Kim, S. Hun (ed). 'Eurovision Forum Handbook'. Darmstadt, Germany, 2007.

Kim, Y. 'Ways to BAM' [in Korean]. Collecton of 1st and 2nd SKBF Lectures, Shanghai, China, 2009.

Kim, Youngbong and Eunhae Hwang. *The Yohan Tokyo Christian Church's Twenieth Anniversary*. Tokyo: Yohan Tokyo Christian Church Press, 2008.

'Korean Church Statistics. www.kreanchurchyp.com.

Korean Ministry of Education, Science and Technology. 'Multicultural Children's Study Status'. www.mest.go.kr, 2007.

Korean Mission Leaders Forum. 'Memorandum of 9th Korean Mission Leader Forum'. www.kwma.org, 2009.

Kraft, Charles H. *Anthropology for Christian Witness*. Maryknoll, NY: Orbis Books, 1996.

Ladd, George Eldon. *The Gospel of the Kingdom: Scriptural Studies in the Kingdom of God*. Grand Rapids, MI: Eerdmans, 1998.

Lee, Moonjang. 'Change of Mission Paradigm: Issues of Korean Mission in the 21st Century' [in Korean]. In *Issues of Korean Mission in the 21st Century: Surak Forum Compendium, Korea, Nov 2005*, 14-31.

Levinskaya, Irina. *The Book of Acts in its First Century Setting.* Grand Rapids, MI: Eerdmans, 1996.

Ma, Julie C. *When the Spirit Meets the Spirits: Pentecostal Ministry among the Kankana-ey Tribe in the Philippines*. Frankfurt: Peter Lang. 2000.

_____. 'Church Planting: Pentecostal Strategy for Mission'. In Kay Fountain (ed). *Reflections on Developing Asian Pentecostal Leaders: Essays in Honor of Harold Kohl.* Baguio, Philippines: APTS Press, 2004, 323-55.

Mandryk, Jason. *Operation World: The Definitive Prayer Guide to Every Nation.* 7th Ed. Gerrards Cross, UK: WEC International, 2011.

Moses, Dennis D. *Leadership and Church Structure in the Pulpit and Out.* Columbus, GA: Brentwood Christian Press, 2000.

Murdock, Steve. 'Cuttings the Purse Strings: How to Avoid and Overcome Paternalism'. *Evangelical Missions Quarterly* 45:1 (January 2009): 66-71.

Norrish, Howard. 'An Evaluation of the Performance of Korean Missionaries'. In *Issues of Korean Mission in the 21st Century: Surak Forum Compendium, Korea, Nov 2005*: 132-151.

Oh, G.T. 'Koreans' Perspective on Migrant Workers: Focus on Work Places'. Study presented at Shinchon Forum 22, 2007.

Park, C.E. 'Foreign Workers' Present Reality and Multicultural Policy Agenda'. Study presented at Shinchon Forum 22, 2006.

Pierson, Paul. 'Non-Western Missions: The Great New Fact of Our Time'. In Patrick Sookhdeo (ed). *New Frontiers in Mission.* Exeter: Paternoster Press, 1987.

'Receiving Mission Workers to Europe: What Every Church Should Know'. www.welcomeproject.net

Reyburn, William D. 'Identification in the Missionary Task'. In W.A. Smalley (ed). *Readings in Missionary Anthropology II.* Pasadena, CA: William Carey Library, 1978.

Roxburgh, Alan J. T*he sky is falling!?!: Leaders lost in transition*: Eagle, Idaho: ACI Publishing, 2005.

Roxburgh, Alan J. and Fred Romanuk. *The Missional Leader: Equipping Your Church to Reach a Changing World.* San Francisco, CA: Jossey-Bass, 2006.

Rundle, S. and T. Steffen. *Great Commission Companies.* Downers Grove, IL: IVP, 2003.

Russell, M. *The Missional Entrepreneurs: Principles and Practices for BAM.* Birmingham, AL: New Hope Publishers, 2010.

Santos, Narry F. 'Survey of the Diaspora Occurrences in the Bible and of Their Contexts in Christian Missions in the Bible'. In Luis Pantoja, Jr., Sadiri Joy Tira, and Enoch Wan (eds). *Scattered: The Filipino Global Presence.* Manila: Lifechange Publishing, 2004.

Sarna, Nahum M. *Exploring Exodus: The Original of Biblical Israel.* New York: Schocken Books, 1986.

Schein, Edgar H. *Organizational Culture and Leadership.* San Francisco: Jossey-Bass, 1992.

Schwartz, B. 'Christian Origins: Historical Truth and Social Memory'. In A. Kirk and T. Thatcher (eds). *Memory, Tradition and Text: Uses of the Past in Early Christianity.* SBL/Semeia Studies No. 52. 2005.

Seo, M. 'Business Activities in the Kingdom of God' [in Korean]. Unpublished manuscript, 2009.

Shore, Bradd. *Culture in Mind: Cognition, Culture, and the Problem of Meaning*. Oxford: Oxford University Press, 1996.

Sipe, James W. and Don M. Frick. *Seven Pillars of Servant Leadership: Practicing the Wisdom of Leading by Serving*. New York: Paulist Press, 2009.

Sjasstad, Larry A. 'The Costs and Returns of Human Migration'. *Journal of Political Economy* 70:5 (1962), 80-93.

Spencer, S. *Mission and Migration*. Calver, UK: Cliff College Publishing, 2008.

Stegemann, E.W. and W. Stegemann. *The Jesus Movement: A Social History of Its First Century*. Trans. O.C. Dean, Jr. Edinburgh: T&T Clark, 1999.

Strauss, Claudia and Naomi Quinn. *A Cognitive Theory of Cultural Meaning*. Cambridge: Cambridge University Press, 2008.

Taylor, William D. 'From Iguassu to the Reflective Practitioners of the Global Family of Christ'. In William D. Taylor (ed). *Global Missiology for the 21st Century: The Iguassu Dialogue*. Grand Rapids, MI: Baker Academic, 2000: 3-13.

'The "Foreigner" in Our Midst: Hopes and Fears for Europe'. EEA's Authorization Team. www.europeanea.org, Spring 2007.

'Theme Three: Mission and Postmodernities'. In Daryl Balia and Kirsteen Kim (eds). *Edinburgh 2010: Witnessing to Christ Today*. Oxford: Regnum, 2010.

Tizon, Al. *Transformation after Lausanne: Radical Evangelical Mission in Global-Local Perspective*. Oxford: Regnum Books, 2008.

Train and Multiply. *Student Activity Guide: For the Trainer to Use with Each Student*. Surrey, Canada: Project WorldReach, 2001.

Tunehag, M. 'God Means Mission: An Introduction to Business as Mission'. Unpublished manuscript, 2008.

Tunehag, M., W. McGee and J. Plummer. 'Business as Mission, Occasional Paper No. 59'. Pataya, Thailand: Lausanne Committee for World Evangelism, 2004.

Uhm, Kiyoung. *The Kingdom of God: Christian Freedom*. Shanghai: Shanghai Korean Community Church, n.d.

Van Gelder, Craig. *The Essence of the Church: A Community Created by the Spirit*. Grand Rapids, MI: Baker Books, 2000.

Von Harnack, Adolf. *The Mission and Expansion of Christianity in the First Three Centuries*. New York: Harper and Brothers, 1961.

Walls, A. and C. Ross. *Mission in the 21st Century*. London: Darton, Longman & Todd, 2008.

Wan, Enoch. 'The Phenomenon of Diaspora: Missiological Implications for Christian Missions'. In Luis Pantoja, Jr., Sadiri Joy Tira, and Enoch Wan (eds). *Scattered: The Filipino Global Presence*. Manila: Lifechange Publishing, 2004.

Won, Moo H. 'Korean American Pluralism: The "1.5" Generation'. In Sang Hyun Lee and John V. Moore (eds), *Korean American Ministry*. Louisville, KY: PC USA, 2006, 215-229.

Yamamori, T. and K. Eldred (eds). *On Kingdom Business: Tranforming Missions Through Entrepreneurial Strategies*. Wheaton, IL: Crossways, 2003.

Zerubavel, Eviatar. *Social Mindscapes: An Invitation to Cognitive Sociology*. Cambridge, MA: Harvard University Press, 1997.

Contributors

Tereso C. Casiño currently is Professor of Missiology at the School of Divinity, Gardner-Webb University, Boiling Springs, North Carolina, U.S.A. Formerly he he served in the faculty of Torch Trinity Graduate School of Theology, Seoul, Korea. He also served as Managing Director of Cape Town 2010 Data Mining Team, the digital research unit of the Communications Department of The Lausanne Movement, while charing the North American Lausanne Diaspora Missiology Educators Forum.

Peter Chang has been serving in Bonn, Germany as a missionary of the University Bible Fellowship (Korea) since 1980. During this period, he has ministered university students in Bonn and on other European campuses through Bible study and preaching. As an ordained minister, he currently serves as the Director of the Europe UBF. His academic training includes PhD in Pharmacy from Bonn University (1984).

Sam Cho served as Professor of Management at Yanbian University of Science and Technology in China for many years. He is currently serving as a strategic consultant on Business As Mission, while continuing his networking role with Interserve.

Sungho Choi is currently serving as Dean of International Development and Lecturer at Wales Evangelical School of Theology, UK. His received theological training at University of Wales, Lampeter.

Do Myung Chun is Pastor in charge of Portuguese Ministry in United Korean Presbyterian Church of Sao Paulo, Brazil. He immigrated to Brazil in 1971 and practiced medical mission as a general surgeon for a decade. He is currently enrolled in D. Min course at Fuller Theological Seminary.

Jae Ryun Chung is the lead pastor of Point5 Community at the Onnuri Community Church, Seoul, Korea. Being a 1.5 diaspora generation in the United States, he returned to Korea for ministry. He is currently pursuing a PhD degree at the Drew University.

Chulho Han is dedicated as a mobilizer for youth mission with Mission Korea. He served IVF Korea and IFES as East Asia Regional Graduate Secretary. He currently directs Mission Korea Partners since 2010, after successful leadership of Mission Korea conference for many years.

Matthew Jeong served as a missionary in Pakistan, and as Area Director North, and later as director of Ministry Development of Interserve International. He is currently National Director of Interserve Korea.

David Chul Han Jun serves as Fouding Director of Friends of All Nations in Korea since 2001. His ministries include Korean Harbor Evangelism, OM Ship, Mission in South Africa and World Concern in the past, and presently One Mission ECC Shepherds ministry to Vietnam and Philippines. He completed a D.Miss. degree at Fuller Theological Seminary and now teaches at Seoul Theological Seminary.

Min-Young Jung, after many years of ministry both in Indonesia as a Bible translator and in Korea as director of Global Bible translators (Wycliffe Korea), has served since 2002 as International Coordinator of the Asian Diaspora Initiative, a strategic initiative of Wycliffe International to engage Asian diaspora churches for the cause of Bible translation. Currently he is Associate Director of Wycliffe International, while providing supervision over the Asian Diaspora Initiative.

Byung Yoon Kim is Professor of Intercultural Studies at Philippine Baptist Theological Seminary and Asia Baptist Graduate Theological Seminary, Baguio City, Philippines. He founded Asia Vision Short-term Missions Project 2015 and is currently serving as International Coordinator.

S. Hun Kim is a reflective practitioner and researcher on mission and diaspora/migration with Oxford Centre for Mission Studies, UK. After completing Bible translation in the Azeri language at Wycliffe, he has served as Diaspora Consultant with Wycliffe and as Director of the Korean Research Institute for Diaspora, Oxford. He is a member of (Lausanne) Global Diaspora Network.

Soon Geun Lee is the founder and one of the co-representatives of the Korean Diaspora Forum. He served as Senior Pastor of the Korean Church in Baltimore, U.S.A for many years. He has now returned to Korea to establish a diaspora mission in Korea.

See-Young Lee is Former Vice Foreign Minister and Ambassador of the Republic of Korea to the UN, France, Austria and Senegal. He also served as President of Jeonju University and Visiting Professor of the Graduate School of International Studies of Seoul National University, and currently as Chair Professor of Handong Global University, Korea. He also serves as Chairman of the International Board of COME Mission.

Julie C. Ma taught at Asia Pacific Theological Seminary, Philippines, and currently serves as Research Tutor at Oxford Centre for Mission Studies, Oxford, UK. She also served in the General Council of the Edinburgh 2010.

Wonsuk Ma was Vice President for Academic Affairs at Asia Pacific Theological Seminary, Philippines. Currently he is David Yonggi Cho Research Tutor and Executive Director of Oxford Centre for Mission Studies, Oxford, UK.

Steve Sang-cheol Moon is a graduate of Trinity Evangelical Divinity School, Deerfield, IL, USA with a Ph.D. in Intercultural Studies (1998). He is currently director of the Korea Research Institute for Mission, Seoul, Korea. He also teaches missions at the Hapdong Theological Seminary, Suwon and other seminaries both in Korea and abroad.

Doug K. Oh is a former president of Hapdong Theological Seminary in Korea. He is currently President of the Presbyterian Theological Society in Korea, and also teaches Church History at Hapdong Theological Seminary.

Minho Song is Senior Pastor of Young Nak Korean Presbyterian Church of Toronto. Previously, he taught Missions and New Testament at Asian Theological Seminary, Quezon City, Philippines. Currently, he serves as adjunct professor at Asia Research Institute of Language and Culture, Handong Global University, Korea, and at Asian Theological Seminary, Philippines.

Jonathan Tran is Assistant Professor of Theological Ethics in the Department of Religion at Baylor University, in Waco, Texas, USA. He is author of *The Vietnam War and Theologies of Memory: Time and Eternity in the Far Country* (Wiley-Blackwell, 2010), *Foucault and Theology: Power, Witness, and Christianity* (T&T Clark, forthcoming 2011).

Enoch Wan is Director of the Doctor of Missiology programme, Western Seminary, Portland, Oregon and Pesident of the Evangelical Missiological Society, North America.

REGNUM EDINBURGH 2010 SERIES
Series Listing

David A. Kerr, Kenneth R. Ross (eds.)
Edinburgh 2010
Mission Then and Now
2009 / 978-1-870345-73-6 / xiv + 343pp (paperback)
2009 / 978-1-870345-76-7 / xiv + 343pp (hardback)

No one can hope to fully understand the modern Christian missionary movement without engaging substantially with the World Missionary Conference, held at Edinburgh in 1910. As the centenary of the Conference approaches, the time is ripe to examine its meaning in light of the past century and the questions facing Christian witness today. This book is the first to systematically examine the eight Commissions which reported to Edinburgh 1910 and gave the conference much of its substance and enduring value. It will deepen and extend the reflection being stimulated by the upcoming centenary and will kindle the missionary imagination for 2010 and beyond.

Daryl M. Balia, Kirsteen Kim (eds.)
Edinburgh 2010
Witnessing to Christ Today
2010 / 978-1-870345-77-4 / xiv +301pp

This volume, the second in the Edinburgh 2010 series, includes reports of the nine main study groups working on different themes for the celebration of the centenary of the World Missionary Conference, Edinburgh 1910. Their collaborative work brings together perspectives that are as inclusive as possible of contemporary world Christianity and helps readers to grasp what it means in different contexts to be 'witnessing to Christ today'.

Claudia Währisch-Oblau, Fidon Mwombeki (eds.)
Mission Continues
Global Impulses for the 21st Century
2010 / 978-1-870345-82-8 / 271pp

In May 2009, 35 theologians from Asia, Africa and Europe met in Wuppertal, Germany, for a consultation on mission theology organized by the United Evangelical Mission: Communion of 35 Churches in Three Continents. The aim was to participate in the 100th anniversary of the Edinburgh conference through a study process and reflect on the challenges for mission in the 21st century. This book brings together these papers written by experienced practitioners from around the world.

Brian Woolnough and Wonsuk Ma (Eds)

Holistic Mission

God's plan for God's people 2010 / 978-1-870345-85-9

Holistic mission, or integral mission, implies God is concerned with the whole person, the whole community, body, mind and spirit. This book discusses the meaning of the holistic gospel, how it has developed, and implications for the the church. . It takes a global, eclectic approach, with 19 writers, all of whom have much experience in, and commitment to, holistic mission. It addresses critically and honestly one of the most exciting, and challenging, issues facing the church today. To be part of God's plan for God's people, the church must take holistic mission to the world.

REGNUM STUDIES IN GLOBAL CHRISTIANITY

(Previously GLOBAL THEOLOGICAL VOICES series)

Series Listing

David Emmanuuel Singh (ed.)
Jesus and the Cross
Reflections of Christians from Islamic Contexts
2008 / 978-1-870345-65-1 / x + 226pp

The Cross reminds us that the sins of the world are not borne through the exercise of power but through Jesus Christ's submission to the will of the Father. The papers in this volume are organised in three parts: scriptural, contextual and theological. The central question being addressed is: how do Christians living in contexts, where Islam is a majority or minority religion, experience, express or think of the Cross? This is, therefore, an exercise in listening. As the contexts from where these engagements arise are varied, the papers in drawing scriptural, contextual and theological reflections offer a cross-section of Christian thinking about Jesus and the Cross.

Sung-wook Hong
Naming God in Korea
The Case of Protestant Christianity
2008 / 978-1-870345-66-8 / xiv + 170pp

Since Christianity was introduced to Korea more than a century ago, one of the most controversial issue has been the Korean term for the Christian 'God'. This issue is not merely about naming the Christian God in Korean language, but it relates to the question of theological contextualization—the relationship between the gospel and culture—and the question of Korean Christian identity. This book examines the theological contextualization of the concept of 'God' in the contemporary Korean context and applies the translatability of Christianity to that context. It also demonstrates the nature of the gospel in relation to cultures, i.e., the universality of the gospel expressed in all human cultures.

Hubert van Beek (ed.)
Revisioning Christian Unity
The Global Christian Forum
2009 / 978-1-870345-74-3 / xx + 288pp

This book contains the records of the Global Christian Forum gathering held in Limuru near Nairobi, Kenya, on 6 – 9 November 2007 as well as the papers presented at that historic event. Also included are a summary of the Global Christian Forum process from its inception until the 2007 gathering and the reports of the evaluation of the process that was carried out in 2008.

Paul Hang-Sik Cho
Eschatology and Ecology
Experiences of the Korean Church
2010 / 978-1-870345-75-0/ 260pp (approx)

This book raises the question of why Korean people, and Korean Protestant Christians in particular, pay so little attention (in theory or practice) to ecological issues. The author argues that there is an important connection (or elective affinity) between this lack of attention and the other-worldly eschatology that is so dominant within Korean Protestant Christianity. Dispensational premillennialism, originally imported by American missionaries, resonated with traditional religious beliefs in Korea and soon came to dominate much of Korean Protestantism. This book argues that this, of all forms of millennialism, is the most damaging to ecological concerns.

Dietrich Werner, David Esterline, Namsoon Kang, Joshva Raja (eds.)
The Handbook of Theological Education in World Christianity
Theological Perspectives, Ecumenical Trends, Regional Surveys
2010 / 978-1-870345-80-4/ 759pp

This major reference work is the first ever comprehensive study of Theological Education in Christianity of its kind. With contributions from over 90 international scholars and church leaders, it aims to be easily accessible across denominational, cultural, educational, and geographic boundaries. The Handbook will aid international dialogue and networking among theological educators, institutions, and agencies. The major objectives of the text are (1) to provide introductory surveys on selected issues and themes in global theological education; (2) to provide regional surveys on key developments, achievements, and challenges in theological education; (3) to provide an overview of theological education for each of the major denominational / confessional traditions; and (4) to provide a reference section with an up-to-date list of the regional associations of theological institutions and other resources.

David Emmanuel Singh & Bernard C Farr (eds.)
Christianity and Education
Shaping of Christian Context in Thinking
2010 / 978-1-870345-81-1/ 244pp (approx)

Christianity and Education is a collection of papers published in *Transformation: An International Journal of Holistic Mission Studies* over a period of 15 years. It brings to life some of the papers that lay buried in shelves and in disparate volumes of *Transformation,* under a single volume for theological libraries, students and teachers. The articles here represent a spectrum of Christian thinking addressing issues of institutional development for theological education, theological studies in the context of global mission, contextually aware/informed education, and academies which deliver such education, methodologies and personal reflections.

J.Andrew Kirk
Civilisations in Conflict?

Islam, the West and Christian Faith 2011- 978-1-870345-71-2

Samuel Huntington's thesis, which argues that there appear to be aspects of Islam that could be on a collision course with the politics and values of Western societies, has provoked much controversy. The purpose of this study is to offer a particular response to Huntington's thesis by making a comparison between the origins of Islam and Christianity; the two religions that can be said to have shaped, in contrasting ways, the history of the Western world. The early history of each faith continues to have a profound impact on the way in which their respective followers have interpreted the relationship between faith and political life. The book draws significant, critical and creative conclusions from the analysis for contemporary intercultural understanding, and in particular for the debate about the justification of violence for political and religious ends.

REGNUM STUDIES IN MISSION
Series Listing

Kwame Bediako

Theology and Identity

The Impact of Culture upon Christian Thought in the Second Century and in Modern Africa

1992 / 1-870345-10-X / xviii + 508pp

The author examines the question of Christian identity in the context of the Graeco–Roman culture of the early Roman Empire. He then addresses the modern African predicament of quests for identity and integration.

Christopher Sugden

Seeking the Asian Face of Jesus

The Practice and Theology of Christian Social Witness in Indonesia and India 1974–1996

1997 / 1-870345-26-6 / xx + 496pp

This study focuses on contemporary holistic mission with the poor in India and Indonesia combined with the call to transformation of all life in Christ with micro-credit enterprise schemes. 'The literature on contextual theology now has a new standard to rise to' – Lamin Sanneh (Yale University, USA).

Hwa Yung

Mangoes or Bananas?

The Quest for an Authentic Asian Christian Theology

1997 / 1-870345-25-8 / xii + 274pp

Asian Christian thought remains largely captive to Greek dualism and Enlightenment rationalism because of the overwhelming dominance of Western culture. Authentic contextual Christian theologies will emerge within Asian Christianity with a dual recovery of confidence in culture and the gospel.

Keith E. Eitel

Paradigm Wars

The Southern Baptist International Mission Board Faces the Third Millennium

1999 / 1-870345-12-6 / x + 140pp

The International Mission Board of the Southern Baptist Convention is the largest denominational mission agency in North America. This volume chronicles the historic and contemporary forces that led to the IMB's recent extensive reorganization, providing the most comprehensive case study to date of a historic mission agency restructuring to continue its mission purpose into the twenty-first century more effectively.

Samuel Jayakumar

Dalit Consciousness and Christian Conversion

Historical Resources for a Contemporary Debate

1999 / 81-7214-497-0 / xxiv + 434pp

(Published jointly with ISPCK)

The main focus of this historical study is social change and transformation among the Dalit Christian communities in India. Historiography tests the evidence in the light of the conclusions of the modern Dalit liberation theologians.

Vinay Samuel and Christopher Sugden (eds.)

Mission as Transformation

A Theology of the Whole Gospel

1999 / 0870345133/ 522pp

This book brings together in one volume twenty five years of biblical reflection on mission practice with the poor from around the world. The approach of holistic mission, which integrates proclamation, evangelism, church planting and social transformation seamlessly as a whole, has been adopted since 1983 by most evangelical development agencies, most indigenous mission agencies and many Pentecostal churches. This volume helps anyone understand how evangelicals, struggling to unite evangelism and social action, found their way in the last twenty five years to the biblical view of mission in which God calls all human beings to love God and their neighbour; never creating a separation between the two.

Christopher Sugden

Gospel, Culture and Transformation

2000 / 1-870345-32-0 / viii + 152pp

A Reprint, with a New Introduction, of Part Two of Seeking the Asian Face of Jesus

Gospel, Culture and Transformation explores the practice of mission especially in relation to transforming cultures and communities. - 'Transformation is to enable God's vision of society to be actualised in all relationships: social, economic and spiritual, so that God's will may be reflected in human society and his love experienced by all communities, especially the poor.'

Bernhard Ott

Beyond Fragmentation: Integrating Mission and Theological Education

A Critical Assessment of some Recent Developments
in Evangelical Theological Education

2001 / 1-870345-14-2 / xxviii + 382pp

Beyond Fragmentation is an enquiry into the development of Mission Studies in evangelical theological education in Germany and German-speaking Switzerland between 1960 and 1995. The author undertakes a detailed examination of the paradigm shifts which have taken place in recent years in both the theology of mission and the understanding of theological education.

Gideon Githiga

The Church as the Bulwark against Authoritarianism

Development of Church and State Relations in Kenya, with Particular Reference to the Years after Political Independence 1963-1992

2002 / 1-870345-38-x / xviii + 218pp

'All who care for love, peace and unity in Kenyan society will want to read this careful history by Bishop Githiga of how Kenyan Christians, drawing on the Bible, have sought to share the love of God, bring his peace and build up the unity of the nation, often in the face of great difficulties and opposition.' Canon Dr Chris Sugden, Oxford Centre for Mission Studies.

Myung Sung-Hoon, Hong Young-Gi (eds.)

Charis and Charisma

David Yonggi Cho and the Growth of Yoido Full Gospel Church

2003 / 1-870345-45-2 / xxii + 218pp

This book discusses the factors responsible for the growth of the world's largest church. It expounds the role of the Holy Spirit, the leadership, prayer, preaching, cell groups and creativity in promoting church growth. It focuses on God's grace (charis) and inspiring leadership (charisma) as the two essential factors and the book's purpose is to present a model for church growth worldwide.

Samuel Jayakumar

Mission Reader

Historical Models for Wholistic Mission in the Indian Context

2003 / 1-870345-42-8 / x + 250pp

(Published jointly with ISPCK)

This book is written from an evangelical point of view revalidating and reaffirming the Christian commitment to wholistic mission. The roots of the 'wholistic mission' combining 'evangelism and social concerns' are to be located in the history and tradition of Christian evangelism in the past; and the civilizing purpose of evangelism is compatible with modernity as an instrument in nation building.

Bob Robinson

Christians Meeting Hindus

An Analysis and Theological Critique of the Hindu-Christian Encounter in India

2004 / 1-870345-39-8 / xviii + 392pp

This book focuses on the Hindu-Christian encounter, especially the intentional meeting called dialogue, mainly during the last four decades of the twentieth century, and specifically in India itself.

Gene Early

Leadership Expectations

How Executive Expectations are Created and Used in a Non-Profit Setting

2005 / 1-870345-30-4 / xxiv + 276pp

The author creates an Expectation Enactment Analysis to study the role of the Chancellor of the University of the Nations-Kona, Hawaii. This study is grounded in the field of managerial work, jobs, and behaviour and draws on symbolic interactionism, role theory, role identity theory and enactment theory. The result is a conceptual framework for developing an understanding of managerial roles.

Tharcisse Gatwa

The Churches and Ethnic Ideology in the Rwandan Crises 1900-1994

2005 / 1-870345-24-X / approx 300pp

Since the early years of the twentieth century Christianity has become a new factor in Rwandan society. This book investigates the role Christian churches played in the formulation and development of the racial ideology that culminated in the 1994 genocide.

Julie Ma

Mission Possible

Biblical Strategies for Reaching the Lost

2005 / 1-870345-37-1 / xvi + 142pp

This is a missiology book for the church which liberates missiology from the specialists for the benefit of every believer. It also serves as a textbook that is simple and friendly, and yet solid in biblical interpretation. This book links the biblical teaching to the actual and contemporary missiological settings with examples, making the Bible come alive to the reader.

Allan Anderson, Edmond Tang (eds.)

Asian and Pentecostal

The Charismatic Face of Christianity in Asia

2005 / 1-870345-43-6 / xiv + 596pp

(Published jointly with APTS Press)

This book provides a thematic discussion and pioneering case studies on the history and development of Pentecostal and Charismatic churches in the countries of South Asia, South East Asia and East Asia.

I. Mark Beaumont

Christology in Dialogue with Muslims

A Critical Analysis of Christian Presentations of Christ for Muslims from the Ninth and Twentieth Centuries

2005 / 1-870345-46-0 / xxvi + 228pp

This book analyses Christian presentations of Christ for Muslims in the most creative periods of Christian-Muslim dialogue, the first half of the ninth century and the second half of the twentieth century. In these two periods, Christians made serious attempts to present their faith in Christ in terms that take into account Muslim perceptions of him, with a view to bridging the gap between Muslim and Christian convictions.

Thomas Czövek,

Three Seasons of Charismatic Leadership

A Literary-Critical and Theological Interpretation of the Narrative of Saul, David and Solomon

2006 / 978-1-870345484 / 272pp

This book investigates the charismatic leadership of Saul, David and Solomon. It suggests that charismatic leaders emerge in crisis situations in order to resolve the crisis by the charisma granted by God. Czovek argues that Saul proved himself as a charismatic leader as long as he acted resolutely and independently from his mentor Samuel. In the author's eyes, Saul's failure to establish himself as a charismatic leader is caused by his inability to step out from Samuel's shadow.

Jemima Atieno Oluoch

The Christian Political Theology of Dr. John Henry Okullu

2006 / 1-870345-51-7 / xx + 137pp

This book reconstructs the Christian political theology of Bishop John Henry Okullu, DD, through establishing what motivated him and the biblical basis for his socio-political activities. It also attempts to reconstruct the socio-political environment that nurtured Dr Okullu's prophetic ministry.

Richard Burgess

Nigeria's Christian Revolution

The Civil War Revival and Its Pentecostal Progeny (1967-2006)

2008 / 978-1-870345-63-7 / xxii + 347pp

This book describes the revival that occurred among the Igbo people of Eastern Nigeria and the new Pentecostal churches it generated, and documents the changes that have occurred as the movement has responded to global flows and local demands. As such, it explores the nature of revivalist and Pentecostal experience, but does so against the backdrop of local socio-political and economic developments, such as decolonisation and civil war, as well as broader processes, such as modernisation and globalisation.

David Emmanuel Singh & Bernard C Farr (eds.)
Christianity and Cultures
Shaping Christian Thinking in Context
2008 / 978-1-870345-69-9 / x + 260pp

This volume marks an important milestone, the 25th anniversary of the Oxford Centre for Mission Studies (OCMS). The papers here have been exclusively sourced from Transformation, a quarterly journal of OCMS, and seek to provide a tripartite view of Christianity's engagement with cultures by focusing on the question: how is Christian thinking being formed or reformed through its interaction with the varied contexts it encounters? The subject matters include different strands of theological-missiological thinking, socio-political engagements and forms of family relationships in interaction with the host cultures.

Tormod Engelsviken, Ernst Harbakk, Rolv Olsen, Thor Strandenæs (eds.)
Mission to the World
Communicating the Gospel in the 21st Century:
Essays in Honour of Knud Jørgensen
2008 / 978-1-870345-64-4 / 472pp

Knud Jørgensen is Director of Areopagos and Associate Professor of Missiology at MF Norwegian School of Theology. This book reflects on the main areas of Jørgensen's commitment to mission. At the same time it focuses on the main frontier of mission, the world, the content of mission, the Gospel, the fact that the Gospel has to be communicated, and the context of contemporary mission in the 21st century.

Al Tizon
Transformation after Lausanne
Radical Evangelical Mission in Global-Local Perspective
2008 / 978-1-870345-68-2 / xx + 281pp

After Lausanne '74, a worldwide network of radical evangelical mission theologians and practitioners use the notion of "Mission as Transformation" to integrate evangelism and social concern together, thus lifting theological voices from the Two Thirds World to places of prominence. This book documents the definitive gatherings, theological tensions, and social forces within and without evangelicalism that led up to Mission as Transformation. And it does so through a global-local grid that points the way toward greater holistic mission in the 21st century.

Bambang Budijanto

Values and Participation

Development in Rural Indonesia

2009 / 978-1-870345-70-5 / x + 237pp

Socio-religious values and socio-economic development are inter-dependant, inter-related and are constantly changing in the context of macro political structures, economic policy, religious organizations and globalization; and micro influences such as local affinities, identity, politics, leadership and beliefs. The three Lopait communities in Central Java, Indonesia provide an excellent model of the rich and complex negotiations and interactions among all the above factors. The book argues that the comprehensive approach in understanding the socio-religious values of each local community is essential to accurately describing their respective identity which will help institutions and agencies, both governmental and non-governmental, to relate to these communities with dignity and respect.

Young-hoon Lee

The Holy Spirit Movement in Korea

Its Historical and Theological Development

2009 / 978-1-870345-67-5 / x + 174pp

This book traces the historical and theological development of the Holy Spirit Movement in Korea through six successive periods (from 1900 to the present time). These periods are characterized by repentance and revival (1900-20), persecution and suffering under Japanese occupation (1920-40), confusion and division (1940-60), explosive revival in which the Pentecostal movement played a major role in the rapid growth of Korean churches (1960-80), the movement reaching out to all denominations (1980-2000), and the new context demanding the Holy Spirit movement to open new horizons in its mission engagement (2000-). The volume also discusses the relationship between this movement and other religions such as shamanism, and looks forward to further engagement with issues of concern in wider society.

Alan R. Johnson

Leadership in a Slum

A Bangkok Case Study

2009 / 978-1-870345-71-2 xx + 238pp

This book looks at leadership in the social context of a slum in Bangkok from an angle different from traditional studies which measure well educated Thais on leadership scales derived in the West. Using both systematic data collection and participant observation, it develops a culturally preferred model as well as a set of models based in Thai concepts that reflect on-the-ground realities. This work challenges the dominance of the patron-client rubric for understanding all forms of Thai leadership and offers a view for understanding leadership rooted in local social systems, contrary to approaches that assume the universal applicability of leadership research findings across all cultural settings. It concludes by looking at the implications of the anthropological approach for those who are involved in leadership training in Thai settings and beyond.

Titre Ande

Leadership and Authority

Bula Matari and Life - Community Ecclesiology in Congo

2010 / 978-1-870345-72-9 xvii + 189pp

This book proposes that Christian theology in Africa can make significant developments if a critical understanding of the socio-political context in contemporary Africa is taken seriously. The Christian leadership in post-colonial Africa has cloned its understanding and use of authority on the Bula Matari model, which was issued from the brutality of colonialism and political absolutism in post-colonial Africa. This model has caused many problems in churches, including dysfunction, conflicts, divisions and a lack of prophetic ministry. Titre proposes a Life-Community ecclesiology for liberating authority, where leadership is a function, not a status, and 'apostolic succession' belongs to all the people of God.

Frank Kwesi Adams

Odwira and the Gospel

A Study of the Asante Odwira Festival and its Significance for Christianity in Ghana

2010 /978-1-870345-59-0

The study of the Odwira festival is the key to the understanding of Asante religious and political life in Ghana. The book explores the nature of the Odwira festival longitudinally - in pre-colonial, colonial and post-independence Ghana - and examines the Odwira ideology and its implications for understanding the Asante self-identity. The book also discusses how some elements of faith portrayed in the Odwira festival could provide a framework for Christianity to engage with Asante culture at a greater depth. Theological themes in Asante belief that have emerged from this study include the theology of sacrament, ecclesiology, eschatology, Christology and a complex concept of time. The author argues that Asante cultural identity lies at the heart of the process by which the Asante Christian faith is carried forward.

Bruce Carlton

Strategy Coordinator

Changing the Course of Southern Baptist Missions

2010 / 978-1-870345-78-1 xvii + 268pp

In 1976, the Southern Baptist Convention adopted its Bold New Thrusts in Foreign Missions with the overarching goal of sharing the gospel with every person in the world by the year 2000. The formation of Cooperative Services International (CSI) in 1985 and the assigning of the first non-residential missionary (NRM) in 1987 demonstrated the Foreign Mission Board's (now International Mission Board) commitment to take the gospel message to countries that restricted traditional missionary presence and to people groups identified as having little or no access to the gospel. Carlton traces the historical development along with an analysis of the key components of the paradigm and its significant impact on Southern Baptists' missiology.

Julie Ma & Wonsuk Ma
Mission in the Spirit:
Towards a Pentecostal/Charismatic Missiology
2010 / 978-1-870345-84-2 xx + 312pp

The book explores the unique contribution of Pentecostal/Charismatic mission from the beginning of the twentieth century. The first part considers the theological basis of Pentecostal/Charismatic mission thinking and practice. Special attention is paid to the Old Testament, which has been regularly overlooked by the modern Pentecostal/Charismatic movements. The second part discusses major mission topics with contributions and challenges unique to Pentecostal/Charismatic mission. The book concludes with a reflection on the future of this powerful missionary movement. As the authors served as Korean missionaries in Asia, often their missionary experiences in Asia are reflected in their discussions.

S. Hun Kim & Wonsuk Ma (eds.)
Korean Diaspora and Christian Mission
2011-978-1-870345-91-0

As a 'divine conspiracy' for Missio Dei, the global phenomenon of people on the move has shown itself to be invaluable. In 2004 two significant documents concerning Diaspora were introduced, one by the Filipino International Network and the other by the Lausanne Committee for World Evangelization. These have created awareness of the importance of people on the move for Christian mission. Since then, Korean Diaspora has conducted similar research among Korean missions, resulting in this book. It is unique as the first volume researching Korean missions in Diasporic contexts, appraising and evaluating these missions with practical illustrations, and drawing on a wide diversity of researchers.

GENERAL REGNUM TITLES

Vinay Samuel, Chris Sugden (eds.)
The Church in Response to Human Need
1987 / 1870345045 / xii+268pp

Philip Sampson, Vinay Samuel, Chris Sugden (eds.)
Faith and Modernity
Essays in modernity and post-modernity
1994 / 1870345177 / 352pp

Klaus Fiedler
The Story of Faith Missions
1994 / 0745926878 / 428pp

Douglas Peterson
Not by Might nor by Power
A Pentecostal Theology of Social Concern in Latin America
1996 / 1870345207 / xvi+260pp

David Gitari
In Season and Out of Season
Sermons to a Nation
1996 / 1870345118 / 155pp

David. W. Virtue
A Vision of Hope
The Story of Samuel Habib
1996 / 1870345169 / xiv+137pp

Everett A Wilson
Strategy of the Spirit
J.Philip Hogan and the Growth of the Assemblies of God Worldwide, 1960 - 1990
1997 /1870345231/214

Murray Dempster, Byron Klaus, Douglas Petersen (eds.)
The Globalization of Pentecostalism
A Religion Made to Travel
1999 / 1870345290 / xvii+406pp

Peter Johnson, Chris Sugden (eds.)
Markets, Fair Trade and the Kingdom of God
Essays to Celebrate Traidcraft's 21st Birthday
2001 / 1870345193 / xii+155pp

Robert Hillman, Coral Chamberlain, Linda Harding
Healing & Wholeness
Reflections on the Healing Ministry
2002 / 978-1- 870345-35- 4 / xvii+283pp

David Bussau, Russell Mask
Christian Microenterprise Development
An Introduction
2003 / 1870345282 / xiii+142pp

David Singh
Sainthood and Revelatory Discourse
An Examination of the Basis for the Authority of Bayan in Mahdawi Islam
2003 / 8172147285 / xxiv+485pp

For the up-to-date listing of the Regnum books see www.ocms.ac.uk/regnum

regnum

Regnum Books International

Regnum is an Imprint of The Oxford Centre for Mission Studies
St. Philip and St. James Church
Woodstock Road
Oxford, OX2 6HR
Web: www.ocms.ac.uk/regnum